D1706223

DAVID M. LEVY, Professor of Clinical Psychiatry at Columbia University, is also attending psychiatrist at the New York State Psychiatric Institute and a psychiatrist with a private practice in New York City. He is a graduate of Harvard University (1914) and of the University of Chicago Medical School (1918). He has lectured at the University of Illinois (1920-22), the University of Chicago (1923-27), Smith College (1924-30), the New School for Social Research (1928-39), and the New York Psychoanalytic Institute (1936-41). Other positions have been Attending Neurologist and Director of the Mental Hygiene Clinic for Children at the Michael Reese Hospital, Acting Director of the Illinois Institute for Juvenile Research, Chief of Staff of the New York Institute for Child Guidance, and Attending Psychoanalyst at the Psychoanalytic Clinic for Training and Research. During World War II he served as consulting psychiatrist in personnel for the Office of Strategic Services and in 1945-46 he was Director of the Information Control Division Screening Center in Germany. He is a member of many professional organizations and has been President of the American Orthopsychiatric Association. His publications include many articles in professional journals and a number of books: *Sibling Rivalry* (1937), *Maternal Overprotection* (1943), *New Fields of Psychiatry* (1947), *Behavioral Analysis* (1958), and *The Demonstration Clinic: For the Psychological Study and Treatment of Mother and Child in Medical Practice* (1959).

MATERNAL
OVERPROTECTION

By DAVID M. LEVY, M.D.

The Norton Library

W · W · NORTON & COMPANY · INC ·
NEW YORK

To A. R. L.

COPYRIGHT © 1966 BY W. W. NORTON & COMPANY, INC.
COPYRIGHT 1943 BY COLUMBIA UNIVERSITY PRESS

First published in the Norton Library 1966
by arrangement with Columbia University Press

Library of Congress Catalog Card No. 66-15313

All Rights Reserved
Published simultaneously in Canada
by George J. McLeod Limited
Toronto

W. W. Norton & Company, Inc. is also the publisher of
the works of Erik H. Erikson, Otto Fenichel, Karen Horney and
Harry Stack Sullivan, and the principal works of Sigmund Freud.

PRINTED IN THE UNITED STATES OF AMERICA

2 3 4 5 6 7 8 9 0

FOREWORD

THE publication of *Maternal Overprotection* in paperback is a gratifying event because it will make available for more years to come a publication still useful as a methodology and as an important human relationship study.

These studies in maternal overprotection were made possible by the special resources and personnel of the former Institute for Child Guidance, New York City. They comprise numerous medical, social, psychometric and special psychiatric investigations — a service afforded only by a large staff of specialized workers. More than 2,000 case records, representing more than a hundred hours of contact per case, were then available. This library of records was essential for the method employed. At the time my purpose was to utilize them for human-relationship studies by a method of "case selection" which would yield records containing the most clear-cut examples of the relationship to be studied besides all the relevant data.

The first step was a selection of cases in which any evidence of overprotection appeared in the record. The next step was a sifting process (Chap. II), classifying the records according to a variety of overprotective forms. Finally a search among the records of "pure" overprotection was made which satisfied the criteria of clear-cut examples and completeness of data.

The word "pure" used in this connection needs explaining. Since maternal feelings vary biologically in a quantitative sense there are numerous factors which may reinforce them besides such factors that are familiar to us through psychoanalytic studies. The assumption is simply that given a high or even an average maternal woman, a number of experiences (e.g. "period of anticipation," "extra hazard" in Chap. VII) may reinforce maternal behavior without assuming that the explanation must necessarily and primarily be a psychoneurosis, as in "compensatory overprotection" based on unconscious hostility to the infant. Otherwise we are put in the curious position of inferring that any large deviation from an average in a normal distribution curve must of necessity be proof of a psychoneurosis. The differentiation of neurotic and so-called "pure" overprotection are considered in the text.

All the manifold data utilized in this study are exposed to the reader as in any experimental investigation. This point was stressed in many of the reviews that followed its first publication. The method of investigation and evaluation was thought to be applicable then as now to numerous other human relationship problems. For this type of clinical research the child-guidance method is particularly appropriate because of the wide range of information it yields. As you read the case studies in the book you will note data classifiable as social, psychometric (tests), psychodynamic (motivational), medical, psychopathological. The data are classified again as derived by means of inquiry, observation, physical and psychological measurement. Methods of investigation are discussed in Chap. I.

The follow-up studies are also a special feature. Patients were studied yearly for three years after treatment and then seven to ten years later. This was done as carefully in the follow-up period as at the beginning of treatment.

Since this study was published I have completed a number of further investigations of maternal feelings, pursuing a number of points raised in this publication. It remains for me, however, a basic undertaking; the assembling and ordering of data in a new enterprise.

DAVID M. LEVY, M.D.

February, 1966
New York, N.Y.

CONTENTS

ACKNOWLEDGMENTS

I AM especially indebted to these former students of the Smith College School for Social Work, who helped accumulate the data pertaining to this study as part of their field service done at the Institute for Child Guidance: Kathleen Andrews, Emma Blomquist, Ruth B. Brown, Christine Brunk, Clare Davis, Margaret A. Figge, Patricia Foley, Mildred Ford, Margaret B. Freeman, Mary C. Gleason, Jean Goldman, Elizabeth Hough, Olive M. Irvine, Martha P. Lewenberg, and Katherine C. Young.

I am also grateful to the following: Dr. Helen Witmer, for her help in supervising and aiding the students' work; Mr. Simon H. Tulchin, I.C.G. staff psychologist, who made possible the collection of data on intelligence and achievement tests for the special study of overprotection and school achievement; Miss Helene Brady, for checking data and secretarial services; Dr. Lawson G. Lowrey, Director, and every member of the I.C.G. staff, for help and suggestions; and the Trustees of the William Alanson White Psychiatric Foundation, for permission to reproduce these studies, which originally appeared in the Foundation's quarterly publication *Psychiatry* (November, 1938; February, November, 1939; February, November, 1941; February, 1942).

I. AIMS AND METHODS

IN THIS investigation an attempt is made to study a human relationship, utilizing for the purpose the resources of the Institute for Child Guidance at New York City. The method employed is to select out of abundant material cases in which such a relationship appears in its simplest and clearest form, to evaluate all pertinent data, and then, in the light of the investigation, to study more complex or "impure" forms.

The aim is to determine the genesis of the particular human relationship and its effect on the personalities involved. Its object, the final goal of all such studies, is to learn how to control or modify the process in order to solve problems in human behavior.

Since the validity of our findings depends on the method of investigation employed, it is important to describe it in detail. Indeed, our first problem in the field of human relationships is that of methodology. The difficulties are best revealed by considering the methods of investigation available for the solution of our problem—maternal overprotection. We want to know how a mother gets to be overprotective; how her child is affected by living with that type of mother; how to clear up actual and prevent potential difficulties that may result. Furthermore, we want to gain out of our investigation new technical weapons for the study of other human relationships.

It is generally accepted that the most potent of all influences on social behavior is derived from the primary social experience with the mother. If a mother maintains toward the child a consistent attitude of, let us say, indifference and hostility, the assumption is made that the child's personality is greatly affected thereby. His outlook on life, his attitude towards people, his entire psychic well-being, his very destiny is presumed to be altered by the maternal attitude. Life under a regime of maternal indifference develops a psychic pattern of quite a different mold than under a regime of maternal overprotection. Psychiatrists regard the difference as great as though the children concerned lived in entirely different worlds. Indeed, two children of the same parents, whose mother exhibits a different attitude toward each, manifest on that basis alone profound differences in personality. If human behavior is influenced so markedly by maternal attitudes then surely the most important study of man as a social being is a study of his mother's influence on his early life. The play of social response between mothers and children would then represent the foundation of social life, and its investigation the pivotal attack on the problem of social behavior.

Now the conviction that the destiny of the individual rests in the hands of his mother (or mother-substitute) is based on the thesis that the social forces operating on the infant affect his entire life. This belief is fairly common to investigators in human psychology regardless of their generally conflicting viewpoints.

The Watsonian psychologists find in the conditioned response ample proof that the child's innate behavior is arranged into patterns that determine by his second year of life how he will act in his twentieth. They regard mother love so powerful (and so baneful) an influence on mankind that they would direct their first efforts to mitigating her powers.

Though in striking contrast with the schools of Watson, Pavlov, or Bechterew in viewpoint and method, psychoanalytic investigators similarly ascribe paramount influence to the early years of life. Such influence is derived from the Oedipus complex, the nucleus of all human relationships, and the erotogenic zones. Indeed, the Oedipus complex is in a sense a derivative of erotogenic zones, because the desire to possess the mother and hold her as the prized possssion against all rivals results from an investment of the child's body with pleasure in which the mother is constantly playing the important role. Through nursing she invests the mouth area with pleasure; through fondling and stroking, the skin area, and so on. The child is thereby constantly charged with intensely pleasurable sensations within the mother-child relationship, a bond which according to the pleasure principle he fights hard to maintain and yields only and in as little measure as possible under dire necessity. The Freudian baby, like the Watsonian baby, grows up in a world determined largely by maternal love.

The Adlerian school likewise, regards the "style of life" already well established in early childhood. Starting with the energy emanating from the power-drive, the stage of life is set by the maternal attitude. In the case of the "spoiled" child, for example, the desire for the top role is developed into a monstrous powerlust, because the mother created a life for her baby in which it was fed with constant attention, devotion, and obeisance. He grows up, therefore, with a fixed pattern of domination, trying to adapt to the world in the only way he knows. The role of nursery despot finds its repercussions later on in difficulties with work, with friends, with marriage.

Child-guidance workers, committed to no special school of thought, utilizing whatever concepts appear workable in their attempt to solve the diverse problems of maladjustment in children, are also of the same mind in regard to the importance of infantile experience in shaping personality. Their views especially bolster up the preceding viewpoints not only because of the rich clinical experience on which they are based, but also because of their inclusive methods of study. Since the latter represent the groundwork of this investigation, they require further description.

The methods employed in the present-day child-guidance units of this country arose out of the tussle of psychiatry with the problems of delinquency. The historical account of the extramural psychiatrist in his new venture is beyond the scope of this treatise. It is important to note that the American enterprise which eventually made delinquency a branch of the general problem of maladjustment represents largely a development and combination of methods, in contradistinction to those European clinics that represent the application of a theory. The distinction is important. The preparatory work in the American field has been directed to the utilization of general medicine, applied psychology, sociology, special psychiatry, and the organization and training of special workers within each field for a combined attack. The evaluation of methods and distribution of effort among the different workers on any given case are the current problems of the staff. At present the investigation of an individual problem in maladjustment includes a social, physical, psychometric, and psychiatric examination. Observations are made in the office, at home, school, and playroom. Various individuals that have contact with the patient are interviewed, besides members of the family concerned.

The strength of the "American method" (as it is sometimes called by European workers) lies in its inclusiveness, its development of competent specialized workers, and its receptivity and absorption of contributions from any source. It musters for the attack specialized workers along a wide front. Its method is analogous to that of general medicine which utilizes for the advantage of the patient facts gleaned from research in physics or chemistry, pathology or physiology, bacteriology or sociology.

A child presenting a problem in school retardation may reveal through the usual methods of study a visual trouble, a special defect in muscular coördination, poor preparation in arithmetic, superior intelligence, poor mechanical ability, a fright neurosis, exposure to parental disharmony, an overindulgent grandmother, and a severe father. However the specific problem of school retardation may be explained as a result of the dynamic operation of this or that combination of factors in the case presented, three facts are clear. 1. School retardation, though the immediate reason for referral, is one of a large number of difficulties in social adjustment that our patient presents. 2. Without the advantage of special examinations, significant findings important to the welfare of the patient might be missed entirely. 3. Therapeutic attack of a wide range is essential, involving procedures as diverse as muscle training, special tutoring, family rehabilitation, and psychotherapy. The case sample given is typical in its complexity of all others.

The child-guidance method represents in its ideal form a coördination of all available clinical tools, expertly manipulated for the purpose of investigating and therapeutically modifying human behavior. Ideally, therefore, it is the method *par excellence* in the field. It is proof against psychologic absurdities that take root only in complete ignorance of medicine. It is proof against medical absurdities that by neglecting the study of social situations find germinating dementia praecox in every case of shyness, or a lesion of the central nervous system in every sudden personality shift.

Its weaknesses are inherent in organization methods and in the multiplicity of tools utilized. The former are revealed when case turnover becomes a paramount issue and case studies become dull and dead routine. Weaknesses of the latter form are revealed when the case record becomes an accumulation of superficial data that gives a false impression of thoroughness because of bulk. Moreover, a weak member of the staff may throw the entire combination out of gear. The medical examiner who overlooks, let us say, a brain tumor gives false weight to the interpretation of behavior based on findings in other fields; so also does the mental tester who fails in his diagnosis of mental deficiency, the psychiatrist who fails to unearth a crucial experience, the social worker who receives and accepts false information. But problems in organization and in competency of personnel do not affect the logic of the method applied.

The strength of the psychoanalytic method, utilized as an exclusive technique, lies in the constantly increasing skill accruing to the successful worker with this "microscope" of psychodynamics. In contrast with the child-guidance method it is a concentrated attack along a main front. It utilizes sociological and medical data as it perceives them expressed in the psychic life of the patient. The psychoanalyst may say that social data accumulated by special investigators in the child-guidance field are of importance in the life of the child only in so far as they become part of its psychic expression; hence whatever value they have is incorporated by psychoanalysis.

This amounts to saying that the psychoanalyst is interested not in what the child experiences, but how he experiences it. Needless to say, a direct study of the social life of a child, a study of experiences on which his psyche operates, presents another approach and, hence, sheds further light on his mental life. In the developing field of child analysis there is evident an increasing utilization of the mother and the home as a source of information for experimental data. It is obvious that psychic assimilation of experience is only one side of the picture. The availability of data derived through examination of the child's mental and physical capacities and incapacities, through social psychiatric studies of the individuals who form his most intimate life experiences, is clearly of tremendous advantage in the investigation of mental processes.

The psychoanalyst utilizes, to be sure, whatever data he has available in the study of the child. On the medical side, for example, he usually makes sure that the patient is organically sound, or at least he becomes informed about the patient's physical handicaps. There is a significant difference, however, in the handling of data in another field by the worker whose thinking, no matter how skilled, is confined to one point of view. Consider, for example, the case of an adolescent girl whose problem in social adjustment is related to clumsiness. She does well in school, is popular with girls, and has a healthy relationship with her parents. In sports and dancing, however, she is unsuccessful and for that reason has avoided going to parties. Periods of despondency, feelings of difference, and occasional crying spells have been observed recently by the parents. The family physician has pronounced her health excellent.

Now, in the absence of physical findings, the psychoanalyst or the worker with any other exclusive psychodynamic method would proceed each along his line. Each would become receptive to his particular psychodynamic aspect of the problem and would draw on wisdom derived from experience with similar cases and knowledge of the literature on the subject. The implication is simply that prolonged experience and familiarity with any special method to the exclusion of all others might deprive the patient of advantages to be exploited in the related fields. Actually, a number of patients referred to the Institute, with a record of several negative physical examinations and with clumsiness as one of the complaints, showed evidence of mild spastic palsy. The finding of this organic factor influences every other approach to the case. The psychoanalyst made aware of the finding may retain his interest in the psychodynamic aspect of the organic lesion. But it remains the business of child guidance to exploit neurology as well as psychoanalysis as part and parcel of its method.

The example cited is used to illustrate the fact that the combination of methods used in child guidance is of practical and theoretical importance. Each field of endeavor may be strengthened by contributions from the other. One may argue that there is no limit to the elaboration of methods; it is only expedient that one should become as expert as he can with the tools at his command, and learn to coöperate with other specialists. The answer can only be a statement of the experience in child guidance, namely, that the present combination of methods represents basic and minimum requirements for the study and treatment of problems in social behavior.

Further, each type of examination, whether physical, psychometric, or psychiatric, is enhanced in value when constantly oriented to the problem of social adjustment. A physician who finds on examination that his patient, a girl of nine, reveals an upper incisor tooth with a slight overbite would ordinarily make nothing of it. Alert to the psychologic implications of even the slightest anatomic variations he now observes that the patient's smile is somewhat "taut" and lacks "muscular" spontaneity; that when talking, her lip movements show limited excursion; and that on several occasions she covers her mouth with spread-out fingers. All these movements are designed to prevent exposure of the crooked tooth. The child tells that her younger sister who has pretty teeth smiles "big," but she smiles "little." The tremendous consequence of her response to a slight dental malalignment is demonstrated by the fact that since early childhood the patient consciously manipulated lips and hand during conversation, thereby setting up a barrier to "natural" social experience. The consequence of the increased self-consciousness, the years of increased tension of lips, the dynamic interplay of these factors within the total life situation, are part of a coördinated study in which the value of the psychoanalytic method is enhanced.

The psychoanalytically trained worker operating in a child-guidance field will be made more alert to influences on psychic life contributed by physical findings, mental tests, social investigations, and various direct clinical observations. He will learn also many ways of reinforcing his therapy and modifying his technique. On the other hand, through his contribution, the physical examiner, psychologist and social worker will become sensitized to the psychodynamic aspects of their data.

In reviewing the several methods of investigating human behavior, it will be noted that the child-guidance method in practice is primarily a combination of clinical procedures; that is, in contrast with the experimental method, it does not attempt to control the conditions it seeks to study. The statement is true only in a general way, for like clinical medicine any number of details in its investigation are the results of controlled conditions. Examples are furnished by various measuring and testing procedures in the physical and psychometric studies. It remains true, however, that, like clinical medicine, child guidance is primarily an art and not a science. The more methods of precision, the more scientific advantage it has, the stronger an art it is. But, like medicine, an art it always must remain because it is engaged in the practical business of modifying the behavior of individuals, a business in which there are varying degrees of individual skill, new combinations of factors in every case, numerous practical moves that must be made in which prediction is impossible. The purpose of research within the child-guidance field is to increase the precision with which such moves can be made.

Research workers in social behavior of children have relied on various modifications of the experimental method, usually in the form of standardizing conditions for a test situation; or treating with statistical devices various data collected from observations or interviews. When material of the latter form is derived from clinical studies, the method is usually to compare the data pertaining to the group originally investigated with that of another group acting somewhat as the "control" animal in biologic experiments. The clinical findings in a group of delinquents are compared, for example, with the findings in a group of nondelinquents of similar social and economic status. Significant differences in the frequencies of data in the groups are then interpreted as contributing factors or causal agents in the creation of delinquent behavior. "Check" or contrasting groups are used as necessary measures of the significance of the data. However plausible "broken homes," for example, may appear as a "cause" in the delinquent group, the finding of that condition as frequently in the nondelinquent group weakens the argument considerably. Now it may be argued, that regardless of statistical findings, broken homes do not contribute to the security of the individual, they produce discordant factors to good social adjustment, and that they are provocative of difficulties in behavior of which delinquency is one of the symptoms. This may of course be true. "Broken homes" are of all types. In the delinquent group there may be many unbroken homes far more discordant than the broken homes of the nondelinquent group. The frequency of the finding of "broken homes" in both groups remains, nevertheless, a valid figure, easily checked by similar studies. The functional value of the term is given full meaning only by intensive study of the individual.

Individual psychodynamic studies present another source of material for research in addition to data yielded by the experimental and statistical method. Such studies may yield data experimentally verifiable. They may also, by amassing case records, be handled statistically, at least in certain phases of the work. Psychoanalytic investigators fortify certain observations with statistical data and also suggest how theories may be checked by the experimental method. For example, as a check on a psychoanalytic theory that neurosis is a consequence of anxiety engendered by severity of birth, Freud suggests a study of the frequency and severity of infantile fears in relation to easy and severe labors. Another psychoanalyst suggests the use of an instrument to measure the contraction of the *sphincter ani* muscle as an aid to the study of certain personality traits. In the main, however, the psychoanalyst has come to depend on a method of investigation peculiar to his own field. The material for study is for the most part a by-product of a primary therapeutic problem, usually the treatment of neurosis. Since the therapeutic method has as one of its technical aims the development of increasing skill on the part of the analyst in order to break down the patient's psychological barriers to a free expression of his most intimate thoughts and experience, data previously unknown to research are now available. These data are criticized by various workers as prejudiced products of highly biased investigators. They assert that the practical problems of treatment require active interpretation and the resulting associations swing usually to the particular theory of the interested analyst. Further, the material out of which general conclusions about the human psyche are drawn comes from a highly selected group, that fraction of psychoneurotics that can afford treatment.

Without entering into the details of this controversy it is necessary to point out that free association as developed by psychoanalysis remains for all time a contribution to method, certainly the most valuable of all methods today in psychodynamics regardless under whose banner it is employed. Obviously a first essential in the investigation of a human being is a method that will make possible his most complete self-revelation. The individual's conscious desire to coöperate in such a venture has been shown often enough to be merely a good beginning of a difficult experiment.

The question of the limitation of psychoanalytic contributions derived solely from the study of psychoneurosis is especially important to investigators who utilize check groups as controls. The present reply of psychoanalysts is that such checks are actually at hand since analyses have been made of normals and various maladjusted individuals other than neurotics. The earlier and still the main contention is that a study of the psychoneurotic reveals the dynamics of the normal psyche more clearly than a study of the normal himself. The psychoneurotic reveals the process as an open conflict which in the so-called normal is "closed." The normal is less penetrable by the psychoanalytic method for that very reason. His social adjustment amounts to a cured neurosis in which there is, therefore, increased difficulty of disclosure. Furthermore, he lacks the main incentive for analysis, the discomfort that drives the neurotic to treatment. Contributions to psychodynamics by direct study of the normal are best made, therefore, by the analysis of children, in which psychic processes may be studied developmentally.

Study of the psychoneurotic has given strength to a growing conviction that the vast majority of problems in maladjustment whether revealed in the form of neurosis, psychosis, delinquency, or "behavior problem," are adaptations of individuals endowed with similar mental mechanisms. Child-guidance studies of family groups demonstrate in the main various exaggerations of parent-child and sibling relationships common to all family life.

The study of exaggerated or "abnormal" forms has thus far contributed more to our knowledge of normal problems in adjustment than direct study of normals. Indeed the study of the maladjusted is the best preparation for the study of the adjusted. It reveals in sharp relief the points of stress in normal behavior that exclusive study of the normal can never do. Also it directs the investigator to the crucial problems that normals must contend with when the normal becomes the object of investigation.

Contributions to knowledge of normal behavior by study of the abnormal may be described in terms analogous to medical science, in which the study of the sick has contributed more to knowledge of health than the direct study of the healthy. In medical science there remains, however, the flourishing field of physiology whose method is chiefly an experimental attack on the problem of the normal functioning of the body. Further, the pathologist is much more comfortable when his deductions are consistent with findings in physiology. He often employs experimental evidence of physiologists as a main support.

The upshot of the argument of workers in the general field of maladjustment boils down really to an exigency. We try to do the best with what we have. The most convincing evidence in science is that derived by experiment. Under certain given conditions certain results will follow. Anyone skillful enough to repeat the experiment will, if the evidence is true, come out with the same result. But our material does not ordinarily lend itself to the controlled conditions required by laboratory procedures. A study of mothers who have marked difficulties with their children is best checked against a study of mothers who have little or no difficulties with their children. But mothers don't present themselves for study unless they have difficulties, and although willing to answer superficial questions or even fill out questionnaires, they are not ready to submit to the intensive examinations required for thorough investigation. Difficulties in acquiring normal samples as controls may be solved some future day. When they are, the results of our present-day investigations will have to stand scrutiny from a new point of vantage. It is important now to turn to the highest possible advantage the material we possess.

In the study of maternal overprotection, control of all conditions for the purpose of an experiment would require complete isolation of mother and child. Even if this could be done, and all conditions ideal from the viewpoint of the observer were maintained, certain uncontrolled factors would always complicate the procedure. Even assuming laboratory control of the child from birth, the mother's entire past life would influence the controlled social situation in various ways. Hence, the experimental findings, though supplying objective and accurate overt symptomatology of a maternal overprotective relationship, would leave unsolved the problem of its genesis, for that problem is involved in the mother's own early experiences in life. The experiment proposed, assuming a valid technique for measuring the results, would consist in the elimination of all other complicating social contacts. The experiment would thus represent an attempt to study a human relationship by isolating it. Similar check experiments would have to be made with other types of mother-child relationships for comparison of results.

Leaving out of consideration the problem of the genesis of the maternal attitude, let us assume that we can at least recognize such attitudes and select mothers who display them to a marked degree. We then isolate the pair so that the child is thoroughly and consistently exposed to its mother with the attitude we wish to study. If, say, the attitude is one of overprotection, we infer that whatever modifications of personality it is capable of effecting will be done in "optimal" fashion under the conditions of isolation. The experiment represents a social monopoly of the child by the mother. The effects of the overprotective attitude are not diminished by a father, teacher, companions, servants, or by various competing outside interests.

A number of experiments of the same type will aid in ruling out the influence of constitutional and other factors in the child. In time we should conceivably be able to say, on the basis of our experiments, that the effect of an overprotective attitude on children is thus and so, regardless of health, size, strength, intelligence, emotional make-up, and the rest. We would thus succeed in isolating those personality factors in our group of children, however diverse in other respects, that would be common to them as a result of maternal overprotection.

After a period of years the experimenter might widen the range of social life for his subjects and follow them through school life and through marriage. He might then make certain conclusions about the effect of maternal overprotection on all the usual problems in social adjustment; on how his subjects adapt themselves to work, love and play; on how they manage as friends, husbands, fathers; on how the personality traits resulting from growth in the medium of the overprotecting mother have shaped their destinies.

The hypothetical experiments described represent a method of studying human relationships by selecting one in which the complex factor to be investigated appears in exaggerated form. The exaggeration is effected by selecting a mother in whom the overprotecting attitude is pronounced. However, by artificially removing all other social relationships that might complicate the problem, all influences that might mitigate the overprotection are removed. The overprotection is thereby made to flourish luxuriantly like a plant in a hothouse, by selecting a favorable seed to start with and providing an optimum medium for growth removed from all competition in the normal habitat.

An important assumption for the experiment and for the investigations recorded in this book is derived from clinical study and common observation; namely, that the maternal overprotective attitude is a very common one, very likely universal. Hence, when a child is exposed to it in magnified form we are favored with an opportunity of observing the operation and results most clearly. Later on we may then be able to discern the activity within this relationship though it appears in a minute degree.

Details of experiments in social behavior that cannot be made, and that appear to be unwarranted manipulation of human beings, have not been set down in these pages as interesting speculation. They represent situations that may be actually approximated in the life about us. Such experiments are being made all the time.

Our first problem after accumulating a wealth of case material is to select carefully case studies in which the relationship to be studied happens to exist in a form most readily available for the purpose of investigation. The material at hand must contain numerous studies of various relationships. After selecting cases for a particular study we may be in a position to enrich further case studies through knowledge of the limitations of our library of human records, by more complete investigation of symptomatology and of maternal background factors, only elaborating our inquiries at any point on the basis of leads furnished by the investigation.

In our hypothetical experiment we set up the conditions of a mother-child monopoly in order to study the effect of overprotection by isolation and magnification. How far really can we approximate the experimental situation in actual practice? Take the case of a mother who soon after the birth of her child manifests a strong overprotective attitude. She "lives only for her child." Her life is devoted to it. She is uncomfortable whenever she is away from it, if only for a few minutes. She allows the husband to have little or no share in her baby's training. It is her baby, not his. She threatens to leave the house if her husband dare lay a finger to the child. The husband's role as father is negligible and remains so throughout the life of the child. The mother's career becomes more and more exclusively maternal. Her sexual and social difficulties with the husband increase. They no longer go out together. The baby, later the child, becomes the everlasting excuse for the gradual elimination of the wifely role. Social life, previously active, becomes more and more restricted. When the child goes to school the mother accompanies him there, long past the time when the neighbors' children are on their way alone. She helps him with all his studies, allows him no friends for fear they will contaminate him, and is quite uncritical in her attitude toward him.

The clinical picture presented is a fair composite of a number of the cases selected for this investigation. It shows how, once an overprotective attitude is well developed, a mother-child monopoly gradually comes to fulfillment. When the mother finds in her child the solution for all her emotional needs, she gets caught by a social bond that automatically loosens all the others. She then creates the conditions of the hypothetical experiment.

In the same way, by selecting of cases fulfilling optimum conditions for study, any type of relationship may be studied. What is the influence on personality, for example, of brother-rivalry? Let us carefully review all our clinical studies in which such rivalry loomed large in the life of patients and select out of them those in which that relationship dominated most completely. Utilizing the relationship studied as the focus of our investigation, we must then evaluate all other data in terms of the (now) primary relationship. Has a previous experience of maternal overprotection increased or decreased the intensity of the rivalry? In how far is difference in intelligence a factor? All the data in our records must be examined in the light of the relationship studied, and their significance must be determined by comparison with other groups used as check or contrast studies and also by their logical and progressive dynamic relationship derived as far as possible from the direct associations of the patient.

It seems evident that in the study of human relationships as intimate as those of family life, intensive study of a handful of cases, selected because the relationships depicted are unusually clear, yields more knowledge than a statistical study of several thousand unselected cases. Our position is like that of a chemist who in first learning to analyze a metal picks out ores which by common observation contain in the purest form the metal to be studied. After learning to analyze it, he is then able to isolate the metal from complex mixtures regardless of its quantity or combination with other agents. Analogously, the first cases of maternal overprotection to be analyzed are those in which the relationship appears in the largest "quantity" and in the simplest form. For "quantity" the criteria of selection are clearness in the statements of overprotection and a fair unanimity in the finding—at least one lay observer besides staff members. Since a psychiatrist might interpret as evidence of maternal overprotection numerous details in any mother-child relationship, selection of cases on that basis would include numerous mild and complex forms, too elusive for the original study. The lay observation is accepted also only when it is clean-cut. The statement, "I suspect the mother might baby him too much," is inadequate. The statements, "His mother never lets him out of her sight," "The boy is fourteen but she treats him like a kid of five," indicate clearly enough that the cases are open to investigation.

Selection of cases in which there is general agreement and clear evidence of the problem gives little difficulty compared with the task of selection for simplicity or "purity." The criterion is evidence indicating that the overprotection is of a "wanted" child. The reason for making this criterion is a practical one. The overprotection of an unwanted child reveals evidence of maternal rejection, a mixture in which the overprotection nevertheless predominates in the clinical picture. By utilizing the criterion, "wanted child," experience has shown that selection favors cases in which the overprotecting factors are the most consistent. In short, the criterion used enables a selection of relatively pure forms on the basis of the clinical data in our records.

A dynamic classification based entirely on maternal attitudes might reveal that mothers consistently overprotective are relatively freer of hostile elements in relationship to children than those who show evidence of excessive maternal care with a mixture of rejection. In the latter group the overprotection is considered compensatory, derived from a feeling of guilt because of unconscious hostile attitudes toward the offspring. If psychoanalytic studies were available for all the mothers in the "pure" group, they might reveal also that their excessive care of children had some roots in unconscious hostilities, even though objective evidence did not break through. For the purpose of the investigation, we know at least that the maternal influences to which our patients were subject differ in consistency in the two groups.

The various clinical types of overprotection and further inquiry into problems of selection will be found in succeeding chapters and in the footnotes.

Our aim at this point is to stress the advantage in the study of human relationships of the method of selecting "pure" forms— forms in which the relationship may be seen most clearly, and studied in relation with all pertinent data. The richer our case material, the better the opportunity for discovering case studies that approximate as nearly as possible the requirements of ideal human experiments. The combination of methods developed in the field of child guidance has made possible the data secured for our investigation. Findings that emerge are checked whenever possible with contrast and control groups and with the contributions of other investigators.

II. CASE SIFTING

THE problem of case selection, a fundamental problem in the study of human relationships, may be illustrated by an analogy. Let us consider again the example of the chemist who has set himself the task of identifying iron. He will first select ores in which by common observation the iron exists in "purest" form. After various observations and experiments he learns to identify the metal so that he can determine its presence even though it exists in compounds in a minute degree. He is no longer dependent on crude observation or "practical" opinions. He has established identifying and objective criteria, which in the course of further experimentation become more and more refined. Having established the identity of his metal, the chemist may determine its behavior in various combinations. However difficult the analysis of the chemical reactions, he is at least certain of the metal he wishes to study.

In the study of human relationships as exemplified by maternal overprotection, we have advanced to the stage of establishing criteria of identification. Future investigators will refine the means of identification and study relationships of forms purer than those selected in our investigation. However crude our material may appear in the light of future refinements of method, it remains our task to work out the various factors that help to explain the development and formation of the maternal overprotective relationship, utilizing the data available by present methods of investigation. We will then be in position to consider the various influences that modify the relationship in a therapeutic way.

By the method of selection a large number of cases of overprotection were weeded out. Some of these were eliminated because of inadequacies in the investigation—evidence inexplicit, inferences without facts, data incomplete. Included in the group sifted out for technical reasons were also cases evidently of maternal overprotection in which the number of interviews was too small to check the original investigation, to determine maternal attitudes clearly, or to initiate therapy.

Of the findings in the social investigation, those referring to the mother's attitude, to early childhood experiences, and to sex were most frequently altered by continued contacts and increasing confidence of the mother in the social worker and psychiatrist. In a few cases such attitudes were inferred from the facts which appear self-evident.

Actual facts about childhood, concerning early responsibilities, treatment by parents, economic struggles, and similar social data, are obtained with relative ease in early interviews. Attempts on the part of informants to present in a rosy light experiences of hardships, of cruel parents, and the like, may represent their psychic adaptation to childhood memories. As in psychoanalysis, a chronological sequence of data reveals further and further admissions of feelings of bitterness, frustration, and affect hunger.

Data on marital sex adjustment are most likely to be withheld in early interviews and generally are the last to be revealed. Since the minimum period of contact with the families comprising our study is about two years, there was ample opportunity to complete this evidence.

All cases of largely nonmaternal overprotection were weeded out. These included children overprotected by fathers, siblings, grandparents, or other relatives. In a number of the maternal overprotective forms, there often is a reinforcement of the maternal attitude by others. Such cases are included in the main study. Where the overprotection is largely nonmaternal, the cases are treated separately. Relatively few cases of marked paternal overprotection were found, although cases of paternal favoritism, shown usually to a daughter, are very common. There are several possible reasons for this infrequency. It is very rare that fathers are in as frequent social contact with children as are mothers. Cases in which the parental roles are reversed so that the father stays home and does the housework while the mother goes out to work are oddities. The opportunities for a constant overdose of paternal contact are therefore limited, especially in the important infantile years. Where a relatively strong father-daughter overprotection occurs, the problems arising may not affect the child so that it will be referred for treatment. There are a large variety of difficulties that do not become overt or available for treatment until adult life, if ever. Children are more likely to be referred for acts of aggression—quarreling, disobedience, temper tantrums, rebellious behavior—than for excessive obedience and submission. When overprotection results in an apparently successful parent-child relationship, especially in the form of a model child, the problems are more likely to become manifest when adaptation to adult life without parental support becomes necessary. A number of children, nevertheless, are found in our maternal overprotection group who are obedient and well-behaved. They happen to be referred from sources outside the home, for reasons to be discussed under the question of referral.

Overprotection by a grandparent, especially a grandmother, maternal or paternal, living in the patient's home, is a frequent finding. Such cases are complicated, especially when the mother is still striving unsuccessfully to free herself from the daughter relationship and her marital adjustment finds in the presence of the grandmother a constant stumbling block. When the grandmother successfully absorbs all parental authority, the child has a means of escaping parental modification, yet displays a pattern of behavior that differs from pure maternal overprotective forms. When overprotection is largely maternal though abetted by grandparents, the case is naturally included for study since it satisfies the criteria of selection.

A fair number of cases were found in which maternal overprotection though no longer present at the time of selection existed in marked degree during infancy or until the advent of a second child. A striking example is afforded by an immature parental pair who were constantly at the beck and call of their first child, a daughter; brought her about for all the neighbors to admire; and then discarded her like a forgotten doll when the baby arrived. A typical intense jealousy and open hostility against the newcomer was the reason for referral. Later it will be shown how sibling rivalry appears to be generally proportionate to the degree of maternal overprotection and the degree of threat at the time of the birth of the rival.

The most frequent clinical type of maternal overprotection has been referred to in Chapter I. It is found in the group in which the overprotection masks or is compensatory to a strong rejection. It will be considered separately.

There remain a number of mild and mixed forms that require description. Early overprotection followed by rejection is an example. Theoretically, a frank rejection of a child may be followed by "pure" overprotection, though we have no cases to illustrate that sequence. A mother absorbed in a first child and indifferent to the second may, after a dangerous illness of the second child has necessitated much nursing care on her part, shift about in her attitudes. Such cases are of the guilt-overprotection form. There are children, also, who experience temporary periods of overprotection, or alternating periods of overprotection and rejection, or mixtures of overprotection and severity. In this connection, those children also should be included who are seen by their mothers for brief periods of time during the day, yet, in the time available, receive strongly overprotective care. They are often children of professional women. The latter act as though they must make up for their hours of absence from the child through the intensity of their devotion in every minute of contact.

"Mild" maternal overprotection is presumably an attenuated form and very common. A quantitative distribution of overprotective manifestations would show, no doubt, a graduated progressive series. In the mild forms, however, many extraneous problems complicate evaluation and selection. Since we are dealing with mothers of various cultural backgrounds and of different economic and social groups, patterns of maternal behavior with children, correctly estimated as overprotective in one group, may in another group be typical phenomena. Breast feeding over a period of two years, for example, may be a symptom of overprotection. On the other hand, it may be typical behavior in certain cultural groups.

We are saved from this difficulty by the study of extreme forms in which the requirement of case selection by a lay observer, besides professional workers, is a decided help. For our so-called "pure" cases are evidence of maternal overprotection within the mothers' own groups.

A clinical classification of overprotection includes 1. *pure*, 2. *guilt*, 3. *mixed*, 4. *mild*, and 5. *nonmaternal* forms.

This investigation is concerned primarily with the "pure" form. The 20 cases selected are referred to throughout the text as Group I. (Summaries of the cases appear in the Appendix.) Examples of "guilt overprotection" are best deferred to a later chapter where they may serve as contrasts to our group. Examples are cited to illustrate cases eliminated for technical reasons and overprotection of mild and mixed varieties.

An only son of an aggressive, dominating mother is referred because of poor school work and withdrawal from group activities. He is a submissive, obedient, immature thirteen-year-old "mamma's boy"—a good case for study of maternal overprotection of the dominating type. Unfortunately the mother gives little background history and refuses to keep office appointments. Besides, the statements of overprotection are conflicting and inferential or mild; for example, the school teacher "suspects" he is both pampered and abused at home; the mother says she spoils him "somewhat," the boy "thinks perhaps" the mother babies him too much.

A seven-year-old girl is referred for enuresis. On the basis of a long period of "anticipation" (the child was born four years after marriage though contraceptives were never employed), a series of severe illnesses in early childhood, including mastoiditis with surgical interference, and some evidence of maternal over-solicitude at the time of investigation, maternal overprotection was inferred. But the criteria of selection were not established and social data were inadequate.

An example of overprotection in which the mother plays a minor role is afforded by an eleven-year-old boy referred because of quarreling and disobedience at home. In school his conduct and achievement are good. He lives in a woman's world, indulged by two sisters, the younger nine years his senior, and his mother. The father deserted five years ago. As the mother has worked outside the home for some years, the overprotection is largely by the sisters. The boy "takes complete possession" of the household of women who are always at his service.

An example of maternal overprotection that varied with external factors is shown by Mrs. R. When her first child was four years old, her second died of pneumonia following a cold. After that event she became overprotective of the surviving child, especially during his frequent colds. After the birth of a third child, her overprotection of the first considerably diminished.

Intensification of maternal care initiated by conditions in the child of severe illness, accident or deformity is a very common occurrence in family life. That mothers tend to favor the weaker, sicklier and generally more dependent child is an honored lay observation. Some mothers describe the response to the child during a severe illness in terms of a distinct change of attitude as in the remark, "Until he had that sickness I didn't realize what being a mother meant."

No doubt a study of a group of relationships of mothers with deformed or defective children would reveal examples of most intense overprotection. There are several reasons for eliminating this group. First, the method is primarily a relationship selection in order to throw light on universal mother-child dynamics. Selection by deformity of the child reveals complex maternal reactions that vary from marked overprotection complicated with feelings of guilt over imagined responsibility or proof of family taint to various forms of rejection. These reactions are to a special type of problem. Where physical deformity or illness occurs in case studies selected by the criteria specified, their influence is evaluated along with other data.

Overprotection during infancy followed by rejection is well illustrated in the case of a six-year-old girl referred because of fighting, quarreling, and constant show-off behavior. Born of doting parents, constantly caressed and petted, kept at the breast eighteen months, she was shown in triumph and spoiled by relatives and neighbors. During several illnesses the father and mother took turns walking the floor with her all night. The weaning process was a difficult one, starting with peppering the nipples and achieved finally by forced feeding.

At the age of four the patient's world collapsed, the central position usurped by a baby sister. The father told her about the wonderful surprise and took her to the room where she saw baby sister at "her breast." The patient screamed, shouted, "Damn you, get away from my ninny," ran to the baby and tried to kill it. On two other occasions she was caught trying to throw the baby out of the window.

Until the birth of the second child, the patient was cheerful and happy, though troublesome because of excessive demands for attention. After the experience described, she became "mean and nasty."

The case may be used to illustrate the value of "magnified" human material, besides serving as an example of a mixed form of maternal overprotection. The patient, following her loss of "first place" in the household, was kept continually provoked by the same conditions that represent a very common lot for many children, though in a milder degree. The conditions were: 1. constant exposure to the sight of the parents doting on the second child; 2. hearing unfavorable contrasts that grew in frequency as the patient became more difficult, for example, "This is a good baby, you are bad"; 3. loss of attention by relatives and neighbors now concentrated on the new "sensation."

By the criteria of selection, the case described is not included because at the time of study the patient was no longer overprotected. In a number of the cases selected by our criteria, it will be apparent that the overprotection does not remain consistent throughout childhood. In the example cited, the complete shift in overprotection to the newcomer is evidence of the inconsistency of the maternal response to her first-born. The mother discards number one for number two with the ease of a primitive parent. A number of case studies are at hand in which a mother, ignorant and emotionally immature, overindulges her infant, creates an excessive dependency on her, and when, as a result, the child becomes difficult, discards it. Such easy release does not occur in the so-called pure cases. Numerous attempts by mothers to become emotionally free of the infant who grows up to overburden the family with tyrannical demands ordinarily end in failure.

Maternal release from the infant who becomes difficult after overprotection during the first two years may represent a strong desire of many overprotective mothers, even though never acted out as in the example given. Our so-called "pure" cases of overprotection are "pure" only in their overt clinical manifestations. Whatever the psychic attitudes may be, or, in other words, whatever the mixture of love and hate elements in the maternal attitude, we can say of the "pure" group that it represents one in which maternal behavior is most clearly and consistently expressed in overprotection. When a struggle for release by either mother or child from the bonds of the powerful overprotective relationship becomes apparent, the overprotective features may be concealed. Hence, a number of cases are lost in the sifting process because at the time of the original investigation they did not satisfy the criterion of clear evidence of overprotection observable by a layman. Hence, our selection of "pure" cases is limited to those of children actively overprotected at the time of study.

A distribution of the clinical groups of overprotection has been made by Miss Freeman. Taking 526 seriatim from the files of the Institute, she finds 96 cases that fall readily into the five groups listed. Thirty of the 96 satisfy the criteria of maternal overprotection of a wanted child in which the evidence is decisive and agreed to by lay and professional observers (Group I). Twenty-eight are cases of maternal overprotection mixed with rejection, in which the clinical evidence shows predominance of overprotection (Group II). Twenty-one are cases of maternal overprotection in infancy followed later by rejection (Group III). Twelve are examples of mild maternal overprotection (Group IV), and five are cases of non-maternal overprotection (Group V).

Experience of investigators in allotting cases to the clinical groups indicates that with increasing care more and more cases are weeded out of the "pure" forms (Group I). The experience is consistent with theoretical anticipation. In the distribution of mother-child relationships selected by clinical evidence of overprotection and rejection, both common findings, we would expect to find mixtures more frequent than pure forms. A distribution of cases of overprotection and rejection, leaving out nonmaternal forms, would show "pure" overprotection on one end of the distribution curve, "pure" rejection on the other, with the mixed forms making up the bulk of cases between. Naturally, the most careful sifting would tend to show more impurities in the end groups and increase the frequency of the mixed forms. With the knowledge derived from this and similar investigations, future study of our own case material will no doubt reveal impurities in the so-called "pure" group. For the present we may say that it reveals, at least, more consistent and clear cases of overprotection than do the other groups. The factual data of overprotection for the so-called pure group appear in the following case histories.

MATERNAL OVERPROTECTION DATA

CASE 1 (MALE, 8 YEARS [1])

Excessive contact: When he was an infant mother could never leave him for a instant. When he was two years old, she had moods of despondency because she could not get away from him. She feels worried and unhappy when patient is out of her sight. Has been sleeping with him the past six months because he has called her. Lies down with him at night. Extra nursing care has been required because of his frequent colds. Mother says they are attached together like Siamese twins.

Prolongation of infantile care: Mother dresses him every day (age 8), takes him to school every morning and calls for him every afternoon. When at school in the morning she pays the waiter for his lunch and tells waiter what to give him. Breast fed 13 months. Mother fed him the first five years. Mother still goes to the bathroom with him and waits for him. Mother insists on holding his hand when they walk together. Resents his walking alone.

Prevention of independent behavior: He has one friend whom mother takes him to see every two weeks. Mother does not allow him to help in housework for fear he'll fall and break a dish, etc.

Maternal control: Mother must have a light burning for him until he falls asleep. He goes to bed at 10 P.M. Mother always gives in to him; does everything for him; is dominated by him. He spits at her and strikes her.

CASE 2 (MALE, 14 YEARS)

Excessive contact: Mother moved to her present home so she could watch the patient from her window while he walked to school.

1 Age given is at time of referral.

Prolongation of infantile care: Mother continued bottle feeding until he was 3½ years old because he didn't want to give it up. Mother bathed and dressed the patient until he was six and helps to bathe and dress him even now (age 14).

Prevention of independent behavior: Mother prevents his working in spite of recommendations (age 16).

Maternal control: He is extremely "impudent and defiant of authority." Since age 6 when frightened, and until age 14, the patient did not allow the parents to go out in the evening or leave him at home. He refuses to go to school, keeps late hours, and refuses to get out of bed in the morning.

CASE 3 (MALE, 6 YEARS)

Excessive contact: As an infant, the patient was ill the first six weeks in the hospital. Mother was afraid he was not getting enough attention, cried and begged to let him sleep with her; she would lie and watch him in her arms most of the night, Extra nursing care necessary the first year because of boils.

Prolongation of infantile care: The patient was bottle fed to age 4. Mother still dresses and washes him.

Prevention of independent behavior: He sleeps in a cot in parents' room. They are afraid to let him sleep alone (age 6). Mother always protects him against neighbors when they blame him for fighting. Refuses to let him do chores.

Maternal control: Patient is disrespectful and disobedient.

CASE 4 (MALE, 4 YEARS)

Excessive contact: The patient had much nursing care because of numerous colds, and excessive attention to his feet (pronation). He never slept well; cried all the time. "Kept someone always busy pushing the cradle." Everyone tells her, says mother, that she pays too much attention to him, but she feels she has to as she is with him so much.

Prolongation of infantile care: Mother still dresses him; prepares his clothes for toilet (age 6 years, 5 months).

Prevention of independent behavior: He is constantly with mother; refuses to leave her side or to return to kindergarten, or play outside the house unless she is with him. She is afraid to let him run upstairs as he gets out of breath. He is not allowed to visit in other homes.

Maternal control: Patient rules the household by his screaming and imperative voice. Mother will comply with his demands rather than let him scream. He swears at her, kicks and strikes her. He pushes away food he doesn't want and says, "It stinks." He comes in to lunch whenever he pleases.

CASE 5 (MALE, 13 YEARS)

Excessive contact: Mother has slept with him the past three years. Up to age 7, she never let him go out with any adult (even father) except herself.

Prolongation of infantile care: When the patient is disobedient she puts him to bed in the afternoon, even now. She still prepares special food for him when he refuses to eat. She still sits by and coaxes.

Prevention of independent behavior: Mother delayed his schooling until he was seven because she did not like him to leave her. She blocks the plan of sending him to boarding school. She kept him from having friends or learning bad things from other children. When he was sent to camp at 14, the mother visited him on the second day, found that his feet were wet and took him home.

Maternal control: General obedient, submissive response to maternal domination. Uses aggressive methods to maintain his dependency on the mother, insisting she walk to school with him, et cetera.

CASE 6 (MALE, 10 YEARS)

Excessive contact: Mother slept with him until he was six years old. During the entire five years, the mother and patient lived alone with practically no other contacts.

Prolongation of infantile care: The patient was breast fed to age 3, with the excuse, "You know he was all I had."

Prevention of independent behavior: The mother changed the patient to another school because the walk there was a little shorter. Until age 8 she never allowed him to play with other children because they were rough. He is now allowed to play with boys in front of the father's store. Mother hired an older boy to accompany him to school because he complained that the boys molested him.

Maternal control: Anxious, obedient child. Accepts mother's domination. Accepts mother's infantile methods of dicipline without protest. Mother's "slightest disapproval" is very effective in making him mind. He wants to do exactly what the mother does, helping her with the housework, and is overresponsive to her approval or disapproval.

CASE 7 (MALE, 11 YEARS)

Excessive contact: Mother still sleeps with the patient. She takes him along, wherever she goes, even now. Much nursing care was necessary throughout his infancy and childhood because of illness. The patient spends all his spare time with mother.

Prolongation of infantile care: The patient was breast fed 11 months.

Prevention of independent behavior: The patient's social life is exclusively with mother and sister.

Maternal control: Always very obedient to the mother.

CASE 8 (MALE, 7 YEARS)

Excessive contact: Since the birth of patient, mother has always insisted on staying at home with him, and has stopped all her previous social activity. She gives him constant attention and devotion, has "lost herself" in the patient.

Prolongation of infantile care: The patient was breast fed 11 to 12 months.

Prevention of independent behavior: Mother continually watches the patient from the window. Goes to the school frequently to protect the patient against supposed discrimination, and whenever he receives poor grades.

Maternal control: "Overly obedient to an exacting and nagging mother."

CASE 9 (FEMALE, 4 YEARS)

Excessive contact: Mother's social life is almost entirely monopolized by the patient. Extra care has been necessary because of various illnesses.

Prolongation of infantile care: The patient was breast fed 16 months. The mother still coaxes and feeds her, and still dresses her.

Prevention of independent behavior: The mother refused to let her help with any housework when the child was eager to do so.

Maternal control: The patient refuses to come in from play. It is often 11 P. M. before the mother can get her to bed. Patient turns off the radio after the parents have turned it on, is disrespectful and disobedient.

CASE 10 (MALE, 12 YEARS)

Excessive contact: There is frequent kissing and fondling. The mother practically never let him alone during infancy. She kept him away from all but a few adults because she was afraid of infection. Patient still sleeps with the mother when father is out of town (continued to age 13).

Prolongation of infantile care: Patient was breast fed 12 months. Mother still waits on him, gets water for him, butters his bread, etc.

Prevention of independent behavior: Mother has prevented his bicycling, making his own friends, and has generally prevented the development of responsibility.

Maternal control: The patient is disrespectful and impudent to the parents. He constantly demands mother's service, and had a temper tantrum at the age of twelve because she didn't butter his bread for him. He resents giving up his chair for mother. He leaves the table and refuses to eat when he doesn't get the biggest piece.

CASE 11 (MALE, 10 YEARS)

Excessive contact: The patient gets constant nagging attention from the mother, with added devotion from the grandmother in his first four years. Mother stopped numerous social contacts to devote herself to the patient. She often prevents him from reading in order to talk to her.

Prolongation of infantile care: Patient was bottle fed to 21 months. Mother still wants to bathe the patient. He locks the bathroom door and won't let her come in. She stays outside and gives him directions. She always gets his hat and coat for him.

Prevention of independent behavior. Mother is unable to prevent his going with the boys in the streets, etc., because of his disobedience.

Maternal control: The patient is disrespectful and impudent to the parents. He teases and bullies mother. He sleeps on a single bed in parents' room or on a couch in the living room, regardless of their wishes. He turns off the radio when the parents wish it on. He refuses to stay at home nights, leaves at will, returning usually at 10 P. M. He eats meals when he pleases. He slaps mother in temper (latest instance at age 13).

CASE 12 (MALE, 15 YEARS)

Excessive contact: Mother has always "served and watched over" the patient. Up to about age 10, if she left him for more than ten minutes he cried and called for her. She makes many trips to his room during the night to see if he is sleeping quietly or is restless.

Prolongation of infantile care: The patient was breast fed 14½ months. Mother shines his shoes for him. She is constantly after him about cleanliness, studies, going to bed, etc.

Prevention of independent behavior: Mother never allowed him to play in the streets or associate with other children. She tries to prevent his playing chess or reading detective stories.

Maternal control: The patient is disrespectful and impudent to parents and sister. When he loses his temper, strikes his mother; teases and bullies her. He spitefully tramps with muddy shoes on clean floor, cuts his suits, etc.

CASE 13 (MALE, 14 YEARS)

Excessive contact: There was much nursing care by mother because of patient's numerous illnesses in infancy and childhood, up to age 7.

Prolongation of infantile care: The patient was breast fed until the age of two.

Prevention of independent behavior: Mother uncritically defends the boy against schoolteachers. He is given no responsibilities at home. Mother refuses to accept that suggestion. Mother opposes his working hard on the basis that he will have enough hard work when he is grown up. She does not allow him to bring friends to the house.

Maternal control: Patient keeps his own hours. He goes to the movies whenever he wishes and the mother has his meals ready for him when he comes home. He is disobedient and impudent to mother, orders her around. Insists that she find his shirt, his shoes, etc.

CASE 14 (MALE, 5 YEARS)

Excessive contact: Much nursing care was necessary during the patient's infancy due to his frequent colds. Mother has always watched over the children, she says, "as through a microscope."

Prolongation of infantile care: Mother dresses the patient entirely. He was breast fed 12 months, when mother stopped because of pregnancy. He was bottle fed 2½ years.

Prevention of independent behavior: The patient is never allowed to play except in mother's sight. Though it is only a short distance to the school, mother takes him there and calls for him every day.

Maternal control: The patient swears at mother, kicks and pinches her.

CASE 15 (MALE, 7 YEARS)

Excessive contact: The patient cried so frequently during the day that mother fondled him continuously after his second week. "I always had him around me; even when cooking I would have one hand on the stove, the other on the carriage—anything to stop his screeching." Whenever the mother goes out, she always takes the child with her.

Prolongation of infantile care: The patient was breast fed 18 months. Mother still helps him dress.

Prevention of independent behavior: The mother visits the school weekly to check on the patient's progress. She had him transferred to a school so that he doesn't have to cross street car tracks. He is allowed to play only within sight of the mother.

Maternal control: Docile and submissive, obedient adjustment to mother and to his younger brother.

CASE 16 (MALE, 14 YEARS)

Excessive contact: None after the long nursing period.

Prolongation of infantile care: The patient was breast fed 18 months.

Prevention of independent behavior: The mother is uncritically protective of the patient and makes excuses for whatever he does. She objects to the boy's going to work, even though he would live at home, because he would be away from her.

Maternal control: The patient does as he pleases; goes to the movies frequently regardless of mother's wishes. He is unmanageable at home.

He refuses to do any chores. He dominates the mother and sister; they have always done things for him to prevent rows.

Case 17 (Male, 13 Years)

Excessive contact: On account of the children, mother rarely goes out, for her "the door to the outside world is closed"; whenever she goes out she must come back immediately.

Prolongation of infantile care: Mother has always done things for the patient he could have done for himself. For the first time (patient age 15) she refused to get him a glass of water and told him to get it himself. She has him lie on a couch when he looks tired, and keeps the other children out of the room. She gets up several times a night to see if he is all right.

Prevention of independent behavior: He is prevented from making friends in the neighborhood because the boys are "too tough." At 15, he is not allowed to take any toys out of the room alone. Mother refuses to give him an allowance in order to supervise the spending of every penny.

Maternal control: Mother says he tyrannizes over her by being dependent on her for everything, and nagging, yet he is obedient as to bedtime, etc., and never openly rebellious to her.

Case 18 (Male, 16 Years)

Excessive contact: Mother "shares his every experience." They always go to the movies together. They have practically no social life out of each other's company.

Prolongation of infantile care.

Prevention of independent behavior: Mother goes to the movies and explains the subtitles to him in such a way that "there is no danger of his mind being poisoned." She never allows him to join in outdoor sports for fear of injury, except recently, when he insisted on playing baseball with other boys, she accompanied him. She takes up the cudgels for him in every school difficulty; constantly writes letters, makes visits, and has become the school nuisance. She helps him with every school subject.

Maternal control: Remarkably obedient and submissive to maternal domination, even accepting her refusal to let him play ball with other boys at the age of 16.

Case 19 (Male, 12 Years)

Excessive contact: The patient was absent from mother for the first time at age 13 when he was sent to camp for two weeks ("and able to do everything"). He had much nursing care between the ages of seven and eight because of infantile paralysis. Mother does not go out on account of her son.

Prolongation of infantile care: Mother still feeds him, helps him dress, slaps him when he is "naughty," sleeps in the same room with him though in separate beds. She is constantly helping him do things he can do himself, even helping him into the bathtub (paralysis of right leg). He was breast fed 13 months.

Prevention of independent behavior: Mother has discouraged friends by not allowing him to invite them to the home.

Maternal control: Completely accepts mother's "babying." Obedient and docile. He tries to compel mother to accompany him to school.

CASE 20 (MALE, 4 YEARS)

Excessive contact: There is still much fondling, sitting on mother's lap, constant kissing. Because she would not leave her children, the mother, until recently, rarely went out with her husband.

Prolongation of infantile care: Mother still dresses him (until modified by treatment, at age 5).

Prevention of independent behavior: The patient refuses to play with other children, preferring always to be where mother is.

Maternal control: Very obedient, does exactly as he is told. "Too good." "Is downcast if mother forgets to kiss him." Very considerate of mother and solicitous of her in all her moods.

DESCRIPTIVE DATA OF THE CHILDREN STUDIED IN REGARD TO SEX, AGE, INTELLIGENCE, HEALTH, ECONOMIC STATUS. AND DELINQUINCY

Sex: Nineteen males; one female.

Age span (at time of referral): 5 to 16 years; median age is 10 years. Four children are age 4 to 6 years; five are 6 to 10 years; ten are 10 to 15 years; one is 16 years old.

Intelligence test classifications: two are dull; five are of adequate intelligence; thirteen are superior or very superior. Of the twenty, fourteen are in school; of this number, two have repeated grades because of failure to pass, and one is doing poor work (attributed to language handicap), though in proper grade. The remaining eleven of the fourteen are doing average or superior work, according to school grades.

Health: Excepting one boy with paralysis of a leg, there are no deformities in the group. Details of medical histories and physical examinations are given in chapters III and VIII.

The economic status of the group is "adequate" in eight cases; "marginal" in twelve; "dependent" in none.

Delinquency: Truancy occurs in one case; stealing in three; of the latter, stealing in two cases is from the mother only.

Behavior problems are of prevailingly an aggressive type in twelve cases; submissive in eight.

As compared with other I. C. G. cases, the group is younger, more intelligent, of higher economic status, and less delinquent.

III. EXCESSIVE CONTACT

MATERNAL overprotection is synonymous with excessive maternal care of children. Its manifestations in the mother-child relationship have been grouped, according to the manner in which they occur, under four headings. Three of these concern maternal activity primarily and paraphrase the common observations: 1) "the mother is always there"; 2) "she still treats him like a baby"; and 3) "she won't let him grow up" or "she won't take any risks." These expressions are rendered into the groupings: 1) excessive contact; 2) infantilization; and 3) prevention of independent behavior. All the manifestations of overprotection as revealed by maternal activity are classifiable under the three headings, excepting those which denote anxious behavior.

Maternal anxiety or oversolicitude is indicated in our groupings only when revealed by objective behavior in the mother-child relationship. Since oversolicitude is always manifested in one or more of the three categories already enumerated, the problem of its inclusion is partly solved. Thus, oversolicitude will be manifested by refusal to take risks for the child, by excessive nursing care during illness, and the like. The data furthermore indicate the amount of oversolicitude as measured generally by the type of activity prevented by the mother, the extent of infantilization, the amount of contact. In our study we are limited to factual evidence of overprotection.

The advantage in handling factual data is obvious. The evidence is well defined, hence, more convincing; comparisons of the signs of overprotection are easily made for each case and studied in relation to other phases of the investigation. Nevertheless, the significance of the manner in which oversolicitude is manifested cannot be captured by a record of its objective overprotective manifestations. The child who is ill with a mild case of measles may be exposed to a mother whose harassed look, exaggerated response, tense embracing, and tearful exclamations, "Oh, my baby, my poor sick baby," give evidence of more intensive overprotection than that of a mother in a similar plight, also overprotective, yet emotionally more controlled. The difference in the two mothers is brought out in our study only in so far as the intensity of response is proportional to the factual data. Assuming that the facts recorded under excessive contact, infantilization, and prevention of independent behavior are equal in two given cases, there remains a difference in the quality or intensity of behavior that is not recorded. There is no way of telling with the data at hand how the child's personality is affected by this qualitative difference. At this stage of development in our human relationship studies we must be content with gross differentiation.

The fourth criterion of overprotection is lack or excess of maternal control. The former indicates a breakdown in the mother's ability to modify her child's behavior. In extreme form, the mother is quite subservient to the demands of her nursery despot who has retained full possession of the mother's attention and services as in the first year of life. The latter indicates excessive maternal domination of the child.

When overprotection is revealed by all four criteria, the picture presented is well portrayed by a mother who holds her child tightly with one hand and makes the gesture of pushing away the rest of the world with the other. Her energies are directed to preserving her infant as infant for all time, preserving it from all harm and from contact with the rest of humanity. For her child she will fight hard, make every sacrifice, and aggressively prevent interference with her social monopoly. Her aggression, directed so strongly against the intruder, yields, however, before the child. Towards him she is submissive; her discipline falters when he becomes assertive in the latter half of infancy, and is gradually destroyed.

The picture presents a composite of eleven out of the twenty "pure" cases. It summarizes instances of maternal overprotection in which the negative aspect of the fourth sign, "lack of maternal control," is present. In the remaining nine cases, eight children show an excessively submissive relation to the mother, are obedient to her, and very dependent.

In the one group the general picture is that of inadequately modified behavior in respect to infantile power over the mother. The infantile aggression is manifested in having one's way, dominating every situation, manipulating the scene in order to be the central figure, displaying temper when crossed. The overprotection may be described as a process in which infantile power, unmodified, expands into a monstrous growth that tends to subjugate the parents.

In the second group, the dependency phase of the infant's relation to the mother is fostered through lack of development or overmodification of the dominating phase. In regard to infantile aggression, the overprotection in the second group is a process of constriction rather than expansion—a constriction in the growth of aggressive tendencies.

In their clinical manifestations of overprotection, mothers show a distinct difference in the two groups. Mothers of the dominating children are indulgent; mothers of the submissive children are dominating. The statement as it stands is merely a description implied by the meaning of the terms employed. For if a child is submissive to his mother, it is implied that he readily yields to her demands, that he keeps away from the company she forbids, that he goes to bed on time, and the like. She appears to be dominating the child, and the child is submissive to her. On the other hand, if a child goes to bed when he pleases, eats only what happens to suit his fancy, the fact that his behavior toward his mother has been consistently undisciplined implies that she has been consistently indulgent. The fact that the mother has indulged or dominated is implied in the description of the child's behavior as undisciplined or submissive. The question remains, is the type of maternal overprotection determined primarily by maternal attitude or by the type of response in her offspring? Before we can attempt an answer we must study the significant phases of overprotection in detail, as well as the backgrounds of the mother and child, and their response to family life. So far, at least, a study of manifestations has revealed two distinct relationships in the maternal overprotective forms.

Excessive contact, the inseparability of mother and child, is the first and foremost evidence of maternal overprotection. When contact is excessive, infantilization and prevention of the child's independent growth are natural outcomes. In fact, some behavior items might be classified in any one of the first three groups. Take, for example, the item "breast-fed eighteen months." It denotes excessive contact, infantilization, and also, in so far as it prevents adaptation to the more "mature" manner of feeding at eighteen months, prevention of "independent" growth. The items is classified only under infantilization because it indicates factually that the mother is continuing a practice past the usual time in her social group. Classification in other groups would be an inference. Consider the item, "The mother goes nowhere without her son (now age 12)." There is no question of the classification "excessive social contact." It is also fair to infer that the making of friends, hence, "independent growth," is prevented by this arrangement. However, the mother may not have actively prevented her boy from forming friendships. He may himself have made no efforts or may even have refused to do so. If she had actively prevented him, then that item would be so classified. There are overprotective mothers, certainly, who, though wishing to absorb the entire social life of their offspring, do not actively prevent their forming other social contacts. If the children of such mothers differ from those whose friendships have not been allowed to develop, then our classification will help to reveal the significant differences determining or resulting from variations in the stress of overprotective patterns.

Excessive contact is manifested in continuous companionship of mother and child, prolonged nursing care, excessive fondling, or sleeping with the mother long past infancy. We do not have norms statistically established for all these activities. Obviously gross differences from generally known maternal behavior are then alone reliable.

Social and physical contact are differentiated in order to determine the special influence, if any, of body contact. Of the forms of physical contiguity, sleeping with the mother presents the longest and potentially the closest form of contact. We might anticipate that in puberty, especially under the overprotective regime, incestuous conflict would then be overtly expressed; and that where social contact is excessive, though without close physical contact, incestuous conflict would be expressed through an indirect symptomatology.

Besides excessive social contact, sleeping with the mother occurred in six of the group of twenty. These six are all boys and when first examined ranged in age from 8 to 13. Three were older than 12 years; the remaining three were ages 8, 10 and 11, respectively. Since all but one had been treated or followed up at least two years since the initial study, we had three patients now as old as 14, 15 and 16. (For follow-up studies ten years later see Chapter X.)

The oldest of these adolescents is generally submissive to his mother, is called "sissy" and "mamma's boy" by his school companions, avoids boys' games, is very neat and clean, and afraid to fight. His mother regards him as "sweet, affectionate and considerate" (at 13). There was excessive contact in his first year of life because of his constant crying and the mother's fear that he would die since he was "delicate and underweight." He does not mix with other boys and is constantly at home after school hours, usually reading. He has also received extra care because of his frequent complaints of fatigue. He has occasionally slept with the mother (up to age 15); there has been little or no fondling.

The overprotection has been chiefly indulgent, though mixed with domination. For example, the mother had him get a glass of water for himself for the first time when he was fifteen years old. At the same time, if he is naughty she puts him to bed early and punishes him as though he were a small child. In relation to the mother, his symptoms are chiefly of dependency. Puberty is delayed. He has a feminine make-up, high pitched voice and small genitals.

From the age of 14, when sleeping in his own bed he has occasionally walked in his sleep, each time to the mother's bed.

Once, at about age 14½, after he was in bed the mother powdered his back with talcum because of a "heat rash," whereupon he had an erection. The mother told the incident to the father as a sign that the boy "was growing up." The patient is always very modest about his attire.

The next oldest of the seven is a boy of 15 (Case 5), timid and reserved, who, like the previous patient, does not play with other boys and is called "sissy."

The overprotection is largely dominating in this case, and the patient's relation to the mother dependent and submissive. Up to age 7 the patient was always, when not asleep, in the mother's company. The mother has "always kept him in very closely and was afraid to have him mix with other children for fear of diseases and the things he might learn from them." Her plan of overcoming his unhappiness in school is "to simply sacrifice everything and take him out of school and go with him some place where she could be with him all the time." When disobedient, she puts him to bed in the afternoon (then age 13). She has been sleeping with him the past three years (patient's age 10–13 years). Like the previous patient also, physical findings are of a feminine-looking boy, with large hips and high-pitched voice, though genitalia were well developed. There is no overt evidence of sexual response to the mother.

The third boy (Case 10), age 14, is disrespectful and impudent to his parents. Physically, he is robust and sexually well developed.

Maternal overprotection is chiefly of the indulgent type in this case. There has been excessive social contact, much fondling and kissing, and sleeping with the mother during the father's absences from the home on account of business. The sleeping arrangement was terminated when the patient was age 13 years, 1 month. The father had just left on a trip. The patient came to his mother's bedroom and said he would like to sleep with her; then he suddenly turned pale, and walked out of the room. When later the mother asked him why he didn't want to sleep with her, and why he turned pale, he answered that it "made him sick."

It is interesting that in spite of prolonged physical contact in bed with the mother during adolescence, not one of the three made incestuous attempts, although two of them gave evidence of direct sexual response or conflict. All three were warned and threatened about masturbation. Although allowed to sleep with the mother, they were never exposed to her nakedness. All received more than the usual training in sex taboos.

The three adolescents in Group I do not show evidence of direct sex response to mothers. Such symptoms, when present, were manifested in various peregrinations of the incestuous conflict. It is worth noticing that where the child's relation to the mother is submissive rather than dominating, he is theoretically less likely to be sexually aggressive.

Among the preadolescent children in Group I, a boy (Case 11), when age 10 years, 10 months, embraced and kissed his mother while she lay on a couch and then proposed they do to each other "what dogs do," illustrating with body movements. The overprotection was indulgent. Social contact was excessive in infancy though the child did not sleep with the mother, and there was no undue fondling. The child became an omnivorous reader; the mother would often snatch the book from him to get his company. Indeed, the mother's efforts to keep him in closest contact were fought off by the patient. She still insists on bathing him, but he won't allow it and locks the bathroom door. She remains outside the door and gives him directions. She resents the fact that he refuses to undress in front of her.

Although physical contact in this case is not excessive, the child's frank incestuous proposal is in keeping with the mother's own efforts to encourage his bodily contact and with the child's very dominating behavior.

Eight of the group of 20 cases received prolonged nursing care because of illness. The intensification of overprotection occasioned by jeopardy to the life of the child will be considered later. At this point, the relation of illness to excessive contact is our main concern. A study of medical histories preceding age 7 has been made by Brunk for 30 overprotected and 200 "non-overprotected" Institute cases. These show practically the same number of illnesses and operations per child for each group. The types of illnesses also were quite similar.

In our group of twenty cases, which represents a more carefully weeded list than Miss Brunk's, there are listed 62 illnesses before age 6, and 16 operations. There are 3.1 illnesses per child in contrast with 1.4 of the check group; .8 operations per child in contrast with .25. In other words, the overprotected group had more than twice as many illnesses and three times as many operations as the check group. In regard to accidents, not one was recorded for Miss Brunk's group or ours. There were 20, or one for every ten children, in the check group.

These findings appear consistent with the general observation that overprotective mothers give more accurate and complete development histories of their children than do others, and are more likely to secure medical care and take medical advice (hence, the large number of tonsillectomies). Refusal to take risks for the child, prevention of his independent growth, however great an evil in his social development, is reflected in the absence of one serious accident.

The findings therefore do not lend support to the theory that illnesses *per se* are productive of maternal overprotection. It appears obvious, however, that frequent nursing care means more maternal contact and for the child may be an infantilizing experience; further, if associated with danger to life, it intensifies the overprotective attitude. As reinforcing factors in excessive contact, prolonged illnesses, whether mild or severe, are more important than acute illnesses.

A distinction might be made between maternal response to physical conditions in the child requiring constant contact, yet not threatening to life, and response to acute conditions in the child that may be brief, yet frightening because of the supposed imminence of death. Contrast, for example, two overprotective mothers, of whom one has given very frequent care to a child because it appeared sickly and weak from birth until age 7, though never seriously ill, and the other who had a child requiring no extra care because of illnesses except on three occasions in infancy —bronchopneumonia, a mastoiditis with operative interference, and one convulsion. In the latter case, anxiety about the child and fear of its death would tend toward oversolicitude, that is, exaggerated response to the child's physical state on all other occasions. In the former, anxiety about death would be a secondary response to the chronic though mild illness, which would necessitate and hence intensify the closeness of contact between mother and child. There are mothers, not especially overprotective, yet demonstrating marked oversolicitude during the child's illness, no matter how mild, who have been sensitized by one or more experiences with "death close to the child." On the other hand, there are mothers also, neither overprotective nor overly solicitous about health, who relish the close social contact that the child's illnesses afford.

Given an overprotective attitude, in which closeness to the child is a powerful motive, all conditions requiring nursing care become reinforcing factors. Serious illnesses of the child intensify the oversolicitous phase of the overprotective pattern.

With present limitations in data and our inability to split a relationship into its fine elements, we cannot measure the intrinsic value of the mother's varying experiences with the illnesses of her children and prove how her overprotection takes on various shapes in conformity with different external factors. We can at this stage merely assume that a mother, already prepared to play an overprotective role, and, hence, already disposed toward oversolicitude and excessive contact, will, in the event of illnesses in her offspring, receive an extra push in that direction. It must be remembered that maternal response to the infant's illness is regarded not as a genetic factor but as a strengthening element in an attitude already present, weighting it, however, with the measure of the external event.

An example of marked apprehension about illness and excessive contact, reinforced by the special form of organic difficulty in her child, is well demonstrated by the mother in Case 7. She has never gone anywhere without her 11-year-old son, when he is not at school. She still sleeps with him. In his first year of life he was a colicky baby and received abundant nursing care by the mother. When age 3½ years his life was in jeopardy because of double lobar pneumonia. The doctor told the mother there was little chance for recovery. Empyema was a sequel; a thoracotomy was performed with good recovery. Several months of nursing care were required. At 4 years of age the child began to take on weight rapidly. The genitalia were examined and appeared to be very small. A Fröhlich syndrome was diagnosed and about three years of glandular therapy and weekly visits to private physicians followed. Meanwhile the mother made a daily examination of the genitalia, a practice she still continued at the time of our examination when the patient was 11.

Due to financial difficulties the patient had to receive treatment at dispensaries when age 7. About that time, the patient was demonstrated in a clinic. The mother said she overheard the doctor tell his students that the patient, her son, would die by age 17. The mother then commented, "I knew I had been giving in to him before, but after that I knew I couldn't give in to him enough."

The condition requiring glandular treatment had lasted seven years up to the time of examination. In itself it was not apparently serious to life. The boy was not ill in bed; he attended school regularly and seemed healthy though fat. Yet it afforded the mother a plausible pretext to examine his body daily; made necessary frequent weighing of the boy. In short, it gave tremendous reinforcement to the already existing excessive contact.

On two occasions the death of the child was predicted—once during his lobar pneumonia and again when the fatal words were heard at the clinic. These experiences would act presumably as factors keenly intensifying apprehension about the child's death and would reinforce the mother's general oversolicitude about her son's health.

At the time of our examination the mother protested greatly when she was asked to remain outside the examining room. She said that in all his numerous examinations she had always been present. After much persuasion she consented, remaining close to the examining room door.

In the remaining cases, various mixtures of prolonged contact through nursing care, besides experience of acute, serious illness, are shown. Of eight cases in which illnesses afforded an added reason for excessive contact, in seven the child became an object of solicitude and received extra care because of sickness very shortly after birth. Although health histories of overprotected and nonoverprotected children may not show significant differences in type or frequency of illness (except in the number of accidents), a study of the time distribution of the child's illnesses may prove interesting. In the absence of such a study we may at least indicate the theoretical significance of the distribution of illness as an added stimulus of overprotection.

When a child's sickness follows immediately or shortly after birth, the actual, besides the psychological, threat to the life of the child is greater than if the illness occurs later on in infancy or childhood. If all the child's illnesses come in rapid succession in the first two years of life, maternal contact and solicitude at that time are presumably more intense and productive of overprotection than if the same illnesses are scattered through the first ten years of life. Further, when maternal attachment is increased, through whatever agency, in the first year of the infant's life there naturally follows a lessened ability to yield to the growing independence of the child. The two-year-old is normally given less protective care than the one-year-old. When maternal attachment is intensified by illness during the first year of life, maternal release is hindered and the attitude of the child fixed by the one-year-old relationship. Hence, one must investigate all external factors in the first year of the infant's life that may tend to solidify the overprotection in that period and thereby help to explain the infantilization, an attempt to hold the mother-infant relationship throughout the life of the child.

Further examples of illness in infancy and childhood operating as factors increasing maternal contact and apprehension follow Table I. Unfortunately comparable data for other groups are not at hand. The mere tabulation of incidence of disease, operation, and accident, when viewed as purely external factors, is inadequate. We need complete data not only on time periods, progress of disease, the various phases to which mothers were exposed, the physicians' statements to mothers, but also on incidental factors indicating in detail what the mothers experienced in terms of contact with, and apprehension because of, their children's ailments. Nevertheless, we may say with certainty that in twelve cases in Group I the medical history of the child shows nothing significant in this connection. In the remaining eight cases, the medical data furnish interesting evidence that the overprotection is strengthened through excessive contact and apprehension on the part of the mother. Actual danger of death occurred in four cases: Case 3, asphyxia neonatorum and severe boils; Case 1, bronchopneumonia, mastoidectomy; Case 19, infantile paralysis; Case 14, convulsions, cervical adenitis with high temperature. Apprehension of death because of factors besides actual illness occurred in three others: Case 7, hypopituitarism and doctor's prediction of death from pituitary tumor; Case 13, sickly and weak from infancy to age 7 with vomiting spells, and a convulsion in infancy; Case 17, underweight and "delicate" in the first year of life. In all eight cases there is evidence of prolonged nursing care given by the mothers.

SUMMARY

Since maternal overprotection represents exaggerated maternal care of the child, a study of its overt manifestations is directed to activities that yield factual data. Exaggerations of the usual physical and social contacts, infantile care, and protection against danger, in the rearing of children, are clinically described as excessive contact, infantilization, and prevention of independent behavior. Such activities appear overtly as behavior primarily of the mother. Exaggerations of the usual maternal attempts to modify the child's behavior, observed in the form of discipline and indulgence, are clinically described as domination and indulgence, and the data collected under the caption "maternal control." The latter exaggerations are observed most conveniently in the child's response to maternal control. Of the manifestations of overprotection, the first three are seen as activity of the mother; the fourth as activity of the child. On the basis of differences in manifestation of maternal control, maternal overprotection is classified as dominating and indulgent.

Data of overprotection when classified into four groups show much dovetailing; nevertheless, there are characteristic differences.

Excessive contact is manifested in continuous companionship of mother and child, prolonged nursing care, excessive fondling, and sleeping with the mother long past infancy. The twenty "pure" cases (Group I) contained six boys who slept with their mothers long past infancy, three of them during adolescence. Of the latter, two showed overt evidence of direct sexual response or conflict, though none showed overt incestuous behavior. Of the former, one showed active incestuous behavior. In the remaining fourteen cases of Group I, no overt sexual response to the mother was revealed.

In eight cases, excessive contact was occasioned by prolonged nursing care. A study of the twenty medical histories of Group I and a contrasting group of 200 "non-overprotected" cases shows on the average twice as many illnesses and three times as many operations in the former. The findings are regarded as inaccurate for illnesses, but accurate for operations, since they appear consistent with the general observation that overprotective mothers give more accurate and complete medical histories of children, as also developmental histories, than do others. Not one serious accident occurred to the children in Group I; twenty occurred in the contrast group. Most of the Group I operations were tonsillectomies. In combination with the absence of serious accidents, these findings are at least consistent with the careful medical attention and protective behavior of the overprotecting mothers.

Consideration was given to the problem of prolonged nursing care in ordinary illnesses, of their distribution in time as external factors reinforcing maternal contact, and serious or other frightening conditions, threatening to the life of the child, as factors stimulating maternal apprehension.

EXAMPLES OF ILLNESSES IN INFANCY AND CHILDHOOD AS POTENTIAL FACTORS REINFORCING MATERNAL CONTACT

CASE 3. Child was born asphyxiated, and within a few days had numerous boils over the scalp. Visitors to the ward said, "Look at that poor little baby. I doubt if he will live." The mother was greatly upset, cried frequently and was unable to sleep. She begged and finally persuaded the nurse to let the baby sleep in her bed. The mother would lie awake and watch the baby through the night. The scalp was treated

TABLE I Number of Illnesses and Operations in Group I before Age 7

CASE NUMBER

Illnesses	1	2	3	4	5	6	7	8	9	10	11	12	13	14	15	16	17	18	19	20	
Measles	1		1	1	1	1		1		1		1					1	1	1		12
Chicken pox	1	1									1					1	1		1		6
Pertussis		1			1						1	1				1	1				7
Diphtheria		1		1								1				1	1	1			5
Pneumonia	1	1					1		1												4
Rickets (moderate)			1	1									1	1							3
Frequent colds	1		1	1					1												4
"Colic" in 1st year						1												1			2
"Colitis" or diarrhea				1			1						1								3
Croup	1																			1	2
Convulsions														1					1		2
Tonsillitis			1										1								2
Cervical adenitis						1		1													2
German measles														1						1	1
"Boils"			1						1												1
Otitis-mastoiditis	1							1					1								2
"Sickly and weak"																					1
Fever—unknown origin													1								1
Mumps		1																			1
Vomiting spells													1								1
Total illnesses																					62
Operations																					
Tonsillectomy	1	1	1	1				1	1		1			1	1			1			10
Mastoidectomy	1								1												2
Thoracotomy							1														1
Paracentesis				1					1												2
Circumcision for phimosis								1													1
Total operations																					16

Average number of illnesses per child 3.1   Average number of operations per child 0.8

for nine months. The child had frequent colds. When 2½ years of age, there was much worry because of bow-legs. Mother refused to follow the recommendation that he wear braces. At 4, he had measles and in the same year, because of his frequent colds, a tonsillectomy. (Note bottle feeding to age 4.)

Note reinforcement of maternal overprotection shortly after the birth of the child, through fear of its death at a period when the protective attitude is especially powerful, followed by excessive contact.

CASE 1. Sickly baby; "croup" when teething; bronchopneumonia at 14 months; frequent colds and sore throat to age 6; mastoid operation at 5; measles at 5½; a tonsillectomy at 6, followed shortly by chicken-pox.

The history shows general physical conditions requiring extra care in infancy, with factors intensifying such care through life—threatening conditions in infancy (bronchopneumonia) and childhood (mastoid operation)—a good setting for the increased maternal apprehension that follows.

CASE 19. Infantile paralysis at 7 years. Doctor did not expect patient to live. Much nursing care for twelve months and since then numerous visits to doctors for treatment of paralyzed right side.

The case illustrates a situation that because of the prolonged nursing period and original jeopardy to life reinforced overprotective factors already present.

CASE 17. Baby underweight and delicate, especially in first year of life. Mother afraid he would die.

CASE 13. Patient "sickly and weak" during infancy and up to age 7. Vomiting spells and one convulsion during infancy. Influenza and pneumonia at 4.

CASE 14. Three convulsions at 14 months of age, with cervical adenitis and high temperature. Catches cold easily. Physician has warned mother against ever exposing the child to draughts. Factors favored apprehension and excessive contact.

CASE 4. No serious illnesses in infancy but numerous colds. Much nursing care by mother, and much attention to his feet because of pronation due to rickets, for which he has worn arches since age 2. Attacks of diarrhea age 3 weeks to 5 months. Tonsillectomy at 19 months.

CASE 9. Colic and much crying first half year of life. Mild diphtheria at 2 years. Tonsillectomy at 2 years, 4 months, and within a few months, several paracenteses of ear drums; treatment of ears and sinuses weekly since that time.

The last five cases cited are typical instances of conditions shortly following birth, that call on the mothers' protective tendencies at an especially crucial time, i.e., in the infant's most helpless period. Assuming a "typical" maternal attitude, such conditions would weigh the balance in favor of overprotection. Assuming a previously conditioned overprotective attitude, they would reinforce the overprotection. It is not difficult to visualize how, starting the maternal career with a sickly infant who has one or more serious acute illnesses, a mother's whole orientation to the social experiences of the child is affected. However, in the twenty instances of "pure" overprotection not one case reveals infantile histories as an exclusive source of maternal overprotection. In the cases of so-called "mild overprotection," the favoring of the child sickly in infancy is, of course, a common finding.

IV. INFANTILIZATION

INFANTILIZATION consists in the performance of activities in the care of a child beyond the time when such activities usually occur. Infantilization refers also to continuity of the same type of care ordinarily modified in later years. Breast feeding an infant of two years, for example, may in a given cultural group represent maternal activity that usually ends at nine to twelve months. Completely dressing a five-year-old child may represent activity which, at that age, is usually modified to helping with regard to a few items of clothing (for example, tying shoelaces and assisting with difficult buttons).

The data of infantilization concern feeding, dressing, bathing, washing, punishing and various kinds of behavior typical for children of younger years. Glaring examples are shown by a mother who helps her thirteen-year-old son dress; and by another who still butters bread and gets water for a twelve-year-old; by another who punishes a thirteen-year-old son by putting him to bed in the afternoon. Such examples are typical of many others illustrating the behavior of mothers who have prolonged the infantile method of handling into the older years.

Mothers in Group I demonstrate singly or in combination three types of infantilizing activity. Commonest is the continuation of breast feeding, a prolongation of the mother-infant relationship. Five mothers showed this type of infantilization with little or no evidence of the other forms. Six mothers gave evidence of prolonged breast feeding in combination with other forms.

The other two types of infantilization show a difference of degree, in which the child has a greater measure of control. A mother may wait on her child "hand and foot," yet may allow him to bathe and dress himself. In the gradual relinquishing of infantile care, breast feeding first gives way, then bodily care, and finally, the "waiting on" the child for services he can perform himself. The last form of infantilization includes services that adults may perform for each other, services that some of our overprotected children demand. Yet the same children may prevent the mother's insistent efforts to continue bathing and dressing them.

The infant has less share in the determination of length of breast feeding time than in the other forms of infantilization. He may himself aid in prolonging the status of mother as servant, playing in this respect an aggressive dominating role. He may yield to infantile bodily care, aiding thereby the maternal domination.

Of the children in Group I older than 10 years, there are three, each age 13, whose infantilization includes infantile punishment and help in eating and dressing. The overprotection is dominating; the relation to the mother submissive. In the forms of infantilization we are given another measure of maternal overprotection, a measure of the degree of modification from infantile care; and also a measure of the child's adaptation to this behavior.

Of the kinds of infantilization described, breast feeding is most easily measured against check groups. Miss Brunk's group of 27 cases of overprotection in which length of breast feeding time is given contains 12 cases or 45 percent in which the period is twelve months or longer, as compared with 15 cases or 9 percent in a check group of 170 non-overprotected. In her total case number, 30 overprotected and 200 non-overprotected, exclusive breast feeding (that is, no milk other than mother's) occurred in 53 percent of the former, and in 17 percent of the latter. In our own Group I, breast feeding twelve months or longer occurred in 10 cases (50 percent). Of these, four were breast fed eighteen months; one, twenty-four months; and one, thirty-six months.

As an additional check group, Miss Freeman studied seriatim records of 526 Institute cases, not excluding overprotected children, and found 32 percent of breast-feeding cases twelve months or over. Two other check groups (Terman's [1] 589 gifted children and Woodbury's [2] 20,504 unselected cases from industrial

---

[1] Lewis M. Terman, ed., *Genetic Studies of Genius* (Stanford, Calif., 1926), p. 182.
[2] Robert M. Woodbury, "The Relation between Breast and Artificial Feeding and Infant Mortality," *American Journal of Hygiene*, II (1922), 668–87.

cities) show a distribution in length of breast feeding similar to the Institute's check group of 526 cases. Both Dietrich's [3] group of 998 private maternity cases, and Schlossmann's [4] group of 721 cases show no breast feeding after the twelfth month.

A further check on the relation of maternal attitude to length of breast feeding time is made by selection of cases on the basis of long and short feeding. If we select 100 children on the basis of a long breast-feeding period (twelve or more months), we should find, if overprotection is the important factor in prolonging the period, more overprotected children in this group than children who are not overprotected. On the other hand, if we select a very short breast-feeding period (one month or less), we should expect comparatively fewer overprotected than non-overprotected children.

When the maternal attitude is known to be hostile to the child (maternal rejection), we would anticipate increase in the number of short periods, decrease in the number of long periods. Miss Freeman selected 100 long and 100 short breast-feeding cases, using no other selective criterion.

She found 50 "rejected" children in the one month group; 20 rejected in the twelve-month-or-longer group. Her figures for the overprotected children are 19 in the one-month group; 49 in the twelve-month-or-longer group (see Table II).

TABLE II

Maternal attitude	LENGTH OF BREAST FEEDING	
	1 month or less	12 months or longer
Rejection	50	20
Overprotection (pure, mixed, mild and nonmaternal)	19	49
Guilt overprotection	16	12
Neither rejection nor overprotection	15	19
Total number of cases	100	100

[3] Henry Dietrich, "An Analysis of a Series of Case Records Relative to Certain Phases of Breast Feeding," *Journal of the American Medical Association*, LXXIX (1922), 268–70.

[4] A. Schlossmann, "Offentliches Gesundheitswesen über die Zunahme des Stillwillens," *Klinische Wochenschrift*, III (1924), 69–81.

Freeman groups all overprotection forms together except "guilt overprotection," since in the latter evidence appears that strong rejection elements are present. In mixed overprotection, the maternal attitude is consistent throughout the infancy of the patient and hence is rightly included with the pure forms in breast-feeding studies.

Of the various factors that might affect length of the lactation period, Freeman found little or no significance in differences of nationality (divided into American-born, foreign-born, Jewish and non-Jewish), or in the child's sex or intelligence. Children who were "wanted," according to mothers' statements, showed a slightly greater preponderance in the long-feeding group than children who were "unwanted." Frequency of short as contrasted with long breast-feeding periods were affected also but slightly by illnesses during pregnancy or difficulty of delivery.

"Only" children as contrasted with older, mid, or youngest children showed no significant difference in long or short breast-feeding time when those "only" children who were separated from the mother for reasons of economic, physical or social necessity (death or desertion of the father, illness of mother, illegitimacy of child) were substracted from the totals.

Certain factors operating in favor of long breast-feeding time, that is, large families and young mothers, would operate against long periods in the overprotected groups, since in such groups there are many only children and mothers relatively old for primipara. In Group I, for example, the average age of mothers at the time of giving birth to the patient is 27, in contrast with the average of 23 in Freeman's check group. Furthermore, the percentage of families of only children in Group I is 50, in contrast with the Institute for Child Guidance percentage of 22 (237 only children in 1,084 families referring a child).

In spite of factors militating against a long period of lactation, the overprotecting mothers keep their infants at the breast longer than mothers in the other groups. The average for the Group I breast feeders is fourteen months, as compared with averages of four to nine months in the five check groups. Further, only one of the twenty in Group I failed to use breast feeding (because of eclampsia). All the evidence available indicates that the overprotective attitude is significantly correlated with a relatively long breast-feeding period.

The detailed evidence at hand indicates further that prolongation of breast feeding by the mothers in Group I is a prolongation of the pleasure of having the child at the breast, a difficulty in separating from the child at this stage, or returning to the breast when the child balks at the transition to cup or bottle. A number of mothers in Group I continued breast feeding regardless of the physician's advice or the criticism of neighbors.

In Case 7, the mother cried when on account of her illness she had to wean the baby at eleven months. She explained her fears: "You feel they are taken away from you." A mother (Case 6) who kept her child at the breast for three years, in spite of strong protests of friends, defended herself by saying, "You know he was all I had." Breast feeding was prolonged because mothers "hated to start weaning" (Case 10, breast feeding twelve months; Case 16, eighteen months); and because the child refused to take the bottle (Case 9, breast feeding sixteen months).

In Group I, furthermore, there are four instances of unusually long periods of bottle feeding. After weaning by physician's advice at ten months, bottle feeding was continued to twenty-one months (Case 11. "Because of the child's insistence" bottle feeding was continued to thirty months, after weaning from the breast at twelve months (Case 14). In the single case where feeding was exclusively by bottle (Case 17), weaning was delayed until about forty-two months "because he didn't want to give it up." In Case 2, weaning from the breast occurred at eleven months; from the bottle at forty-eight months.

Mothers who prolong breast or bottle feeding display an interesting contrast when the problem of weaning comes up. One group actively prolongs the act; the other yields to the child when it resists separation from breast or bottle. A significant difference in the overprotective attitude may be focused at this point; for the one attitude is an active one, the other passive. In the former, the prolongation is primarily initiated by behavior of the mother; in the latter, by behavior of the infant. In the former, the mother "refuses" to release the infant; in the latter, the infant will not release the mother. Hence, we may speak at this early stage of an active and passive form of maternal overprotection.

In six Group I cases, mothers gave as reason for the prolongation of feeding, difficulty with the process of weaning: "the child's insistence" (Case 14); his refusal to "give it up" (Case 17); "refusal to take the bottle" (Case 9); difficulty at the start (Case 2); the bother of weaning (Case 16); the "hatred" of or "inability" to start (Case 10). In five of these cases, the overprotection was consistently indulgent. In the sixth (Case 17), the overprotection was a mixture of indulgence and domination. Likewise, in five of the six cases, the child's attitude to the mother was impudent and disobedient, that is, aggressive; in the sixth, the attitude was mixed (Case 17).

The findings have at least suggestive value and are in agreement with the general maternal attitude. They point to the value of further investigation of the weaning process as an indication of maternal orientation in the mother-child relationship. They show further that even in this form of infantilization the baby is not a purely passive agent.

The length of time a mother allows or keeps her child at the bottle presents a problem that differs from breast-feeding time. A nursing mother is much more "tied down" than a mother who feeds artificially. Further, it is easier to make up a twenty-four-hour milk formula as a nearly exclusive diet than to add or substitute vegetables, fruit, and cereal mixtures. Indeed, it has been shown that prolonged bottle feeding may be a sign of neglect, an easy way out of certain feeding responsibilities.

In contrast with length of breast-feeding time, Brunk found a high frequency of prolonged bottle feeding in her check group. It is noteworthy that in Group I all children but one who were bottle fed had a preliminary long period of exclusive breast feeding.

The problem of the influence of attitude on length of lactation is complicated by a number of social, racial, economic and physical factors. By various methods of selection and comparison with check groups such factors have been ruled out. All comparisons show certainly that selection by attitude shows a significant difference; and that selection by other factors (except obvious social factors—for example, illegitimacy of the child), shows insignificant differences.

Further, the argument that attitude-influence is important is strengthened by examples showing a special need or wish on the part of overprotective mothers to prolong the nursing period. On the other hand, in the case of rejecting mothers, examples are at hand showing special hostility to the whole process of feeding a child by the breast—attitudes traced to various sexual conflicts that render breast feeding a disgusting or hateful performance.

A study of the influence of attitude in determining length of breast-feeding time is more difficult for short than for long periods. In the latter, organic factors that interfere with nursing are ruled out by the length of the period itself. Of the reasons given in 100 cases of breast feeding one month or less, illness or mouth deformity of the child occurred four times; infant's refusal to nurse, three; illness of mother, nineteen; insufficiency of milk or poor milk composition, twenty-two; separation of child from mother for economic reasons, twelve. There remained but four mothers who stated that they stopped nursing of their own volition (because of "laziness," "disgust," or "worry"). But it is well known that mothers who are opposed to nursing will avail themselves of any excuse to stop, and in many cases it is difficult to ascertain the validity of the organic factor as a deterrent. Nevertheless, the fact remains that one hundred cases selected for very short feeding periods contain fifty cases of maternal rejection. Put in other words, a quick way of gathering records of maternal rejection is by selecting cases in which breast-feeding time is one month or less.

In general, all factors favoring rejection of the child tend to shorten, all factors favoring overprotection tend to lengthen, the breast-feeding act. When overprotection is compensatory to rejection—that is, a reaction against feelings of guilt over hostility to the infant—the overprotection is less likely to be manifested in prolonged breast feeding than in other forms. The last statement, an inference from clinical experience, is in keeping also with the findings in Table XI (page 68).

A consideration of the factors involved in the one phase of breast feeding we have studied, namely, its total duration up to the time of weaning, reveals the complexity of the general problem. First, we may bulk together various social and organic barriers to breast feeding. These concern actual deformities of the infant's mouth or mother's breast, illnesses and social factors that cause separation of mother and infant. Even when there is an apparently necessary separation of infant from breast, maternal attitude may be a primary or secondary factor. This is obvious when, for example, breast feeding is limited to a few weeks because of the child's illegitimacy. Under such circumstances, mothers may yield to family persuasion, aid in getting rid of the child as a burden, or cling to it in spite of everyone. In the case of inverted nipples and other local conditions of the breast, maternal attitude is important whenever an attempt is made to continue the feeding in spite of impediments. Obviously, also, conditions exist which prevent breast feeding regardless of attitude.

The physician's requirement that breast feeding terminate at a certain period might be mentioned at this point. Though pediatrists may differ as to the exact optimal duration, their advice generally is to go on at least for five months. This factor, therefore, does not affect our findings in the one-month group. It was shown, moreover, that prolonged feeding in the overprotecting group was not affected by advice of physicians, relatives, or neighbors.

A second set of factors is concerned with the physiology of lactation. Mothers differ in regard to duration, speed, and volume of flow at any one nursing period, total duration, and milk composition. A number of these factors, probably all, are affected also by the infant's response to the breast. Consider, for example, a breast feeding in which volume is small, flow is rapid for several minutes and then very slow. The infant may respond with vigorous sucking only during the easy flow. If the infant is not encouraged, or efforts are unsuccessful in getting the breast emptied, then an important stimulus to lactation—the empty breast—is lost. It is unnecessary to cite further examples. A number have been furnished in a previous investigation. They demonstrate that all factors which tend to shorten the time at each breast-nursing period, or the frequency of the periods, especially by substitution of the bottle for the breast, are factors that aid in shortening lactation.

Given mothers of poor ability to lactate as regards flow and volume, there remains a big margin in which the desire to nurse the child may operate favorably upon the duration of breast feeding. On the other hand, regardless of lactating ability, the period may be terminated by a hostile attitude. Assuming an attitude but slightly hostile or favorable to breast nursing, it seems logical to assume that the ability to nurse with ease, as a physiologic advantage, might be sufficient to favor the longer nursing period.

Milk composition or insufficiency as a cause of early termination of breast feeding was given in twenty-two of one hundred cases. Present-day knowledge of the influence of physiologic or psychic factors on the chemistry of human milk offers little advantage to our study. A number of individual investigations emphasize the direct influence of emotions on the ability to lactate. However, once a hostile attitude to nursing occurs, numerous factors which remove external stimuli to breast secretion (for example, failure to encourage complete nursing, quick removal of the breast from the infant who dawdles, early use of substitute feeding, skipping a feeding) complicate the problem of primary effect on the secreting cells.

A third factor concerns the maternal attitude to the breast-feeding act. There are mothers frankly hostile to the infant, for whom breast feeding is a pleasurable experience. On the other hand, an overprotecting mother may regard the act as a loathsome ordeal. In the one hundred short feeding cases but one mother gave "disgust" at nursing as the reason for its early termination. The emotions of disgust experienced while suckling a child ordinarily are attended by feelings of guilt. The cause of the short period is then rationalized as "insufficient milk," "too nervous to nurse," and the like. The feelings of guilt are not based necessarily on guilt feelings over the attitude to breast feeding but on the repressed experiences basic to them. In the five cases in which we have psychoanalytic material on this point, the disgust had its roots in sexual conflicts involving the sucking act, in the development of the attitude that breast feeding is filthy, and in a strong and bitter hostility to the passive feminine role.

We have no studies of the genesis of increased pleasurable sensations at breast feeding. In the ordinary act, pleasure is attributed to the relief of breast tension (in which respect the breast resembles other emunctory organs) and to stimulation of the nipple area. There is ample evidence in girls that pleasurable sensations from nipples are heightened by special experiences (as in stroking or masturbatory play with nipples usually in conjunction with genital stimulation). Further, we have instances of girls observing mother nursing the baby, (in those cases in which the breast-feeding act is naturally, even proudly, exposed to the family,) and responding with envy of the mother-role, an envy that would tend to heighten the importance, probably also the feeling of pleasure, in their own later nursing experience.

If a cursory inquiry of the attitude to breast feeding among twenty-four acquaintances is representative, mothers are generally glad to wean as soon as the doctor permits. In the group of twenty-four only two regarded the act as pleasurable, five as at least unpleasurable, the remainder as something more or less of a mild nuisance, neither especially pleasurable nor unpleasurable.

In the Group I mothers, data on this question are lacking. We are not in a position to infer, therefore, how far pleasurable sensations during breast feeding were influential in prolonging the act. Evidently, judging by the duration of breast feeding, they had an ample supply of milk (with one exception). Lactating ability as a hormonal influence on the overprotective attitude is a factor that has not yet been studied.

The fourth and presumably the most significant factor in the study of the time phase of lactation is the mother's attitude to the infant. It has already been shown how overprotection tends to prolong, rejection to shorten, the period. A consideration of the first three factors indicates that the first, comprising obvious organic and social reasons for terminating the act, can be selected out for group comparisons. Also, that a number of such "reasons" are at least complicated by the maternal attitude.

In the second factor, which deals with the physiology of lactation, it was shown also that attitude is an important consideration in the attempt to make the most of one's ability to lactate. Utilizing the examples given, it may be argued that as a determining factor local sensations of pleasure or displeasure must at least reinforce the maternal overprotecting attitude when the act is pleasurable; and the rejecting attitude when it is unpleasurable.

TABLE III

TOTAL DURATION OF BREAST-FEEDING TIME IN OVERPROTECTED AND NON-OVERPROTECTED CHILDREN

| Time in months | OVERPROTECTED | | NON-OVERPROTECTED | |
	No. of cases	Percent	No. of cases	Percent
Less than 1	2	7	36	20
1–5	6	21	71	37
6–11	9	31	70	36
12–17	9	31	13	6
18–23	3	10	1	0.5
24 or longer	0	0	1	0.5
Total	29	100	192	100

In Table III, there is a consistent and significant correlation of overprotection and long breast-feeding time.

In the check group of non-overprotected I.C.G. cases, there appears a decrease in the percentage of long breast feedings (that is, twelve months or longer) in the economically favored groups. The small number of cases in the overprotected group does not allow splitting up in small divisions. However, comparison by economic status shows (Table V) that the overprotected group contains more families in the "adequate" and "comfortable" groups than does the check group (73 and 61 percent, respectively). Hence, the economic factor, if operative in the overprotected group, would tend to diminish the frequency of long feeding. But this is not the case, since the overprotected group contains 41 percent, and the non-overprotected 7 percent of long feedings. The overprotected group used for comparison in Tables IV and V contains 21 families of "adequate" or "comfortable status." The latter shows nine cases or 43 percent of long feeding.

The economic factor would, if at all, influence the figures in the overprotected group in the direction of shorter breast feeding periods.

TABLE IV

PERCENTAGE OF TOTAL DURATION OF BREAST-FEEDING TIME AND ECONOMIC STATUS

	OVERPROTECTED				NON-OVERPROTECTED			
Time in months	Dependent	Marginal	Adequate	Comfortable	Dependent	Marginal	Adequate	Comfortable
Less than 1	0	0	13	0	35	18	15	23
1–11	50	67	47	50	53	69	79	77
12–23	50	33	40	50	12	11	6	0
24 or longer	0	0	0	0	0	2	0	0
Total	100	100	100	100	100	100	100	100
Total number of cases	2	6	15	6	17	56	89	22

Tables II to IV, inclusive, are compiled from Brunk's Tables XIV, XV, and XVI.

TABLE V

PERCENTAGE DISTRIBUTION BY ECONOMIC STATUS OF OVERPROTECTED AND NON-OVERPROTECED IN TABLE IV

	Dependent	Marginal	Adequate	Comfortable
Overprotected (29 cases)	7	20	53	20
Non-overprotected (184 cases)	9	30	43	18

Table VI shows that, however the divisions on nationality are made, the overprotected groups show higher frequencies in the longer breast-feeding periods.

A further check on nationality factors has been made by comparing nativity of parents in short and long feeding groups; and of American born, Jewish and non-Jewish groups (Tables VII & VIII).

TABLE VI

PERCENTAGE OF, BREAST-FEEDING CASES AS RELATED TO NATIONALITY
OF MOTHER

Time in months: Overprotected	American non-Jewish	American-born and foreign-born Jewish	Non-Jewish foreign born
Less than 1	8	10	0
1–5 inclusive	23	30	0
6–11 inclusive	38	20	33
More than 12	31	40	67
Total number of cases	13	10	6
Time in months: Non-overprotected			
Less than 1	21	13	20
1–5 inclusive	41	39	31
6–11 inclusive	36	44	31
More than 12	2	4	18
Total number of cases	69	62	55

Table VII confirms the findings in Table VI of similar distribution of Jewish and American born non-Jewish groups. If, of the other groups, we add the representatives of south and central Europeans (Italian, Polish, Hungarian, Roumanian, Armenian, Spanish) and compare them with north Europeans (German, Irish, Swedish, Finnish, Scotch, English, Belgian), the results show relatively more frequent long feedings in the former group (26 long feedings, 7 short feedings, compared with 7 long and 23 short feedings).

Within these groups the Italians and Poles show preponderating numbers of long feedings (18 long, 6 short); the German and the English-speaking group, short feedings (19 short, 7 long). Assuming that these differences would hold for large groups, we would have to make correction for nativity in the overprotecting group. This is unnecessary in Group I because the American and Jewish group form a large bulk of the cases.

That foreign born tend to nurse longer than American born (whether Jewish or non-Jewish), a tendency shown also in Table VIII, is confirmed by Miss Freeman's findings.

TABLE VII

LENGTH OF BREAST-FEEDING TIME AS RELATED TO NATIONALITY OF MOTHER

	LENGTH OF BREAST FEEDING	
	1 month or less	*12 months or longer*
Nationality of mother	*(No. of cases)*	*(No. of cases)*
Jewish	35	34
American Non-Jewish	26	26
Italian	5	13
German	8	2
Polish	1	5
Negro	2	4
Hungarian	3	1
Irish	2	2
Roumanian, French	2	2
Swedish, Finnish	3	0
Armenian, Russian	0	3
Porto Rican, Lithuanian	0	2
Canadian, Scotch	5	0
Spanish	1	2
English	4	3
Chinese	1	1
Belgian	1	0
Not stated	1	0
Total	100	100

TABLE VIII

LENGTH OF BREAST-FEEDING TIME IN AMERICAN AND FOREIGN-BORN MOTHERS

	LENGTH OF BREAST-FEEDING TIME		
	1 month or less	*12 months or longer*	
	(No. of cases)	*(No. of cases)*	*Total no. of cases*
American born:			
Jewish	13	7	20
Non-Jewish	27	22	49
Foreign born:			
Jewish	22	28	50
Non-Jewish	36	39	75

Short over long in American-born group—1.4
Short over long in Foreign-born group—0.86

The belief that mothers tend to nurse their male children longer than females is not borne out by Miss Freeman's studies.

Further, the proportion of total long and short feeding cases shows a sex distribution very similar to a large unselected I.C.G. group. The proportion of males to females in Table IX is 59 to

TABLE IX

LENGTH OF BREAST-FEEDING AND SEX OF NURSLING

	1 month	*12 months*	*Total no. of cases*
Male	57	61	118
Female	43	39	82

Of the males, percentage in short-feeding group—48
Of the females, percentage in short-feeding group—52

41; the proportion of males to females in 1,004 Institute cases is 62 to 38. Hence, the disproportion of males in overprotected Group I does not explain the long period of time at the breast is that group.

So far, the available data show that differences in economic status, nativity, or sex of child do not account for the long breast-feeding time in the overprotected children.

In Miss Freeman's study of the relation of ordinal position to length of breast-feeding time, only children occurred more fre-

TABLE X

LENGTH OF BREAST-FEEDING TIME AND ORDINAL POSITION

Ordinal position	*1 month or less* (No. of cases)	*12 months or longer* (No. of cases)
Only child (of one child families age 5 years or older)	36	19
Youngest	25	20
Middle	13	28
Oldest	25	31
Not stated	1	2
Total	100	100

quently in the one-month group than could be accounted for by chance.

The mid child appears with significant frequency in the long-feeding group. The conjecture that the frequency distribution in this table may be explained by physiological difference of maternal age at the time of lactation may be checked partly by Miss Freeman's data. The proportion of long feeding in families of two or more children is highest for the middle child, next for the oldest, and lowest for the youngest.

The high proportion of short feedings for the only children is not explainable by difference in age of mothers at the time of giving birth. The difference in average age with the mothers of "oldest" children is but two years (25 compared with 23). Further, when corrections are made for obvious causes of short feeding (illegitimacy, death or desertion of father, illness of mother, her

TABLE XI

MATERNAL ATTITUDE IN FIFTY-FIVE CASES OF ONLY CHILDREN

	BREAST FEEDING	
Attitude	1 month or less	12 months or more
Overprotection	14	17
Rejection	19	1
Neither	3	1

age in one case), there remain fifteen of the only children in the one-month and ten in the twelve-month group. Similar study of "oldest" children does not support the theory that frequency in short feedings in mothers of only children is based on physiologic handicap in ability to lactate.

Within a check group of only children, the significance of maternal attitude in influencing length of feeding time is apparent.

TABLE XII

	BREAST FEEDING	
Attitude	1 month or less	12 months or more
Overprotection	11	17
Rejection	22	1

Table XI is Miss Freeman's Table XVI. The overprotection cases include also "guilt overprotection" which logically belong in the second group. On the basis of Miss Freeman's data, the corrected figures would be those of Table XII.

According to Table XIII, there appears to be an increase in the lactation period with increase in size of family, as grouped in four divisions. This increase may lend support to the inference

TABLE XIII

LENGTH OF BREAST-FEEDING TIME AND NUMBER OF SIBLINGS

	LENGTH OF BREAST-FEEDING TIME		
Size of family	No. of cases 1 month or less	No. of cases 12 months or more	Percentage Long feedings
One child	36	19	35
One of 2 children	29	25	46
One of 3 children	13	20	61
One of 4 or more children	21	34	62

that within certain limits the ability to lactate progresses with increase in number of offspring.

Besides maternal attitudes, certain physical and social factors relating to pregnancy have been compiled by Miss Freeman (Table XIV) for long and short feeding groups.

The factors of "illegitimacy" and of maternal attitudes have been discussed previously. Difficulties during pregnancy and birth show a consistent though not statistically significant difference, indicating less worried, healthier pregnancies and easier births for the long-feeding group.

The item "accidents in pregnancy" refers only to accidents sufficiently serious to become a complication, as fracture. The "psychic accidents" of pregnancy-falls and slips symptomatic of conscious or unconscious wishes to abort—were not investigated.

Summarizing, we find that infantilization consists in performing activities in the care of a child long past the usual time. Bodily care including dressing, feeding, and waiting on a child are types of infantilization easily observed. Instances are given in three Group I children, each age 13, whose mothers still help them dress and eat. Special consideration has been given to breast feeding since it is the most fundamental requirement in maternal care and an activity measurable in terms of time (duration in months). In half the Group I cases, breast feeding lasted 12 months or longer, and in six of these, 18 to 36 months. In various check groups, the highest percentage of breast feeding, 12 months or longer, was 32 percent.

A check on the relation of maternal attitude to duration of breast feeding in months, made by selecting 100 long (12 months

TABLE XIV

Maternal attitude

	Male	Female	Wanted	Unwanted	Illegitimate	Normal pregnancy	Accidents in pregnancy	Sickness in pregnancy	Mother worried during pregnancy	Premature birth	Instruments used	Difficult delivery	Normal delivery	No overprotection or rejection	Rejection	Pure overprotection in infancy	Guilt overprotection	Non-maternal overprotection	Mild maternal overprotection
100 cases breast fed 1 month or less	57	43	37	46	9	52	2	20	23	5	23	39	54	15	50	14	16	2	3
100 cases breast fed 12 months or more . .	61	39	52	32	1	63	1	17	15	2	21	27	65	19	20	37	12	3	9

or longer) and 100 short (one month or less) cases, shows 49 overprotected, in contrast with 20 rejected children, in the long-feeding group, and 19 overprotected, in contrast with 50 rejected children, in the short-feeding group, Table II.

In the determination of duration of breast feeding, the overprotective attitude was found to be more significant than the following factors: nationality, economic status, ordinal position of the child, "onlyness," sex of child, age of mother at time of birth, illness of mother or child.

V. PREVENTION OF SOCIAL MATURITY

PREVENTION of independent behavior, the third criterion of maternal overprotection, refers to active prevention of children's growth in the direction of self-reliance. In Group I all but two mothers show varying degrees of such activity. Of these two, one tries to prevent her ten-year-old son from going with other boys, but cannot because of his disobedience; the second has no need of actively preventing, because her four-year-old son refuses to play with other children, preferring to remain close to her side.

Of the items listed under active prevention, some are closely related to infantilization, for example, compelling the child to sleep in the parents' room though he has a room of his own (Case 3) and taking the child to and from school every day (Case 14); some to excessive contact, for example, delaying the child's schooling a year in order to have him longer at home (Case 5) and allowing the child to play only within mother's sight (Cases 14, 15, 8).

In general, the maternal activity is a continuation of behavior towards the infant, which reinforces closeness and infantilization, with the added gesture of pulling the child back, and of preventing his growth into more independent behavior. Further maternal activity preventing the child from developing responsibility and fighting his own battles consists in constantly taking up his defense, in guarding him from social contacts outside the home, in trying to overcome on his behalf any possible hardship.

The maternal gesture of excessive contact and infantilization, the gesture of holding the infant tightly in one's arms and preserving for all time his status as nursling is now endangered by his growth into childhood. As the demands of reality, which include the child's own increased range of movements, compel some form of maternal release, the gesture changes to that of holding the child's hand, pulling back as he struggles away from the nursery, and pushing away the world about him. The details of the mother's activity in this phase of overprotection enable us to visualize this world with her eyes. The mother may perceive, in every form of social life her child must enter, great danger to his life, contamination of his morals, cruel lack of recognition of his superiority, besides competition with her own wish to dominate and possess. The usual maternal qualms when the child leaves the nursery for the school and embarks on new social adventures, and the usual maternal tendency to soften the critical attack on the child is represented in the third phase of overprotection, largely as an exaggeration. In prevention of the child's growth toward independence, we are witnessing again normal maternal behavior in magnified form.

Within the home, activity hindering growth of more responsible behavior is concerned largely with the matter of chores and school work. Refusal to let the child help with housework is explained by mothers on the basis of fear of accident to the child, fear of his breaking dishes, and the like. Since in the city, especially, there is great variation in such requirements, household chores present a difficult point of comparison with other groups. It should be noted, at least, that available data in Group I show a consistency with other details in that the children are either spared or prevented from developing responsibility even in this regard.

Homework on school subjects offers the overprotective mother an opportunity for helping the child, one that is readily seized. Maternal care continues in coaching, frequent visiting of school to the point of becoming a nuisance, taking up the cudgels against the teacher's criticism and attempting to fight the child's battles for him in the classroom and on the playground.

Aside from maneuvers to release the maternal hold exercised by the child himself, with little if any paternal assistance, the release required by attendance at school presents the strongest early threat to the overprotective relationship. Previous maternal attempts to reinforce the earliest infant relationship through excessive contact, an intensification of the mother-child bond, must be renewed when the growing child, weaned from the breast, demonstrates the beginnings of independent behavior through growth in muscular activity, speech, and self-assertion.

At this stage, maternal overprotection becomes largely an infantilizing process, a process that carries on the earlier maternal activity in spite of its maladaptation. It is part of the struggle exemplified by prolonging "forever" the situation in which the baby is at the breast. In the period when infantilization is especially in evidence, in the second, third and fourth years of infancy, various compromise formations occur, depending on the power of the overprotection, and of the struggles of the child for release. However, whatever form such compromises may take, the child remains closely within the maternal setting. Leaving aside the father's influence, two new situations arise that for the first time require maternal adjustment to the child in settings outside the family circle. One of these, the school situation, is usually inescapable. The other, formation of friendships, may be combated throughout childhood.

When the range of the child's activities stretches beyond the family circle, the overprotecting mother may reach out in every possible direction to insure safety and appreciation for her offspring, and prevent any freedom of movement that will jeopardize her monopoly.

The latter form of maternal behavior is comprehended by the third criterion of overprotection. Unfortunately for the child, it operates in preventing the benefits of outside influences that make for growth in social adaptation, in satisfaction through meeting one's own problems, in fighting one's own way. In so far as adaptation to school and friends may act as an antidote to the infantilizing influence of overprotection, its possible benefits may be prevented.

Data on prevention of independent behavior appear in nineteen of the twenty Group I cases. The remaining case (20) is that of a boy, age 4, who refuses to play with other children and hence requires no overprotective maneuvers of prevention in that regard. In one other case (11), a boy of 10, maternal efforts to prevent social contacts are overcome through disobedience.

Though some data on the criterion studied appear in all but one case, they are not complete. It must be remembered that our records are selected on the basis of overprotection. They are not prepared to meet the requirements of special investigation. The available data are, nevertheless, all the more striking for that reason.

In regard to schoolteachers, the data available show feelings of hostility or derogatory attitudes on the part of the mother in four cases (8, 18, 13, and 10), too frequent appearance in the classroom or writing of letters to the school in four cases (8, 18, 10, and 15), representing five mothers in all.

It is fair to assume, therefore, that for most of the mothers of our group the school situation is accepted. Rather than opposition to the schoolteacher, the activities recorded are more in the nature of coaching and generally insuring the success of the child in the classroom, besides the employment of measures to prevent risk of accident while walking to school. Since we do not have a check group for comparison on this point, we do not know if five mothers of the sixteen who have children in school represent a relatively high percentage of mothers demonstrating hostile attitudes and frequent appearance with complaints in the classroom. The larger number of Group I mothers seem to accept the school situation and to limit the overprotection, in regard to school, to efforts outside the classroom.

One of the Group I mothers (1) regards the school hours as a well-earned period of rest, a period in which she is happy to be released from the "domination" of her son. The attitude toward school as a release from, at least, boisterous behavior or nagging attention of children is a finding common in many ordinary mother-child relationships. Its presence in the overprotective relationship is overt evidence of a change in attitude towards the child, a new maternal orientation to be considered later in Chapter X. Certainly if overprotective mothers conceal a feeling of relief when the school takes over a protective and pedagogic function for the child, they have little need of manifesting guilt feelings, as sending the child to school is one of the social mores—an accepted reality.

The advantage of education, an important consideration, reinforced by strong educational drives in a number of Group I mothers, appears to control maternal ideas about the child in school. The wish to hold the child to the role of infant is superseded in the school situation by the wish to develop the child into an outstanding student.

The mother's educational drive will be considered in a later chapter on maternal background factors (Chapter VII). In the present phase of our study, we may note her stress on homework, even her strict disciplinary function in this regard, in spite of numerous indulgences in other relations. The response of the child to the pressure of her authority at this point helps to explain various other discrepancies in the child's response to the overprotective pattern. Children are quick to learn the parents' point of tolerance, the point at which all evasions and infantile maneuvers are without effect. Even in extremely undisciplined children we note certain dutiful responses. Indulgent overprotective mothers may be inflexible in regard to certain conventions and practices of their children.

Response to the authority of the teacher on the part of children who tyrannize and dominate the household, children who on the basis of all their experience in life are most poorly adapted to classroom discipline, is explainable partly on the basis of their inability to escape the necessity of conforming to the social scheme of education, and to a different maternal attitude.

When difficulties in classroom conduct arise, we shall see behavior consistently in line with the response to overprotection. In general, however, it is true of our group, that when intelligence is adequate to achieve success in school, a contrast of good classroom behavior with difficult behavior at home occurs, a contrast so great that some teachers are surprised to learn that their very polite and successful students are causing so much trou'   't home.

Of the fifteen children age 7 years or older in Gr‹
at grade, six above grade, and three (one on ac‹
are retarded one grade, respectively according
two of the fifteen have had to repeat a grad'

high percentage of superior educational achievement, as compared with the bulk of Institute cases.

Study of educational achievement reveals an interesting finding which may help in tracing the pattern of overprotection in regard to schoolwork. Review of the interests, school grades, and achievement tests of Group I children shows, in spite of variation in intelligence and economic levels, relatively high success in language (vocabulary, composition, "English"), poor scores in arithmetic, and special interest in reading, a feature in significant contrast with our check group.

Excellence in vocabulary is easily understood in view of constant association of the child with an adult. The absence of friends, especially in early childhood, a further effect of the overprotection, may have special significance in this regard.

Since in our group of twenty all but one are males, we are concerned with the attitude towards vocabulary employed by members of the boys' social group. The usual attitude is hostile to "big words"; association with the group fosters the use of boys' slang, disfavors "feminine" words, especially of endearment, and also generally descriptive language. Association with boys, particularly in early childhood when growth in language is rapid, acts as a deterrent to rapid absorption of adult vocabulary through group pressure and through lessening the amount of time spent with the mother. During school life, daily play with children after school hours, added to time spent in the classroom, allows a relatively small portion of time for the mother, in contrast with the situation in early infancy. The increasing amount of time spent away from the mother, representing in the life of the child thousands of hours of companionship with children, allows for a variety of psychic influences which the overprotection may nullify. These psychic influences are most readily comprehended by the process of identification, a process whereby the individual makes as his own the attitude of others. An example is afforded by Case 18, in which the son's attitude toward teachers, friends, sex, and vocation is identical with his mother's attitude.

Identification with the boy's own group would result in inacting in opposition to the overprotection, to infantile response to caresses, to playing the baby, to absorption of adult vocabulary; that is, in regard to adult vocabulary the child would tend to utilize as part of his speech only those expressions that the group would tolerate. With a strong group identification, the situation in the earlier phase of boy-language versus home-language might be so altered that oral vocabulary develops only according to the pace set by the group. The language spoken by the child during the period of strongest group identification would then show least similarity with that of the mother. This explains generally a number of cases in which the child's speech differs so remarkably from that of the parents. The boy's identification with his companions thus affects his receptivity to adult language. Companionship acts as a deterrent to amassing a large vocabulary through the time factor also. It absorbs innumerable hours that the overprotected child spends in reading, home study, and conversation with adults.

In many children, whose interest in reading and social contact with adults gives them a larger vocabulary and wider range of information than the average, several results are easily discerned. There is a greater ease in conversation with adults, and often a preference for adult company. In school, compared with children of equal intelligence (as determined by tests), there is greater facility in speech, in comprehending and absorbing reading matter. In school subjects the advantage applies directly to reading, spelling, composition; less directly to history.

It is probably the advantage in verbalization and ease with subjects in which reading facility is important that gives these children a feeling of superiority to others in the public school. Such advantage applies, of course, to all sorts of children not necessarily overprotected. It helps to ease adaptation to the classroom, especially in the earlier grades. When the child has superior intelligence the advantage becomes tremendous, and the satisfaction in school achievement an important consideration. That is one of the reasons for marked excellence in schoolwork in some of the overprotected children of Group I; a reason for attempting to keep the mother out of the sacred precincts of the school where his high standing in work and conduct is in marked contrast with undisciplined behavior at home in Case 12; a reason for the frank enjoyment of examinations in several; a reason for the marked discrepancy in behavior at school and at home. There remain other considerations for excellence in schoolwork and conduct on the part of overprotected children who are rebellious and difficult at home. These will be reviewed in a later chapter.

The advantages in the study of school subjects enumerated do not apply, however, to arithmetic. It is the most purely "disciplinary" of school subjects. In mathematics, reading ability and vocabulary have the least application. Hence, we often hear from boys whose verbal ability, range of information, and praise from adults lend them a superior attitude, an expression of surprise that some of their schoolmates who appear to be dolts nevertheless achieve high marks in all school subjects, including arithmetic. It is fair to infer that the overprotected boy of the aggressive type would take least kindly to a subject which is as difficult for him as it is for others, that in some cases, he would refuse to pay much attention to it, and would give greater effort to "easier" subjects.

Two other considerations on our findings in regard to difficulty in arithmetic (a confirmation of an old clinical observation about the overprotected boy) might be worth mentioning. Several mothers who coached their sons with homework had to leave the arithmetic problems to the child in the more advanced grades because they found the work beyond them. Further, children who play with others, and who are sent on errands involving some computation, may have more experience with number concepts that may give them an advantage over the overprotected children. The inferences are suggestions for the accumulation of further data on this point.

In the foregoing discussion, reference has been made to the importance of friends as an influence counteracting overprotection. The formation of friendships by the child is directly prevented or discouraged by Group I mothers in twelve cases; it is unnecessary because of the child's refusal to make friends in three cases; and is indirectly prevented through the mother's refusal to allow participation in outdoor games in one. Of the four remaining, one child makes friends in spite of the mother's protests.

The effect of the overprotective relationship on the social life of children in Group I is most clearly revealed by the fact that all twenty have difficulty in forming friends or in having normal friendly relationships. The direct problems of the overprotected children are reserved for later study. The maternal side of this development must now engage our attention.

Six mothers (Cases 10, 12, 5, 6, 16, 17) prevented their children from making friends in early childhood for reasons that the other children are tough, profane, might teach bad habits, or communicate disease. In maternal activity of this type, there is implied an overvaluation of the child with increased fear for his life and his morals and, most importantly, a fight for the mother-child monopoly with its goal of complete possession.

It must appear evident at this stage of the investigation that in every adventure in which the child may engage various intensities of maternal overprotection are revealed. Within the group of so-called "pure" overprotection, gradations are readily discerned. Thus, in the maternal attitude to the child in school, our theoretical expectation of extreme resentment toward the school was fulfilled in five cases, the others showing various gradations from compromise to complete acceptance. So also in response to friends. Attempts involving complete prevention of friends occurred in six cases; in others, various compromises occurred. Four mothers allow the children to play with others on condition that they are always within sight. Most extreme of these, is a mother (Case 1) who allows her child a friend to whom she takes him on a visit once every two weeks. The maternal need of constantly being "there," even during the child's play with other children, is in every one of these cases consistent with activity relating to the school, as Table XV indicates.

TABLE XV

MATERNAL ACTIVITY AS MANIFESTED TOWARDS CHILD'S FRIENDS AND SCHOOL

CASE 1

Child's Friends. He has one friend whom mother takes him to see every two weeks. (Age 8.)

School. Mother takes him to school every morning and calls for him every afternoon. When in school mornings she pays the waiter for his lunch and orders for him in advance.

CASE 14

Child's Friends. Child never allowed to play with other children except within mother's sight. (Age 5 years, 11 months.)
School. Though it is a short walking distance, mother takes him to school and calls for him every day.

CASE 15

Child's Friends. Allowed to play with other children only within mother's sight. (Age 7 years, 5 months.)
School. Mother visits school weekly to check child's progress. Mother had child transferred to a school so that he wouldn't have to cross street car tracks.

CASE 8

Child's Friends. In his play with other children, mother continually watches her child from the window. (Age 7 years, 4 months.)
School. She goes to the school frequently whenever he receives poor grades, and to protect him from supposed discrimination.

Maternal activity in the instances noted appears largely as measures to insure the child's safety. The child may go to school but only under the mother's protection. The child may play with other children but mother must look on. Such measures are in contrast with those illustrated by the six mothers who entirely prevent social contact with other children and with two mothers who allow the child to make friends provided he doesn't bring them home (Cases 13 and 19). Of the latter, the overprotection in one (Case 13) is remarkably indulgent, with uncritical defense of the child and a frank expression of the desire to keep him a baby and hold on to him until he reaches the age of thirty-five. However, there is little maternal activity outside the home; no intrusion into school or playground; no effort to control selection of friends. Overprotective maneuvers are confined to the home. The efforts to prevent independent behavior consist of uncritical defense of the boy's attitude to school, discouraging study to prevent his working "hard," and keeping him free from any household responsibilities. Later, in studying the background factors in this case, we may understand how the overprotection took on this particular pattern. For the present, we may note a social determinant in keeping the boy's friends out of the house—namely, a small apartment in which the mother keeps also two dogs.

The second case (19) is one of marked maternal domination in which the refusal to let the child invite friends home practically prevents the formation of friendships, since the boy has infantile paralysis and cannot join in boys' play. It belongs, therefore, to the group of mothers who attempt to prevent all social contact with other children.

Examples of excessive contact are most extreme in the group of six mothers who have, at least in the first eight years of the life of their sons, entirely prevented contact with children. Examples follow:

TABLE XVI

"EXCESSIVE CONTACT" MANIFESTED BY MOTHERS WHO PREVENT SOCIAL CONTACT WITH OTHER CHILDREN

CASE 10. Boy, age 12. Practically never let him alone during infancy. Kept him away from all people except a few adults because, she said, of fear of infection. She still sleeps with him.

CASE 6. Boy, age 10. During his entire first five years, mother and patient lived together with practically no other contacts. Mother slept with him until he was 6 years old.

CASE 5. Boy, age 13. Up to age 7, mother never let him out of the house with anyone but herself, even excluding the father. She has slept with him the past three years.

CASE 12. Boy, age 15. Up to his tenth year, if mother "left him for more than ten minutes, he would cry and call for her." She has always "served and watched over him." She makes many trips to his room at night to see "if he is sleeping quietly or is restless."

CASE 17. Boy, age 13. The mother says that for her "the door to the outside world is closed"; whenever she goes out, she must come back immediately. Still occasionally sleeps with her son. Excessive contact in infancy, especially in first year because of his delicate health.

Selection of cases on the basis of sleeping with the child after he has reached school age, as the most objective criterion of excessive contact, yield six out of the twenty cases in Group I. These six include four of the five cases in the preceding table (10, 5, 6,

17). The others include the case of a mother (1) who allows her son contact with one other child every two weeks, and the case of a boy, age 12 (7), who has no friends, refusing to leave the mother's side.

These findings indicate that if in our criteria of maternal overprotection we make sure that "sleeping with the mother long past infancy" is represented as an item in "excessive contact," the cases resulting may represent the purest examples of mother-child monopolies, for they would contain criteria of excessive contact, infantilization, and prevention of independent behavior in the highest degree.

When an overprotecting mother sleeps with her son even until age 7 or older is maternal overprotection intensified? The answer is not revealed by our data since they indicate merely that when the factor "sleeping with the child" is used as a selective basis within Group I, the most intensive examples of overprotection are sieved out. Further trials in the use of other items in the same manner did not yield as extreme samples. The item of "sleeping with the child" may be merely symptomatic of certain maternal trends dynamically determined long before maternity exists, trends which are to be considered in Chapter VII. Nevertheless, it appears reasonable to infer that aside from all other factors tending toward maternal overprotection, the close physical contact, resulting from the years of sleeping with the child in which the overprotective attitude is formulated, would of itself intensify all tender, possessive and protective attitudes towards it.

In three cases the children have no friends outside the family through no apparent maternal attempts at prevention, but through the children's own refusal (Cases 10, 4, 7). Two of these are submissive, obedient children, one an aggressive, rebellious child (4). The latter shows in his contact with the mother a marked dependency and also a strong dominating tendency. She must be there wherever he is, a filial response that reveals dependency in its aggressive, dominating aspect, consistent with the whole pattern of the indulgent overprotection.

Certain interesting aspects of the manifold forms of overprotective patterns and of special interest in treatment are revealed in the children who without maternal intervention refuse to have social relations with others. The mother of one of them (Case 7) has, in fact, encouraged his making friends. On one occasion she left him with a group of boys playing ball. Within five minutes, her twelve-year-old was back at her side pleading to remain.

The pattern of overprotection in which a mother tries to release the strong mother-child bond created in the earlier years has been noted in those extreme forms described in Chapter II in which overprotection in infancy is followed by rejection. In consistent forms of "mild" overprotection many instances of such release are discerned. They are represented by mothers who, though overprotective, are not submerged in the relationship. These mothers see clearly the ill effects of the dependency and may make strenuous efforts to effect a release. Their objective is partly self preservative, preventing further encroachment on their own freedom to develop other relationships and possible danger to the marital state; partly, increasing alarm over the excessively close attachment of the son; partly, a derivative of the maternal attitude that operates on behalf of the child's need for growth in independence at the cost of increasing sacrifice of a mother-child monopoly.

Even in Group I patterns we have some evidence of maternal efforts at release. Case 7, therefore, is important in indicating that symptomatology yields knowledge not only of the extent of monopolistic formation but also of activity that aims to prevent its further growth.

We may anticipate the section on treatment at this point by utilizing the entering wedge supplied by mothers who are at the stage of attempting various forms of release from a now overpowering human relationship. In Case 7, early prevention of social contact was unnecessary as an overprotective device because the subject clung tightly to his mother. At about the age of twelve his mother tried to encourage social contact. That fact presents a favorable therapeutic direction because the social worker may now operate along the lines established by the mother. The worker has the advantage of the mother's coöperation in a first attack on the monopoly because the direction is already set. The social therapy starts its attack whenever possible along the lines of release. In general, the more abundant the evidence of efforts to get release from the mother-child bond (especially on the part of the mother), the more hopeful the outlook. When release phenomena are manifested entirely by the child, therapy must centralize on the mother since otherwise her efforts will vitiate the treatment. Indeed, she may bring the child for treatment largely because she wants help in quelling his rebellion against overprotection.

Thus far maternal activity in regard to the child's social contacts reveals efforts directed at prevention or regulation, or at maintaining a status in which such efforts are unnecessary. As in other mother-child relationships, we see in this instance various differences in the values of the mother-child equation. Some mothers have to exert much effort, others very little, to prevent the child from making social contact with others. On the other hand, children vary in their response from little to extreme effort in the direction of social contact. Should the child succeed in spite of the mother, then various efforts at regulation ensue with varying degrees of success.

Two Group I children (Cases 11, 16) made friends in spite of the mother. Both are of the dominating, undisciplined types in an indulgent, overprotective pattern. One (Case 11) has fought against all infantilizing influences, and evinces the strongest example of dominating behavior. At the age of ten he keeps what hours he pleases, eats meals when he wishes, slaps his mother when angry, and is impudent and disrespectful to both parents. His contact with boys, in spite of the mother's protest, is an expression of his general disobedience and dominating tendencies. The other child (Case 16), age fourteen, is likewise unmanageable, does as he pleases, keeps his own hours and dominates both mother and sister. In both boys the aggressive, dominating response to the overprotection overrides attempts at preventing social content. Nevertheless, as will be shown later in both cases, there is difficulty in making friends because of attempts to play the dominating role with the "gang" as with the mother.

The sharpest contrasts in all overprotective patterns are afforded by the two sets of responses described. In Case 7, for example, response to the overprotection is in the form of dependency on the mother for social life, avoidance of all other social contacts, marked stability as a student; in general, a perfect adaptation to the maternal order of dutiful child, affectionate son, and obedient, industrious school boy. In Case 16, however, response to the overprotection is chiefly of a dominating type (the direction of activity is the opposite of Case 7's); his drive to dominate every situation makes for undisciplined behavior, selfishness, and instability. To have his own way in all things is a symbol of activity that acts counter to almost all the mother's plans. His aggressive domination destroys the mother-child monopoly she has tried to create, and transforms it into a relationship in which he is master to a subservient family. In contrast with Case 7, whose response is a passive adaptation with strong mother-identification resulting in submissive stability, his response is an active adaptation with a wild, unmodified growth in aggression and, hence, in undisciplined behavior. Lack of modification of aggressive tendencies is seen also as lack of emotional control, with a typical series of related problems.

A pattern involving both phases—the boy (Case 7) who avoids friends and clings to the mother and the boy (Case 16) whose disobedience carries him into the gang against his mother's wishes— is illustrated by Case 4. Here, the boy manages to have both friends and mother, by insisting that mother come along when he plays with his friends. His compromise consists in domination— by having the mother when he wants her, "ordering" her to come —and in dependency—by having the mother present in the groups of boys as his protector.

There remain three cases in Group I which have not been considered in regard to the maternal attitude towards the child's social contacts. The previous seventeen are covered by the captions "total prevention" (six cases); "partial prevention" (including three cases in which children are allowed to play only within mother's sight, two who are not allowed to bring friends home, one whom mother takes on a fortnightly visit to a boy—six cases); "unnecessary" (three cases); "friends in spite of mother" (two cases).

Of the remaining, one (Case 2) played with smaller boys only because, the mother explained, he could get his own way with the younger ones and they laughed at the funny things he said; at fourteen, however, he made no friends of his own age. The second (Case 3) prefers playing with girls although he plays with boys also. The third, a girl, made friends easily until age four and a half years. At that time a neighbor scolded her for quarreling. Since that time she has refused to play with other children unless the mother accompanies her.

A comparison of the number of friends among groups of children, divided according to the mother-child relationship into "overprotected," "rejected" or "neither," has been made in Table XVII. A random selection of 117 seriatim records were taken. Out of this group, 27 cases were selected as overprotected (all maternal forms); 23, rejected; 46, neither; the remainder, not classified. Table XVII shows a trend of increasing number of friends as we go from the "overprotected," to "rejected" and to "neither." Group I is added for comparison in the first column.

PERCENTAGE OF CHILDREN HAVING COMPANIONS, CLASSIFIED ACCORDING
TO MATERNAL ATTITUDES OF REJECTION AND OVERPROTECTION

Companions	Group I (overprotected)	Overprotected (all forms)	Rejected	Neither
None or One	65	63	52	33
Two or More	35	37	48	67

In the group of mothers who prevent their children from having companionship with others, the problem of their own social contacts arises. Later it will be shown how mothers who have invested all their emotional values in the child tend to withdraw from their previous social connections. If overprotecting mothers have friends, it seems logical to assume that among them they are likely to find someone at least who may have a child with whom they may entrust their own. One such instance has been recorded previously. To elucidate this problem Table XVIII was drawn up by Miss Andrews to show relationship of parents and their children's social contacts, in 117 "unselected" cases.

This table shows a distinct general tendency for children to be as sociable as their parents are, measured roughly by the number of companions. It brings to focus again the importance of parental activity as a determiner of the child's adaptation to human relationships. (See also Table XXXI, page 97.)

TABLE XVIII

SOCIAL CONTACTS OF PARENTS AND CHILDREN

Parents with no social contacts outside of home (45 families)
Of their children
- 44 percent have no companions
- 11 percent have one companion
- 45 percent have few or many companions

Parents with few social contacts outside the home (50 families)
Of their children
- 30 percent have no companions
- 22 percent have one companion
- 48 percent have few or many companions

Parents with many social contacts outside the home (23 families)
Of their children
- 22 percent have no companions
- 17 percent have one companion
- 61 percent have few or many companions

TABLE XIX

GROUP 1: MOTHER'S ATTITUDE TO SCHOOLTEACHERS

CASE 8. Mother feels boy is a genius and school authorities are against him. Frequently in school to protect him against supposed discrimination and to boost his marks.

CASE 18. Mother sends "countless letters and notes remonstrating against school's abuse of the patient." Believes school very unappreciative of her son.

CASE 11. "Mother frequently resorts to getting the school to help her enforce" her authority. She complains to the teacher when patient disobeys.

CASE 13. Mother thinks teachers are not sufficiently understanding of her son's nervousness. Always defends boy against schoolteachers.

CASE 1. Regards school as a well earned period when she need not worry about son and yet is not exposed to his domination (patient then age 8). (Change in maternal attitude about this time.)

CASE 10. Mother objects to our interviewing school for fear school will regard patient a problem. Very strong attachment to one school-teacher. Regards school personnel as shallow in intelligence and sensitivity.

CASE 12. Patient has warned mother against appearing in school where his record is excellent. She wants to complain to teachers about his behavior at home and get their help in disciplining him.

CASE 15. Mother goes to school weekly to check on patient's progress and when she can't go, she sends the father.

In three cases the children have not reached Grade I; in the remaining nine, maternal attitudes to teachers show nothing unusual.

TABLE XX

GROUP I: CLASSROOM BEHAVIOR, STUDIES, AND INTERESTS

CASE 8. Age 7 years, 4 months; Grade II. Very good in *reading;* average in *arithmetic;* A conduct. Interest chiefly in play.

CASE 17. Age 13 years, 9 months; Grade VII. Constant difficulty with *arithmetic*. Scholarship averages B; conduct C. Disciplinary problem. Attitude to schools marks: "As long as I get by, that's all I care about." Interest chiefly in *reading*. Keeps scrapbook of newspaper clippings. Interested in visits to Museum of Natural History. Slight interest in mechanical toys.

CASE 18. Age 16 years, 5 months; Grade X. A in English and French; fails in *algebra*. Chief interest is in reading. Avoids sports.

CASE 11. Age 10 years, 11 months; Grade VII. A in work and conduct to Grade VI; then A or B. Not proficient in *arithmetic*. "Only interest is *reading* and roughhousing on the street with a gang of boys." "Has always had a great respect for the authority of the school."

CASE 13. Age 14 years, 6 months; Grade VII. Fair in English. Fails in *arithmetic* in which he gets special tutoring. Says teachers are all against him. Truant after Grade I. Interest in sports; shows leadership and initiative. Delights in letter writing. An "omnivorous" reader; spends much time reading, even during truancy from school.

CASE 5. Age 13 years, 4 months; Grade IX. Through Grade VIII at 13. A "plodder." Conduct excellent. In tests, especially good in vocabulary; poorest in *mathematics*. Only interests are *reading* and music. Used to read a book a day. Likes to do housework but mother discourages it.

CASE 1. Age 8 years, 1 month; Grade III. Very fond of school. Excellent in study and conduct. Considered better than average only in *language*. Special difficulty in *arithmetic*. Avoids sports.

CASE 10. Age 12 years, 5 months; Grade VIII. Very good student. Superior in all educational tests, though lowest score is in *arithmetic* computation. Voracious *reader*. Interests largely intellectual. Strong attachment to one teacher.

CASE 19. Age 12 years, 10 months; Grade VI. School conduct excellent. Best subjects are history, geography and *reading;* poorest are *arithmetic*, grammar and spelling. In achievement tests scores highest in *language* usage, lowest in "computation." Fond of *reading* and drawing.

CASE 2. Age 14 years, 0 months; Grade VII. Ahead of other children in information acquired through wide reading. Special difficulty in *arithmetic*. In educational tests rates low in *arithmetic*. Very bright in *language*. Marked disciplinary problem in classroom. Chief and absorbing interest in *reading*. Good swimmer. Entertains with singing and dancing stunts.

CASE 12. Age 15 years, 0 months; High School II. Serious, excellent student. Allows nothing to interfere with school routine. Honor grades; two special promotions. Chief interest is *reading* which causes much difficulty with mother who tries to prevent it and get him out of doors as doctor has advised.

CASE 15. Age 7 years, 5 months; Grade I. Poor schoolwork; A in conduct. Most deficient in *arithmetic* and *reading*. Fairly uniform test scores. Interested chiefly in play with girls because boys are too rough.

CASE 16. Age 14 years, 4 months; Grade VI. School truancy and disciplinary problem. Favorite subject is *reading*. In achievements tests, lowest scores are in science, history, and literature. Interests chiefly movies and companions.

CASE 14. Age 5 years, 11 months; Grade I. No conduct problem. Doing well in Grade I. In tests, very superior in *language* development. Likes books and music. Can *read* the titles and distinguish phonograph records. Less interested in toys.

CASE 7. Age 11 years, 3 months; Grade V. Excellent student. "Model" behavior. Highest grades. Interest chiefly in *reading*.

CASE 4. Age 4 years, 9 months; not in school. By tests, superior ability in conversation and *language* usage. Great drive to excel in school work. Sits by the hour copying words he doesn't understand. *Begs to be read to.*

CASE 20. Age 4 years, 5 months; in nursery school. Good behavior in nursery school. Superior in all tests; very superior in tests requiring verbal response; high average in performance type of test, i.e., mental age on Kuhlman-Binet, 69 months; mental age on Merrill Palmer, 55 months. Interested in household chores. Likes to sweep, etc. Much play with younger brother.

CASE 6. Age 10 years, 1 month; Grade III. After doing poor work in earlier grades, now doing excellent work in Grade III. Good conduct. Complains constantly of boys annoying and threatening him at school; a number of these tales proven to be false. Interest chiefly in play with companions. *Likes to be read to* but not interested in *reading*. Likes to draw pictures and shows some artistic ability. Likes to take mechanical toys apart, though can't put them together.

CASE 9. Age 4 years, 5 months; kindergarten. Tested at 4 years, 5 months; showed superior rating (I.Q. 117) on Stanford-Binet (5 years, 2 months) and on Merrill Palmer 4 years 10 months; did especially well on comprehension tests. Tested at 5 years, 4 months, she secures a higher rating (I.Q. 128), the difference explained on the basis of verbalization.

CASE 3. Age 6 years, 1 month; Grade I. Backward in *arithmetic,* and *reading* difficulty due to subnormal intelligence. Nevertheless, apparently enjoys *reading* and writing.

TABLE XXI

SUMMARY

Number of Cases above Grade I	14
Number of these cases with special difficulty in arithmetic or algebra	6
Number of these cases in which scores on achievement tests or school marks are lowest in mathematics	10
Number of these cases in which evidence from test scores (vocabulary, reading comprehension) and school marks shows superiority in English as compared with other subjects	9
For entire group of 20 cases, number showing superiority in all tests requiring verbal ability (as determined by Stanford-Binet, Merrill Palmer, achievement tests, or school marks)	10
Of the 16 in Grade I or above, the number whose outside interest is chiefly reading	10
"Omnivorous" readers	6

It must appear obvious that the children in Group I are highly differentiated in regard to special interest in reading, verbal acceleration, and relatively, arithmetical retardation. The fourteen who are above Grade I contain six "omnivorous" readers. Though the group is small it must be remembered that they represent a "concentrate" of overprotected forms.

Eight of the fourteen have had the advanced Stanford Achievement tests, and are compared with two check groups. As a further aid in this comparison, a second group of overprotected cases (eighteen) and a group of rejected cases (fourteen) have also been utilized. Percentage figures for all groups are tabulated in Table XXVII.

In reading tests both overprotected groups show strong contrasts with the "check" and "rejected" groups and slight though

TABLE XXII

DEVIATION FROM GRADE IN PERCENTAGES

	½ year or less		3 or more years		2 to 3 years		1 to 2 years	
	M	F	M	F	M	F	M	F
Reading								
At grade	33.6	34.4						
Retarded			0.4	2.5	7.2	11.8	13.2	16.0
Accelerated			10.8	4.2	16.4	11.0	18.4	20.1
Arithmetic								
At grade	40.4	45.4						
Retarded			1.2	5.0	8.0	5.9	20.0	20.2
Accelerated			1.6	0.0	6.4	6.7	22.4	16.8

CUMULATIVE PERCENT

	½ year or less		3 or more years		2 or more years		1 or more years	
	M	F	M	F	M	F	M	F
Reading								
At grade	33.6	34.4						
Retarded			0.4	2.5	7.6	14.3	20.8	30.3
Accelerated			10.8	4.2	27.2	15.2	45.6	35.6
Arithmetic								
At grade	40.4	45.4						
Retarded			1.2	5.0	9.2	10.9	29.2	31.1
Accelerated			1.6	0.0	8.0	6.7	30.4	23.5

similar contrasts with the special school group. The overprotected groups are definitely superior in reading ability, as measured by the test.

Three hundred sixty-nine routine achievement tests of I.C.G. cases [1] showing grade achievement by the advanced Stanford

[1] 250 males; 119 females.

Achievement Test differentiated by sex are tabulated in Table XXII. Sex differentiation for reading and arithmetic shows a slight superiority of males in both subjects.

Measured by the degree of retardation or acceleration in units of school years, our check group appears to do best in the subjects

TABLE XXIII

CHECK GROUP OF 369 I.C.G. CASES SHOWING GRADE ACHIEVEMENT ONE OR MORE YEARS ABOVE OR BELOW PROPER GRADE, AS MEASURED BY ADVANCED STANFORD ACHIEVEMENT TEST

	Percent retarded one or more years	Percent at grade	Percent accelerated one or more years
Reading	23.8	33.9	42.3
Arithmetic	29.8	42.0	28.2
Nature and Science	39.1	36.9	24.0
History and Literature	19.2	33.9	46.9
Language	22.1	28.7	49.2
Dictation	22.8	40.4	36.8

"language, history and literature," and poorest in "arithmetic and science." Reading and dictation stand midway. The findings that arithmetic and science are more difficult than other school subjects, at least as determined by achievement tests or school marks,

TABLE XXIV

SAME AS TABLE XXIII SHOWING GRADE ACHIEVEMENT TWO OR MORE YEARS ABOVE OR BELOW GRADE

	Percent retarded two or more years	Percent at grade	Percent accelerated two or more years
Reading	9.8	66.9	23.3
Arithmetic	9.8	82.6	7.6
Nature and Science	12.9	76.0	11.1
History and Literature	4.4	70.9	24.7
Language	9.0	62.0	29.0
Dictation	7.6	74.8	17.6

is a general observation in both "progressive" and "old fashioned" schools. It is consistent with the findings for all our groups excepting the "rejected" (see Tables XXVIII and XXIX).

The check group represented by Tables XXII and XXIII, though selected by virtue of referral for various types of behavior problems, shows a distribution in mental age and intelligence quotient similar to that of the public-school children of New York

TABLE XXV

"SPECIAL" SCHOOL GROUP
(150 Cases)

	Percent retarded one or more years	Percent at grade	Percent accelerated one or more years
Reading	12.0	21.3	66.7
Arithmetic	39.6	33.6	26.8
Nature and Science	43.4	28.3	28.3
History and Literature	20.7	26.2	53.1
Language	16.1	21.0	62.9
Dictation	16.8	23.1	60.1

City. Unfortunately, a good sampling of "non-problem" cases from the public schools is not at hand. A special survey of a private school, utilized in Tables XXV and XXVI, offers another interesting comparison with the other groups.

TABLE XXVI

"SPECIAL" SCHOOL GROUP
(150 Cases)

	Percent retarded two or more years	Percent at grade	Percent accelerated two or more years
Reading	2.7	63.3	34.0
Arithmetic	10.7	77.2	12.1
Nature and Science	19.3	71.0	9.7
History and Literature	6.9	71.7	21.4
Language	6.3	58.0	35.7
Dictation	4.2	67.8	28.0

The special school surveyed is the "Professional Children's School" in New York City, a private school made up largely of juvenile actors and other stage performers. They are of special interest in this study because they live in a world more "verbalized" by the nature of their work, interests, and more frequent contact with grown-ups than an average group of children.

This group shows greater disadvantage in "arithmetic" and "science" and greater acceleration in reading than our check group. In reviewing the achievement scores of the special-school group, it is interesting to note a progressive advance in subjects as they become more purely verbal.

The group contrasts in reading are clearly shown in Table XXVII. The overprotected groups show highest acceleration in

TABLE XXVII

COMPARATIVE DEVIATION OF ALL GROUPS IN READING, IN PERCENTAGES

(Advanced Stanford Achievement Tests)

	Retarded one or more years	At grade	Accelerated one or more years
Overprotected: Group I (8 cases)	0.0	50.0	50.0
Overprotected: Larger group (18 cases)	5.6	44.4	50.0
Rejected group (14 cases)	28.6	57.1	14.3
Check group (369 cases)	23.8	33.9	42.3
Special-school group (150 cases)	12.0	21.3	66.7
	Retarded two or more years	At grade	Accelerated two or more years
Overprotected: Group I (8 cases)	0.0	50.0	50.0
Overprotected: Larger group (18 cases)	5.5	55.6	38.9
Rejected group (14 cases)	7.2	85.6	7.2
Check group (369 cases)	9.8	66.9	23.7
Special-school group (150 cases)	2.7	63.3	34.0

reading. Next comes the special-school group, then the check group, and finally the "rejected" group. The latter group is composed of I.C.G. cases selected on the basis of overt evidence of maternal hostility.

If one argues that all our data on reading achievement are consistent with the degree of social contact of mother and child, the point is well sustained by the findings. For the overprotected group stands highest, and the rejected group lowest in the list; the intervening groups being rightly placed in accordance with that criterion.

The observation by Zachry [2] that children with special reading difficulty are frequently "rejected" is confirmatory evidence.

The special-school group and the overprotected group show a greater degree of retardation in arithmetic than the others. In

TABLE XXVIII

COMPARATIVE DEVIATION OF ALL GROUPS IN ARITHMETIC, IN PERCENTAGES

(Advanced Stanford Achievement Test)

	Retarded *1 or more years*	*At grade*	*Accelerated* *1 or more years*
Overprotected (Group I)	37.5	12.5	50.0
Overprotected (Large group)	22.2	33.3	44.5
Rejected group	21.4	64.3	14.3
Check group	29.8	42.0	28.2
Special-school group	39.6	33.6	26.8

	Retarded *2 or more years*	*At grade*	*Accelerated* *2 or more years*
Overprotected (Group I)	25.0	50.0	25.0
Overprotected (Large group)	11.1	77.8	11.1
Rejected group	0.0	98.8	7.2
Check group	9.8	82.6	7.6
Special-school group	10.7	77.2	12.1

severer retardation (two or more years) the overprotected groups are more frequently represented than all others. On the other hand, while they show also a higher percentage of acceleration, the contrasts are by no means as clear as in "reading." Nevertheless, it is interesting that a comparison of percentages in the latter half of Table XXVIII (severe retardation) shows in regard to arithmetic, the exact reversal of the findings in reading. In the former, the "rejected" group are highest, next comes the check group, then the special school group, and last, the overprotected groups.

The curious position of the "rejected" group in regard to arith-

[2] Personal communication from Dr. Caroline B. Zachry.

metic is brought out most sharply in Table XXIX, where it is the only group showing less retardation in arithmetic than in reading. Of the remaining three groups, the overprotected show the highest

TABLE XXIX

READING-ARITHMETIC RETARDATION RATIOS FOR ALL GROUPS

	Retardation 1 or more years	Retardation 2 or more years
Overprotected—Group I	0.0:37.5	0.0:25.0
Overprotected—Large group	5.6:22.2	5.5:11.1
Rejected group	28.6:21.4	7.2: 0.0
Check group	23.8:29.8	9.8: 9.8
Special-school group	12.0:39.6	2.7:10.7

discrepancy of reading skill and arithmetical ability as measured by the test; the check groups, the least.

Table XXX shows a tendency towards a larger number of companions in the higher economic levels.

TABLE XXX

CHECK-GROUP STUDY OF NUMBER OF COMPANIONS IN 177 I.C.G CASES [8]

Dividing ages of the 117 children in 5–8 years (inclusive), 9–13, and 14+, the group 9–13 ("gang age") has the highest percentage of few or many companions (93%). The group 14+ has 73%.

As compared with boys, the girls had a smaller percentage of "many companions," though as high a percentage of "few companions."

> "Many friends": boys, 71 per cent
> "Many friends": girls, 29 per cent

Grouped according to economic status, the percentages of number of companions follow (98 cases):

	Many	Few	One	None
Comfortable	33	16	10	19
Moderate	32	16	11	19
Marginal	21	48	28	3
Dependent	14	20	6	48
Total cases (percentage)	28	25	18	27

[8] Compiled by Miss Kathleen Andrews.

TABLE XXXI

GROUPED ACCORDING TO THE SOCIAL CONTACTS OF PARENTS
(118 CASES)

Of the 45 children whose parents have "no" social contacts:
44.4% children have no companions (20 cases)
10%—5–8 years; 45%—9–13 years; 45%—14+ years
11.1% children have one companion (5 cases)
20%—5–8 years; 40%—9–13 years; 40%—14+ years
24.4% children have few companions (11 cases)
27%—5–8 years; 46%—9–13 years; 27%—14+ years
20% children have many companions (9 cases)
34%—5–8 years; 32%—9–13 years; 33%—14+ years

Of the 50 children whose parents have few social contacts:
30% children have no companions (15 cases)
33%—5–8 years; 40%—9–13 years; 27%—14+ years
22% children have one companion (11 cases)
27%—5–8 years; 46%—9–13 years; 27%—14+ years
36% children have few companions (18 cases)
11%—5–8 years; 62%—9–13 years; 27%—14+ years
12% children have many companions (6 cases)
33%—5–8 years; 17%—9–13 years; 50%—14+ years

Of the 23 children whose parents have many social contacts:
22% children have no companions (5 cases)
60%—9–13 years; 40%—14+ years
17% children have one companion (4 cases)
25%—5–8 years; 25%—9–13 years; 50%—14+ years
22% children have few companions (5 cases)
60%—9–13 years; 40%—14+ years
39% children have many companions (9 cases)
11%—5–8 years; 33%—9–13 years; 56%—14+ years

SUMMARY

Thus we find that "prevention of independent behavior" is manifested in overprotective measures that prevent the child from undergoing risks customary in the social group to which the child belongs. Such measures appear as a direct outgrowth of infantilization, adding to the active efforts at infantile care, protection against the child's social development beyond the range of immediate maternal care. They operate against all outside influences that make for growth in social adaptation.

Maternal infantilizing behavior in the case of the growing child comes in conflict with, especially, the school situation and friendships outside the home.

Maternal response to the school situation was revealed in hostile attitudes to schoolteachers, in ensuring the child's success by frequent appearance and consultation in the classroom, in coaching and disciplining the child's schoolwork at home, in walking with the child to and from school. For the most part the mothers accepted the school situation and demonstrated overprotection in extra coaching, discipline, and precaution against accidents on the street and playground.

Some overprotecting mothers, who otherwise indulged, showed markedly contrasting behavior in their discipline of the child's schoolwork; and, likewise, children, who otherwise rebelled, in responding to such discipline on the part of the mother and to the general discipline of the classroom.

As compared with the bulk of Institute for Child Guidance cases, the overprotected children who are at school show superior educational achievement, relatively high scores in language, poor scores in arithmetic, and special interest in reading. For further investigation of this point, a second group of overprotected children (besides Group I) was compared with a large check group (369 I.C.G. cases), a special-school group (150 juvenile actors and other "professional" children), and a group of rejected children (14 cases). The "rejected" group alone showed less retardation in arithmetic than in reading. Of the remaining groups, the overprotected showed the highest discrepancy of reading skill and arithmetical ability.

The advantage of the overprotected children in reading ability and vocabulary tests (regardless of intelligence level) was explained by close association with the mother, identification with her, absence of competing group contacts and influences opposing receptivity to adult language. The initial ease with subjects requiring verbalizing ability and later reading skill has least application to arithmetic and natural science. The relatively low grades in the latter subjects were explained largely on that basis. Further explanations were found in the mother's inability in coaching arithmetic as compared with other subjects and in the fact that the overprotected children were not allowed to go on errands, experiences involving money transactions.

The importance of social contacts as a counteracting influence to overprotection is discussed. The formation of friends by the children of Group I mothers is directly prevented or discouraged in twelve cases, indirectly prevented by refusing permission to play outdoor games in another, and unnecessary, because of the child's refusal to make social contacts, in four cases.

All twenty Group I children have special problems in forming friendships.

As in other phenomena of overprotection various gradations in the intensity of maternal activity in controlling the child's social activities are discerned. These vary from total prevention of play with other children (six cases) to compromises in which the child is allowed to play with others, but only when the mother is there (four cases), or in which the child may not bring his playmates home (two cases). Special efforts to encourage the child to make friends occur in one case.

All four mothers who prevent their children from playing with others unless they are present show special and unnecessary precautions in accompanying the children to school and making frequent visits to the classroom.

Of the six mothers who prevent their children from having any companionship with others, five show evidence of excessive contact of unusual degree, including sleeping with the child (all boys, ages 10, 12, 13, 13, and 15, respectively).

By experimenting with the various possible combinations of data in the "pure" cases of overprotection, it is found that the purest samples are secured by selecting cases in which, besides the other criteria, the item "sleeping with the child long past infancy," is included under "excessive contact."

Social contacts outside the home are prevented in three cases by the children themselves. One of these duplicates the maternal compromise patterns described by insisting that the mother be present whenever he is with his playmates. Such cases illustrate how children may themselves attempt to create or ensure the continuance of the mother-child monopoly. Attempts to release the child from the close bond to the mother are seen typically in normal family life and commonly in overprotective forms. Even in Group I cases, evidence of similar attempts are found. It is important, in collecting data of maternal overprotection, to include such findings for purposes of therapy, since the mother's efforts toward releasing herself from the burden of the overprotective relationship may constitute an entering wedge into the mother-child monopoly.

A tabulation of the number of playmates of children of over-protecting, rejecting and "other" mothers has been made. Divided into groups of "none or one" and "few or many," the table shows a trend of increasing number of playmates as we go from the "over-protecting" mothers, to "rejecting," and to "neither."

A study was also made to determine if there is a relationship between the number of companions of parents and children. The study revealed a distinct tendency towards increase in number of companions of the child with increase in the number of social contacts of the parents.

The findings are consistent also with the observation that in case of pure overprotection the mother narrows down her social life to the child.

Evidence of attempts on the part of mothers to release children from overdependency upon them appears frequently in normal mother-child relationships and in the "mild" forms of overprotection. Evidence of the same type, though less frequent, appears also in Group I mothers. It is important to determine especially maternal efforts at release from the burden of overprotection, since active social therapy is directed with advantage at "points of release" already established.

VI. MATERNAL CONTROL

THE fourth criterion of maternal overprotection, lack or excess of maternal control, contains data derived primarily from the behavior of the child, data indicating a defect in maternal discipline. The inclusion of such findings may be questioned since they do not show evidence directly of maternal activity and appear to be a resultant of the forms of maternal overprotection previously described. Nevertheless, they show those aspects of maternal care that involve discipline of the child and are most readily observed directly through the child's activity rather than the mother's. Instead of describing acts, for example, in terms of "the mother allows this or that," or "dominates the child in this way or that," we may collect objective data on maternal control in terms of the child's activity. Furthermore, it is difficult to learn in any given act how much the mother has "allowed," or actively indulged the child, and how much the child has appropriated as a privilege fought for against parental opposition.

Overindulgence is a weakness in maternal control. It consists in yielding to the wishes or actions of a child or submitting to demands ordinarily not tolerated by most parents. It is the commonest evidence of "spoiling." A demarcation line between the mother's inability to deny the infant's wish and her later apparently unwilling submission to his tyranny is difficult to draw. The former situation, one of willing active catering to the child, is overindulgence in a true sense. Submitting unwillingly to his excessive demands is a passive form of indulgence. Allowing the child to eat whatever he wishes, to sleep regardless of hours, because one "doesn't wish to deny him anything" is typical of the former; surrender to the child's insistence in these matters, of the latter. In either situation, whether of willing or unwilling submission to the child's demands, the child appears to be active, the mother passive. Yet in the overindulgent act, the mother may be as actively overprotective as in the other forms.

The extreme example of overindulgence is that of complete maternal surrender to the child, to the point that the child's merest wish becomes the mother's absolute command. In such a hypothetical case, the child represents a deity on whose altar the mother willingly sacrifices her life. Maternal obeisance of that type would then be transformed into a psychosis in which every sense of proportion is perverted by the maternal attitude. All the social orientations of the mother, as wife, housekeeper, worker, member of various social groups, would completely deteriorate. She would live only for the purpose of fulfilling the wishes of her offspring, submitting to his demands for certain kinds of food, and later, toys, clothes or money, or surrendering to his refusal to conform to requirements of eating, time of sleeping, bowel and bladder control, and later to requirements of home work, elementary politeness or deportment. This quality of maternal overprotection differs sufficiently in its expression from the other forms to require special formulation.

Overindulgence shows a distinct resemblance to other forms of overprotective phenomena. Theoretically, one may argue that excessive contact, infantilization and refusal to take risks for the child likewise represent evidence of overindulgent behavior. However, in sorting out the data there is little difficulty in differentiating items for the fourth criterion, as a review of the maternal overprotection data in Chapter II will show. Items that show closest similarity to lack of maternal control have to do with infantilization when they concern especially prolonged breast or bottle feeding or helping the child with bathing or dressing long past infancy. In Case 2, for example, the mother continued bottle feeding until her boy was 3½ years old because "he didn't want to give it up." She helped to bathe and dress him until age 14, at the time when he was referred for treatment. Such activities may be regarded as evidence of overindulgence on the part of the mother. Presumably, she refuses to give up the pleasure of handling her son as an infant, and prefers to continue bottle feeding long past the weaning period. On the other hand, one may assume as readily, on the basis of the facts given, that the mother did not yield to her wish to prolong the child's infancy but to a stubborn refusal on the part of the infant to give up the bottle. Furthermore, excessive bottle feeding, as an easy way of avoiding the more troublesome diet, may occur in maternal rejection of infants. The facts recorded under infantilization can be interpreted per se as evidence only of a prolongation of infantile care.

A final and most significant reason for separating data on infantilization from data on overindulgence is revealed by five cases in Group I in which there is no evidence of overindulgence, yet strong evidence of infantilization. Data on overindulgence are, hence, not merely an elaboration of data on infantilization but present a type of maternal activity that may be distinct from the other forms of overprotection.

There are in Group I nine children who are overly disciplined rather than indulged. All but one of them has been infantilized to some degree—at least prolonged infantile feeding and dressing.

Unfortunately, evidence of excessive maternal control is not found in our records in as great detail as evidence of lack of maternal control. This is understood in view of the fact that the latter represents undisciplined behavior of which the mother complains and for which the child may be referred. On the other hand, excessive obedience to parents is unlikely to be regarded as a problem.

Complete maternal submission, as described in the fictitious example given, is not found in any of our cases of maternal overprotection. Various forms and degrees of overindulgence are present, but are not extreme as in the hypothetical case. Nevertheless, in eleven of the twenty Group I cases, there are numerous instances of remarkable submission to the tyranny of infantile demands. Two questions present themselves: first, why are these parents willing to take as much punishment as they do from their children; and second, why does the submissive maternal attitude to the infant's undisciplined behavior fall short of the extreme instance?

An answer to the second question is found in the development of an impossible situation in the family life at a certain stage in the growth of the unmodified, aggressive infant. Even should the father remain submissive to a life in which the whims of the child dominate the family activity, the mother at some point or other can no longer hold out. As a matter of self-defense, she is compelled to turn against the "monster." The numerous and incessant complaints of the mother against all she "has had to endure," in spite of all the sacrifices she has made, attest to this situation. A review of the data indicates how difficult the situation becomes. Besides disrespectful behavior, insulting refusals to comply with the parents' requests, the mother is also spit at and slapped (Case 1); not allowed to go out in the evening because the child refuses to let her go (Case 2); compelled to prepare meals whenever the child wishes to eat regardless of meal times, to have food that is disliked thrown to the floor (Case 4); compelled to sleep in the bed the son chooses (Case 11); hit, teased and bullied, annoyed by muddy shoes on newly scrubbed floors (Case 12); kicked, pinched, and sworn at (Case 14).

Rebellious, defiant, tyrannizing behavior toward mothers occurred in eleven cases of the twenty. In each case, difficulties began in infancy and increased with the growing aggression of the child. Yet only three of the eleven mothers sought help directly because the child made life intolerable for them. Of the remaining eight cases, three were referred for reasons other than rebellious behavior (Case 4 by mother through a settlement worker because the child, age 4, could not be persuaded to stay in kindergarten without the mother; Case 9, age 4, by mother through advice of the family physician because the child was afraid of the dark; Case 13, age 14, by a visiting teacher because of school retardation.) Five were referred for rebellious behavior primarily by agents other than the mother, with or without her coöperation (Case 2 by a visiting teacher, Case 3 by a settlement house psychiatrist, Case 10 and Case 14 by fathers, Case 17 by a public-school vocational counselor).

After referral of the aggressive children, regardless of the reason originally given or the agency that made examination possible, complaints by mothers of the suffering they endured followed regularly. The mothers of this group appeared to relish the opportunity to give expression to the "punishment" they had to undergo.

Nevertheless, they regularly interfered with treatment, tried to spoil the growing relationship of child and psychiatrist, and, presumably, to control the interviews, especially in the early stages. Several mothers, after expressing great satisfaction at release from the tyranny of a child exerted every effort to restore the status that preceded the treatment period. Indeed, in reviewing the therapeutic history one discerns clearly that the entire group of overprotecting mothers were caught hard and fast in the relationship even when some of them put forth strenuous efforts at release. The situation is revealed in high light in Case 12, in which the mother, driven to desperation by the tyrannical role of her son, moved the entire household during the night, while the son was visiting at the home of a relative. She hoped in this way to prevent his return since he did not know the new address. Yet in a few days the mother brought him back.

A study of the mothers who displayed such remarkable tolerance to the undisciplined behavior of their children and a general unwillingness to accept help for that problem does not show evidence of general submissive attitudes. On the contrary, they show in relation to their husbands and friends distinctly dominating tendencies. Their own childhood, marital and social experiences are recorded in detail in Chapter VII. At this point it is worth noting that in submitting to their children they demonstrate in their adult life an exceptional relationship.

Some reasons for unwillingness to refer the children for treatment are found in the prevailing parental resistance to the admission that the child is a problem. That attitude is based on the difficulty in admitting one's failure as a parent and in overcoming illusions about the child. Overprotective parents do not differ essentially from others in this respect. Parental pride and overvaluation of the offspring naturally militate against the admission that the child is more of a problem than other children or that the parent has failed to bring it up properly. The repeated assurances on the part of the overprotecting mothers that the child is badly behaved in spite of all they have done for it, as a defense against the possible accusation that the fault is theirs, seems merely an exaggeration of usual parental behavior. All influences that exaggerate maternal love act to strengthen these very tendencies that would prevent or defer the referral of the child as a problem.

In the maternal overprotective relationship, the admission of the child's need for treatment becomes especially difficult since the mother, by absorbing the child, has not shared any responsibility in its upbringing. She has taken on herself the entire burden of rearing, hence also the burden of admitting her complete failure when she initiates referral of the child for treatment.

As referral data indicate, mothers have not sought help in the case of tyrannizing youngsters until years have elapsed and then in most cases have done so through the initiation of others and against their own original protest. Refusal to refer because of incestuous conflicts arising out of too exclusive mother-son relationships is clearly portrayed in some cases.

Besides the reasons given for late referrals or refusal to refer, there are chance factors that operate in each case. These are the chance knowledge that resources for treatment are available, and the chance that the child's difficulty will affect an individual who recognizes the problem, knows that agencies for treatment are at hand, and who helps initiate referral to the agency.

The type of symptoms presented by the child is also an important influence in the choice—and in the selection of cases—for referral. Review of such data shows that not one child was referred directly by a parent for submissive behavior, in contrast with referrals of "rebellious" children. Obviously, too, teachers, social workers, and physicians who deal with children are more likely to regard as a problem the child who is impudent, disobedient, and difficult to manage than one who is sweet and submissive.

The data limited to symptomatology of maternal overprotection reveal no clue that enables us to explain the divergence of maternal control in its two forms. Why, with apparently similar overprotecting phenomena of excessive contact, infantilization, and prevention of independent behavior, do some cases of maternal overprotection take on the indulgent and others the dominating form? Later investigations into maternal background and constitutional factors [1] of the children may throw more light on this question.

Theoretically, a sharp contrast may be drawn between over-protecting mothers who dominate and those who indulge. The former express to the fullest degree that phase of maternal love that corresponds to possession of the love object. The latter represent in exaggerated degree the phase of surrender to the love object. The former attempt with great concentration of energy to mold the child according to the maternal conception, thwarting any expression that is not in the determined direction. The latter abandon themselves to the child's emotional development however it proceeds, making feeble attempts to modify insistent behavior. The former act as though saying, "This is my child. He must do whatever I wish"; the latter as though saying, "I am his mother. I will do whatever he wishes."

Both exceed the usual parental overvaluation of the child. The former, however, attempt to constrict its personality, to trim it to the desired shape; the latter allow the child's personality to expand, giving luxuriant growth to infantile tendencies.

The behavior problems of the children are consistently rebellious and aggressive in indulgent overprotection; submissive and dependent in dominating overprotection. However, the child's share in the direction of maternal maneuvers is more clearly observed in relation to the fourth criterion than to the others. Granting that all overprotecting mothers start with strong infantilizing behavior, it is easy to understand how the child's response may swing the overprotection into the dominating or indulgent form. If the child responds with sweet submission to infantilizing behavior, the dominating tendencies of the parent are unhindered and strengthened. If the child rebels against discipline, the submissive tendencies of the parent are brought into evidence. We need start only with the premise of excessive maternal love. In a milder degree, if the child yields readily, the control exerted by

[1] A subsequent study showing a constitutional factor as a possible explanation of submissive behavior has been made. David M. Levy, "Aggressive-Submissive Behavior and the Fröhlich Syndrome," *Archives of Neurology and Psychiatry*, XXXVI (1936), 991–1020

the mother in the first year of life continues in the form "dominating mother—obedient child." If he rebels, he is given his way and the maternal domination in the early months gives way to overindulgence. In a milder form such variation in parental response is typical of family life in general.

When the dominating activity of the mother will suffer no modification regardless of the rebellious behavior of the child, an impasse results. Assuming an inflexible dominating tendency, the children, theoretically, would make one of two adaptations—complete submission or continual warfare. Cases may be cited to illustrate such family patterns. However, they do not illustrate maternal overprotection; they demonstrate maternal personalities in which the need to dominate usurps all other tendencies. In such cases there may be little or no evidence of maternal love. On the basis of the selective criteria for this study, one case (18) was included in which the dominating phase of maternal care is especially pronounced. It differs from the others in the form of expression used to illustrate the overprotection and in the absence of any data on infantilization. The teacher who referred the patient wrote that the "mother has her clutches on the child." The various observers expressed chiefly evidence of extreme maternal domination. At first investigation, the case appeared unlike the others, but it was included since it satisfied the selective criteria. The absence of data on infantilization is an interesting differentiating point. A study of the case in detail shows a remarkable lack of warm maternal response, of demonstration of affection, of any evidence of overprotection except in the form of domination.

The inclusion of this case indicates the impurities in our original sifting, and the need of establishing more accurate criteria. It illustrates, also, as experience has shown, that the presence of one or two criteria of maternal overprotection may not necessarily prove an overprotective relationship, and that the "purest" forms show all four essential components.

The method we employed in the study of a human relationship began with a device for the selection of so-called pure cases in order to reveal the relationship in a form most readily available to investigative procedures. Clearness of delineation rather than quantity of material became the first requirement in the cases finally chosen. Nevertheless, it is clear that the method of selection was a crude one since it depended on a rather subjective process. "Everybody" who knows the family, laymen and experts, says that the child is overprotected. Selecting on that basis, however emphatic or unanimous the opinions of the observers, must represent merely a method out of which criteria for objective selectivity may be formulated. Various observers point to this and that child as overprotected. We first make sure of their language and their agreement, then we study the relationship and find that it consists of essential components. When this is done we have established new criteria and can select cases in a more precise manner.

Under *maternal control* are included all available data of maternal discipline. Such control in Group I mothers is manifested by exaggerations of normal maternal domination or indulgence of the child, and described as overdomination and overindulgence.

Overindulgence consists in yielding to the wish or actions of a child or submitting to his demands to an extent not tolerated by most parents. Overindulgence appears in active form through willing catering to the child's whims or wishes, and in passive form through surrender to the child's demands. Overindulgence in its extreme form would be manifested by complete maternal surrender to the child.

Both phases of maternal activity in the control of children can be studied most conveniently in an indirect way; *i.e.,* by collection of data on the response of children in this phase of maternal overprotection. Since children of overindulgent mothers display various rebellious symptoms disturbing to parents, they are more likely to be referred for treatment than children of overdominating mothers, since the latter are obedient and submissive.

In the Group I cases, nine children appear to be overdisciplined. All but one have been infantilized also to some degree. The absence of infantilization in the one case leads to a doubt of its proper inclusion in a group of so-called "pure" cases, since instances of maternal overdomination, without other evidence of overprotection, represent an essentially different type of mother-child relationship.

The activity of the child in initiating maternal overprotection appears more striking in the overindulgent than in any other phase of overprotection.

Eleven of the twenty Group I mothers who overindulge show numerous instances of submission to the tyranny of infantile demands. Some explanations of this maternal tolerance are set forth and data presented showing how, in spite of long citations of what they have had to endure, only three of the eleven overindulgent mothers sought help directly.

Data on Excessive Maternal Control

CASE 5. Boys call him "sissy." They take his belongings away from him; he never fights back. Wants his mother to walk to school with him (age 13). No temper tantrums or cross words to mother but when angry "goes off and sulks," then often returns to kiss mother and ask her forgiveness. Timid and seclusive in school. Does not accept invitations of friends. Industrious student. Clean, neat, obedient, and polite. Has often washed the dishes and cleaned the house, although mother has never required it; in fact, she is opposed to it. Accepts meekly punishment of going to bed in the afternoon, even now (age 13).

Referred by a settlement-house social worker because child is teased so cruelly by other children who regard him as "sissy."

CASE 6. Teachers complain that he tattles on other children in school. Always fearful and timid with other boys; they take his candy away from him and beat him up. He never fights back. Still clings very closely to mother and is loath to leave her in the morning for school (age 10). Whenever late coming home, he makes numerous apologies to mother. Responds strongly to the slightest disapproval. Shows considerable distress if either parent shows displeasure. Has needed very little discipline, according to the mother. Meekly accepts punishment, such as going to bed an hour earlier. Honest, truthful, obedient, polite, extremely neat. Throughout the treatment, patient's lack of aggression was considered the important problem.

Referred by a social worker because of fears.

CASE 7. Never disobedient to mother except when she tried to make him play with other boys; he then ran back to mother and clung to her. "Model" deportment at school and at home. Completely submissive to mother.

Not referred as a behavior problem.

CASE 8. Obedient, clean, well-mannered, overly polite, quiet boy. No evidence of temper tantrums or disobedience. Dominated completely by mother.

Referred by father through psychiatrist for special study of children of a parent with manic depression. Problems: restless behavior, dawdling at table.

CASE 17. In relation to mother is usually sweet, affectionate, kindly, considerate, though with occasional bad temper. Says he never wants to leave mother. Rebellious behavior in the classroom; quarreling with other boys and with next sibling. Tells mother every thought and everything that happens to him. Runs errands for mother; tidies up the place for her.

Referred by a public-school vocational guidance teacher with mother's coöperation because of rebellious behavior at school.

CASE 18. Mother forbids any athletic activity, and though the boy is 16 years old he yields to her demands except on one occasion when mother allowed him to play ball; she then accompanied him to the baseball field to see that he didn't get injured. Though mother will not allow him to go to the movies alone, he does not protest. Works long hours at home on his studies. Always "such a good baby." Girls regard him "like a sister." Interviewed with mother; never speaks for himself.

Referred by a school principal, in spite of mother, because of "sissy" behavior and an overdominating mother.

CASE 19. Gets on well with other children who take a protective attitude towards him. Very obedient and polite; eats what he is given, goes to bed on time. Teacher says he is a charming boy who "ought to have been a girl." All infantile habit problems managed without difficulty. Problems are entirely those of infantile dependency and irresponsibility.

Referred by mother through family physician because of school retardation.

CASE 20. A 4-year-old boy submissive to a 2-year-old brother who protects him in fights. Very solicitous of mother's moods; inquiries worriedly if she seems tired or upset. Mother considers him "too good" in that he seldom opposes the young brother's domination. She wishes he would not be so considerate of her and others' feelings. He is never destructive or quarrelsome; obeys the commands of mother and father quickly. When his requests are refused he appears sad but doesn't ask again. Enjoys doing housework, sweeping very carefully with a toy broom. Plays chiefly with a girl younger than himself. Eats well, though slowly, whatever is given him, preferring food that he is told is good for him. He makes numerous efforts to keep the baby role and insists that he is the baby.

Referred by mother through a mothers' club, originally because of enuresis and thumb-sucking.

VII. MATERNAL AND PATERNAL
FACTORS

IN GENERAL, our discussion of the problem of genetic factors has dealt thus far with certain conditions that act as external stimuli, reinforcing maternal protective tendencies originally present, or, in a sense, congealing it so that the maternal attitude to the baby in its earliest months of life remains more or less fixed—impervious to its normal gradual dilution in response to the growing child. Such external factors have to do especially with the illnesses of the offspring, which in some cases threatened its life and in others were so arranged in time and frequency as to help bind the mother more closely in the critical early months.

In studying the maternal factors, we must explore the influences exerted in every phase of the mother's life on the overprotective relationship. This leads us to a study of experiences related to the period immediately preceding the birth of her offspring, to her marital and social life, and to her childhood. Again all our data will be oriented to the problem of the overprotective relationship. We should possess psychoanalytic investigations of mothers and children living in the relationship studied in order, especially, to determine how the maternal instinctive tendencies and the response to them by the child have been shaped—to aid in understanding the influences we are investigating by direct study of the psychic life.

PERIOD OF ANTICIPATION

Assuming a "normal" desire for children, all types of experience that thwart or threaten the possibility of pregnancy or its successful termination are potent sources of increased maternal longing. Mothers who suffer the trials of prolonged anticipation of the firstborn, of long periods of relative sterility, or spontaneous miscarriages, or stillbirths, are rendered obviously more apprehensive and protective in their attitude toward the offspring than if childbirth occurred without these circumstances.

Significant data relating to the "period of anticipation" follow. One case is included in which abortions were artificially induced in the early years of marriage. This was followed, however, by a long period of relative sterility, to end about fifteen years after marriage with the birth of the patient. Included also are two cases of severe organic complications of pregnancy (4 and 17), and one with severe emotional disturbance due to the husband's desertion (6).

Eleven mothers in the group experienced one or more instances of relative sterility (5 cases), death of offspring (3 cases), or spontaneous abortion (3 cases) preceding the birth of the patient—an unusually large number of such instances in a group of 20 [1] Adding the other instances described we have 13 out of 20 mothers whose histories prior to the birth of the overprotected child indicate an unusual "period of anticipation."

The data presented have significant meaning as factors favoring overprotection only on the assumption that the child was wanted. This assumption is based on the mother's statement, and will be scrutinized later. A long period of anticipation, numerous gynecological examinations, hopes raised only to fall, feelings that one is doomed to sterility, that it must be a punishment for sin, guilt-fed wishes that examination of the husband will reveal that he is to blame—these are typical responses to the experience of "relative sterility." The enhanced feeling toward the infant is easily comprehended. The normal overvaluation of an infant is increased. Extra precautions for its care follow apprehensive feelings. These are magnified also by a conviction that no other pregnancy will follow.

Responses during the "period of anticipation" are well illus-

[1] Check studies of the I.C.G. records show but four children born as late as three years or longer after marriage, to 104 mothers who had not used contraceptive measures. Another check study for abortions or death preceding birth of a patient yielded 15 percent of such instances in 200 cases. However, no differentiation between spontaneous and induced abortions was made. For spontaneous abortions, the only type comparable to the overprotective group, the percentage 15 is, therefore, high.

trated in our records. After a first miscarriage, two years followed before a second pregnancy occurred. It went to term (Case 8). There was much anxiety about it. The only pregnancy that followed—in the past eight years—resulted in a second miscarriage. The mother accused her husband of having syphilis, claiming that

TABLE XXXII

PERIOD OF ANTICIPATION OF BIRTH OF PATIENT IN 20 CASES OF "PURE" MATERNAL OVERPROTECTION

Case no.	Ordinal position [a]	Data on period of anticipation [b]
1	only	
2	only	Mother examined because of sterility and much treatment to overcome it. Patient born in 10th year of marriage. Mother then age 33.
3	only	Fear of sterility. No contraception. Patient born in 4th year of marriage.
4	only	Caesarian birth due to nephritis. Only pregnancy, since doctor warned against danger of further impregnation.
5	2/2	No contraception. Patient born five years after first child. A five-month spontaneous miscarriage five years after the birth of patient was the last pregnancy.
6	only	Husband deserted during pregnancy. Depression.
7	2/2	First pregnancy resulted in stillbirth. First child a girl aged 13, had infantile paralysis at the age of 8 months and was subnormal. The patient was born four years after marriage. Fear of sterility.
8	only	Miscarriage preceding and following the birth of patient. Fear of sterility. Mother 41 years of age when patient was born.
9	only	
10	1/4	
11	only	
12	1/2	
13	1/2	Birth of patient preceded by death of first child (at 7 months).
14	1/2	Spontaneous miscarriage preceding birth of patient. Fear of sterility and treatment for it.

TABLE XXXII (*Continued*)

PERIOD OF ANTICIPATION OF BIRTH OF PATIENT IN 20 CASES OF "PURE"
MATERNAL OVERPROTECTION

Case no.	Ordinal position [a]	Data on period of anticipation [b]
15	1/2	A seven-month stillbirth preceded birth of patient. There was a spontaneous miscarriage following.
16	1/2	
17	1/3	Eclampsia with temporary loss of vision of several days duration, and convulsions. Illness continued about two months after birth.
18	only	Several induced abortions, then no contraception and accepted sterility by age 37. Pregnant at 40, about 15 years after marriage. Thrown from horse during pregnancy.
19	only	One spontaneous miscarriage preceding birth of patient.
20	1/2	

[a] Under *Ordinal Position*, "only" means an only child; 1/3 means first of three children; 1/2, first of two children, etc.
[b] Blank space indicates nothing unusual in period of anticipation.

he was responsible. He yielded to her insistence and had an examination, which revealed no evidence of disease.

After several induced abortions in the early years of marriage—the only instance in Group I, Case 18—preventive measures were stopped. But years of sterility followed, and the mother stated that she was fully resigned by the time she reached age 37 to a childless marriage. She became pregnant at age 40 and felt that "destiny ordained her maternal urge should be satisfied by giving her a child late in life." Her precautions in safeguarding the patient, an only child, are remarkable even in our highly overprotective group.

An example of a combination of factors of "anticipation" in the period preliminary to the birth of the patient is well illustrated in Case 7. The mother feared sterility because her husband, a widower, had had no children. She was always anxious for a boy and during her first year of marriage, when living near the seashore, often wrote "Marty" in the sand, the name of her hoped-for son. A first pregnancy was terminated by stillbirth. A girl, the first viable child, had infantile paralysis at the age of eight months, resulting in a paralysis of the leg, and was subnormal. The patient, the last child, was born in the fourth year of marriage.

A preliminary period of barren years is a different type of experience from a series of pregnancies that end in disaster. The feeling of hopelessness and "impotence" is greater in the former. A pregnancy that aborts raises a hope at least that another pregnancy will ensue and that it will go to term. The difference in maternal attitude resulting from a period of anticipation featured chiefly by waiting, contrasted with a period featured chiefly by disappointment, cannot be determined from our data. It would seem that the mothers who suffered a long period of sterility are especially concerned with that phase of overprotection that concerns risks to the life of the child (Cases 2, 8, 14, 18). More data are necessary for the study of this differentiation.

So far we have treated our material on the assumption that a child was wanted and that a normal maternal need was magnified by a period of tantalizing waiting and disappointment. But suppose our reliance on the mothers' statements as to frustration is false; or that, at least, an unconscious wish to be unencumbered by pregnancies or children was a motivating influence. There is supporting evidence for this viewpoint in our records. Two mothers postponed for a long time an operation recommended as a cure for their sterility. Another rode horseback, thereby endangering the pregnancy by a possible accident—which actually occurred.

Studies of maternal attitude by the method of psychoanalysis indicate that hostile feelings towards pregnancy and children are universal in our culture. Such feelings vary in a quantitative sense, like physical energy, and likewise, a counteracting force, repression, that enables the individual to check the dangerous activity impelled by these feelings, and also to conceal recognition of them. The reader is referred to the psychoanalytic literature for further elaboration of these principles of human behavior.[2] Their application to the problems raised in this section, however, is easily comprehended. It is possible that a mother, consciously yearning for a

[2] Georg Groddeck, *The Book of the It* (New York, 1928), pp. 22-23. J. C. Flügel, *The Psychoanalytic Study of the Family* (London, 1926), p. 160.

child but unconsciously hostile to her destiny as the impregnated female, might accept a period of sterility all too readily. In that sense, the reason given for postponing an operation designed to cure the sterility—because of fear of death, inconvenience, and the like—would be regarded as a rationalization, and a concealment of the hostility to pregnancy. Indeed, as Groddeck asserts, the sterility itself would be explained on the same basis as a state psychically determined.

Reasoning along the same line, all maternal overprotection could be regarded as compensatory to unconscious hostility, and its quantitative variation simply an index of the strength of the compensatory device. So-called "pure" overprotection would be pure only in the sense that its manifestations are consistent in every phase of maternal care, whereas the group labeled "compensatory" or "guilt" overprotection show inconsistencies or special emphasis on one phase of the mother-child relationship.

Reasoning along the same line, differences in maternal feelings related to constitutional factors would be regarded simply as increasing or diminishing the compensatory device. This consideration would be necessary since it is known that the same conditions —for example, infidelity on the part of the husband—are followed by increased maternal protection in some women and by rejection of the child in others. The difference in reaction is then attributed to differences in make-up, the overprotective reaction being the reaction of maternal types.

The "psychopathology" of maternal overprotection resembles obsessional neurosis more than any other—in the compulsory quality of the behavior, the stubborn resistance to therapeutic modification, and the high degree of responsibility that characterizes the overprotecting mother. This resemblance also would lend support to the theory that maternal overprotection represents a type of neurosis, in which especially processes of guilt result in exaggerated maternal care.

Before considering other possible neurotic elements in mother-child relationships, it is important to weigh the possibility of a "pure" overprotection, pure not only in the consistency of the clinical symptoms, but also in the sense of an excess in maternal response not primarily determined by psychic conflict. Granting a normal maternal response to the helpless infant, one readily grants an increased response to an increased helplessness. That the sickly infant evokes more care and concern than the healthy one requires no explanations in terms of neurosis, nor the fact that a previously healthy infant elicits through a sudden convulsive seizure increased maternal behavior. Numerous conditions act primarily as an aggregate of powerful stimuli that evoke a correspondingly powerful maternal response. So also with various frustrations of pregnancy. They would especially increase the longing for a child in maternal women and it can be shown that Group I mothers displayed in the main especially consistent maternal behavior in their relationship with siblings during their premarital life. When feelings of guilt are to be found in "pure" overprotection, as they are likely to be in any mother-child relationship, they may therefore be secondary factors, and not primary determinants, as in the "impure" cases. Otherwise we would be in the precarious position of maintaining that when a response in a human relationship is increased above normal the increase is effected only through a neurotic mechanism.

Applying the question to the three instances encountered in the group, we have certain data that may help in our inferences. In Case 14, the mother did not accept the advice of several physicians to have a minor operation for the cure of sterility. This refusal might be considered evidence proving a lack of good faith in her avowed wish for pregnancy, even though such operations are never represented as certain of success. There was, however, a special fear of operations, a fear reinforced by her husband's attitude. The physician's advice to go to the country for a rest was naturally preferred as a cure of sterility to an operation, and shortly following this trip a pregnancy actually ensued. Hence the real test of willingness to undergo an operation in case the trip to the country was not followed by pregnancy could not be made. We are ignorant of the factors that made impregnation possible after the mother's rest, as also of the spontaneous miscarriage that preceded the birth of the patient.

In Case 3, as in the previous one, the mother said she had been very anxious to have a child. She said she was very disappointed when pregnancy had not occurred in the first year of marriage. An operation was advised, but she postponed her decision. After some months, however, she consented, underwent the operation, and two months later conceived. Six years elapsed, following the birth of her child, when he was referred to the Institute. In that period of time she had not conceived again and refused to consider a second operation which had been advised, and accepted by her, as a fair promise of another pregnancy.

We have the problem of considering, as evidence of opposition to the wish to be pregnant, postponement of the first operation, and also refusal to have a second. The fact that, regardless of wavering, the operation was accepted is proof rather that the operation was feared, as it was, and that a hope that pregnancy would occur in time, regardless, was strengthened. Furthermore, the operation was performed in the fourth year of marriage, a period of testing not unduly prolonged.

The fact that the mother was illiterate and recognized that condition as an especial proof of the need for a child should be mentioned. She couldn't read and was all the more "lonely for a child." Through the child she longed to fulfill the gratification of her eager wish for an education, in competition with her literate brothers and sisters.

Her refusal to become pregnant a second time because it would involve another surgical procedure offers an interesting problem in the overprotective relationship. The situation differs from that of a woman who frankly, though opposed to the maternal role, satisfies the demands of her conscience or of her husband and family by producing one child—and then no more. Her one child is all the concession she intends to make. When the desire for the maternal state is powerful, as in the group of overprotective mothers, the coming of a child may, in some instances, represent a complete fulfillment. In fact, it may preclude further pregnancies. In this way the mother-child monopoly becomes established in its truest sense, allowing no competing influence, even in the form of another child. The necessity of an operation, or complications of pregnancy or of childbirth would then be readily exploited as deterrents to further pregnancy. Quite a number of two-child families are explained by mothers on the basis that it isn't fair that a child be an only child, and a brother or sister should be provided. In fact, a number of children are adopted for that reason. Among overprotecting mothers this consideration would naturally be very important, since the needs of the child are overvalued.[3]

The third instance (Case 18) of a period of relative sterility in which the question of conflicting feelings toward pregnancy was raised, occurred in a mother who was 40 years old at the time of the pregnancy that resulted in the patient's birth. During the pregnancy she rode horseback and was thrown. Thereafter she was afraid that something "happened to the foetus." In this case the presumptions of hostile feelings towards the pregnancy are strong. They are strengthened by the fact that the mother was unwilling to have children in the early years of marriage, that she had several induced abortions, and when a period of sterility set in, she was quite content. At age 37 she felt the certainty of sterility. When she became pregnant at 40, she felt that "destiny ordained her maternal urge." The conflicting attitudes towards pregnancy are evident, and the inference clear that her feelings of guilt were enhanced by the early abortions, by the fear that sterility was a consequent punishment, and that the accident had been brought about by her own insistence on riding horseback when pregnant— even without assuming that the accident was determined by unconscious motivation. In fact, other considerations in this case make its inclusion in the group of "pure overprotection" questionable. It has been discussed previously in regard to the impurities found in relationship studies by the first sifting process. The mother described is the only one in the group who had abortions performed because she frankly did not want children. She is a questionable selection in terms of the criterion of "wanting a child," because when her pregnancy came so late in life, her "wanting a child" was in the form of accepting her destiny as a mother, rather

[3] In this connection it is interesting that of the 20 children in Group I, 10 are only children, and 8 are from two-child families, although the average number of years the mothers were married, at the time the children were referred for treatment, was 11 years (median, 11). Contrasted with the 90 percent of 1 and 2 child families in this group, is 42 percent of 1 and 2 child families in 427 I.C.G. cases used as a contrast group. See M. P. Lewenberg, "A Study of the Marital Relationships of Overprotecting and Non-overprotecting Mothers."

than a longing to be one. The selection is questionable also in terms of the spontaneous and definite expression of overprotection in its usual forms. In her case the expression given by the teachers who knew the mother well was some variation of the remark made by one of them—"she has fastened her clutches on the child." Though accepted in the group of "pure" overprotection, in view of the unanimity of description by the workers on the case, of the mother's excessive supervision and protection of the patient, the remark differs from all the other expressions of overprotection. This mother differed from the others also in a distinctly paranoid attitude. Her overprotection was an extension of this attitude in the mother-child relationship. She was constantly on the alert to protect her son against any criticism, writing innumerable letters of protest to the school principal concerning the supposed ill treatment by teachers and companions, lack of appreciation, and so on. She had serious difficulties in her own career as a nurse and later as actress for the same reasons, "laying down the law" to the stage director, claiming her talents were not appreciated, and the like. A review of her case abstract in the appendix will reveal other abnormalities of behavior. In her case we have a magnification of that phase of overprotection that involves overvaluation and defense of the child against the hostile world. The data of her overprotecting behavior are comprised under the headings of protection, as fear against danger, and domination, with nothing specifically under "excessive contact" and "care." In her blend of maternal feelings the aggressive and protective elements outweigh the love elements. It is an "impure" variety of overprotection.

MARITAL FACTORS: SEX

When husband and wife are sexually compatible and have social interests in common they thereby set up a number of conditions that operate against a mother-child monopoly. The fact that they have a life of their own as husband and wife withdraws certain time and energy from the parental relationship. A wife devoted to her husband cannot be exclusively a mother. In a more fundamental sense, the release of libido through satisfactory sexual relationship shunts off energy that must otherwise flow in other directions—in the case of our group, in the direction of maternity. The child must bear the brunt of the unsatisfied love life of the mother. One might theoretically infer that a woman sexually well adjusted could not become overprotective to an extreme degree. Certainly she would not make the relationship to the child her exclusive social life. There are four presumably sexually well-adjusted mothers in the group of 20 that comprise our "pure" group.[4]

There is certainly definite evidence that the sex difficulties of our mothers have, at least, reinforced the overprotective relationship. In one case it was clear to the mother that her overprotective attitude became intensified after learning of her husband's infidelity. From her own point of view she had more love to give and also, having lost her husband, wanted to make sure she would never lose the children. Such instances are common enough, but not sufficient to explain the original overprotective attitude, for it appears clear from our studies that the difficulty in the sexual adjustments acts chiefly as a strengthening factor rather than a causal one. As will be seen later, a large number of mothers in this group also curtailed their general social activity after the coming of the child. Four mothers in our group of twenty samples of "pure overprotection" are apparently sexually well adjusted. Of the remainder, all have difficulties in sexual life, varying from passive adaptation without pleasure to various methods of preventing sexual activity. One mother is receptive to sexual activity, she says, but her husband has been for years in a penitentiary—the one criminal father in our group (Case 16); another is a widow (Case 19); and one is divorced. Both the latter, however, were averse to sexual activity.

Typical responses are quoted from the records: "Mother was repelled by sex relations and felt a revolt against her husband after the act" (Case 8). "She does her duty by her husband. She always loved her children more than her husband and discarded him after they were born. He was frankly jealous of the children" (Case 17). "Father is impotent. Mother finds fault with him because of her

---

[4] I am aware of other instances of mothers who overprotect their children though sexually well adjusted and much in love with their husbands; whose overprotection is nevertheless of the "pure" type. They did not manifest the extreme degree of overprotection of our samples but were better able to tolerate remedial measures and to accept the husband's role as father of the child.

lack of satisfaction, and also because she wants more children. The husband says that she frequently cries because of her lack of satisfaction" (Case 11). "Mother has been sleeping with her son the past three years and has had no sex relations with the husband. The husband is easy to get along with and a good provider" (Case 5). "Mother is frankly sexually frigid" (Case 1). "Mother passively submits to the husband's sexual demands though she has never had any pleasure in the sex relationship" (Case 10). "Mother has always been averse to coitus, using various pretexts and evasions to prevent it. Husband has complained to his mother-in-law trying to get her help to make the wife have sex relations with him" (Case 2). "Mother considers sex activity disgraceful" (Case 12). The examples given are sufficient to indicate that there is a remarkably high degree of sexual maladjustment in the group. However, not all the mothers are sexually inadequate. Four appear to be well adjusted and another was sexually responsive to her husband before he was taken away from her.

An attempt was made to see if any differences in the type of overprotection or in the background factors occurred between mothers who at least dutifully submitted to sexual requirements of marriage and those who used measures to prevent the act. Nothing significant was found on this point. Contrast studies in regard to the rate of sexual maladjustment have been made. Lewenberg compared 45 overprotecting mothers with 45 non-overprotecting mothers, the cases taken at random from the files. Her contrast group showed 46 percent sexual maladjustment as compared with 87 percent of the overprotecting group. In a study of 35 rejecting mothers Figge found sexual incompatibility in 66 percent—25 out of 35 cases.[5]

Where difficulties prevent outlets of energy in one direction, a compensatory flow in another is readily understood. This time-honored idea has been utilized to explain the exaggerated mother

[5] Figures in Katharine Bement Davis, *Factors in the Sex Life of 2200 Women* (New York, 1929), a questionnaire study, show 30 percent sex maladjustment in 881 wives, computed from her Table VII, page 72; G. V. Hamilton, *A Research in Marriage* (New York, 1929), a combined questionnaire and interview study, shows 46 percent; Louis M. Terman, and others, *Psychological Factors in Marital Happiness* (New York, 1938), 33 percent.

love of widows, of mothers of only children, of mothers who, for whatever reason, have only their children to look after. It does not explain why, under the circumstances given, some mothers reject their children, or continue, even intensify, a previous rejection. The explanation of simple compensatory increase in mother love, through blocking other channels of expression, is used typically in cases where maternal love was previously in evidence.[6]

Why sex maladjustment occurs so frequently in our groups of overprotecting mothers is a problem difficult to solve without psychonanalytic data. At this point it may be said that the overprotecting mothers were found to be aggressive women, as was consistent with their strong maternal behavior. Other data that may throw some light on this problem will be considered in sections dealing with personality traits of the mothers and fathers of the overprotected children.

Marital Factors: Social

Consistent with our findings on sexual incompatibility, there is little social life in common among the parents of the overprotected children in Group I. "Practically no social life together," "They do nothing together," "Rarely go out together," "Little social life in common," are items typical for all but five of the group of 20. Of these five (Cases 6, 10, 14, 16, 19) two are, however, sexually incompatible. Of the four who are presumably sexually responsive, three are also socially compatible with their husbands.

The rate of social disharmony or, least, of curtailment in mutual social activity, seems high. This finding is not to be explained by a generally impoverished social life due to economic or cultural factors, since the majority of mothers in Group I—three-fourths— were socially active before marriage. Nor is it to be explained by infidelities or extramarital social activity of the fathers, since they represent on the whole a faithful and stable group of men. The explanation is not to be found entirely in the sexual incompatibility, for it is a common observation—and there are two instances

6 J. C. Flügel, *The Psychoanalytic Study of the Family* (London, 1926), pp. 157, 158. "The love of parents to children stands in reciprocal relationship to the parents' other interests and affections."

also in our group—that many husbands and wives have an active social life together, in spite of sexual disharmony.

A study of the general social activity of Group I mothers (aside from their role as parents) may offer an explanation of the restricted social activity with their husbands. For in the curtailment of contacts with friends, women diminish thereby the social life of their families. This applies especially to our group, since the husbands have been largely dependent for social relationships on their wives. Of the entire group, three mothers continued an active social life after marriage (Cases 1, 4, and 10); four had little or no social life before or after marriage, in the sense of visiting and having friends visit the home (Cases 3, 15, 16 and 18). Of the remaining 13, 12 greatly curtailed all social activity after marriage. Of these, the child was given as the reason for withdrawing from previously formed friendships, in eight cases (2, 5, 8, 11, 12, 17, 19, and 20). The method varied from immediate and conscious withdrawal to a gradual detachment from other social contacts after the birth of the child. Restriction of social activity after marriage because of lowered economic status are the reasons given by three others (Cases 9, 13, and 14). In the remaining case (7) the parents never left the children alone or visited or went out anywhere together without them. In terms of continuing contacts with old friends, curtailment or complete withdrawal from social activity was determined by nine of 14 mothers in this group, on the basis primarily of the mother-child relationship.

Where almost complete limitation to the society of the child occurred, the overprotective data appear especially striking in material on infantilization—besides, obviously, one excessive contact —as though the pattern was woven for a permanent mother-infant relationship. Attempts at preventing the child from making friends with other children also featured the activities of this group. On the other hand, maternal activity in the schoolroom, as an example of protecting the child from the danger of competing in the world outside the home, was not striking.

It was noted that several mothers of the group of 20 had little or no social contacts before or after marriage. Two of these were clearly suspicious of other people, a suspicion that involved the teacher's attitude to their children. They constantly complained that the child was not treated fairly, and so on, and their frequent visits to the school became a nuisance. The question arose whether, in at least one of our cases, the overprotection was not "pure" but a paranoid state that embraced the child, since the data were largely in the form of "prevention of independent behavior." There is clearly a difference in the dynamics of protecting the child against extramaternal experiences when this activity represents an outgrowth of the original absorption in the infant, and when it represents an extension of a generally suspicious attitude manifested long before marriage. Overprotection of the latter type shows especially evidence of "excessive contact" and "prevention of independent behavior," since these data are consistent with social isolation. Theoretically, we would expect, in contrast with mothers who are truly excessively maternal—"pure overprotection"—a paucity of data on infantilization. Naturally all cases of "pure overprotection" involve more than the usual amount of "guarding against the stranger," but such an attitude is a derived and not a primary phenomenon.[7]

MATERNAL FACTORS: AFFECT HUNGER

A first review of the childhood experience of mothers in our 20 (Group I) examples of maternal overprotection revealed a number of glaring accounts of privation of parental affection and of childhood play. Lack of maternal love featured the lives of most. Hough, using groups of 31 case records, each, of overprotecting and non-overprotecting mothers, found a larger proportion of cases of unhappy childhood in the former, a difference, however, not statistically significant. Hough's "control" group was selected by taking records seriatim from the files, and simply eliminating those containing evidence of overprotection. Foley [8] studied this problem by

[7] In Lewenberg's study, social maladjustment was found in 88 percent of the marriages of overprotecting mothers, and in 38 percent of the marriages of non-overprotecting mothers (45 cases in each group). Figge's figures in social maladjustment for groups of 35 rejecting and 35 non-rejecting mothers were 70 percent and 40 percent respectively (S.C.S. in S.W. 2,248, 1932).

[8] In Foley's articles, examples are given to illustrate the classification of her groups. By affection was meant that "the mother received affection and attention as a child

applying the factors "no affection" and "early responsibility" to three groups of mothers—"overprotecting," "rejecting," and "neither." After this process a much larger contrast was discernible between the overprotecting and the neutral group, the former showing 68 percent, the latter 15 percent, of the criteria "no affection" and "responsibility."

In considering privation of parental love in the 20 Group I mothers, a first selection was made of the five cases in which death of the mother occurred in childhood and was not followed by a sustaining mother-substitute. The first selection is based on the concrete nature of the evidence rather than severity of privation, since it is clear that a living mother who denies love creates a privation of greater severity than occurred in one or two of the five cases selected.[9]

CASE 12. Her father died four months preceding her birth. Her mother died when she was ten years old. She had loved her mother, and though treated kindly by an older sister with whom she lived, felt keenly the loss of her mother. With choking sobs she told how she used to envy children when she heard them say "father" or "mother." One of seven children.

CASE 14. Her mother died in her infancy. She was brought up by a strict, unaffectionate grandmother. She was very fond of her father who, however, was away from home on business much of the time. Her childhood memories were filled with longing for a mother, and phantasies of being loved by a mother. One of four children.

---

and that she considered her childhood happy." By "responsibility" was meant that the mother was overburdened as a child with household cares. It is easy to differentiate these terms, since records can be found with sufficient elaboration of childhood experiences. As to their accuracy, one may say that the general tendency of adults is to give a happy version of their childhood memories, hence more thorough studies of the parents might alter their original accounts and increase the number of unhappy childhoods.

Foley found that "lack of affection" in the childhood of mothers occurred with greatest frequency in the overprotecting group (68 percent of 41 mothers), less in the rejecting group (42 percent of 19 mothers) and least in the "neutral" group (15 percent of 40 mothers). A check by Thompson on Foley's study shows but a slight preponderance of overprotective mothers in the category "no affection, responsibility." However, the classification of so large a proportion of overprotection in her records (50 in 100 cases taken seriatim from the files), a finding so discrepant from other studies, was due to her intentional inclusion as evidence of overprotection its manifestation in its mildest and mixed forms.

[9] In the case citations that follow, the words "she" and "her" refer to the mother of the patient, the words "mother" and "father" to the grandparents of the patient.

CASE 15. Her father died when she was two, her mother, whom she loved, when she was eight years old. Then she and her brother lived with a "grouchy" uncle who made her stop school at the age of ten, to help with the housework. At fourteen, he sent her out to work in a factory. At fifteen, she ran away from home and supported herself until marriage. Her grandmother, who lived with the uncle, treated her kindly. One of two children.

CASE 17. Her father deserted in her infancy. Her mother died when she was four years old. She was placed in a home and then on a farm where she was made to work and was punished frequently. When eight years old, with the help of a farm laborer, she escaped, walking four miles to a railroad station. She traveled to the home of an older brother who placed her in a convent, where she remained until age nineteen. In this convent she had, as her sole object of love, a doll. She described with strong feeling her grief when this doll, surrendered unwillingly as a temporary gift to a child ill with measles, was burned in the fire. Youngest of seven children.

CASE 18. Her mother, whom she loved, died when she was seven years old. Thereafter she lived with a kindly, affectionate grandmother who died when she was nine. Several placements with sisters followed until age twelve, when she lived with her father, whom she admired, and a step-mother whom she regarded as mentally deficient. From the age of sixteen years she earned her own living until marriage, starting work as a governess. One of nine children.

A second group comprises four cases featured by the death of a father in childhood.

CASE 6. Her father, with whom she had very little contact, died when she was nine years old. She was the only girl in a family of four children, loved and protected by her mother and brothers.

CASE 8. Her father died in her childhood. Her mother gave little or no affection and was often depressed. A hard early life due to poverty. She worked as a housemaid during adolescence. Second of eight children.

CASE 16. Her father, hard-working, uncommunicative, saw very little of the children and died when she was eight years old. Her mother, a strict disciplinarian, had her committed to an institution when she was fifteen years old, to prevent her marriage. Only girl in four children.

CASE 19. Her father died when she was four years old. After that her mother ran a boarding house, and had little time for the children. Nevertheless she felt loved by her mother and regards her childhood as happy. Oldest of three children.

Insofar as the death of a parent in childhood is in itself a source of privation of affection, the two groups include nine such cases. Of these, two are questionable, and certainly not severe instances, since a satisfying relationship with the surviving parent or siblings occurred. The remaining seven cases represent examples of severe privation of parental love.

A third group comprises five cases in which evidence of privation occurs in an intact family group, in relation with the mother.

CASE 1. She had to work hard as a child, doing housework from the age of six, and helping in the care of the children. When age eleven years she was sent out to work. At twelve her father had her give nursing care to the mother during confinement. She resents strongly privations in her childhood exacted by her stern, "cold" father, whom, nevertheless, she admires and by whom she was regarded as the favorite child. Her mother was completely dominated by her father and played rather a dependent role in relation to her children. Third of six children, the oldest of the three girls.

CASE 4. Her mother was considered "mentally backward," unable to cook or manage the household, leaving much responsibility to her from early childhood. Her father was "tyrannical," refused to let her play with dolls, and exacted absolute obedience. She married, she said, to get rid of his tyranny, yet she admires him greatly and was considered his favorite. Oldest of three children.

CASE 10. She received no affection from her mother, with whom a hostile relationship existed from early childhood. She was strongly attached to a dominating though kindly father, who died when she was fourteen years old. Third of five children.

CASE 13. Both her parents were very strict and gave little or no evidence of affection. She had household responsibilities and helped in the care of the younger children from early childhood. As a girl, vowed that if she ever had children she would be very lenient with them.

CASE 20. She had a dominating and neglectful mother and a father who played a passive role. Her childhood was "very unhappy." Starting at ten years of age she worked during vacation and after school hours. When age thirteen she quit school to work in a factory and help support the family. She is the second of three children, all girls. The older is alcoholic, the younger epileptic and has been under "her charge" since age fourteen.

A fourth group comprises cases of intact families in which an affectionate relationship was established with the mother, but not with the father.

CASE 2. Her father was a strict disciplinarian, whose "rages" frightened the children. They turned to the mother for protection from him.

Her mother was the dominant family figure and received full devotion and loyalty from the children. At eleven she left school to help support the family. The fourth of ten children, all of whom visit each other frequently and represent a loyal affectionate family.

CASE 7. She was fond of her mother, but hated her father because he was stern and brutal to her and punished her severely. As a child she worked on the farm. Third of ten children.

The fifth group comprises cases in which a more or less affectionate relationship was established with both parents.

CASE 5. She was very fond of her mother. When age two, her father refused to live with the mother, left home, but remained in the neighborhood. She used to visit him weekly, remembers him with affection, which changed to antagonism in her adult life. She quit school and went to work when thirteen years old to help support the family. She was the seventh of fourteen children, of whom six died in infancy.

CASE 9. Her father, a carpenter, was a very irregular worker because of ill health. To supplement the family income her mother, evidently the dominant parent, took in boarders. She remembers an affectionate relationship with both parents, who, however, had little time for the children. She was evidently favored, since she was the only child allowed to remain in school until the fourth year of high school. She was the third of five children.

CASE 11. She was kept home as a child, to help with the housework and could attend school only at night. At thirteen years she went to work in a factory. Her mother was the dominant parent and handled all the money. She regards her relations with her parents as affectionate. Sixth of seven children.

Within this group of 20 overprotecting mothers there are an unusual number of instances of severe privation of parental love. The basic or maternal relationship is severely affected in 12 cases, both maternal and paternal in nine, and either, in 16. Even in the group of cases where an affectionate relationship is recorded, there is evidence of some impoverishment of parent-child relationship in terms of contact, due to undue requirements of responsibility in childhood (Case 11), the mother's occupation (Case 9), the father's absence from home and the large number of siblings (Case 5), and the need for going to work in childhood or early adolescence (Cases 5 and 11).

It should be noted also that the death of one or both parents up to the age of 12 years occurred in nine cases.

The impoverishment in the child of all those positive feelings implicit in parental love—recognition, security, affection, sympathy, and the like—has been called "affect hunger." The term was derived from clinical studies in which various symptoms demonstrating exaggerated need of love were traceable to early love privations.[10] The assumption that love is a basic need of the child, a need unfulfilled by care and protection alone, can be readily utilized as an aid in explaining an overprotective relationship. For, assuming an insatiable hunger for love, based on early privations, its gratification through maternity would engender a relationship of the closest degree.

The insolubility of affect hunger in marriage could be explained in two ways. In one, the husband may be regarded as unable, through a mature love, to satisfy a requirement made possible only in maternity, namely, the establishment through the child of a new childhood for the mother, free of all early privation.[11]

The second explanation is in terms of our data—the high degree of sex and social incompatibility in the marriages of the overprotecting mothers. As a solution of affect hunger, the marital relationship failed in the large majority of cases, and hence offered no offsetting influence to the exaggerated maternal behavior.

We are left with the problem of these difficult marriages. It is easy to understand how, when a maternal overprotective relationship is established, a bad marriage will help to reinforce it. But why is there so high a degree of incompatibility in the marriages of this group? Also, a previous study has shown that a history of affect hunger in the life of the mother occurs with a fair measure of frequency among rejecting mothers. Furthermore, two of the marriages in the overprotecting group are distinctly happy and harmonious. In the type of study pursued, absolute differences do not occur; nevertheless the problem remains, why in the event of a difficult marriage some women turn to their children with more,

[10] David M. Levy, "Primary Affect Hunger," *American Journal of Psychiatry*, XCIV (1937), 643–52.
[11] An inference would follow from this argument that insofar as the husband could satisfy the needs of a wife suffering from affect hunger, he could mitigate her overprotecting tendencies. He would then play the role of an older, loving, indulgent, husband-father.

others with less, devotion. The material of the next section dealing with the personalities of the mothers in Group I may help in solving the problem presented.

MATERNAL FACTORS: RESPONSIBILITY

The overprotecting Group I mothers represent predominantly responsible, stable, aggressive women. To a number of them, other members of the family, as well as friends, come for help and advice. Summaries of the findings in the records follow.

CASE 1. She had a life of responsibility from early childhood, helping with the housework and care of the children at six years of age. She attended evening high school 3½ years. Her whole family depend on her and "never do anything without consulting her."

CASE 2. She left school at 11 years to help support the family, and worked in the same factory until her marriage at 23. All her brothers and sisters (9) still consult her "as the one naturally in charge of the family situation." She is considered an "aggressive, dominating person."

CASE 3. The oldest of five children, she was kept at home to help with the housework while the others went to school. Later she worked in a factory until marriage at age 27, helping to earn money for the family. She is considered "aggressive and a climber." She is very ambitious for her son's education.

CASE 4. As her mother was mentally "backward," she had much household responsibility from early childhood. After graduating from high school she worked as a clerk for two years until her marriage. "Always a leader," active in mothers' clubs, president of one. Many people come to her for advice. "She is the kind of woman who looks after other people's troubles and does not attend to her own."

CASE 5. She quit school at 13 to help support the family. She worked in a store over five years until her marriage, at which time she had been promoted to the position of cashier. An aggressive woman who resisted all treatment plans for her son.

CASE 7. She worked hard on a farm in childhood. She has always been competent, self-reliant, aggressive, and since her husband's death has made a good living by sewing.

CASE 8. Born of poor parents in a large family she had many household cares in childhood. As a girl had job of housemaid for neighbors. She came to this country at the age of 20, took training as a nurse, studied hard, and received her diploma when age 23. She worked as a nurse until age 39 when she married. She used to sing in a church choir, was ambitious to become an actress and had strong cultural ambitions. Aggressive.

CASE 9. Always ambitious for an education; her family, in spite of poverty, managed to keep her in high school until she graduated at 17. She then held a job for two years, changed to a better one which she held for six years. In this job she was imposed on to do extra work because, she says, she was too timid to assert herself. Active in a women's lodge, she became president for a term. She was also president of a mothers' club. Earlier in marriage, she took full charge of her husband's store, to enable him to make supplementary income. Her friends have always come to her for advice. She says, "And what I can do to them if they get nasty is a shame." She feels that fate has been unfair in preventing the development of her artistic career.

CASE 10. Though ambitious for an education she had to quit school at 14 to get a job. She became active in labor movements and was president of a philanthropic organization. She has "always loved" to look after people; her brothers and sisters have always relied on her for help and advice. She tried to dictate the methods of treating her son, gave details of how he should be examined, and so on.

CASE 11. She had to work hard as a child, because of poverty. Always ambitious for an education, she went to night school for some years and always tried to pose as an educated person. She held a job in a factory for ten years, was promoted to the position of "forelady," and was the one worker who was "not afraid to talk to the boss."

CASE 12. A very aggressive, dominating woman, "extremely self-sufficient," taking no one's advice, making all decisions for her husband and children. As a child she was "entirely lacking in shyness." At 17 years of age she worked in a factory and held jobs until her marriage at 26.

CASE 13. When her parents tried to prevent her marriage she eloped. She has completely dominated her husband. As the oldest child she played a responsible role to the three younger children and was the mother's "assistant manager."

CASE 15. She was taken out of school to help with the housework at 10. At 14, she worked in a factory. At 15, she ran away from home because of her uncle's severity, worked as a waitress, saved money, and had had a year's training as a "practical nurse" when she married.

CASE 16. She left school when in the sixth grade to work in a factory. Held the same job six years. In spite of her mother's strong opposition to her husband, even commitment to an institution, she married him. She was always "self-willed, capable and proud."

CASE 17. Placed on a farm where she had to work hard and was punished severely, she ran away at the age of eight years and managed to go to her brother's home by train. He placed her in a convent where she remained until age 20. Then she became a successful worker in a factory and continued employment there until her marriage at age

25 years. She has always shown much initiative, self-reliance, and responsibility. As a wife she has played chiefly a maternal and protective role.

CASE 18. She has been self-maintaining since age 16 years, first as a governess, later, through her own savings for training, as a graduate nurse. She is ambitious to be an actress and has played some minor roles. She lost one job by "laying down the law" to the manager. She is generally very aggressive and dominating.

CASE 19. After graduating from college, she took a secretarial course and held one job for eight years, a second for seven years. Always the responsible member of the family. The others still turn to her for help and advice.

CASE 20. From age ten years, she worked after school hours and during vacations. She quit school to work in a factory at thirteen. In her teens she had the major share in the care of an epileptic sister and took the responsibility of having her committed to an institution. "She has remained the responsible member of the family," always called in when there is trouble.

All but two of the 20 cases have been included as examples of women who have played roles in life characterized by aggressive and responsible behavior. Of the remaining two cases, one is characterized by submissive and responsible behavior (Case 6), a woman who always played a dependent role. The other (Case 14) is characterized also by responsible behavior, but the data are inadequate to determine the aggression.

The entire group of 20 may be characterized as responsible, 18 as both responsible and aggressive. The term "responsible" in this connection is attested by helping, beyond ordinary chores, with the housework and care of siblings in childhood; by helping to support the family through steady employment before marriage; by self-maintenance through steady employment, saving money for education, and other evidence of stable, competent, reliable care or support. There is little difficulty in determining the responsibility of the group in the manner indicated, since it occurs in high degree. When "household cares early in childhood" is described, it amounts to a serious curtailment of childhood play. Stability of employment is seen in the number of years at steady work, a range of 2 to 16 years or longer. There is also a surprising number of instances in which the same store or factory job was held for 5 years or longer (12 years in Case 2, probably 12 years in

Case 3, 5 years in Case 5, 6 years in Case 9, 10 years in Case 11, 9 years in Case 12, 6 years in Case 16, 5 years in Case 17, 15 years in two jobs in Case 19).

Since every mother in the group had to help the family through work in or outside the home, the measure of responsibility in this regard is easily ascertained. Stability in terms of supporting others is thereby demonstrated—a stability that is evident in the over-protecting behavior. The overprotecting mothers are certainly stable, scrupulous, serious, ever watchful in the care of their children; apparently stable also in their work as employes.[12]

Since work outside the home is determined largely by the economic factor, a simple enumeration of jobs is not as significant in this study as stability in employment, for which, unfortunately, we have no control studies of I.C.G. cases. This does not alter the finding of unusual stability in the group; it does not enable a comparison of this point with other groups.

A feature of the responsibility described, of special interest in terms of the overprotecting behavior to follow in motherhood, is its aggressive or active quality. For the responsible attitude determined by the measure of stability in work is not merely the stability of acquiescence, of obedience. It appears to be an active helping out, a responsible attitude in a truly maternal sense. The description of the help given to the family in Case 6 will illustrate this point, since it is in marked contrast with the rest of the group. In the case cited, the mother was the only daughter in a family of four children, worked conscientiously at home, later in factories, and, after marriage, on her own as a seamstress. The work was done, however, as a dutiful daughter, dependent always on an authoritative person, represented before marriage by mother and brothers; later, when her husband absconded, by a social worker. Typically her marriage was arranged for her. She remained stable, responsible, but highly dependent on others. Note in contrast the instances in which the situation is reversed in the others. "Her whole family depended on her," they "never do anything without her," "they still consult her," "she is the one naturally in charge of

---

[12] In Foley's groups the percentages of mothers playing a responsible role before marriage, as defined in this section, are as follows: 90 percent of 41 overprotecting mothers; 41 percent of 19 rejecting mothers; 65 percent of 40 "neutral" mothers.

the family situation," are phrases that occur in some form or other in seven cases (1, 2, 3, 9, 10, 19, 20); other evidence of aggressive, dominating behavior in 18 of the 20 cases.

The active or aggressive feature of responsible behavior may be regarded as distinctly maternal, representing the active helping out on the mother's part in the mother-child relationship. Eighteen of the 20 overprotecting mothers played a maternal role in the sense of an aggressive responsible role from childhood. The records are lacking in material dealing with direct maternal behavior, in the sense of spontaneous mothering of children during childhood. Even in the absence of such data the conclusion seems warranted that the overprotecting mothers showed, in the main, strongly maternal behavior from an early age.[18]

Maternal Factors: Thwarted Ambitions

In the data relating to responsibility there are a number of notations having to do with the mothers' ambitions for education or a career. One of the effects of educational privation in the parent is seen in strong ambitions for the education of the child. Fulfillment through the child of the parent's thwarted ambition is easily comprehended and directly stated by the parents themselves—to "make up" to the child what they themselves were denied. One readily comprehends the possibilities in this regard of an increased valuation of the child, through increased identification with it. Other features of the overprotective relationship are in themselves sufficient to explain strong ambitions for the child, as the esteemed love object and as a protective measure in the struggle for existence. The thwarted ambitions of the parents would represent an additional factor. The records reveal 12 cases (1, 2, 3, 4, 5, 8, 9, 10, 11, 14, 15, 18) in which this factor appeared. Lewenberg's study of thwarted ambitions showed a higher percentage in an overprotecting group than in a control group, a difference, however, not statistically significant.

The attempt to experience through the child the satisfactions of

[18] Since in this group stability could be determined readily through the record of jobs held by each member of the group, correlation of jobs before marriage and overprotection might be inferred. However, the check studies referred to show no significant difference on this point, though, presumably, the necessity of working for a living increases an attitude of responsibility.

demands necessitated by an experience of love-hunger would theoretically be enhanced by any other privation; hence the significance of a thwarted career would, under such circumstances, be of much greater import than if love-hunger were absent.

Affect hunger and strong maternal "tendencies" are basic findings in the life histories of the overprotecting mothers. Of the two findings the latter occurs in the group with greater frequency, and in the absence of the former. Hence it is not necessarily its derivative. Certain cases of affect hunger reveal a marked overvaluation and attachment to a love object. The love object may be understood in terms of the original hunger for maternal love, protection and support. The excessive demands, so typical of affect hunger cases, are seen in the light of the child's need of "contact" and "care." Variations in the pattern of demands can be understood in terms of varying stresses in the familiar criteria of maternal care; in the one case for constant proximity and caresses (contact), another for money and indulgence (care and overindulgence), another for constant reassurance (protection against loss of love), and so forth.

Presumably the concept of affect hunger could be employed to explain both the excessive need of love and the aggression of the overprotecting mothers, since the experience of affect hunger has been found in relation with a high degree of aggressive behavior. However, affect hunger occurs also in rejecting mothers, explained, in such instances, as an attempt on the part of the mother to play toward the husband the role of demanding child, in competition with her own children. Since the overprotecting mothers in one group showed maternal tendencies in childhood, an assumption was made that the influence of affect hunger in the direction of overprotection was effective only in definitely maternal women. This assumption would have to be tested by a study of early maternal behavior in rejecting mothers who had experienced affect hunger—a study not yet at hand.

MATERNITY AND AGGRESSION

Aggressive behavior, as we understand the term, is part and parcel of maternal behavior. The aggression in relation to the infant is involved in various dominating, protecting, and training activities. Since basic maternal behavior is essentially similar in birds and mammals, including man, a study of the aggressive aspect of maternity in animals is worth recording. This behavior is seen especially in fighting enemies of the offspring, but is manifested before the necessity of attacking intruders occurs. According to Whitman it is manifested in certain birds before the eggs are laid, even before the nest is built. Among pigeons, aggression is shown as soon as the place for a nest is found. "This pugnacious mood is periodical, recurring with each reproductive cycle, and subsiding like a fever when its course is run." [14] Whitman states that the period of aggression covers the three stages of building the nest, sitting on the eggs and rearing the young. He describes similar cycles of aggression in fish.

The numerous descriptions of maternal aggression in animals have to do with the protecting function of maternity, and represent a necessary biologic adaptation for survival of the young. The various forms of maternal behavior may be described in terms of protecting and giving. Apparently the giving function has often been used as synonymous with the word "maternal," including activities in which aggressive behavior appears indirectly as in nursing, body care, and the like. Stress on the giving function of maternal behavior involves also the idea of sacrificing one's interests on behalf of the child, of submitting to its needs. It has given rise to theories of feminine passivity and masochism.[15] There has been a tendency to regard maternity in the light of femininity, and hence to dwell on those aspects of maternity consistent with that psychology. The aggressive phase has thus come to be regarded as evidence of masculinity. Theories of femininity, emphasizing especially passive, receptive behavior in women, in keeping with her role in overt sex activity, have embraced all of her functions, and hence have confused feminine and maternal behavior.

Aggressive behavior, manifested in its protecting phase, is an integral part of the maternal pattern. It is distinctly maternal.

[14] Charles Otis Whitman, "Animal Behavior," *Biological Lectures, 1898, from the Marine Biological Laboratory, Wood's Hole, Mass.* (Boston, 1899), pp. 285–358, in particular p. 323.

[15] Helene Deutsch, "Significance of Masochism in Mental Life of Women," *International Journal of Psychoanalysis*, XI (1930), 48–60; Sandor Rado, "Fear of Castration in Women," *Psychoanalytic Quarterly*, II (1933), 425–88.

In the cases of "pure" overprotection there is consistent exaggeration of both the giving and the protecting function. De Groot's [16] observation that highly maternal women are often sexually maladjusted is consistent with our findings. She attributes the difference, however, to their high degree of masculinity. She states that the woman achieves active love, and satisfies her masculinity in relation to her child, in nourishing and caring for it, later educating it. This statement is tantamount to making maternal behavior synonymous with masculinity.

There is evidently a relationship between aggressive and maternal behavior. De Groot's observation that very feminine women are usually poor mothers appears logical in view of the fact that hardly one of the overprotecting mothers in Group I can be so described. Further, it appears consistent with the observation that there may be a clash between maternal and sexual drives; a high degree of maternity developing at the expense of femininity.[17]

The cleavage between sexual and maternal behavior is sharply demarcated in animals. Previous to more recent endocrinologic studies of maternal behavior, many investigators regarded nursing and mother-love to be derived from the sexual instinct. Ceni [18] writing in 1927, showed in various ways that maternal impulse has no relation to female sex processes. Using hens in his experiments he found that the maternal impulse survived castration; implanting an ovulating ovary in a mothering hen stopped the maternal impulse; during pregnancy there was a hypoactivity and involution of the ovaries, during the period of heat the highest degree of ovarian activity; also that when through glandular implants he obtained maternal behavior in roosters, they stopped all sexual activity. Wiesner and Sheard,[19] working with rats, found also that experimental removal of the ovaries during pregnancy or postpartum had no effect on maternal behavior. Yerkes [20] quotes

[16] Jeanne Lampl De Groot, "Problems of Femininity," *Psychoanalytic Quarterly*, II (1933), 489–518; 513.

[17] Helene Deutsch, "Mütterlichkeit und Sexualität," *Imago*, XIX (1933), 15–16.

[18] C. Ceni, "Die endokrinen Faktoren der Mütterliebe und die psychische Feminierung von Männschen," *Schweizer Archiv für Neurologie und Psychiatrie*, XXI (1927), 131–42.

[19] Bertold P. Wiesner and Nora M. Sheard, *Maternal Behavior in the Rat* (London, 1933).

[20] Robert M. Yerkes and Ada W. Yerkes. *The Great Apes* (New Haven, 1929), p. 263.

Madame Abreu and gives his own observations of three female chimpanzees who stopped sex relations from the time they gave birth until they weaned the baby.

Although such sharp delimitations of sexual and maternal behavior are not observed in humans, there is evidence in women of sexual and maternal cycles, as of menstrual cycles, according to the investigations of Benedek.[21]

The overprotective mothers manifested from childhood aggressive and helping tendencies, both characteristic of maternal behavior; the question now arises as to its biologic nature. Although maternal types are differentiated by common observation, there is no scientific study of this problem. It has been demonstrated in animals that maternal behavior is highly dependent on hormonal influence, also that differences in this regard may occur in virginal animals living in isolated cages. Numerous experiments have been performed in which maternal behavior has been produced by implants of glands or the administration of glandular extracts—in virgin, in spayed female, even in male animals. Thus Ceni implanted various glands in the abdomen of a rooster, who thereafter displayed maternal behavior, getting chicks under his wings, exactly like a hen. Corner [22] produced both growth and lactation of the mammary gland by administering extracts of the pituitary gland of sheep to spayed virgin rabbits. Similar results were achieved in rats, dogs, cows, and sows.[23] By such methods male rats were induced to make nests, retrieve and lick newborn rats, and show other evidence of maternal behavior.[24] By using extracts of the urine of pregnant women—antuitrin S—Tietz [25] was able to induce definite loosening of the fur in virgin rabbits, a proof of

21 Therese Benedek and Boris B. Rubenstein, "Ovarian Activity and Psychodynamic Processes," *Psychosomatic Medicine*, I (1939), 245–70.

22 G. W. Corner, "The Hormonal Control of Lactation," *American Journal of Physiology*, XCV (1925), 43–55.

23 Fritz Grüter and Paul Stricker, "Über die Wirkung eines Hypophysenvorderlappenhormons auf die Auslösung der Milchsekretion," *Klinischer Wochenschrift*, L (1920), 2322; Fritz Grüter and Paul Stricker, "Recherches expérimentales sur les fonctions du lobe antérieur de l'hypophyse," *La Presse Médicale*, LXXVIII (1929), 1268.

24 M. McQueen Williams, "Maternal Behavior in Male Rats," *Science*, LXXXII (1935), 67–68.

25 Esther B. Tietz, "The Humoral Excitation of the Nesting Instinct in Rabbits," *Science*, LXXVIII (1933), p. 316.

maternal behavior, since female rabbits pull out the fur of their abdomen for nesting a day or two before parturition. A nonpregnant rhesus monkey, who had previously been quite indifferent to a guinea pig that lived in the same cage, became quite maternal toward it, after injections of anterior pituitary hormone. She carried the guinea pig in her arms, tried to suckle it, and fought off anyone who tried to take it away. The glandular injections resulted also in hypertrophy of the uterus and mammary glands.

The specific hormone involved in these experiments was isolated from other anterior pituitary hormones, and named prolactin by Riddle.[26] He identified it as the hormone capable of producing broodiness—clucking and nesting—in actively laying hens, and depressing the ovary. He recognized it as the active agent that initiated lactation in mature mammary glands, and increased the activity of crop glands in pigeons. He was able through its use to induce clucking in certain roosters, and in non-laying hens, though nesting behavior did not follow. Using the conclusion of Wiesner and Sheard that in rats the same hormonal factor was responsible for lactation and maternal behavior, and the retrieving test—collecting the scattered young—as its expression, he induced maternal behavior in virgin rats by injecting prolactin—after "priming" the ovaries.

Further evidence of hormonal influence on maternal behavior is derived from observations and experiments in pseudopregnancy, a condition in which all the concomitants of pregnancy are present without a foetus. Such states can be induced by copulation with a sterile male,[27] by copulation late in heat,[28] and by tapping the cervix with a blunt instrument.[29]

The condition occurs frequently and spontaneously in animals,

[26] O. Riddle, R. W. Bates, and S. W. Dykshorn, "The Preparation, Identification and Assay of Prolactin—a Hormone of the Anterior Pituitary," *American Journal of Physiology*, CV (1933), 191–216; O. Riddle, R. W. Bates, and E. L. Lahr, "Maternal Behavior Induced in Rats by Prolactin," *Proceedings of the Society for Experimental Biology and Medicine*, XXXII (1935), 730–34; O. Riddle, R. W. Bates, and E. L. Lahr, "Prolactin Induces Broodiness in Fowl," *American Journal of Physiology*, CXI (1935), 352–60.

[27] Grüter and Stricker, *op. cit.*

[28] J. R. Slonaker, "The Effect of Copulation, Pregnancy, Pseudopregnancy and Lactation on the Voluntary Activity and Food Consumption of the Albino Rat," *American Journal of Physiology*, LXXI (1925), 362–94.

[29] Wiesner and Sheard, *op. cit.*

and has been observed particularly in dogs, simply because they are so readily available for observation. A number of hysterical pregnancies in women are probably misdiagnosed pseudopregnancies.[30]

Loisel [31] described the behavior of a nonpregnant hybrid bitch who showed evidence of periodic lactation and maternal behavior, restless searching about as though for pups, making nests out of paper or straw. Given three young rabbits, she licked and tried to suckle them during such periods. They occurred after each menstruation. Lang [32] described similar behavior in two virgin bitches, whose maternal activities stopped when swelling of the mammae subsided—in two to three weeks.

Studies of pseudopregnancy, like studies of prolactin-induced behavior, are of special value in revealing manifestations of maternal behavior without an external stimulus. They are pure studies of a drive, that is, of specific activities impelled exclusively by internal stimuli. They indicate the powerfully endogenous nature of the phases of maternal behavior, in clear activity, without the presence of the object for which they are to function.

A sufficient number of examples have been used to illustrate the highly biologic nature of maternal behavior. Its integral components are biologic, not psychogenic. Its aggressive features may be regarded as a protective framework for the insurance of suckling and rearing during the infancy of the animal, just as the aggressive features in the sexual behavior of males may be regarded as an insurance of the insemination of the female. The active, initiating characteristic of male aggression in sexuality is most closely analogous to the drive, in maternal behavior, to get something to suckle and mother.

There are natural variations in the strength of the component maternal drives in animals, which may be comparable to human behavior. Certain hens, for example, are good layers, but poor sitters. Using the retrieving test, and new-born rats as the stimulus,

[30] R. Hofstätter, *Über eingebildete Schwangerschaften* (Berlin, 1924).

[31] Gustave Loisel, "Relations entre les phénomènes du rut, de la lactation, de la mue et de l'amour maternel chez une chienne hybride," *Comptes Rendus Hebdomadaires des Séances et Mémoirs de la Société de Biologie*, LX (1906), 255–58.

[32] H. B. Lang, "A Note on Maternal Behavior in Two Female Virgin Dogs," *Psychiatric Quarterly*, V (1931), 649–51.

Wiesner and Sheard showed a variation of maternal drive in virgin female rats. Of 250 females used, 80 percent showed no response in the first five minutes. Of the 20 percent who showed a response, there was a variation from irregular and aimless picking up of young to immediate retrieving similar to the behavior of lactating females. Similarly when the newborn rats were left for twenty-four hours with the virgin females, each in a separate box, there was an increase in the number of retrievers, a similar variation, in retrieving behavior, and in a small number of instances, nest building—further, there was no relation of retrieving to oestrus.

In the case of puerperal rats, again a variation was found in maternal drives, when the mother was supplied with a succession of foster young. Some females would retrieve only small young, others small and large, and for varying periods of time, revealing thereby different intensities and durations of the components of maternal drive.

Variations in maternal behavior of girls, in which some become "neighborhood mothers," preferring the care of a baby to any other pursuit, are consistent with the finding of such constitutional variations in animals. In other words, some women may be more naturally maternal than others, and manifest such differences at an early age.

The attempt to show that aggressive behavior is part and parcel of maternal behavior and that variations in this regard may indicate natural differences in maternal make-up, does not preclude the influence of social and psychic factors. There is a varying degree of plasticity in the different components of maternal behavior.[33]

Wiesner and Sheard have shown experimentally the effects of external stimuli on various components of the maternal drive in the rat. By supplying the mother with successive litters of young,

[33] The study of comparative maternal functions in animals shows a remarkable variety of forms with increasing specialization in every phase. First to be discriminated is the deposition of seeds in which every variation from the stage of free to specific environment occurs, from indiscriminate scattering (exotokes of Giard), with apparently no protection, to selection of favorable sites (concealment, shelter, temperature, oxygen) and protection of the site from enemies, to sex specialization and maturation of the seed within the body of the female (endotokes). Mammalia thus represent a high degree of specialized processes for the purpose of overcoming risks of survival of the young by means of sex differentiation, nesting of egg inside the body, and specialized nutrition (lactation). See note 36, following.

they prolonged the maternal response including lactation up to 429 days, representing about 20 times the normal period of maternal behavior. During the period of lactation, rats, dogs, or monkeys are easily induced to care for alien young. Instances of ducks mothering chicks are items of common observation. It would seem that in animals as among humans various external influences can vary the intensity of the maternal drive. An actual manifestation of overprotection with a resulting increased dependency on the mother has been described in the case of two monkeys, with exaggeration of both the giving and the protecting phase.[34]

The expression of aggression in maternal behavior, in which the giving function, its very core, is diminished or even absent, is seen in various forms. Of these the following may be differentiated: the dominating mother who gives no love but whose dominating tendencies embrace every social relationship; the dominating mother who utilizes only her children, or a particular child, as an object of domination, though without love—disguised often as conscientious motherhood; the thwarting or denying mother, whose aggression appears in the form of oppositional tactics—as a projected asceticism; the spiteful mother, jealous of her children for having more opportunities or pleasure than she had in childhood, jealous of a daughter because of looks, or charm, or intelligence, jealous of a son because of his sex; the brutal or sadistic mother who utilizes every opportunity to punish, deride, or embarrass her offspring.

These are various types of rejecting mothers who must utilize the children as outlets for inner emotional difficulties. The dynamic mechanisms comprise numerous restorations of the mother's unsolved childhood experiences, or of old hostilities to cruel or denying parents; intense jealousies of brother or sister; the experience of being thrust aside or belittled in social life by more at-

[34] O. L. Tinkelpaugh and C. J. Hartman, "Behavior and Maternal Care of the Newborn Monkey (Macaca mulatta—'M. Rhesus')," *Journal of Genetic Psychology*, XL (1932), 257–87; see especially pp. 274–77. In both instances a presumably normal mother was observed at the same time as the overprotective mother. The first overprotective mother "was the slave of her baby," "almost from the first." When she and a "normal" mother were on top of a shed and their babies of the same age walked toward its edge, the overprotective mother alone rushed over and carried her baby back. She also carried, cuddled, and showed greater affection to her baby than the other mother showed to hers. Differences and similar results in the offspring were described in a second pair of monkeys.

tractive or intelligent children, inside or outside the family; various masculine drives and sexual complexes.[35]

The same type of unconscious hostilities may, however, be expressed in exaggerated love and protection. One may conjecture that the direction is determined by the relative intensity of the maternal drive. Given the same quantum of unconscious hostility, the direction towards hostility or love will be determined by the weakness or strength of the maternal tendency. Thus instances of maternal oversolicitude based on unconscious hostility to the child may represent an intensification of a true mother-love, rather than its entire structure.

MATERNITY AND LACTATION

In 1905, Giard [36] proposed the interesting theory that among mammals lactation is the source of maternal love, a source of symbiosis that unites mother and child. He regarded the sucking child as a source of pleasure to the mother, through releasing tension in her breasts. The feeling for the child would thus be based an a series of positive conditioning experiences through pleasurable release of tension.

His theory has been attacked in many ways. Rabaud,[37] for example, showed experimentally that in puerperal rats maternal behavior in the form of carrying new-born rats back to the litter occurred in pregnancy, in any phase. Animals in a state of pseudopregnancy are also a case in point. Wiesner and Sheard showed that maternal activities occurred in rats even though lactation stopped, in fact, even when the mammillae were destroyed during pregnancy.

Although observations and experiments disproved lactation as a source of maternal love, they do not diminish the value of Giard's theory when utilized as a powerful reinforcement of the mother-child "symbiosis." In the studies of long and short breast-feeding

[35] Karen Horney, "Maternal Conflicts," *American Journal of Orthopsychiatry*, III (1933), 455–63; H. W. Newell, "The Psycho-dynamics of Maternal Rejection," *American Journal of Orthopsychiatry*, IV (1934), 387–401.

[36] A. Giard, "Les Origines de l'amour maternal," *Bulletin de l'Institut général de Psychologie*, V (1905), 3–32.

[37] Etienne Rabaud, "L'Instinct maternel chez les mammifères," *Journal de Psychologie*, XVIII (1921), 487–95.

periods, the proportion of overprotecting attitudes was found significantly correlated with the former. However it was not possible to factor out the stimulus-value of the lactation experience in itself.

Since lactation is stimulated by prolactin, like other maternal functions, there may be a relationship between lactation function and general maternal function. If this is proven to be true, then the ease of lactation on the part of the overprotecting mothers, besides their attitude toward breast feeding, may represent hormonal influence.

MATERNITY AND THE MASCULINITY COMPLEX

Freud regards maternity primarily as a derivative of the sexual instinct, and the child, as love-object, a substitute for a longed-for penis. The girl's infantile sexuality, at first, like the boy's, directed to the mother, is thrown into a state of turmoil when first awareness of the penis occurs. In the usual case the girl develops penis envy, considers herself "castrated" and, in a state of hostility to the mother, for which the usual denials of love and gratification have prepared her, turns to the father, hoping to derive a penis from him. This transformation also occurs in her play with dolls. At first they represent children, merely objects upon which she releases activities exercised on her by the mother. Later, when the desire for a penis begins, the doll represents a child by the father. "The feminine situation is only established when the wish for a penis is replaced by the wish for a child." [38] Through a son alone the mother attains "undiluted satisfaction" and "the most complete relationship between human beings," since through him she is able to transfer all her suppressed ambitions and derive "the satisfaction of all that has remained of her masculinity complex." [39]

The maternal drives, according to Freud, thereby have a dual basis; one purely biological, its source in sexual hormones; the other purely psychological, its source in the ideas of the child. These are derived by observing and contrasting differences in genitalia, and concluding that they have been brought about by

[38] Sigmund Freud, *New Introductory Lectures on Psychoanalysis* (New York, 1933), p. 175.

[39] *Ibid.*, p. 182.

castration. The girl's previously formed hostilities to the mother are then intensified, since the mother is regarded as the responsible agent of the castration, and, in pursuit of the illusory penis, she turns her love to the father.

Freud's theory of maternal behavior is in marked contrast with his theory of sexual behavior. For the latter his orientation, as to its origin, is simply biological, and rests on the discovery of sexuality in the infant; on the proof that sex life does not arise full-blown in puberty, but starts practically with life itself. He sees, however, no evidence of maternal behavior in the little girl, as an early expression of the mature maternal "instinct." Though he uses observations of marked activity in the sex life of certain female animals to question the naïve use of the word passivity as a synonym for femininity, he employs none of the observations of maternal behavior of animals on behalf of his theory of maternal function in humans. Otherwise he would not propose a theory that, by inference, would limit so basic a drive as the maternal to human society alone, since its complex psychic origin could not be ascribed to animals.[40]

Though unnecessary in explaining the origin of maternal love, the theory of penis envy is useful in explaining its intensification and, also, the maternal preference of males. There are 19 boys and one girl among the overprotected children of Group I. A predominance of males is found in similar studies.[41] Favoring the boy, especially the first-born son, is a common observation in our culture. A high degree of aggression in the female, however con-

[40] The difficulty comes from regarding the maternal as a derivative of the sexual drives, as they were once regarded in biology. The love of mother for baby is not seen in terms of primary maternal function but must be represented as a transformation of sexual function, which is primary. Actually the reverse could be argued, and, in a teleological sense, more reasonably—that the sexual drive is subservient to the maternal, that maternal love would ensue regardless of previous sexual behavior, castration, or Oedipus complex. As previously noted, the maternal drive in animals is not affected by removal of the ovaries. It occurs in virginal female animals isolated in laboratory cages. It arises spontaneously in states of "maternal tension," as in states of pseudopregnancy or states artificially produced in either sex by injection of appropriate hormones. Experimental evidence relating to the strength of drives indicates that the maternal is much stronger than the sexual. See H. W. Nissen, "A Study of Maternal Behavior in the White Rat by Means of the Obstruction Method," *Journal of Genetic Psychology*, XXXVII (1930), 377–93.

[41] Hough, Lewenberg, and others.

sistent with a high degree of maternal behavior, is blocked in numerous other ways; hence the utilization of the son as a means, through identification, of satisfying unfulfilled ambitions and aggressions, is quite comprehensible. The universality, in our culture, of penis envy in females, is a generalization not yet established. However, it must be a very frequent phenomenon— and in normal children.[42]

The gratification of a strong maternal drive may be enhanced through a male child by various psychic experiences. The theory of penis envy helps to explain reinforcing factors in maternal overprotection, in regard to the marked predominance of male children and of aggressive mothers in that group. That a high degree of aggression in females is in itself prognostic of overprotection is not to be inferred. Rejecting mothers, whether of sons or daughters, are also more likely to be aggressive, than others. It may be that aggressive women are more likely than others to be either overprotecting or rejecting of children. The direction would then be determined by the strength of the maternal drive. The point is not proven, but it is consistent with the observation recorded that overprotecting mothers showed constant maternal behavior from childhood.[43]

THEORY OF MATERNAL OVERPROTECTION

The theory that emerges from the material presented in this chapter and the preceding one is simply that "true" maternal overprotection occurs in naturally maternal women whose behavior as mothers has been intensified by the operation of certain psychic and cultural forces. By "true" overprotection is meant exaggerated maternal love, that is, overprotection which is not determined primarily by neurosis. By "naturally maternal" is meant a strong maternal drive. Evidence for this feature in the group investigated lies in manifestations of behavior consistent,

[42] David M. Levy, " 'Control-Situation' Studies of Children's Responses to the Difference in Genitalia," *American Journal of Orthopsychiatry*, X (1940), 755–62.

[43] It is a question whether psychoanalytic studies of overprotecting and rejecting mothers would help to settle this question. For assuming that in both groups a high degree of penis envy would be found, its manifestation in excessive love or hate of a male child would then have to be related to a constitutional factor.

throughout the lives of most of them, with both the giving and protecting phases of maternal function. Evidence of specific maternal behavior in childhood, as well as proofs of a constitutionally maternal type, is lacking.

The psychic forces in operation are represented by such powerful agents as affect hunger, experience of relative sterility, or their equivalents in the "period of anticipation"; death-threatening illnesses in the life of the child; marital sexual incompatibility. The cultural-social forces are represented chiefly by the experience of meeting harsh realities too early in life, through deaths of parents, or poverty, or both, necessitating the substitution of work for childhood play, and of premature responsibility. However, the attitude towards such experiences is based, by assumption, on a strong maternal tendency. Other factors in our culture that play into the hands of the potentially overprotecting mother are represented by the high degree of freedom given to mothers in influencing the life of the child, and in the superior role given to the male. In regard to preference for the male child, the psychic influence of penis envy was assumed to be a primary determining factor.

The question will arise as to the validity of a generalization based on so small a number of cases, regardless of sizable control and contrasting groups. The defense given in Chapter I may be repeated here, that by the method of selection of "pure" samples of a human relationship, we are dealing with samples of behavior that approach the requirements of an experiment. Stated rather boldly, the 20 cases, selected out of more than 2,000 by the criteria described, have become 20 experiments, rather than 20 random case studies. Furthermore the findings have been confirmed by other investigators.

Since our theory represents in the main the utilization of psychic forces by a constitutionally maternal personality,[44] its general application to the field of psychosomatics should be noted. It may be true that the maternal drive, a drive so basic to survival, has a higher degree of resemblance in man and animals than the

[44] The women who suffered affect hunger and also seemed to resemble each other closely in regard to aggressive, responsible behavior and sex frigidity became either overprotecting or rejecting mothers; this finding led to consideration of a constitutional determinant.

sex drive. Certainly there is a remarkably close resemblance of the criteria of maternal care used in this study in all mammalian behavior. The sexual life of man may be determined by psychic and cultural influence to a much higher degree than the maternal life. If experiments on humans will show decisive effects of prolactin on maternal attitude—that is, will go beyond a physiological effect, as the induction of lactation, into a psychologic effect, as in animals—the primary hormonal determination of maternal behavior will be proved. Even if this occurs, it will not follow necessarily that the same rule applies to all other human drives.

PATERNAL FACTORS: DISCIPLINE

The fathers of the overprotected children in Group I may be generally characterized as submissive, stable husbands and providers who played little or no authoritative role in the life of the child. They offered little counteracting influence to the overprotection, after their several attempts to discipline the child were firmly resented by the mother. The phrase "discipline of the child was left entirely to the mother" appears in 13 of the 20 records. In three instances, fathers aided the overprotection by indulging or infantilizing (Cases 1, 10, 19); in two they interfered with the mother's attempt to discipline (Cases 2 and 3); and in two others there was little contact with the child because of absence from the home (Cases 16 and 18). In the entire group there was not one instance of a dominating father.

Check groups are not available for comparison. An early attempt to collect data on the role of the father in regard to discipline of the child, though the data were meager, left a strong impression that in the American home discipline is left pretty much in the hands of the mother. The father is more likely to be pressed into service by the mother as occasion requires than to assume an active role. Up till the child's puberty, at any rate, he is, if affectionate, an indulgent father, and, if not affectionate, rather inactive.

However, whether indulgent or indifferent, he tries to meet issues when they are brought to his attention, or when they force themselves upon him. He will, when necessary, see school teacher, doctor, or camp councilor, give reproof, praise, or instruction. In all these functions, however, the wife plays a very responsible part. It depends on her, to a large extent, how important a role, as father, her husband plays. When she assumes a high degree of responsibility with the children, he seems content to leave matters in her hands. When she appears helpless and calls on him constantly for aid, he takes on an important role. His paternal influence in general, until the child's adolescence or later, appears to be determined largely by her.

The fathers of the children in Group I had to deal with mothers who monopolized the child. Their rather ready adjustment to that situation is not difficult to understand, in view of our typical cultural patterns of family life. These fathers appear, however, readily adapted to such complete surrender of the paternal role by virtue of their generally submissive traits. Of the group, for example, 12 fathers maintained an affectionate relationship with the child (Cases 1, 2, 3, 5, 7, 8, 10, 14, 16, 17, 19, 20).[45] Of these one (Case 1) played like another child with his son, complaining to his wife when the son annoyed him, and used by her to hold the child while she did the spanking. Three of the 12 were much more attentive than the usual father, bathing and dressing the child in infancy (Cases 2, 3, 19); they were described, in one case (3) as "more like a mother than a father." Discipline, however, was left entirely to the mother.

The remaining eight displayed much devotion and interest, playing with the child, bringing gifts, attempting discipline in a few instances only to be prevented by the mother, even adding to the maternal indulgence, but never playing an authoritative role. We have the record of one of the affectionate fathers who tried to overcome the maternal overindulgence by persuasion, by appealing to his son to hold a job even if it was unpleasant, in spite of her insistence that the boy should quit whenever he complained.

Five fathers in the group showed little or no affection to the

[45] Includes a father (Case 7) who died when patient was 8 years old; a father (Case 19) who died when patient was 11 years old; also a father (Case 10) who changed and became disciplinary when patient was about 12 years old.

child. In three (Cases 11, 12, 13) [46] this behavior is probably a response to being excluded from participation in parenthood. The same explanation may partially account for the behavior of the remaining two (Cases 9 and 15). A good example of a response to nullification of the parental role is seen in Case 12, of a father who was interested and affectionate during the infancy of his son. His attempts at discipline were sharply thwarted by his wife, and, after warning her several times that she would regret her indulgence, he kept strictly out of the picture. Later as the boy grew more unruly, she would call on the father to discipline the boy, but he refused, using the pretext of illness or fatigue. Within this group of five fathers, the picture of the father-son relationship is of indifference, or impatience, though not overtly of hostility.

In three instances (Cases 4, 6, 18) there was no paternal influence because the father was out of contact due to desertion (6), divorce (18), and in one case (4) work at night. Though in the cases cited the children had no contact with the father due to external causes, there were others in which this factor must also be considered. In the main, the paternal influence was cited even when the father saw the child but once a week, and for only a portion of the life of the child. In five other cases, making eight in all, various circumstances prevented contact with a father, besides those already mentioned; father's death when patient was age 8 years and 11 years, respectively (Cases 7 and 19); father's commitment to a penitentiary for some years (Case 16); father's employment at night since the birth of the patient, though spending Sundays with him (Case 1). Finally in one instance the mother divorced, but remarried when patient was 1 year old (Case 13). The stepfather has been included along with the other parents, but presumably the position of stepfather may be considered as an added factor in explaining the weakness of the paternal role.

We now have a number of explanations—cultural, psychologic, and social—of the low degree of paternal influence in the overprotected group. Certainly, it is apparent, even in the absence of check studies, that the fathers had a remarkably small share in the

[46] A stepfather is included since he married when patient was 1 year old (Case 13). In Case 6, the stepfather was not considered, since the child was older.

rearing of the children in Group I. In eight cases external events left the child exclusively, or almost so, in the mother's hands. In the remaining cases, the fathers adjusted with little or ineffective protest to the mother-child monopoly. The important influence of the father, in his authoritative role, and, as a counteracting agent to maternal infantilization, indulgence, and overprotection, in its strict sense, was thus either nullified or used merely to strengthen the overprotection.

To these facts must be added the derogatory attitude of the child towards the father, which was in several instances fostered by the mother, thereby reducing the paternal influence to its lowest degree.

PATERNAL BACKGROUND FACTORS

In the summaries which follow, a consistent pattern of submissive adaptation is revealed in the group of the fathers of the overprotected children. Data are not available in two cases, in which, however, the father had no contact with the child because of desertion (Case 6), and divorce preceded by separation for a number of years (Case 18). In three other cases, the relation of the father to his parents is not disclosed; however, a generally submissive adaptation to life is evident.

CASE 1. Youngest of three. Still the spoiled darling of his mother, who brings him a bag of fruit daily. Submissive husband. Steady worker as government clerk.

CASE 2. Oldest son, mother's favorite, antagonistic to father, a steady, overconscientious worker. In same firm 15 years. Married his wife when he was afraid he would lose his job.

CASE 3. Illiterate and least successful member of his family. Has concealed his illiteracy from his son. Accepts fact that he is stupid. Steady worker.

CASE 4. Steady, low-salaried worker as government clerk. Took the job because of steady employment and afraid to take chance with other type of work. His mother was dominating and his father, like himself, submissive to her. Unusually submissive husband.

CASE 5. Timid and seclusive as a boy. Favorite of his mother, and antagonistic to his father. A very steady, conscientious worker, "never happy" when away from the shop.

CASE 6. Deserted during wife's pregnancy.

CASE 7. Submissive son of a dominating mother. Very stable worker. Held last job 32 years before his death.

CASE 8. One of eight children. Favorite of mother and after his father's death remained at home on the farm longer than any of the others, working for his mother. Didn't marry till her death, when age 41 years. Kindly, sympathetic, steady, responsible worker. Last job as shipping clerk 7 years.

CASE 9. Second of seven children and mother's favorite. Steady worker, good provider. Died when patient was five years old. As a child very mischievous and "the family fighter." Truant from school when age 13 years because he didn't like his teacher.

CASE 10. Always very respectful and obedient to an authoritative father. Steady, responsible professional man.

CASE 11. Sickly until age 10 years. Very obedient boy, never active in sports. Father's word was law and he never disobeyed. Responsible, steady, serious worker. Psychic impotence.

CASE 12. Hard-working, plodding, conscientious. The only worker who got along with an irascible employer. Only son and favorite child of his mother. As a husband considered "an angel," who gives everything to his wife, as previously to his mother.

CASE 13. Stepfather since patient was one year old. A quiet, retiring, stable individual. A good worker and always afraid he will be fired. Completely under his wife's domination.

CASE 14. "A timid soul." Nervous indigestion. Overconscientious worker, always yields rather than argue or fight.

CASE 15. Oldest of four, in a family still ruled by a very dominating mother, who makes all the important decisions.

CASE 16. Described as a decent but weak individual whose difficulty was attributed to easy submission to others. Was his mother's favorite. Very dependent on wife. Irregular, unstable worker.

CASE 17. Third of five children. Quiet, stable, and a good provider. Submissive son of a "dominating woman who wanted to manage the entire family down to the third generation."

CASE 18. Data inadequate. Wife allowed no interview with him.

CASE 19. Closely attached to his father. Always submissive to his wife. 16 years her senior.

CASE 20. Steady, reliable worker. Good provider. Son of a dominating mother and very attached to next older sister. Eighth of nine children. Described as a weak personality dominated by his efficient wife. Stable worker.

The group yields seven instances in which the fathers were the favorite children, five in which they were obedient sons of dominating mothers, and three in which they were obedient sons of dominating fathers. Of the 18 husbands interviewed, there is only one instance in which evidence of difficulties due to aggressive behavior occurred (Case 9).

In view of the main trends revealed in their personalities, their selection of dominating women and of maternal women appears a logical and determined choice. With few exceptions (Cases 16 and 18), the fathers were also stable and responsible workers. In contrast with their responsible, aggressive wives they may be described as responsible and submissive. That they were selected as husbands appears, therefore, equally consistent, especially when we add the factor of affect hunger, so frequent in the history of the overprotecting mothers—a factor that would determine selectivity in favor of kindness, sympathy, and devotion. Assuming a strong maternal drive in the mothers of the group and certain freedom in range of choice, the selection of men of a dependent type of personality becomes the more likely. Certainly the factors that favored the development of aggressive, maternal, love-hungry women, and of submissive, responsible men, would, at the same time, favor their selection of each other.[47]

GRANDPARENTAL FACTORS

The usual patterns of interfering grandparents are found also in the families of the overprotecting mothers: the indulgent grandparent, relieved of the responsibilities of parenthood, who enjoys the process of spoiling a grandchild; the grandmother, jealous of her daughter-in-law, who regards her son's child as her own; the grandmother who still maintains a maternal hold on married daughter and grandchild. Their activities were of sufficient importance to merit citation in five cases. To the overprotecting factors in Case I were added indulgent relatives, especially the maternal grandmother, who had frequent contact with the child. She brought gifts frequently; augmented the maternal indulgence by

[47] In regard to the role played by the parents of the mothers, it was shown previously that a fair portion of the group had a small share of any parental attention. However, the records allow judgment as to the dominating role played by either parent in the cases of 17 of the overprotecting mothers. In these their mothers played a dominant role in 12, fathers in 5 cases. In an 18th case, the dominant role was played by the grandmother. The mother was a favorite child in two instances, both, of the father

resenting any corrective measures, and often said to the child, "If your mama whips you, you tell me."

In Case 4, the maternal grandmother has continued to lavish the patient with affection and food since infancy and thinks it great fun to be ordered around by him.

All four grandparents, besides the relatives, greatly admired the patient and indulged her (Case 9). However, they do not see her frequently.

A maternal grandmother who lived with her daughter, helped in the indulgent overprotection of the patient (Case 11), and blocked the mother when she attempted discipline, with the words, "Don't hit my child." She also scolded the daughter on these occasions.

A paternal grandmother who visited the home daily (Case 15) was frankly hostile to her daughter-in-law. She interfered with any attempt at discipline, was always around when the child played in the back yard, screamed at any boy who threatened him, and also, like the mother, was overindulgent.

The instances listed above are all examples of maternal indulgent overprotection, which may help to explain the mother's difficulty in coping with the grandmothers, since both were indulgent. There were numerous instances of bickering between mother and grandmother, but no instance in which the mother controlled the situation. A difficulty in adjusting the problem lay also in the mothers' attitude of responsibility towards their own mothers. Where this attitude was not present (Case 15), the relation between mother and paternal grandmother was a long drawn-out battle.

Summary

As potent sources of increased maternal longing for a child, varieties of experience threatening the possibility of successful termination of pregnancy were gathered from the records of the overprotecting mothers. Of the 20, 13 yielded such instances: long periods of sterility (5); death of offspring (3); spontaneous miscarriages (3); and serious complications of pregnancy (3), preceding the birth of the patient.

An attempt was made to determine from available data whether unconscious wishes for the state of sterility operated in the instances given. It appeared likely in one case. The question was considered as to whether overprotection of any variety must be considered a neurosis, a compensatory reaction to unconscious hostility to the child, based on feelings of guilt and resembling obsessional neurosis. It was argued that such a position would refute the possibility of a normal maternal response, since if a normal response may be assumed, its increase in the presence of stronger stimuli must also be assumed.

Sixteen instances of sexual maladjustment were found in the group, a relatively high frequency as compared with check groups. In itself the difficulty was regarded as a strengthening factor of the overprotection, by the method of simple compensatory increase in mother love through blocking other channels of expression.

Fifteen instances were found in which there was little social life in common among the parents of the overprotected child. Of the five remaining cases in which there was a good general social relationship, two were sexually incompatible. The severe curtailment in mutual social activity, as in the mother's own general activity, was determined in most instances primarily by the mother-child relationship. Where the mother's social life was limited almost entirely to the child, the overprotecting data appeared especially striking with regard to infantilization and to attempts to prevent the child from making friends with other children.

Of the 20 overprotecting mothers, severe privation of parental love in their childhood was found in 16. Of these the death of one or both parents occurred in nine. Of the four cases in which an affectionate relationship with parents was recorded, there was evidence of some impoverishment of affection in terms of contact in three. The privation of all those positive feelings implicit in parental love, called "affect hunger," was regarded as an important consideration in understanding the overprotecting relationship, since the child could be utilized as a means of satisfying the abnormal craving for love resulting from affect hunger.

All but two of the 20 overprotecting mothers (Group I) were responsible, stable, and aggressive. The responsible attitude was manifested in stability of work, measured by steadiness of employment, and also in active helping out. The active or aggressive feature of the responsible behavior was regarded as a distinctly maternal type of behavior; it characterized the lives of 18 of the 20 overprotecting mothers since childhood.

Though evidence of thwarted ambitions for a career occurred in 12 instances in the group, the number checked by studies of contrast groups was not considered, in itself, significant.

Of the two basic findings—affect hunger and strong maternal tendencies—the latter occurred with greater frequency and in the absence of the former. It was assumed that the influence of affect hunger in the direction of overprotection, since it occurs also in rejecting mothers, was effective only in definitely maternal women.

In a number of studies of maternal behavior, the aggressive elements involved in its protecting phase were either overlooked or regarded as evidence of masculinity, since woman was considered almost exclusively in terms of femininity. The giving phase of maternal behavior, in the same terms, was regarded as evidence of passivity and masochism. This psychologic theory is analogous to a biologic theory, formerly maintained, that nursing and mother-love were derived from the sexual instinct. Numerous experiments in animals have shown that maternal behavior occurs in castrated females and, in fact, that ovarian activity results in the diminution, and is depressed by, maternal activity. Such studies showed also that maternal behavior in animals is highly "hormonal," and that, in rats, the same hormonal factor, prolactin, was responsible for lactation, and the basic maternal drives.

Studies of pseudopregnancy, a condition in which all the concomitants of pregnancy are present, though the foetus is lacking, represent pure studies of maternal drive. They indicate the powerfully endogenous nature of maternal behavior, in clear activity, without the presence of the object for which they are to function. Such studies illustrate the highly biologic nature of maternal behavior.

As in humans, variations in the component maternal drives occur in animals, even in virgin rats, and are measurable. They show also a high degree of plasticity in the presence of external stimuli, in fact, to such a degree that, for example, the lactation period in the rat has been prolonged twenty times the normal by supplying the mother with successive litters of young. Two instances of maternal overprotection in monkeys were cited.

Giard's theory of lactation as a source of mother-love, through the infant's releasing of tension in the maternal breasts, was considered. Although disproved experimentally it was thought to represent a secondary reinforcing agent to the mother-child relationship. Although the overprotecting mothers showed relative ease of lactation, no studies are available to show any correlation of the two factors.

The theory of maternity as a derivative of the woman's penis envy appears illogical in view of the fact that it rests on a wrong biologic basis—ovarian hormones—and on a psychic basis—unconscious pursuit of the illusory penis through father-incest—which appears superfluous as an explanation, in accordance with studies of animals, and in neglecting evidence of maternal behavior in young girls. The theory does help to explain the marked predominance of male children in the overprotected group.

From the studies presented, the theory of maternal overprotection is based on the operation of certain psychic and cultural forces on women constitutionally maternal to a high degree.

The fathers of the overprotected children studied were, in general, submissive, stable husbands and providers who played little or no authoritative role in the lives of their children. They made a ready adjustment to the maternal monopoly of the child, some adding to the infantilizing care (three cases). Twelve, in all, maintained an affectionate relationship with the child, five showed little or no affection, and the remaining three were out of contact due to divorce, desertion, and absence from the home.

A consistent pattern of submissive adaptation was revealed in the backgrounds of the fathers. Seven were obedient and favorite children, five were obedient sons of dominating mothers, and three, obedient sons of dominating fathers. Of the 18 fathers interviewed, there was only one instance in which evidence of difficulty as a husband was due to aggressive behavior towards the wife.

With two exceptions, all the fathers in the group were stable and responsible workers. The group of parents represent a logical choice of dominating maternal women and submissive responsible men.

The usual patterns of interfering relatives were found in the group. In five cases their activities were important in the life of the child, and consisted chiefly in adding to the indulgence of the mother, and weakening her discipline.

VIII. PROBLEMS OF THE OVERPROTECTED

AS WE have seen, the child of the indulgent overprotective mother has a difficult time in social adjustment—presumably in proportion to the extent to which the relationship to the mother has permeated all others. If the picture in infancy held fast in its essential patterns throughout life, the result would be the fixed role of a demanding, selfish, tyrannical person anticipating constant attention, affection and service; responding to denials of his wishes, or to requirements of discipline, with impatience, outbursts of temper, or assault; restless and completely at a loss in solitude when not immersed in a book; gifted in conversation and in the use of every device through charm, wheedling, coaxing, and bullying, in order to get his own way.

Full growth into the infant-monster, or egocentric psychopath, is stemmed by numerous reality experiences, but the basic problem arising out of the indulgent overprotected background, namely, selfish, demanding, undisciplined behavior, is revealed with monotonous regularity. The problem in adjustment of the indulgent overprotected patient is to overcome the need of forcing every situation into the original pattern of his life, the need of being the beloved tyrant of an ever responding mother.

Of the twenty children in Group I, eleven were examples of indulgent overprotection. Their behavior toward the mother was marked by disobedience, impudence, temper tantrums, excessive demands, and the exercise of varying degrees of tyranny. This type of behavior represented the chief complaint of the mother at the time she referred the child. It is a simple continuity of undisciplined infantile response, each complaint registering the line of maternal surrender.

Disobedience and impudence at home, characteristic of the

entire group, follow maternal weakness in compelling respect, and submission to ordinary household requirements. The child refuses to come to meals, finally coaxed to the table he refuses to remain until the meal is over, or to eat what is placed before him; he refuses to come when called, to answer when spoken to. He keeps his own bedtime, comes home late, stays up late, refuses to wear what is required, throws his clothes anywhere, refusing to comply with numerous injunctions from either parent concerning neatness or routine. He is impudent, tells his mother to shut up or go to hell. He criticizes her freely, her manner or appearance, and is generally disrespectful. In one instance—Case 12—a son accused his mother of being pregnant and insisted she had no right to be so.

Although the type of difficulty described so far is frequently observed in family life, it must be remembered that in the group referred to it is relatively more frequent, chronic and severe.

The growth of aggressive components of the personality accelerated by maternal indulgence is seen in commanding, bullying, fighting tactics; in explosive response to thwarting; in the type of impudence described, besides oppositional, rebellious behavior. It is seen also in excessive demands. The demanding behavior serves the purpose, besides that of getting what one wants, of maintaining the dependent relation on the mother, in which respect the indulgent and dominant overprotected are alike. The aggression of the overprotected has its primary aim of maintaining the originally favored position with the mother; it is basically an aggression of dependency.[1]

An eight-year-old (Case 1) ordered his mother around until she was exhausted obeying his commands. He struck her when angry, spit at her when given something he disliked, threw food on the floor when it was not to his taste. He shot a toy pistol close to her face and, although she disapproved, continued doing so until she wept.

[1] Contrast the excessive demands of the overprotected with those of children suffering from affect hunger. David M. Levy, "Primary Affect Hunger," *American Journal of Psychiatry*, XCIV (1937), 643–52. For the latter they appear to express insatiable hunger for things that were missed; for the overprotected, they are exerted to prevent any alteration of things that always were. The one is constantly searching for the nest of paradise, the other is fighting all efforts to push him out.

A four-year-old (Case 4) ruled the household with his screams and compelled the mother's compliance with all his demands. After a period in which he went to kindergarten alone, he refused to go unless his mother accompanied him, or to play outside the home unless she was there. Another four-year-old (Case 9) by means of screaming tantrums compelled her mother to feed and dress her. She would play after supper, refuse to go to bed, often holding out until 11 P.M.

A twelve-year-old (Case 10) had infantile temper tantrums in his twelfth year when his mother refused to butter his bread for him. He still demanded her help in dressing. He lorded it over everybody, and one servant after another left because of his behavior. He summed up his requirements in life very neatly by saying that his mother would butter his bread for him until he married, after which his wife would do so.

After screaming no longer availed, a ten-year-old (Case 11) used the method of nagging, monotonously repeating his demands. He slept whenever he wished, on a couch in the living room, or in his parents' room, regardless of their disapproval. He still occasionally had temper tantrums. He was sullen and impudent to both parents.

When his wish was crossed, a fifteen-year-old (Case 12) struck his mother or sister. During quarrels with his mother he threw dishes about, cut his clothing, and walked on a clean floor with muddy feet. He was openly critical and disparaging of his parents and referred to his father as "the horse." He constantly demanded his mother's attention and so tyrannized over her that on one occasion when he was visiting a relative, she moved to another residence, hoping to abandon him; yet within a day she brought him home.

In complete command, dominating mother and sister, who yielded in every instance rather than endure his scenes, a fourteen-year-old (Case 16) refused to go to school. He lay in bed, ordered his sister to get his breakfast, bring his clothes, and struck her when she disobeyed.

These examples represent the extremes in the group of aggressive, dominating behavior; and also the remarkable tolerance of the parents. The four remaining cases never attained such magnitude; because, doubtless, of maternal pressure. However masochistic the mother appeared in tolerating the child's brutality, it is unfair to conclude that her response was complete surrender. There was always some attempt at modifying the unruly behavior. One mother used to yell at the child (Case 2), another applied the strap (Case 3), others spanked (Cases 2, 9), denied meals (Case 11), nagged and scolded (Case 12). Although such efforts were not described in detail, it seems that a direct relation existed between parental indulgence and dominating behavior. Certainly the highest degree of indulgence, or neglect to modify infantile behavior, occurs in the most extreme samples—Cases 1, 4, 10, 12, and 16.

Limitations in the production of the theoretically extreme tyrannizing infant are explained by such parental modification as occurred. The patterns in some cases are limited to disobedience and impudence, without, however, evidence of freely destructive behavior and assault. The disobedience in some cases does not go so far as complete refusal to obey. Temper tantrums in some cases changed into nagging. As previously described (Chapter III), the sexual activity towards the mother was held in check. Except in one case disobedience did not include refusal to go to school (Chapter VI). The *enfant terrible,* though given remarkable leeway, has been checked somehow in attaining his full dimensions.

Since the indulgence of the child included his emotional expression, there is evidence in all the indulgent overprotected of temper tantrums long past infancy, of free display of sullenness or any change of mood. The ability to adjust to the school situation indicates a greater degree of control than appears at home. Within familiar surroundings, however, evidence of emotional instability is apparent, in the form of moodiness and quick loss of temper. Such response to frustration or denial appears to be a logical outcome, in the case of children who had their own way so much more than others. Given any "constitutional" aberration in this regard, its intensification to a pathologic degree by the indulgent overprotected background is readily comprehended.

The enslavement of the parent by the child is roughly measur-

able by the overt behavior described. Parental tolerance of infractions of household rules, especially meal time and bed time,
besides bits of impudence, are common enough in general family
life. Less frequent is tolerance of outspoken criticism and verbal
abuse—showing a complete lack of respect. Still less frequent is
the situation in which the child orders the parent around, the
latter submitting; and least frequent, one in which the child in-
flicts physical cruelty on the parents. The succession of events
starts with divesting the parents of authority and ends with the
child in command of the parents. It represents an experiment that
demonstrates the response to the growing aggressive infant in a
social medium rich in love and poor in discipline; an experiment
in which the aggressive and demanding phases of the personality
are given full expression.[2]

[2] Selfishness and carelessness with one's possessions, common characteristics of the
indulged child, have been attributed by Alfred Adler to a lack of training in social
sympathy, and to the anticipation that others will take care of everything. Carelessness
in picking up one's clothes means, "Let the others do it." Adler, more than any other
psychiatrist, has described the behavior of the "spoiled" child, who represents so
fitting an example of his theory of the power-drive; and this drive is assuredly given
tremendous momentum by maternal overprotection. Many symptoms of the indulged
child, especially the innumerable irritations inflicted on the adult through selfish,
inconsiderate behavior, besides the dependency and commanding roles, are well en-
compassed by Adler's theory. Its weakness, in relation to this study, lies, first, in his
attempt to fit a priori every attribute of personality to his theory; second, in loose-
ness of definition; and, third, in too much reliance on clinical observation without
statistical aid. His particular "case-orientation" is worth describing and well known,
since he has written extensively and demonstrated his method in numerous clinics
in this country and abroad. In reading a case-record his attention was focused on
every detail. As he read, he would explain each item in terms of the theory and
frequently anticipate further findings on that basis. If they occurred as anticipated, well and good; if not, he would explain the seeming contradiction or accept
the "flaw." Thus he read in the case of an overprotected child that he was a bed-
wetter. He then commented that bedwetting was a frequent problem in the "spoiled"
child and meant a desire to have the mother sleep with him. The bedwetting
was a protest against separation, and in line with the theory of the power-drive.
So also with an instance in which a child sucked its thumb. This was regarded
as a symptom frequently found in spoiled children, and meant a protest against
adult interference. No attempt was made to give the term "spoiled child" any
more definition than it has in ordinary conversation, nor was any study made to
check the accuracy of clinical observation. If by "spoiled" child the type of overprotected child studied in this investigation was meant, neither observation is correct. Thumb-sucking and bed-wetting occur no more frequently in "spoiled" children than in others; in fact, our studies have shown that bed-wetting occurs less
frequently. As to the explanations given, it has been demonstrated that thumb-
sucking is biologic, rather than psychologic, in origin. The cause of bed-wetting is
still highly debatable. It occurs, however, regardless of the particular form of

School

Of the eleven children in the indulgent overprotected group, only three gave difficulty in classroom behavior. In a few instances, their teachers were surprised to learn that they presented any problems at home (Cases 11 and 17). Our first example, an eight-year-old-boy (Case 1), though defiant, oppositional, and brutal in his behavior at home, was an excellent student, fond of school, anxious to get there on time, and always given a score of A in conduct. A fifteen-year-old (Case 12), always serious about schoolwork, allowed nothing to interfere with his routine. He went to summer school for additional credit despite his mother's protest. A five-year-old was considered a model child by his teacher (Case 14).

Where difficulty in adjusting to the classroom occurred (Cases 2, 13, and 16), it followed along the lines of behavior revealed at home; impudence, disobedience, attention-getting. Thus a fourteen-year-old-boy (Case 2) teased the girls in his class, threw paper wads, pushed the line in front of him, said "Shut your mouth" to his teacher, interrupted the examinations, clowned, refused to do any home work, and was the school's prize nuisance. However, he confined his temper tantrums to the home. Another fourteen-year-old-boy did as he pleased in the classroom, was boisterous, frequently left his seat to look out the window, and was frequently a truant. Another fourteen-year-old (Case 16), always disrespectful and undisciplined in the classroom, truanted, at thirteen became a leading member of a gang that created trouble for the teacher. He was transferred to another school because of bad conduct.

---

mother-child relationship. A more important criticism of Adler's theory of the spoiled child is that it makes no provision for the obedient, docile product of the dominating form of maternal overprotection. Such a child comes distinctly in Adler's classification of the loved child—the other classifications being the hated and the deformed—and yet responds to excessive love with a diminution, rather than an exaggeration, of the power-drive. See Alfred Adler, *The Pattern of Life* (New York, 1930); overindulgence causes delayed speech, food fads, bed-wetting; p. 72. See also Adler, *The Case of Miss R.: the Interpretation of a Life Story* (New York, 1929): "Pampering" causes social maladjustment, pp. 7–8; "a strong feeling of inferiority," p. 21; night terrors, p. 24; bed-wetting, p. 25; insomnia, p. 36; constipation, p. 67; homesickness, p. 110; impulsive behavior, p. 154; "the trait to dominate, to tyrannize," p. 168; uncertainty and vacillation in new situations, p. 236.

Since problems of the overprotected child in relation to intelligence and school subjects have been considered in Chapter V, this discussion will be limited to problems of adjustment to the social situation at school. Our first query in regard to the indulgent overprotected is turned to the discrepancy of home and school behavior in eight of the eleven cases. Reversely, why did the patterns of behavior emanating from the mother-child relationship hold consistently in the classroom for only three out of the eleven cases? Before considering an answer to this question it is worth noting the plasticity of personality revealed by our findings. The influence of a monopolistic mother-child relationship that gave rise to the full expectation of special consideration above all others, of tolerance for any infraction of a rule, of freedom to speak and act impulsively—a preparation fully designed to create a total misfit in a formal classroom—nevertheless failed to do so in a majority of instances. Actually some of the children were models of deportment at school and conscientious students.[3]

One answer implicit in the facts is that the primary maternal influence does not fix the pattern of behavior for every relationship. It has been noted also (Chapter VI) that regardless of their indulgence, overprotecting mothers may be adamant as far as schoolwork is concerned. Further, with the aid of maternal coaching, together with advantage in intelligence and verbal skill, the child gains decided prestige in the classroom. This becomes of especial importance, since the overprotected child, as has already been noted, is poor in sports and in social relations with other children. He may prize his school success very highly, enjoy the intellectual combat of the examination, as in Case 11, and may even regard the classroom as his domain, not to be invaded by mother or social worker, as in Case 12.

So far the adjustment to the classroom is explained by the facts that in this particular regard they were not indulged, that they had an initial advantage, and derived distinct satisfaction through success in their studies. It would appear that they were willing to work for the recognition received from the teacher, in contrast with their attitude to the mother.

[3] Similar observations are made of the good behavior of the "spoiled" child at summer camps, with quick relapse into his customary behavior on returning home.

An inference may be drawn that their behavior as obedient children in a classroom satisfied certain requirements, that it furnished security engendered in responding to the authoritative adult, and hence simplified and quieted the turbulent, demanding behavior at home. The fear of other children may also be a factor. For these inferences, however, our records furnish no data.

Although the display of obedience in the classroom was noted as a definite discrepancy from behavior at home, certain earmarks of the overprotective relationship were recognizable. Thus instances are noted even among the good students of periods of distractibility, easy boredom, difficulty in working on an uninteresting subject, attempts to get special praise and attention. However, such problems were not serious and, if one is inclined to insist that the teacher had to be envisioned by the child in terms of the indulgent mother, the indulgence, if any, was secured by good behavior.[4]

Besides the six-year-old referred to, three boys (Cases 2, 13, and 16), each age fourteen years, were disciplinary problems at school. In attempting to explain their behavior the first noteworthy finding is the I.Q. They represent, although above average in intelligence by tests, the lowest three of the group—I.Q.'s 109, 110, and 113—with one exception, a boy age eight, who was "average." The I.Q.'s of the indulged overprotected who adjusted well to the school situation were respectively 117, 128, 133, 140, 141, and 146.[5]

With the exception of Case 1, the well adjusted had relative superiority in intelligence. Furthermore, it remains a question if No. 1 is an exception since, as a study of his case in Chapter IX reveals, a question arises as to whether he belongs in the group of "aggressives." Since the I.Q.'s of the three boys who were unad-

[4] A six-year-old boy in the group studied was below average in intelligence, suffered from reading reversals, and yet was not a disciplinary problem in the classroom (Case 3), nor did he become so up to the age of eight years. In his case the mother, despite her indulgent overprotection, was constantly pressing him to do well in school. Though he frankly loathed the school, in which he did poorly, she compelled him to go. The case affords a good example of the ability of mothers to except certain situations from the general overprotective attitude, and of the child's adjustment to a situation in which he learns that all his tricks are of no avail.

[5] Case 9, though only age 4 years, 5 months, at the time of referral, was a "model girl" in kindergarten.

justed in school indicate high average intelligence, one may infer that with ordinary industry they could have done well in their studies. However, the difficulty in accepting routine tasks, facilitated by the brightness of the others, would not operate so readily in their cases, especially after the lessening advantage of verbal skills in the higher grades. In other words, as compared with the boys having higher I.Q.'s, they would have to work harder to attain success. It was this success, and the pressure exerted on the child by the mother, that explained the acceptance of schoolwork by the overprotected. It is consistent also with this theory that in the three instances cited, maternal discipline in regard to schoolwork was impaired. In one instance the mother was quite complacent about her son's school failure—Case 13. In another (Case 16), as previously noted, despite overprotection there was a long period of neglect because the mother had to work at a job. In a third (Case 2), the father interfered with the mother's attempt to discipline the boy when he refused to do his home work.

Of the nine children classified as "submissive," one only (Case 17) [6] revealed a problem in classroom discipline. This finding is interesting in view of the fact that five of the nine rated "average" or "below average" in intelligence; their I.Q.'s were 85, 88, 97, 105, and "average." The achievement in terms of grade placement and marks of the group of nine are all consistent with their I.Q.'s. Three of them were model boys in deportment.

Hence we find in the overprotected group that the generally "submissive" children responded well to the requirements of classroom behavior, regardless of I.Q. or satisfaction in terms of educational achievement, whereas the "aggressive" children responded well in those instances in which high I.Q.'s and relative ease in achievement prevailed.

FRIENDS

Difficulty in making friendships with other children is a very consistent finding in every member of the group with, probably, one exception. The mother's particular contribution to this dif-

[6] The exception, Case 17, offered a problem in classification, since a mixture of aggressive and submissive behavior problems was revealed.

ficulty has been considered in Chapter V. The table following gives a brief summary statement of the relationship of the over-protected with other children.

TABLE XXXIII

SOCIAL RELATIONSHIP WITH OTHER CHILDREN

Case No.	Sex	Age at time of referral	Comments
1	M	8	Quarrels with other children. Cries if they do not give in to him. He will not play unless his mother is nearby.
2	M	14	He has no friend at school. "An isolated figure." He used to play with boys much younger than himself. Since age 14 years, he has had one friend.
3	M	6	Since he constantly hits, the neighbors keep their children away from him. He prefers to play with girls.
4	M	4	Considered a "pest" by other boys. He tries to play only with older children. The mother has given money to a 5-year-old boy to play with him.
5	M	13	Called a "sissy," he is timid and shy. He never plays with boys on the street. At the age of 13 years, he started going out with other boys.
6	M	10	He was prevented from having friends until he went to school at 6. He has played with boys since age 8 years, and then only with boys younger than himself. Afraid to fight openly, he makes secret attacks and walks by "innocently."
7	M	11	He still keeps away from boys despite his mother's urging. He has never had social contact with any boy.
8	M	7	He was referred because of his difficulty with children. They avoided him because he was so bossy and boastful. In the past six months he has had two playmates. Observed in play with other children, he differed from them in being overly competitive and in using unfair means in order to win.
9	F	4	She played with other children until age 4 years, when the mother of one of them scolded her. Since then she will not play with them unless

TABLE XXXIII (*Continued*)

SOCIAL RELATIONSHIP WITH OTHER CHILDREN

Case No.	Sex	Age at time of referral	Comments
			her mother is present. She has, since then, been bossy and argumentative, takes teasing poorly, and "can't be outdone in any way."
10	M	12	He had no contact with children until age 6 years, and no friends until age 12. He would try to boss them, but was afraid to fight and became timid and cowardly with them. His father gave him many boxing lessons to overcome his fear. Since he has had friends, at 12, he has played the role chiefly of clowning for them.
11	M	10	An unpopular boy without friends, because he always wanted his own way and would play only the role of leader.
12	M	15	He has had no friends because he always wanted his own way. In recent years he has been able to make friends, but only for a short while, because of his quarreling.
13	M	14	Boastful with children, and selfish in play, he used to be called "sissy." In school, he has had no associates because of his reputation as "immoral and dirty." In the past few years, however, he has had a chum, a boy much more sophisticated and wealthy than he.
14	M	5	He has no friends. He is bossy and always fights.
15	M	7	Shy and timid with children, yet he is eager to play with them though doesn't know how. He will break up their games and when they fight, run screaming to his mother. He prefers girls because they are not rough.
16	M	14	He belongs to a school gang of delinquent boys, with whom he steals and truants. In this group, although he is not the leader, he exerts an important influence.
17	M	13	He will not play with boys on the street, because they are too tough. He prefers to stay at home and read. The boys call him "sissy" and "mamma's boy." When he does play with boys who are younger than himself he is quarrelsome and fights.

TABLE XXXIII (*Continued*)

SOCIAL RELATIONSHIP WITH OTHER CHILDREN

Case No.	Sex	Age at time of referral	Comments
18	M	16	Referred because of his difficulty in making friends. He is very unpopular at school. Boys consider him a "sissy" because he will not join in their sports. His attitude is always "critical and supercilious."
19	M	12	He is friendly and popular with boys, although he has never had a chum. This has been attributed to the mother's refusal to allow him to invite any friend to his home.
20	M	4	Excepting a girl younger than himself, he refuses to play with children outside his home. He is afraid to fight and depends on a younger brother for protection against other boys.

The problems vary from complete lack of friends or playmates to some approximation to the norm of companionship in children. Whatever this "norm" is, it most likely is represented by a figure in excess of Andrew's finding [7] for Institute cases—a large majority of instances of "few or more companions" per child. This "norm" is purely statistical. It does not give an account of the difficulties within the relationship. In the overprotected group, probably two in the twenty (Cases 16 and 19) satisfy the statistical criterion. Of these two cases, however, one (Case 16) has contact only with delinquent boys and his mother, and, although liked by his schoolmates and in social contact, has no real playmates. Of the difficulties in making friendly relationships, fear of the group and attempts to dominate account for all but five cases. Thus, quarreling, hitting, refusal to play any role but leader, and bossy behavior are seen in nine cases—Cases 1, 2, 3, 8, 9, 10, 11, 12, and 14; timidity and withdrawal from the group in six—Cases 5, 6, 7, 15, 17, and 20.

In general, the difficulties in all these relationships may be described in terms of domination and withdrawal. Included under the former are the simple aggressive maneuvers—running the whole show, and attacking the dissident; "showing off"—from

[7] Refer to Table XXX (page 96).

boasting to using the group as audience for clowning or other exhibitions; selfish and demanding behavior, refusal to share possessions for the purpose of play, demanding special consideration, constant interruptions in play or conversation. These characteristics—aggressive, cocky, selfish, and show-off—represent an imposition of one's own personality on others, and difficulty in making those compliances necessary for social life. They represent all but one (Case 16) of the children in the overprotected group characterized as aggressive.[8]

The exceptional case (16) must be considered, even though his friendships were with delinquent boys whose exploits landed the patient in an institution, since within his group the patient was recognized and accepted. It will be remembered that besides the problems in the indulgent overprotected that make for difficulty in social life because of egocentric attitudes, isolation from other children through maternal activity was a frequent occurrence. In the give and take of social relationships, learning by experience is an important factor. The problems enumerated—aggressive, cocky, boastful behavior and the like—are a frequent occurrence in any nursery group. The modification of egocentric behavior is part of the problem of normal growth. It functions best when children have opportunities for play with others without undue supervision. Contact with adults exclusively, in the nursery age, is inadequate for such growth, because child and grownup have an orientation different from that of child and child. A child may be well adjusted to grown-ups, and quite unadjusted to children. With the grown-up, problems of frank aggression, fighting, brutal criticism, skill in sport and play, are largely absent. And the qualities that endear the child to his elders, chiefly brightness in verbal response, precocities, physical appearance, and various forms of infantile cuteness and helplessness, are hardly tolerated by the young. The picture of the indulged, overprotected child, whose first contact with children occurs at the age of six when he first enters school, is an example of tragic unpreparedness. In terms of social adjustment to children, he is years behind. His efforts to dominate the group are met with rebuff. When he fights

[8] Case 13, whose difficulty with children was "boastfulness and selfishness," and Case 4 who was a "pest," are included.

his opponents, he is licked. Instances of this pattern are seen both in the indulged and dominated overprotected groups. The result may be avoidance of the group because of fear, or refusal to join in because the dominating tendencies are frequently thwarted. Various patterns of adjustment to this difficulty appear: recourse to younger children or to girls (Cases 2, 3, 6, 15, 17, and 20); friendships numerous but quickly broken (Case 12); attempts to win friends by making show-off behavior acceptable (Case 10); modification of direct aggression into stealthy attack (Case 10), into excessive competitive behavior (Case 8), or into snobbery (Case 18).

Unlike the others, the boy with delinquent companions is an example of overprotection and neglect. For in spite of excessive care in the home, the mother held an outside job, because of economic necessity. Hence the various maneuvers to prevent or control playmates were not employed in this case. The boy learned how to adjust to the gang. Besides satisfying his need of companionship, and his craving for money and possessions, the gang furnished an outlet for his rebellious attitude toward authority. Hence it can be readily understood why, in relation to the gang, he was willing to modify his pattern of tyrannical behavior at home.

The social relationships of the overprotected, despite the handicaps noted (namely, egocentric behavior or timidity, social inexperience in the first six years of life, lack of skill in play, sports and fighting), are by no means static. In Case 2, for example, we learn that the patient had a friend from the age of 14 years. Another (Case 3) started going out with boys at 13. Another, prevented from social contact until age 6 years, started playing with boys younger than himself, after two years (Case 6). Another was reported to have two playmates, although the relationship was difficult, at about age 7 years. The beginning of friendly relationships in the form of fairly steady companionship occurred at about age 11 or 12 years in Cases 10 and 13 and at 13 years in Case 12.

Of the nine boys in the group referred at age 12 or older, all but three developed satisfactory and steady companionship with one boy or more, at or later than age 12.

Disregarding for the moment the type of relationship that developed, the fact is interesting as evidence of the need for special companionship at the beginning of adolescence, and also as evidence that the difficulties preventing previous relationships were no longer in operation for six of the nine cases.

The development of friendly relationships later on in childhood, after early failures, may be understood by differentiating social activities according to their major forms. After the early egocentric play, in which a child keeps to his own activities, although preferably with another child present, joining in play develops. In the stage of early playmates, the overprotected have the greatest difficulty because their strong maternal dependency, manifested in dominating or withdrawing behavior, has had little chance for modification. In the stage preceding and during typical "gang" activities—roughly nine to thirteen, a stage in which fighting and skill in sports are especially important attributes—they are again at a disadvantage. Nevertheless at camps, after an initial difficulty in adjustment (for example, violating camp rules, refusal to do one's share and the like), a satisfactory adjustment was made. The camp experience indicates that the indulgent overprotected are able to modify egocentric behavior under special conditions.

The stage of friendship, a more highly selective process, allows for the best possibility of a social relationship, since the group attitudes may play a minor role. Further, since such friends are selected later in childhood, certain modifications for social life have been made. Hence the possibility of friendships for the overprotected are better with increasing age. In general, the same holds true for all children who for reasons of individual differences cannot accept the rather stereotyped similarities required in usual childhood relationships. A study of the friendships formed by the overprotected during adolescence must wait for Chapter X.

An aggressive relationship with the mother is correlated with aggressive relationships with children. The consistency is surprisingly high. Even the exceptions are not quite against the rule.

In Case 8, the patient is obedient to his mother, yet his difficulties with children are due to bossiness and boasting. However, the patient is indulged rather than dominated by the mother, and acts like the typical indulged overprotected child towards his grandmother, who lives in the home.

The relationships with children and with mothers are compared in Table XXXIV.

A definite consistency will be noted. The obedient, dependent relationship with the mother is correlated with timidity and withdrawal from social contact with children.

An exception is Case 10, an example of aggressive behavior with the mother, cowardly behavior with children. Later on, however, at age 12, he became very forward in social relationships, invited boys to his home and played the role of host and entertainer.

In Case 16 and 19 social relationships of the highest degree of adaptability for the group occur. They are, nevertheless, consistent with the mother-child relationship. Incorrigible behavior at home is matched with some form of leadership among delinquent boys in Case 16.

Popularity through a general friendly attitude occurs in Case 19, without, however, the development of any steady companionship.

In Case 18, the "supercilious" attitude towards boys conceals a definite fear of making social contacts. The attitude is distinctly an identification with his mother.

So far we have seen very consistent difficulties in the social relationships of the overprotected with other children. The possible values of overprotection in this connection may be theoretically inferred. The bossy and demanding behavior might be modified into leadership and assertiveness. Certainly the indulged overprotected should have no shyness in making their complaints heard and going into action to redress a wrong. The self-assurance fostered by the wealth of maternal love might, conceivably, once a social adjustment has been made, strengthen social position. The experience in wheedling the mother with every variety of charm might be utilized, when modified, into acceptable persuasiveness. Superiority in verbalization might make for conversational talent. The dominated overprotected would have an advantage in modifying infantile submission into friendly acceptance, in politeness, and in stimulating helpfulness through a capacity to serve.

TABLE XXXIV

COMPARISON OF RELATIONSHIP

Case No.	Sex	Age at time of referral	With mother	With children
1	M	8	Disobedient, oppositional, insolent, undisciplined.	Quarreling, dominating.
2	M	14	Disobedient, impudent.	Teases girls, pushes the line in front of him at school, "an isolated figure," plays only with smaller boys.
3	M	6	Disobedient, impudent.	Constantly hits other children. Now prefers to play with girls.
4	M	4	Disobedient, impudent, undisciplined.	Unpopular with children because he is a "pest," due to constant showing off. Tries to play with older boys who do not want him.
5	M	13	Obedient, very dependent, accepts and insists on mother's domination.	Shy and timid. Teased as a "sissy." Kept away from social contact with boys until age 13 years. Prefers to stay home.
6	M	10	Obedient, helpful, responsive, very dependent.	He made no social contact with boys until about age 8, and then only with boys younger than himself. At kindergarten—age 5 to 6 years—he refused to play with the other children.
7	M	11	Completely dependent and obedient.	Has kept away from boys despite mother's urging. No friends. Afraid to fight.
8	M	7	Very obedient, and also indulged.	Until about age 7 years, has not been able to make friends with chil-

TABLE XXXIV (*Continued*)

COMPARISON OF RELATIONSHIP

Case No.	Sex	Age at time of referral	With mother	With children
				dren because of boasting and trying to boss. Overcompetitive in games, he uses unfair methods to win.
9	F	4	Disobedient, aggressive, attention-getting, undisciplined.	Very free with children, bossy and opinionated, cannot brook opposition.
10	M	12	Disobedient, impudent, tyrannical, attention-getting.	He had no contact with children until age 6. Was timid and cowardly with children and kept away because he was afraid to fight.
11	M	10	Disobedient, impudent, undisciplined.	In play with other children wants to be the leader and have his own way. Although not barred from the group, he is not liked. "Hangs around the edge of the group."
12	M	15	Disobedient, impudent, bullying, undisciplined.	Always wanted his own way with children and has no friends.
13	M	14	Disobedient, dominating.	Boastful, selfish, used to be called "sissy," later avoided by school associates because of sexual behavior.
14	M	5	Disobedient, impudent.	No friends because of bossiness and fighting.
15	M	7	Dependent, infantile, submissive.	Shy and timid with children, yet eager to play with them and "doesn't know how." He will break up their

TABLE XXXIV (*Continued*)

COMPARISON OF RELATIONSHIP

Case No.	Sex	Age at time of referral	With mother	With children
				games and when they fight, run screaming to his mother. Prefers to play with girls because they are not so rough.
16	M	14	Disobedient, dominating, undisciplined, "incorrigible."	His contacts have been chiefly in the form of delinquent behavior with other boys. Among them he was "outstanding," although not a leader.
17	M	13	Regarded as "sweet, affectionate and considerate," except for occasional periods of disobedience and temper tantrums.	Regarded as "sissy" and "mamma's boy," he prefers to stay home than make friends with the boys. Afraid to fight with the boys his own age, he has made contact with younger boys. With them he is quarrelsome and fights.
18	M	16	Obedient and submissive.	"Supercilious," like his mother, and boys resent his attitude. Refuses to join them in sports. Unpopular.
19	M	12	Submissive, dependent, and irresponsible.	Friendly and popular although he has no close friends.
20	M	4	Obedient and submissive. "Too good."	Excepting a girl younger than himself, he refuses to play with children outside the home. Afraid to fight, and depends on a younger brother for protection against other boys.

Sexual Problems

In Chapter III consideration was given to the sexual response of those children who slept with the mother long past infancy. In the six instances, two showed overt evidence of sex conflict, one, a proposal of incestuous behavior. An instance in which an adolescent "accused" the mother of being pregnant should be included, since the sexual implications, besides the fear of a rival, are obvious. Overt sexual response to the mother constituted a problem in one case (3) in which sexual advances to a girl were also noted.

Active sex play with a child was noted in Case 4—the doctor-enema play; sex play with a sister in Case 10; an instance of exposure of the genitals to a girl in Case 13; tattooing of arms to attract girls' attention in Case 16. Altogether instances of some form of active heterosexual behavior occurred in six cases, all of them in the overindulged group.

Of the instances enumerated, not one may be considered a problem in sex abnormality, since even in Case 10, the case of sex-exposure, the difficulty was temporary. Sex play, concealed as the game of doctor, is common in children, as also masturbatory sex activity among siblings.

As a group, the overprotected show nothing unusual in the frequency of masturbation. The problem of sex was handled by mothers in, probably, typical fashion. Ten mothers ignored the problem or evaded answering the child's questions (Cases 1, 3, 5, 7, 12, 13, 15, 16, 18, and 19). Five gave the usual variety of threats, illustrating the dire results of masturbation (Cases 2, 6, 10, 11, and 17). Of the remaining five mothers, information on their actual methods of handling the problem was not available. It was assumed that four of them regarded the act as childish, but not reprehensible.

Undue modesty about nakedness and reticence about any sexual topic occurred in three cases (8, 12, and 17). In Case 12, the patient expressed shame about the large size of his genitalia, which he regarded as rather a disgrace.

Regardless of overt manifestations of sexual behavior in this group, the fact remains that it constitutes 19 examples of remarkably close mother-son relationships. What was the effect on sexual development? Were the sons so bound to their mothers that they were unable to make a heterosexual adjustment? Did they show evidence of sexual impotence because of the incestuous conflict? Did any become homosexual—on the basis of feminine identification?

The first series of follow-up studies, continuing three years after "closing" the case, include five patients age 16 to 19 years. No evidence of latent or overt homosexuality appears in this group. The second series of follow-up studies, made seven to ten years later, throw further light on the sexual development of our patients (see Chapter X).

In relation to the indulged overprotected, an interesting problem is the influence of relatively uninhibited behavior on sex development. The six cases in which some form of active heterosexual behavior occurred were consistently in the indulged group. Theoretically, we may infer that gratification of sexual impulses would more likely occur in a group generally indulged. We would anticipate greater impatience at prevention of coitus, a willingness, even a demand, that parents give their support to marriage regardless of the earning capacity of the patient. Hence the insistent demands of early gratification would compete with incestuous conflicts, a competition between indulgence and repression.

The apparently successful sexual adjustment revealed in the most recent follow-up studies of these cases may alter the previous theoretical anticipation of the effect of maternal overprotection on the sexual development of male offspring.

In terms of dependency the argument might follow that the son would remain more or less fixed in the role of child, so that he would be as immature in his sex development as in the relationship to his mother. According to this line of reasoning he would remain impotent, not necessarily homosexual, but simply immature, forever tied to his mother and helpless without her. The argument would apply more cogently to submissive rather than to aggressive dependency. No evidence for it exists in the group of indulgent overprotected. Some evidence is at hand among the dominated overprotected.

In terms of identification, the argument would follow that in the overprotective relationship the son is in such consonance with the mother's feelings and attitudes that he would become psychologically feminine. He would become homosexual, therefore, by feminine identification. There is no evidence of overt homosexuality in this series. However, assuming an unconscious homosexuality, then sexual impotence would follow, since, on the basis already assumed, he could not function in a masculine way. Again for this argument there is probably evidence among the submissive, but none among the aggressive.

So far, the fathers have not been considered. However, impotence or homosexuality, when derived through incestuous conflict, would require paternal influence in the form of a dangerous threat to the son. This threat would have to be implied, somehow, even though the fathers in this series played a prevailingly minor role. In the overprotective relationship, the argument would follow that the usual Oedipus problem would be complicated by an increased charge in sexual drive towards the mother. This would follow from the unusual closeness of mother and son, and the weakness of the counteracting influence from the father. A number of results might follow. Of these, theoretically most plausible are: a flight from the mother and a solution through impulsive heterosexuality; impotence through fear of any heterosexual act although without homosexuality; homosexuality through abandonment of heterosexuality.

Of the evidence in these records, there is some support for the first assumption, none for the others. Actual flight of mother from son and son from mother, during the son's adolescence, occurred in Case 12. Flight from the mother during adolescence occurred also in Case 13. In the former case, however, the runaways, which were obviously complicated with incestuous conflicts, were followed by presumably normal heterosexual development. In the latter, it is complicated by the fact that the patient truanted frequently several years before puberty, and that he was generally precocious in sexual behavior.[9]

[9] On this point, Freud's comment is of special interest; see his *Collected Papers* (London, 1933), Vol. II, p. 225. "So long as we trace the development from its

In terms of indulgent overprotection, the explanation of successful, and also early, heterosexual behavior in these patients lies in their refusal to forego any pleasurable pursuit, in other words, lessened inhibitions, or increased self-indulgence. Early marriage, in spite of family opposition and inability to support a wife, as in Cases 2 and 13, is a similar manifestation.

OUTSIDE INTERESTS

Of the 17 children older than four years of age, reading was the main outside interest in 15. In one of the four-year-olds a favorite pastime was copying words out of schoolbooks and listening to stories read by the mother. For the entire group, sports and play with other children were the main outside activities in only two cases. The remaining found their outside interests inside the home,[10] in reading or other activities—music, drawing, workshop, play with toys.

As revealed in the section on "Friends," these activities, chiefly verbal, passive, and individual, run counter to activities facilitating adjustment to other children. They aid intellectual development in so far as facility in reading and verbalization are part of the process. On the other hand, as exclusive preoccupations, they rule out the rough and tumble social experiences of childhood, with all their implications. Of the latter, the development of strength, agility, endurance, and coördination, in mutual and competitive play, urging steady improvement in finer muscular activity as in the game of marbles, or in large muscle skills as in running games and fighting—is quite obvious. The highly evolved neuromuscular performances in sports and numerous mechanical aptitudes are greatly aided by preparation in child-

---

final stage backwards, the connection appears continuous, and we feel we have gained an insight which is completely satisfactory, or even exhaustive. But if we proceed the reverse way, if we start from the premises inferred from the analysis and try to follow these up to the final result, then we no longer get the impression of an inevitable sequence of events which could not be otherwise determined. We notice at once that there might have been another result, and that we might have been just as well able to understand and explain the latter. The synthesis is thus not so satisfactory as the analysis; in other words, from a knowledge of the premises we could not have foretold the nature of the result."

[10] Refer to Table XX (page 88).

hood play. The boy who has missed out in this regard is handicapped. When, through maternal overprotection, or other causes —for example, temporary physical handicaps, social isolation— he misses childhood play and first enters the organized sports that develop around age 10 to 12 years, he finds himself inept and often ridiculed. A typical response to this situation is lack of interest or avoidance of sports.[11]

More important than skill in sports is the growth in social relationships developed out of play with other children. This is especially important for the overprotected: the indulged, whose main problem is selfish, egocentric behavior; and the dominated, whose main problem is dependent, submissive behavior. For the former, therefore, the give and take of play through which the attitude of the other is stressed, has special value; and for the latter, the need of self-assertion and independent behavior.

Habit Problems

Under this convenient term are included problems of adjustment to necessary household requirements, in relation to table, bed, and toilet. Feeding problems occur in 12 of the 20 cases (1, 2, 3, 4, 7, 8, 9, 10, 11, 12, 13, and 14).[12] Of the eight who present no difficulties in this connection, all but one are of the dominated overprotected group. The others manifest the usual variety of problems, ranging from bad table manners, in the form of grabbing and slovenliness, to food refusals. In detail, the problems appear as obvious representations of the indulgent overprotecting relationship. Thus, undisciplined dominating behavior is manifested in the time of eating—for example, having one's own

---

[11] There are, however, certain physical activities in which development in "spontaneous" play offers little advantage, if any. For example, although quite out of contact with other childen until about age 10, a patient (Case 2) became proficient in swimming—an activity in which instruction during adolescence or even later may develop a performance superior to years of untutored experience.

[12] The number of feeding problems recorded in 1,000 I.C.G. seriatim cases was 146—14.6 percent. Of the 1,000, there were 635 boys and 365 girls. The former revealed 80 feeding problems—13 percent; the latter 66—18 percent. The age range of both groups was $3\frac{1}{2}$ to 17 years. The majority of the feeding problems were at age $7\frac{1}{2}$ years and younger.

meals regardless of family schedule, eating between meals, and dawdling; the manner of eating—throwing unwanted food to the floor, grabbing the largest piece, and eating with the fingers; and the manner of talking about food—criticism of the food, and saying, "It stinks." Dependency, turned into aggressive demands, is manifested by refusing to eat unless fed by the mother, as in Case 9, age 4, or the variation of this theme at that age and in older children—having mother coax or beg down the next bite (Cases 4, 9, and 10). Indulgence of the child's whims is seen in finickiness, refusal to eat certain kinds of meat or vegetables, or any food unless prepared to the king's taste (Cases 1, 2, 9, 10, 12, and 14).

Feeding problems are generally very frequent. They are among the commonest manifestations of maternal indulgence, or apprehension, however mild. The daily weighing of the infant may constitute for the mother, especially of a first child, a life-and-death chart. Sudden loss of appetite, frequently due, probably, to nausea at the onset of a mild infection ushers in apprehensive coaxing and food forcing. A true negative conditioned response to food may be developed in some cases.

Feeding problems due to organic factors are not present among the children considered in this section. They do not contain an instance of inappetence. The feeding difficulties are relationship difficulties in the truest sense. However, such problems arise frequently in mother-child relationships in which severe overprotection does not exist.

In "mild" indulgent overprotection, feeding problems are chiefly in the form of coaxing, dawdling, and finickiness. They are of the same variety as sleeping problems in which the child requires the mother's company before it will fall asleep—when this has developed out of established practice. The same is true of problems in dressing, in which the mother gives help past the usual time. The measure of "spoiling" has every gradation, but, in a pure overprotective relationship, however mild, it shows a general consistency in maternal care and closeness.

This consistency differentiates feeding problems, symptomatic of maternal complexes about food, which vary from special indulgence in regard to eating and apprehension based on the child's serious feeding difficulties, to definite neurosis.[13]

SLEEP

Under disturbances of sleep are included night terrors, insomnia, sleep walking and talking. There is one case of insomnia in the overprotected group (Case 6); one of sleep walking (a few instances in Case 17); and two of night terrors (Case 2, onset at six years; Case 9, onset at 30 months). The group frequency is about the same as in other I.C.G. cases.[14]

Other problems related to sleep have to do with irregular hours, due to refusal to go to bed on time, or without mother's company. This problem is recorded for eight patients, all but one (Case 7) in the indulged overprotected group.

BOWEL AND BLADDER CONTROL

There were no problems of soiling in the overprotected group, and but two cases of enuresis, both nocturnal.[15] As compared with the frequency of problems of enuresis at the time of referral for 1,000 I.C.G. cases—22 percent of 635 boys, 16 percent of 365 girls, the figure is low—10 percent. Of the two enuretics, one wet the bed since infancy—Case 3, age six years; the other—Case 20, age four years—had full control at 12 months, and became enuretic after beginning nursery school at 21 months. Of the 20 mothers,

[13] The latter includes a variety of difficulties. In the neuroses of mothers related to feeding the child, a frequent mechanism consists in an unconscious hostile impulse to destroy by means of food. In overprotection compensatory to hostile attitudes, special stress on the child's eating is understood as proof to the conscience of beneficent motherhood—a denial of the tendency to deny, neglect, or starve the offspring; see Hilde Bruch and Grace Touraine, "Obesity in Childhood: V: The Family Frame of Obese Children," *Psychosomatic Medicine*, II (1940), 141–206. Stuffing the child to make it fat may be influenced, naturally, by cultural determinants. In certain groups, or within certain families in any given culture, the fat baby is highly prized, just as obesity generally may have special merit. Mothers or fathers may utilize the child's weight as a source of competition involving their own prestige.

[14] 20 percent, as compared with 18 percent of 635 boys and 17 percent of 365 girls.

[15] A third case (14) of a five-year-old boy who wet the bed occasionally, and only when his mother had him drink hot milk before going to sleep, was not included. In his case bladder control was established by age two years.

17 reported that bladder control was established for their children by age 2½ years. In this group, control in three instances was established by age 13 months—all in the dominated group. In general, the overprotected group were well disciplined in bowel and bladder habits.[16]

This finding, although inconsistent with the general behavior of the indulged overprotected—and with the frequency of feeding problems which occurred in every case, with one exception—may be explained by special features in regard to bowel and bladder training. This was initiated by the mothers in the first year of life, with their usual high degree of care and solicitude, and completed before the period of infancy was over. As compared with the establishment of feeding and sleeping habits, the problem of bowel and bladder training is more mechanical, requiring simple, steady application, and is near solution before the personality has developed into the negativistic period of infancy—about age two years. As contrasted with eating and sleeping, bladder training is less "social." The former are more conducive to conversation, coaxing, and lullabies. As mutual mother-child relationships they are more satisfying, more time-consuming, and go on beyond the infantile years. Bladder training is begun before the child can talk, is in each instance of brief duration and, besides, is very probably regarded by the mother as a necessary discipline. Hence bladder training, in the case of maternal overprotection, may be proof only of careful routine.[17]

Since bladder control is readily disturbed under emotional stress, the return of bedwetting after beginning nursery school in Case 20 represents a common episode. The increase in the frequency of problems of bedwetting during the period of entering

16 Brunk accumulated data on the age of bladder control for 24 overprotected and 152 non-overprotected I.C.G. patients. In the former, 79 percent achieved bladder control by age three years; in the latter, 60 percent—counting "early" as meaning "during infancy." Counting only those cases in which mothers were able to state the year in which control was established, the percentages were 67 and 55 respectively.

17 The argument rests on the assumption that the vast majority of problems in enuresis continuing from infancy are originally due to neglect in training and persist because of specific erotic components, hence more frequent in boys than in girls.

school is revealed in Table XXXV, showing percentages of enuresis cases of 635 I.C.G. boys, at different age levels.

TABLE XXXV

FREQUENCY OF ENURESIS RELATED TO AGE

Age at time of of referral	No. of cases	No. of cases of enuresis	Percent
Below 3 yrs. 6 mos.	18	9	50
3 yrs. 6 mos.– 4 yrs. 5 mos.	18	6	33
4 yrs. 6 mos.– 5 yrs. 5 mos.	15	3	20
5 yrs. 6 mos.– 6 yrs. 5 mos.	36	6	17
6 yrs. 6 mos.– 7 yrs. 5 mos.	47	13	28
7 yrs. 6 mos.– 8 yrs. 5 mos.	63	22	35
8 yrs. 6 mos.– 9 yrs. 5 mos.	49	15	31
9 yrs. 6 mos.–10 yrs. 5 mos.	71	13	18
10 yrs. 6 mos.–11 yrs. 5 mos.	63	14	22
11 yrs. 6 mos.–12 yrs. 5 mos.	54	11	20
12 yrs. 6 mos.–13 yrs. 5 mos.	60	11	18
13 yrs. 6 mos.–14 yrs. 5 mos.	39	7	18
14 yrs. 6 mos.–15 yrs. 5 mos.	44	7	16
15 yrs. 6 mos.–16 yrs. 5 mos.	31	1	3
16 yrs. 6 mos.–17 yrs. 5 mos.	21	1	5
17 yrs. 6 mos.–18 yrs. 5 mos.	6	0	0
Total	635	139	

The distribution of the 60 enuresis cases among 365 girls shows also a falling off in frequency up to 6½ years—beginning at "below 3½ years" the percentages are 25, 40, 30, 14 for each age group as classified above, a rise at age level 6½ years to 20 percent, increasing to 24 at the 8½ year level, and then a gradual falling off with increasing age.

The frequency of enuresis in combination with other common problems shows generally a decrease with increasing age of the group; as would be anticipated from Table XXXVI. The exception, however, is the combination with "stealing" and "lying"— the "delinquency" complaints. It is well known that enuresis is very frequent in the delinquent groups—likewise general neglect.

Alfred Adler has explained bedwetting as a protest against separation from the mother, hence a sign of "spoiled child." He concluded that if the mother slept with the child it would not

Table XXXVI

Frequency of Enuresis in Combination with Behavior Problems, among 635 Boys [18]

Problems	Median age in years	No. of cases	Percent of enuresis	Average percent
Feeding	7½	80	36 ⎫	
Fingersucking	7½	55	25 ⎭	31.0
Sleep disturbance	8½	112	23 ⎫	
Fears	8½	122	22 ⎭	22.5
Negativism	9½	257	24 ⎫	
Sex	9½	151	23	
Speech	9½	82	23	
Temper tantrums	9½	198	21	21.5
"Nervousness"	9½	129	20	
"Timidity"	9½	51	18 ⎭	
"Excess phantasy"	10½	114	19	19.0
"Sensitiveness"	11½	70	21	21.0
School failure	12½	149	15 ⎫	
School truancy	12½	109	17 ⎭	16.0
Stealing	10½	129	30 ⎫	
Lying	10½	143	30 ⎭	30.0

wet.[19] In any given case enuresis may represent a protest, a regression, or other psychic mechanisms. Such instances, however, are related to enuresis occurring at some period of time after control has been achieved, rather than to enuresis continuing since infancy.[20]

[18] Luton Ackerson and Muriel Highlander, "The Relation of Enuresis to Intelligence, to Conduct and Personality Problems, and to Other Factors," *Psychological Clinic*, XVII (1928), 119–27; Margaret W. Gerard, "Enuresis: a Study in Etiology," *American Journal of Orthopsychiatry*, IX (1939). 45–58; Joseph J. Michaels, "The Incidence of Enuresis and Age of Cessation in One Hundred Delinquents and One Hundred Sibling Controls," *American Journal of Orthopsychiatry*, VIII (1938), 460–65; Joseph J. Michaels and Sylvia E. Goodman, "The Incidence of Enuresis and Age of Cessation in One Thousand Neuropsychiatric Patients: with a Discussion of the Relationship between Enuresis and Delinquency," *American Journal of Orthopsychiatry*, IX (1939), 59–71; Joseph J. Michaels, "Parallels between Persistent Enuresis and Delinquency in the Psychopathic Personality," *American Journal of Orthopsychiatry*, XI (1941), 260–74; George J. Mohr and Elinor H. Waterhouse, "Enuresis in Children," *American Journal of Diseases of Children*, XXXVII (1929), 1135–45; Curt Rosenow, "A Note on the Significance of Nocturnal Enuresis with Reference to Intelligence and Delinquency," *Journal of Delinquency*, V (1920), 41–55.

[19] An attempt was made to test this theory in one case by having the mother sleep with her enuretic child. The child continued wetting for weeks.

[20] Sigmund Freud, *Collected Papers* (London, 1933), Vol. III, p. 90.

Cleanliness and Care of Possessions

Body cleanliness, care of clothing and possessions, and general respect for property in the home may be considered under this heading. Data are available for only 11 cases. Of these, four are careless with clothing and possessions, and generally untidy in the home. The remaining seven are described as very neat and clean. The findings are consistent with the type of overprotection. The careless ones (Cases 1, 2, 11, and 13) are all in the indulged group; the careful (Cases 5, 6, 7, 17, and 20) all in the dominated group.

The meaning of the untidy habits of the indulged, according to Alfred Adler, is paraphrased by the remark, "Let the others take care of it." Why bother about putting things back where they belong, when there is always someone to do it for you? Why be careful about your clothes when there is always someone to buy new things? The explanation is consistent with the undisciplined behavior of the overindulged. Carelessness and uncleanliness are used also for purposes of revenge, as in Case 11, in which the patient, during quarrels, cut his clothing, destroyed dishes, and muddied the floor. The use of slovenliness as a mastery motif, in which the person gives express evidence of his presence in a room, by letting his clothes lie about and generally messing things up, is a well-known mechanism, especially among the overindulged. The paucity of data on these problems may be due to the fact that among children, especially boys, such problems may not be taken seriously.

Physical Examination

The group of 20 children was taller and heavier than comparable groups at the Institute. Of the 20, seven—35 percent—were more than 10 percent above normal weight for age and height (Baldwin-Wood tables), four—20 percent—above normal height for age. There was one patient more than 10 percent below normal weight; none 10 percent below normal height.[21] Of the seven above normal weight, only two were quite obese—Cases 7 and 20,

[21] Of 635 I.C.G. boys, 29 percent were above normal weight, 30 percent above normal height, to the extent of 10 percent or more. Forty percent were below normal weight; 30 percent below normal height, to the extent of 10 percent or more.

52 percent and 37.5 percent above normal weight, respectively, and diagnosed "Fröhlich syndrome." The remaining five ranged from 11 to 16 percent above normal weight. Of the 20, twelve were within 10 percent of normal weight, one below, five somewhat above weight, and two quite fat.

As a whole, the group is better nourished and taller than other patients. This is in keeping with theoretical expectations, in view of the high degree of maternal care. Since the group as a whole is well fed and less active in play and sports than other children, a large number of instances of obesity was anticipated. A special predilection for stuffing children as a form of maternity-neurosis is not apparent in our cases, even in the mothers of the two very obese children.[22]

In four instances (Cases 5, 7, 17, and 19), girdle obesity was noted, besides other symptoms of Fröhlich syndrome—gynecomastia, tapering fingers, velvety skin in four, high-pitched voice and hypopituitarism in three. Later studies of three of these patients in adult life revealed no evidence of impaired sexual development. The only one who received glandular treatment could not be traced for follow-up investigation.[23]

Twelve scars were noted in nine cases, chiefly superficial linear scars, the result of accidental injuries. Scars due to forceps injuries were noted in two instances (Cases 3 and 12); to operations in three instances (mastoid, Cases 1 and 9); appendectomy, Case 3; to an old fracture of the nose, one instance (Case 13); to a recent periostitis, one instance (Case 2); a perforated ear drum, one instance (Case 4). Evidence of tonsillectomy was noted in 10 cases.

The relation of these findings to maternal overprotection has

[22] In Bruch and Touraine's cases of 40 children, the obesity range was 25 to 120 percent overweight. On that basis only two of our overprotected group of 20 were obese. The mother-child relationship in their cases represented varying mixtures of overprotection and rejection. They believe that a factor in the obesity was traceable to maternal overvaluation of food—as a proof of love; but they regarded their material inadequate to offer an explanation of its psychogenesis. See footnote 13, above.

[23] In these cases, the possible influence of the maternal relationship on body configuration, or on the delay of puberty, other than that due to the obesity as such, has been conjectured. Our data allow no inference on this point. Reference is made to Karl A. Menninger, "Somatic Correlations with the Unconscious Repudiation of Femininity in Women," *Bulletin of the Menninger Clinic*, III (1939), 106–21.

been noted previously with reference to the frequency of tonsillectomy and the infrequency of fractures.[24] It is interesting that despite maternal vigilance, evidence of superficial injuries was fairly frequent.

Dental anomalies or caries were found in eight cases—crowding, irregular dentition or "overbite" in four; pyorrhea, caries in three. One patient was undergoing orthodontic treatment (Case 18). Dental treatment was recommended in six cases.

There are no data available that allow comparison on dental findings with other I.C.G. groups. The three examples of caries occurred in the children of mothers who were ignorant rather than neglectful.[25]

Visual errors of refraction were found in 11 cases, of which eight were mild. In two cases, mild strabismus also was present. Six patients wore glasses. Of these, errors of refraction were mild in three, and in one, glasses were given to correct an eyeblinking tic (Case 17). In one instance it was thought that the visual difficulty was actually a handicap in sports, like baseball (Case 12, vision 10/100 in either eye, corrected with glasses to 10/15). Otherwise the handicap was due to the danger of wearing spectacles rather than visual acuity.

In terms of overprotection it is evident that the recommendation of glasses for minor errors of refraction would be too readily accepted by the mothers of these patients, and utilized as reinforcement to protective care.

Since comparable studies of vision are not available for other I.C.G. cases, the inference that the frequency of errors of refraction in the group of overprotected children may be related to their special interest in reading cannot be substantiated.

By chance, one child had an acute otitis media at the time of his physical examination. He recovered without complications. One child revealed slightly impaired hearing (Case 20). The difficulty had apparently little to do with his behavior problems, and presented no handicap to school progress.

Evidence of old rickets, in no case severe, was found in seven

[24] See Chapter III, also Table I (page 50).
[25] The most serious case of carious teeth—Case 6—was definitely related to impaired general health.

cases—knock-knees, bowlegs, flaring ribs, Harrison's groove, flat chest, and lordosis.

No serious cardiac or respiratory pathology was found in the group. There was one instance of functional heart murmur, and one of acute bronchitis. Abdominal examinations were all negative.

In two cases organic treatment was clearly related to the improvement in social adjustment. In Case 6 medical treatment was instituted early because of general malnutrition, a mild to moderate error in refraction, and dental caries. There was a noticeable gain in strength and weight within a few months. With improvement in general health, there developed an increasing aggression and a willingness and ability to fight his own battles. There were a few interviews with the psychiatrist. In reviewing the case the improved health of the child was evidently an important factor in his favorable progress. Other factors in this case are considered in the follow-up study in Chapter X.

Case 15 is a better example, since in that case specific medical treatment was the most essential factor. When referred at 7 years and 5 months, one of the complaints was clumsiness. Because of slight incoördination, enlarged cervical glands, slight intention tremor of spread-out fingers, twitching of the eyelids, lips, and fingers during the Romberg test, it was thought advisable to consider congenital syphilis. There were no disturbances of the reflexes. The Wassermann test was positive. The mother was then examined and found to have syphilis. Both received treatment over a period of years until the Wassermann tests were repeatedly negative. There was definite improvement early in the case. By the seventh month of treatment the patient was much more self-reliant and independent. In the eighth month of treatment improved coördination was noted, and attributed to the antiluetic treatment. Correction of his "moderate" myopia apparently aided in his school progress. This advantage was short-lived, however, since schoolwork became increasingly difficult for him because of his inadequate intelligence.

Although numerous factors were involved in the improvement of this patient, it was inferred that the improvement in health was a very definite factor. The psychological value of improvement due to specific medical therapy, especially in relation to psychiatrist and mother, is considered in the follow-up study of this case in Chapter IX.

There were two other cases in which the organic factor had a very important effect as a strong reinforcing agent in the overprotection. In Case 7, the diagnosis of Fröhlich syndrome and the apparently mistaken conclusion that it was due to a pituitary tumor strengthened considerably the previous overprotecting behavior. In Case 19, maternal overprotection was enhanced by an illness, probably encephalitis, which caused a right spastic hemiplegia when the patient was nine years old. There was distinct reduction of movement in the right hand and some disability in walking, although the patient was able to manage very well with crutches. The social effect of the illness was in the direction of infantile dependency.

In a few instances (Cases 10, 11, 14, and 15) the physical examination served to overcome apprehension. This particular problem was considered part of the physical examiner's task, and much time was spent with the mother to overcome apprehension about illness until reassurance on this point was well determined. In one case (14) there was a withdrawal of interest in the whole study after this point. It had to be revived by stressing the other aspects of the case.

The influence of the maternal attitude on physical development may be derived from data presented in this and in Chapters III and IV. Maternal overprotection in the cases presented appears to be related directly to increased breast feeding, to bladder control, to frequency of tonsillectomy, to improved nutrition, probably, to obesity. It may be related indirectly to corrections of errors of visual refraction, though, as in the frequency of tonsillectomies, such corrections may be related to greater attention to physical health and acceptance of medical advice.

BEHAVIOR DURING THE PHYSICAL EXAMINATION

During the physical study, numerous manifestations of personality difficulties were revealed. Some of these were related directly to the overprotective relationship. An eight-year-old (Case 1) refused to enter the examining room. He held on to his mother's skirt and cried, while she chided him for being such a baby. After much coaxing, he entered the room and gagged, trying hard, although unsuccessfully, to vomit. He allowed the examination after he was promised a trip to the country.

Dependency on the mother, which was noted as a major difficulty in this case, was manifested clearly during the physical examination.

Similarly, an 11-year-old boy (Case 7) at first refused to enter the room without his mother. Later he consented, when it was agreed that she would stay in the adjoining room. During the examination, each made several trips to the other. Difficulty of the same type was revealed also in Case 14.

In eight cases (3, 4, 5, 10, 15, 17, 18, and 20) evidence of anxiety during the examination was revealed in the form of crying or other expression of sensitivity at exposure of the body or the genitals. For example, a 13-year-old-boy (Case 17) required a good bit of coaxing before he would remove his clothes. When he was undressed, except for his underwear, he asked several times if that too was really necessary. Otherwise he was pleasant and coöperative.

The notations made of patients' behavior during the physical examination were part of the routine procedure. No special attention was directed to the manifestations of maternal overprotection or other relationship studies. If this had been done, much more pertinent observations would have been made and, possibly, certain typical behavior syndromes would have been established. Consider the behavior during the examination of a 15-year-old adolescent (Case 12). He protested against the examiner's taking notes. He wanted nothing about him written down. He was very ambitious to make the highest possible scores on physical tests. He was not satisfied with his performance on the dynamometer. He insisted on trying it over, again and again. He asked also to repeat the "steadiness test." He said, "Don't forget, we were laughing. That affects the test, doesn't it?" In the "one-minute Romberg test" he opened his eyes after ten seconds. He tried it again but could not keep his eyes closed longer than 15 seconds. He was quite talkative throughout the study, showing off his knowledge and "lecturing" the examiner.

During the physical examination he demonstrated his suspicious attitudes: protest against taking notes, persistence in opening his eyes during the Romberg test, which may be questioned; his strongly competitive behavior—persistence in repetition of tests; his anxiety as revealed in the increased aggression—talking throughout the examination; and his attempt to remain in the dominating role—inability to "submit" to the ordinary procedure of the physical examination, and an attempt to "take charge" by lecturing to the examiner.

Personality problems are revealed with special facility during the physical examination. There are various psychological reasons for this fact. Nakedness, no doubt, is a factor.[26] Notations of "behavior" concerned difficulties in 14 of the 20 cases. It was possible, nevertheless, to complete the examination in every case.

Summary

The behavior of the indulged overprotected children was featured by disobedience, impudence, tantrums, excessive demands, and varying degrees of tyrannical behavior. The characteristics described were thought to represent accelerated growth of the aggressive components of the personality, and related directly to maternal indulgence. Limitations in the production of extreme tyrannical and possessive behavior at home was explained by varying degrees of parental modification, and external factors.

Most of the indulged overprotected children presented no special problems in school adjustment. This discrepancy between behavior at home and at school was explained by an exceptional and disciplinary attitude towards schoolwork on the part of the mothers; by satisfactions in the classroom related to high intelligence, verbal skill, and help through coaching on the part of the children; also, possibly, to their fear of the school group and a gratification in playing an obedient role. In any event, the adjustment of

[26] David M. Levy, "A Method of Integrating Physical and Psychiatric Examination," *American Journal of Psychiatry*, IX (1929), 121–94.

highly indulged children to classroom discipline indicates a high degree of flexibility in their personalities. When difficulties in classroom behavior occurred, they were consistent with the type of difficulty manifested at home.

Three boys who were disciplinary problems in the classroom were less intelligent than the others and their mothers less concerned about schoolwork.

In contrast with the indulged group, the dominated group responded well to the requirements of classroom behavior in every instance, regardless of I.Q. or of school success.

In all instances but one, difficulties in making friendships with other children occurred. The aggressive children showed, with one exception, "domination" or egocentric difficulties, that is, bossy, selfish, show-off, or cocky behavior. The submissive children showed in all cases but one timidity and withdrawal. There was a remarkable similarity of all the children's difficulty in relationship with their mothers and other children.

Successful adjustment of the indulged overprotected child to camp, as to school, would indicate that his difficulty with playmates could be improved, despite maternal overprotection, if opportunity were afforded for early social experience with children. Difficulties in making friendships were attributed to paucity of contact with children in the preschool age and lack of skill in play and sports, besides the problems inherent in the mother-child relationship. Follow-up studies indicated improvement in this regard during adolescence.

Some form of overt sexual behavior in childhood was noted in six instances, all in the indulged group. No problem in sex abnormality was present. The entire group showed nothing unusual in the frequency or form of masturbation.

Despite the very close attachment, including six cases in which children slept with their mothers long past infancy, follow-up studies into late adolescence or adult life failed to reveal an instance of sex abnormality. The theoretical aspect of this finding was discussed and the inference drawn that in maternal indulgent overprotection, the development of heterosexual behavior was hastened rather than delayed, because of lessened inhibitions.

The main outside interest of the overprotected group consisted in reading. There was a notable lack of interest in sports.

Feeding problems occurred in 12 of the 20 cases. The usual variety was manifested; in the form of bad table manners, refusal to eat on schedule, insistence on being fed or coaxed, finickiness, and refusal to eat certain foods. There was no instance of inappetence. Practically all the indulged overprotected were included in this group. The problems were consistent with maternal indulgence in regard to the feeding.

Nothing unusual was found in regard to sleeping difficulties. Problems related to sleep were in the form of refusal to go to bed, on time or without mother's company. Seven of the eight children who manifested such behavior were in the indulged overprotected group.

No problems in soiling occurred. There were but two cases of enuresis. The number was much less frequent than in other Institute cases. This difference was explained by the greater care exerted by overprotecting mothers. The assumption that the vast majority of problems in enuresis are originally due to neglect in training was supported by special data.

Information regarding cleanliness and care of possessions was available for 11 cases. The four who were very careless in this regard were all in the indulged group. Those noted as neat and careful were all in the dominated group.

Physical examinations revealed that the group of 20 overprotected children was taller and heavier than other I.C.G. groups, in keeping with the high degree of maternal care. Of the group, two only may be regarded as quite obese.

Errors of refraction were found in 11 cases. The inference that this relatively large number may have been due to excessive reading could not be determined, through lack of comparable data.

Treatment of organic difficulties seemed clearly related to improvement of social adjustment in two cases. In two others, organic factors were apparently reinforcing to the maternal overprotection. In three cases, findings during the physical examination served to overcome maternal apprehension. It was followed in one case by withdrawal of interest in the entire study.

In the cases presented, maternal overprotection appeared to be related directly to increased breast feeding, early bladder control, frequency of tonsillectomy, good nutrition, and probably obesity. It appeared to be related, indirectly, to correction of errors of visual refraction.

Manifestations of personality difficulties were revealed during the physical examination in 14 of the 20 cases. They were seen chiefly in the form of dependency on the mother, sensitivity, shyness, and bids for the examiner's attention.

IX. TREATMENT, PROGNOSIS, PSYCHOPATHOLOGY

THE METHODS of treatment derive logically from the methods of investigation employed. Direct efforts were made to correct physical disease or defect, psychic disturbance, educational or environmental handicap. In so far as the problems of the child were activated or produced by difficulties in the parents or in others, stress in therapy was placed wherever the indication for it appeared. The procedures employed for the overprotected children may be summarized under the following general principles of treatment.

Psychotherapy.—With the mother, this consisted in an attempt to determine the dynamics and give insight into her overprotecting attitude and the problems it created in the child. She was shown the value of releasing the child from her infantilizing influence.

With the father, an attempt was made to show him the importance of more active interest in the family life, of developing a friendly relationship with his child, and of utilizing his authority as a father.

With the patient, a kind of insight therapy was used to demonstrate to the child his mechanisms of infantile dependency and tyranny, and the importance of playing a more responsible role.

Environmental or manipulative therapy was used to make mother and child more independent of each other.

With the mother, attempts were made to widen the scope of the mother's interests, for example, by entering activities of settlement houses, developing special abilities, joining bridge clubs, forming friendships. These maneuvers were designed to overcome complete centralization of activity on the child, and develop a saner way of life.

With the father, efforts were directed to socialize the relationship between husband and wife, to encourage them to go out together on trips, take vacations together; generally to correct their loss of a previous social relationship and to enable them to have experience together as husband and wife rather than as parents. Mutual activities of father and child were encouraged.

With the patient, attempts were made to separate the child from the mother for varying periods of time, as at camps or boarding school. Outings with the social worker were used to dilute the relationship with the mother through forming a social relationship with another grown-up. Group activities for the patient were encouraged in order to favor social contact with other boys. In general, the object of these maneuvers was to break up the mother-child monopoly, increase the social contacts of the patient, make him less dependent on the maternal relationship and more responsive to social attitudes outside the home.

Educational Therapy.—Under this heading may be included various suggestions and demonstrations in the handling of the patient, chiefly by the social worker. Mothers were shown, for example, how, in specific situations, they did not have to surrender to the child's demands, how they could ignore attention-getting behavior, encourage self-help, and the like.

Case studies show varying patterns of these methods. In one case psychotherapy was stressed to a high degree; in another case, hardly utilized. In most cases various attempts were made to solve marital difficulties by psychotherapeutic methods. In some, however, this problem was left untouched. Essentially the therapeutic problem consisted in an effort to change the mother's overprotecting attitude and by every available resource to develop greater independence within the mother-child relationship.

Psychotherapy of Patients

Direct psychotherapy of the patients of the overprotected group shows a wide range in the number of sessions—from one to 39. Of the 19 patients treated, ten had 5 interviews or less; three, 6 to 10 interviews; two, 11 to 20 interviews; the remaining, 23, 26, 27, and 39 interviews, respectively. It made little difference how many interviews were held or what variations in method were employed by the staff. The results were uniformly unsuccessful.

In general, the methods employed consisted of interviews for the purpose of, first, giving the patient insight into the overprotective relationship, attempting to demonstrate how the problems of the patient were bound up in it; second, showing the importance of developing responsible and independent behavior, encouraging the patient in that direction; third, attempting in this connection to get the patient's coöperation for the "environmental therapy," for example, camp placement, boarding school and the like.

With the indulgent overprotected group it seemed easy to attain a relationship that allowed for chatty conversation, discussion of the events of the day, even an elaboration by the patient of methods used to tease the parents and to get his own way. However, as soon as the attempt was made to have the patient face the problem clearly as to his own conduct, his attempt to hold on to the mother, to dominate by temper tantrums, his insolence at home and the like, there followed various denials, evasions, attempts to change the subject, then lateness in arriving—one-half to three-quarters of an hour late—and finally refusals to come at all. This experience was shared by Fellows and staff members alike. It was described in various ways, for example: "patient is all right in talking about day to day events but he dodges attempts to get at any of his problems"; of another: "efforts at developing insight into his dependent attitude and tyranny failed," "he prevented any intrusion into his problems"; of another: "in avoiding any conversation about his difficulties he used mainly distracting conversation"; of another: "he absolutely refuses to discuss anything remotely bearing on his difficulties." In two instances a method of free association was tried, as in psychoanalysis. It was given up quickly as futile. Various indirect methods were also tried. One psychiatrist especially formulated a theoretical case, showing the whole development of the patient's problems, referring it to a hypothetical person. The patient seemed very interested and enthusiastic. However, as soon as it was put in terms of the patient's own behavior, the uniform series of evasions and finally termination of treatment occurred. Attempts also to throw the responsibility for keeping the appointment on the patient failed. Such permission was readily taken advantage of, and cancellations of appointments followed.

In the patients classified under dominating overprotection, coming late and failure to keep appointments followed in the same way. For these cases the psychiatrists noted chiefly the patient's lack of enthusiasm, of responsibility, of any interest in getting into the problem.

A reason for the uniform failure might be attributed to the fact that the therapists were mostly psychiatrists—Fellows—in their first year of training at the Institute. However, when older psychiatrists took over the treatment in three cases, the results were also unsuccessful. The problem was recognized chiefly as a difficulty in making the child see a problem. Actually the child had no problem as far as he was concerned—except, from the psychiatrist's point of view, of making the problem more severe. For the indulged child wanted more indulgence. The dominated child, if anything, wanted to retain his infantile state.

If the psychotherapeutic method used is to be classified, it could be called an insight therapy of the Adlerian type—that is, a method in which the problem was explained to the child in terms of conscious functioning of the personality along the lines of ego domination; although there was no special allegiance to the Adlerian school. The dominating behavior, for example, was explained chiefly as an attempt to continue the early infantile state, resulting in infantile tyranny of the household, and attempting to enslave the mother. Dependent behavior was explained chiefly in terms of perpetuating infantile helplessness, lack of courage in growing up, in assuming responsibility, and the like. In regard to relationships with other children, the difficulties of the indulged were attributed to their refusal to play any position but Number One, resulting in inability to really enter a relationship. In the dominated group, the difficulty was attributed to fear of self-assertion, because of the dependent infantile role.

It seems clear that the problem in therapy had little to do with the particular variety of interpretation used. They seemed valid enough, as far as they went. Most likely a Freudian analyst, also as any "dynamic" psychiatrist, would have begun in similar fashion, namely, interpretation in terms of conscious ego-functioning.

A clue to the difficulty is seen in the pattern of late-comings, refusals, cancellations of appointments, which occurred in almost every case, and in the fact that cases failed, improved, or were "apparently" cured, regardless of failure in psychotherapy.

In recognition of the weakness of their roles as therapists, in these cases, several psychiatrists recognized a similarity in their own and the father's relationship to the patient. Their authority with the patient was as slim as the father's. Several, therefore, decided to change from insight therapy into a type of "supportive" therapy; that is, to play the role of father. In this role they stopped their previously unsuccessful efforts of "making the patient see the problems of his own behavior," accepted the patient's conversation without interpretation, but encouraged, praised, and admonished. They tried to make the patient feel their interest in his success, their personal satisfaction in his display of independence, their alliance with him as older friend and mentor. But as substitute fathers they suffered the same lot as the real ones; and, in so far as paternal prestige is built up by the mother, they had little coöperation. It can be seen that the discipline of keeping appointments really depended on the mothers. They were unable or unwilling to coöperate, and, in some cases, themselves broke the child's appointments.

PSYCHOTHERAPY OF FATHERS

Psychotherapy of the patient went on simultaneously with psychotherapy of the parents. The need to strengthen the role of the father, or secure his coöperation, was perceived and made an essential part of the first plan of treatment, evolved after coördinating the usual investigations from psychologist, social worker, and psychiatrist. This task was relegated to the social worker, chiefly because the father had to be seen at odd hours, and often outside the office—a cultural datum that has had a significant influence on the choice of therapist and of therapy.

In four cases the social worker's therapy with the father was aided by interviews with the psychiatrist. Of the 19 treated cases, there were no interviews with the father in three. Of the remaining 16, twelve were seen by a social worker for one to eight interviews—average four. Psychiatrists had interviews with eight fathers; one or two interviews respectively in all instances but one. These small number of contacts had, however, distinct effects in some cases.

The beneficial effect of but one interview is seen in Case 1. The father, who had previously had little or nothing to do with the patient, responded quickly to the psychiatrist's statements about the necessity of paternal influence and the danger of an exclusive maternal relationship. He became friendlier with his son, helped him with a stamp collection, went places with him, assumed generally more responsible paternal behavior—in fact, aroused his wife's jealousy. Another (Case 10), as a result definitely of interviews with the social worker, since previously he had played no paternal role at all, became friendlier with his son, assumed much more responsibility for disciplining him, and acquired in reality the status of a father. A third (Case 15), also a father who had previously played no paternal role, developed a real relationship with his son, taught him carpentry, aided him in his school work. He had five interviews with the social worker.

Besides these three successes in changing a paternal relationship, a fourth should be mentioned, although of a different sort. It was the case of a stepfather, the one harsh father in the group—Case 15. As a result of interviews with the social worker, he became less harsh with his son, and encouraged his development of independent behavior.

Interviews with 12 fathers had no effect or, at best, doubtful results. However, in some, no therapeutic effort was made, except to get their coöperation. Where efforts failed the reason seems clear in some instances. The derogatory attitude of the son toward the father was too severe, for example, in Case 12. In that instance, the father took a night job to avoid the family difficulty. The same applies to Case 5, in which efforts of the father to enter into a relationship with his son were defeated by his wife. In several instances the father added to the maternal indulgence—Cases 2 and 3, for example. In Case 4, there were too many indulgent relatives to give the father a chance to effect a change. In one case everything hinged on the father's coöperation—Case 8. He had strong revengeful feelings toward his wife, appeared coöperative at first, but finally canceled all appointments, probably when the problem of his sexual difficulty in marriage was considered.

PSYCHOTHERAPY OF MOTHERS

Psychotherapy of the mother had as its object insight into the overprotective process, especially her own contribution to the problems of the child. It aimed also at release of the mother's feelings, so as to enable her to recognize and tolerate especially feelings of hostility arising out of her relationships, and if possible to resolve them. Problems of sexual maladjustment were also dealt with. Although definite objectives were present in the mind of the therapist, the mother was not held to any particular area, but encouraged to speak freely as she wished. In three cases psychoanalysis was recommended, although efforts to bring it about failed. Psychotherapy was left largely to the social worker in all but one of the treated cases. The range of interviews was 1 to 41.

In some cases it was decided to make the relationship of the social worker to the mother "largely manipulative"; in others the main reliance was on changing the mother's attitude. In cases where improvement in the mother's relationship to the boy in terms of giving more freedom and the like occurred, it was decided, nevertheless, that there was no real change in the maternal attitude. Hence psychotherapy by the social worker, or psychiatrist, or both, followed. For example, in Case 17, improvement in the patient was as follows: allowed to go on errands alone, diminution in temper tantrums, making friendships with boys, asks to help the younger children, improvement of tics. However, the improvement did not continue satisfactorily because, it was thought, the "mother refused to yield to the boy's growth in independence." She was holding him back. A year after the date of referral the psychiatrist took over. He tried to show the mother the various influences brought to bear on her overprotecting attitude, including her early privations, her dissatisfactions in marriage, her sexual maladjustment. Thereafter she refused to return to the Institute.

The typical experience in the treatment of mothers was some modification of the mother-child relationship in response to advice and environmental change, and little or no response to direct psychotherapy. This pattern occurred in 11 of the 19 treated cases (2, 4, 5, 6, 8, 9, 11, 12, 14, 15, and 17). Negative response to all forms of therapy—advice, "manipulation," psychotherapy—occurred in but two cases (10 and 13). Favorable response to all forms of therapy occurred in three cases (1, 3, and 20). Advice and manipulative methods were used as practically the entire therapy in one case (19); psychotherapy exclusively in two (16 and 18).

Usually psychotherapy, although employed from the start, was utilized to further the progress made by other methods. In so far as mothers enabled their children to become more independent, to go places alone, or to have an experience at camp, they became less apprehensive. After a measure of success was obtained, however, they seemed to struggle against further diminution of the protective and dominating relationship. They developed on the whole friendly relationships with the social worker and psychiatrist, were able to express feelings of bitterness and hostility towards husbands, even towards their sons. Some came to rely on the Institute for help in getting school placement for their children, medical service, and the like. Whenever their own contribution to the problem was considered, whenever an attempt was made to have them recognize their own dominating, infantilizing, sometimes "incestuous" relationship with the child, their resistances grew rapidly. Regardless of the outcome of the case, in terms of modification of the behavior of the child, mothers never accepted the role of patient in a single instance, nor changed fundamentally toward the child.

In this respect they behaved exactly like their children, refusing to consider themselves seriously as a problem.

In one case a mother wanted to engage the efforts of the social worker in the task of discharging a school teacher for failure to recognize the brilliance of her son. When the worker refused, she broke all appointments. Another mother was regarded as too complacent in her role as mother and too satisfied with her son to coöperate for treatment. Unable to budge her from this position, the social worker called on the psychiatrist for aid. He interviewed the mother, emphasized strongly the boy's problem and the mother's contribution to it, without avail.

In attempting to explain the failure of psychotherapy in these cases, certain conjectures seem plausible. When the need for treatment was powerful, as in those instances in which the child's oppression made life miserable for the family, mothers were quite ready to utilize definite suggestions or specific advice. When partial relief was secured, the powerful maternal needs were again ascendant. Actually the mothers never asked for "therapy." They wanted to reëstablish the old mother-infant relationship. They wanted the workers to aid in disciplining the child, and in making him obey, so that they could be comfortable in their overprotective relationship. Not one mother asked the worker to enable her son to be free of her, or herself to be saved from her indulging or dominating tendencies. In one instance a mother said to a woman psychiatrist who had her son under treatment, "I let him come, even though I know he likes you." Another said of her child, "I want to keep him this way until he is 30 or 35." These examples illustrate the mothers' struggle to keep their children bound only to them, and in the status of a child, in perpetuity.

Another problem concerns the strong feelings of guilt engendered in the mother when she was able to release feelings of hostility toward the child. Numerous complaints about how badly they were treated, and how much they endured, were poured out early in the interviews. Hostile feelings toward the child came later. Workers handled such feelings, however, with little skill. They reassured the mothers, to be sure, but somehow could not utilize this most important phase of the treatment—the phase in which they had the most opportunity, if ever, to make possible a change of attitude. Once hostile feelings were expressed, they were never mobilized, elaborated, repeated, developed into fullness of expression. They appeared as a single episode and then vanished. Years later, in follow-up interviews, the mothers denied emphatically that they had ever expressed hostile feelings toward their children.

In reviewing these records it is easy, in retrospect, to realize that, aside from the skill involved in the course of treatment, the psychiatrists had far too little respect for the dimensions of the problem in the psychotherapy of overprotecting mothers. It seems clear that once the worker took the role of counsellor and educator, she lost the role strictly of therapist. The worker was unable to relate the mother to herself in this different relationship. Now one can discern the proper orientation of the case for psychotherapy. Whoever is to play the role of therapist in these cases must start from scratch, acquaint the mother with the purpose of treatment, explain the nature of the problem, the difficulty of the task, and her role as patient. Her refusal to accept this role should be reason adequate to forestall direct psychotherapy.

Environmental and Educational Therapy

We have now to consider those endeavors on behalf of the patient classified as educational and environmental or manipulative. Under the former are included giving of advice and information to parents or patient, demonstrating methods of handling, use of books, and tutoring aids. Under environmental aids are included use of camps, boarding schools and social contacts for patient; use of clubs, vacations and other outside interests for parents.

In every case but one (Case 5) one or both of these methods were attempted. The most direct response in treatment also appeared to be related to such handling.

A number of patterns would show typically a favorable change, the improvement maintained for a long period of time, but without that growth in independence anticipated by the staff. Thereupon an attempt at intensive psychotherapy would ensue.

For example, in Case 1, trips with the patient, a camp experience, and demonstrations to the mother of handling the patient, with advice to ignore his excessive demands, to stop her threats and to encourage his independence, achieved results within three months. She had changed her method of coaxing and nagging to definite directions. The son's refusal to eat certain foods was met with indifference. She saw him fight with another boy and did not interfere. His various attempts to browbeat her were without avail. By the fourth month of treatment the mother "took the chance of her life" and let him go on an errand with another boy. The improvement continued, but came to a halt after about eight months of treatment. Thereafter the change was very slow and the mother was rather discouraged.

Other than psychotherapy, the work with the patient was almost entirely "manipulative." It consisted of trips, arranging contacts with other boys, dancing classes, play groups, boys' clubs, the use of camps and sometimes boarding school. Methods were used to raise a sense of responsibility in the patient by having him chosen to be a class monitor, to tutor the younger brothers, and the like. The purpose of such activities was to enable the patient to make contact with others, to develop interests of his own, and to be separated for long intervals of time from the overprotecting mother. As a method of solving the problem of the mother-child monopoly it utilized situations that would presumably enable the child to "grow away from" the infantile relationship. It served another function—to relieve the mother from the burdens of the relationship, benefit the marriage by removing a contentious object, and improve the chances of psychotherapy. In a number of cases it required a great deal of work with both mother and child to make separation possible, even for a two-weeks' stay at camp. The response to such maneuvers was, however, generally favorable. Some mothers regarded the period when the patient was absent at camp as a remarkable relief, as a "second honeymoon." As a method of enabling the mother and father to resume the happier relationship existing before the patient was born, it had definite effect. In such a period one mother realized fully how she had pushed her husband away, and how through her maternal activities she had changed her husband from a gay person to a worried old man. Improvements based on separation were short-lived, however. Remissions followed, but on the whole there was definite evidence of value.

Similar methods employed with the mother had as their object the development of interests outside the home and an improved social relationship with the husband. Mothers were encouraged to play golf, bridge, take music lessons, enter into settlement house activities, do volunteer work in agencies for children, read books, and join classes in English and domestic science. They were encouraged when possible to get help in the care of the children, to attend the movies, and take up dancing again with their husbands. These methods also were generally beneficial. They aided in overcoming the exclusive care and devotion to the child. Cases in which the highest degree of improvement occurred show special utilization of "manipulative" therapy in the form of outside interests for the mother and specific advice in the handling of the child.

"Advice and demonstration" as a therapeutic procedure with mothers consisted in helping them to ignore attention-getting behavior; in changing coaxing and nagging into direct commands; in breaking up the pattern of infantilizing care by direct refusals; and in encouraging the child to become more responsible and independent. Specifically, mothers stopped dressing the child, waiting on him at table, coaxing, babying, explaining everything, shining his shoes. They refused to argue every point and ignored tantrums. They stopped complaining about what a headache the child gave them. They allowed the child to make friends of his own, to go on errands, to go to school alone. Mothers were encouraged also to speak sharply to the child and to use methods of punishment of their own devising. They were encouraged also to bring the father into the picture more and more, not only in a friendly, but also in an authoritative, relationship.

MEDICAL TREATMENT

In so far as any physical handicap stimulates overprotection its correction aids in overcoming overprotection. However, in no case in this series can physical conditions be regarded *per se* as the cause of overprotection, although they may have reinforced it. Their correction may have been of value in modifying this apprehension, and in some cases, apparently, influencing the overprotective relationship. The effect of organic treatment has been considered in the section on "Physical Examination" in Chapter VIII. In two cases (6 and 15), it was an important, probably the most important modifying factor. In a third case also it had definite general therapeutic value (Case 9).

PSYCHOANALYSIS

Observations on the difficulty of psychotherapy with children would apply equally to psychoanalysis of mothers. In three instances where efforts were made to persuade mothers to get psychoanalytic treatment, there were firm refusals. It would be most valuable to have psychoanalytic studies of mothers primarily overprotective. The cases cited in the literature all deal with compensatory forms. Further, in these cases no effort was made to study the extent of the overprotection, its entire field of operation. An attempt to collect case records or summaries of psychoanalysis of pure overprotection was unsuccessful.[1]

GENERAL COMMENTS

A distinct environmental change had a telling effect in a number of cases. Patients also spoke in retrospect about the value of separation from their mothers. Next in importance was specific advice and actual demonstration in the home. Least valuable was psychotherapy.

In evaluating the therapeutic processes, first to be noted is the importance of using methods of separating mother and child and making possible every opportunity for social contacts outside the family for each of them. Second, the increase of the father's prestige in the family has been neglected. The modification in cases where

---

[1] For this purpose, four psychoanalysts, all males, who had 20 or more years of experience in the field, were seen. They were asked to give a rough estimate of the following items: percentage of their women patients, of married women, of mothers, and of mothers whose overprotection was at least consistent with strong maternal tendencies since childhood. The percentages of female patients ran from 30 to 46 percent. The majority were single—percentage range of married, 16 to 25 percent. Of the married patients, the majority had no children—percentage of married women with children 8 to 25 percent. Two of the four analysts reported that they had never analyzed one case of maternal overprotection in a naturally maternal woman. The others reported one each. The estimates given indicate that in the combined practice of four very experienced analysts there were relatively few mothers of any variety.

it was used is very revealing. Third, the most convincing proof to the mother that her methods were wrong were the demonstrations in the home showing definitely that the child responded to other forms of management. Fourth, that psychotherapy has proven useless may mean it functions poorly in such cases or that it was used poorly. From the material examined it would appear very discouraging in the case of the child—less discouraging in the case of the mother. For the latter it would appear necessary first of all to convince the mother that she is a patient, that she has made maternity into a disease, that she has symptoms of it as clearly as organic symptoms, and that there is a possibility of modifying her relationship. The importance for the child must be emphasized, and it must be shown how the relationship to the child has weakened the entire marriage. It must be represented that the treatment is a difficult one and will take time. It appears obvious to conclude that unless direct psychotherapy of the mother is regarded as a serious and intensive undertaking, it would be preferable to rely entirely on other methods.

OUTCOME

At the I.C.G. a record of the results, or the assumed results, of treatment was a routine procedure. When treatment was terminated an estimate of the patient's adjustment was classified under the rubric of "satisfactorily adjusted," "partially adjusted," or "unimproved." Apparently to avoid the assumption that the terms used represented of necessity the results of treatment, they were designated as "closing status." Nineteen of the 20 overprotected cases were under treatment. The closing status was "satisfactorily" —or "successfully"—adjusted in two—11 percent; partially adjusted in nine—47 percent; unimproved in eight—42 percent. 290 I.C.G. "treatment" cases taken seriatim and so classified showed 75 successfully adjusted—26 percent; 150 partially adjusted—53 percent; 61 unimproved—21 percent. The overprotected cases in this series showed a lower adjustment score than the larger group.

In follow-up investigations of 197 of the original group of 290, seen one-half to two and a half years after the close of treatment, the classifications were, in percentage, 30 successfully adjusted, 50 partial, and 20 unimproved.[2] The same method of classification applied to the latest follow-up studies of the 19 treated cases of our overprotected group—9 to 12 years after referral—revealed two cases or 11 percent successfully adjusted, fifteen or 77 percent partial, two or 11 percent unimproved. The results indicate a high degree of improvement, as compared with the larger group. In 15 of the 19 cases, follow-up ratings are available also for a period of one to two years following the closing status. The shorter period is more closely comparable with the group of 197. It shows also a higher degree of improvement—58 percent, partially and successfully adjusted.

An explanation of the high degree of improvement cannot, at this stage, represent much more than an attempt to evaluate some of the variables in the life histories of these patients.

In regard to therapy, it is reasonable to assume that all the efforts expended in developing within the patient satisfactions that curtailed the dependency relationship might have a cumulative effect. It was noted in the follow-up studies that once a gain towards independent activity was achieved, the child fought for it, combating the mother's infantilizing tendencies—see especially Case 4. This situation occurs very frequently in family life, in which the boy, especially, tries to get not only prerogatives, but also responsibilities, beyond his age. Given a start, the overprotected patient tried to hold his gains and fight for further release from the maternal relationship. When the father entered the picture, the patient had an ally in this battle. In general, it appears that despite any fundamental change in attitude, mothers were willing to yield ground, especially when they felt a lessened burden in the relationship due to the child's lessened dependency. Generally, the improvement appeared to be a quantitative change in the area of overprotection. The mother surrendered various infantilizing activities, allowed her son a greater measure of freedom, although she retained the same attitude to the end. Even when patients married or were engaged, the same overprotective attitude pre-

[2] Of 1,053 treatment cases at the I.C.G., closed in the years 1927–32, similar percentages were found—23 satisfactorily adjusted, 53 partially adjusted, and 24 unimproved. Lawson G. Lowrey and Geddes Smith, *The Institute for Child Guidance 1927–1933* (New York, 1933), p. 56.

vailed. Mothers tried to control their sons' choice in marriage, to "spy" on every movement, and maintain the old maternal functions.

The process of maturation apparently serves in itself as an opposing force to the overprotection, reinforced as it is by cultural norms. In one of the most successful cases in the series (Case 20), the picture as presented seems quite within the normal range. When her boy was 15, the mother recognized clearly a change in his behavior. He no longer confided in her. He made social contacts on his own without telling her all the details. She regretted losing the old close and confiding relationship, but accepted the change. She did not want her son tied to her, she said. She never expected to learn "any of his dark secrets," yet she missed his companionship. The boy himself was aware of his growing independence. The adolescent picture presented by him is a frequent one. Mothers fought against it, even competing with girl friends. One of the patients, Case 15 for example, refused to let his mother have social contact with his girl, knowing that she would break up the relationship. Another had to contend with his mother in order to marry, and compromised only by postponing the wedding (Case 5). Another (Case 13) married despite the mother's objections. She then attempted to absorb the new family. After the death of her son, she played the complete maternal role to her grandchild. On the other hand, in one case (2), the mother had a special interest in her daughter-in-law as a protection against the demands of her son.

That improvement in development of the patient occurred despite maternal attitude is attested also by the latest follow-up studies. At that time the range of ages in the 19 treated cases was 14 to 28 years—age range at referral was 4 to 16, median age 10. A change in the maternal overprotective attitude was seen probably in one case (18).[3] Further, the maternal attitude toward the treatment was unfavorable in a therapeutic sense in all but one instance (Case 20). In retrospect, after 10 to 12 years, mothers regarded the treatment as unnecessary, because the child was not really a problem —Cases 1 and 3, for example; they were tricked into referring the

[3] In Case 15, the mother died six years after the case was closed.

child—Case 17; the treatment was of no value—as in Case 2; they regretted or denied ever expressing hostile feelings towards their sons—Case 11 is an example; the Institute would not do what she wanted them to, namely threaten her son—Case 12. Nevertheless, the attitude towards the workers was friendly in all but a few cases, and the service of the Institute considered valuable for aid in getting school placement or camps or medical treatment—for example Case 9. Even when the maternal attitude towards the Institute was friendly, it was never on the basis that a change in maternal attitude had been effected.

In the latest follow-up studies, definitely improved relationship of son and father was seen in 11 cases. Patients had little to say in explanation, except that they understood things better, or it just happened gradually. One patient was more definite than the others (Case 11). The change started, he said, when he was 15 or 16 years old. He worked with his father in the store and learned what it meant to earn money and support a family. His respect for the father grew after that. The change that occurred in relation to the father was in the form of a friendlier feeling, and more particularly, greater respect. This finding is typical of the growth of father-son relationship in normal family life. It is interesting that it occurs also in the families of the overprotected. The relationship aids in overcoming dependencies on the mother through an increasing identification with the father in adolescence and young manhood.

Mention has been made of the favorable growth in heterosexual interests. In the 19 follow-up studies, of 18 boys all but three were interested in and going out with girls. Two had been married, four were engaged, four went with a special girl of their choice. The one female patient in the series had boy friends. Of the three boys who had no companionship with girls, two were each age 16. The other, age 22 years, was handicapped by infantile paralysis (Case 19).

We may conclude that, as a whole, the group shows a normal growth in heterosexual interest and activity.[4]

Among the problems of the overprotected, difficulty in making friendships occurred in all but one instance (see Chapter VIII).

[4] Note also the section on "Sexual Problems" in Chapter VIII.

It was noted also that there was evidence of some improvement in the early follow-up studies. An explanation for this favorable change was given in the preceding chapter. The latest follow-up studies show further improvement. Only one of the 19 had no friends of his own age and sex (Case 14). Of the others, seven had a number of friends although no intimate friendships. Nine had friends and one or more intimate, and two had one or two close friends, although no other friendships. Of those with a number of friends of their own sex—four or more—only one had special difficulties in the relationship (Case 9). This was due to an overly critical attitude, featured by "telling the truth," a mechanism explained in the case abstract as a possible modification of the old dominating tendencies. In another case, the patient was well liked, although his friends, consistent with his mental age, were all younger than he.

Four members of the series, all in the indulged overprotected group, revealed special talents in social relationship. Of these, three were considered very entertaining, witty, the "life of the party," "good mixers" (Cases 2, 4, and 10). One of them (Case 10) had also organized a club at college, and had definite ability of that type. An explanation of this finding in terms of overprotection has been attempted partly in Chapter VIII and in the case abstracts. It was thought the charm in conversation noted for so many of the indulged overprotected was related to the early stress on verbalization, through close contact with the mother; and a modification of the mechanism of getting one's own way into general persuasiveness. The attention-getting devices in the form of clowning, and the like, would undergo further modification in the form of wit and entertaining. At any rate, the life history of the patients enumerated is especially consistent with the theory proposed. To the theory must be added the fact that in each instance there was superior intelligence with special skill in verbalization.

The fourth case (13) was an example of "great ease in making friends." The patient had an unusual variety of warm friends of every age and occupation. He was primarily interested in people, and spent most of his days visiting. He did not bother about the need of a job. He seemed perfectly willing to live off his wife's earnings.

The material available does not allow a theoretical formulation of the dynamics involved in these relationships. One can surmise that on the basis of the explanation advanced in the three cases cited, we have the added factors of especial pleasure in human contact, the naïve and often successful expectation that every person would act as an indulgent parent, and the possible search in every relationship for the lost maternal relationship in infancy.

In the absence of comparable studies it is difficult to appraise the status of the group in relation to friendships. It is clear that a very definite improvement has occurred. There remain seven members of the group who have no close friends, and one who has made no friends at all. Among these, typical instances of the old difficulties remain. For example, in Case 10 there were no real friendships. People were manipulated by the patient chiefly as a theater for his stage, or as recipients of his favors.

It would be interesting to learn of the modifications of the bossy behavior and the withdrawing behavior in our patients that finally made friendships possible. It was difficult to get adequate data from the patients on this point. Unfortunately, the best source of such data, the friends of the patients, were not available for study. The bullying, demanding, and show-off behavior in the indulgent overprotected and the dependent, withdrawing behavior of the dominated, should reveal their earmarks in the older relationships. Certain transformations of the early tendencies have been considered, namely, bullying into leadership; demanding into persuading; showing-off into entertaining. To these we may add a modification of withdrawing behavior into shy, sensitive friendliness; simple dependency into loyalty. In the preceding chapter it was shown how closely the child's relationship to friends followed the relationship to the mother, in certain particulars. It must be remembered also that in the original relationship the warm affections of the child were especially stimulated. It is this element in the later friendships that has not been investigated. We would infer, however, that despite residues of the early demanding, selfish, and dependent behavior, we would find evidence also, when special friendships were favored, of great attentiveness and warmth of feeling.

Attitudes and success in school remained generally consistent, according to the late follow-up studies. The dominated overprotected continued to advance in school in terms of their capacity, in every instance. They were stable, plodding students. Thus, despite an I.Q. of 85, a patient (Case 1) managed to finish the second year at college. He was always a hard worker. Likewise in Case 3, the patient, despite poor scholastic capacity and failures (I.Q. 85), continued through second-year high school. Another graduated from grammar school at 16. He was a poor student but always received an A for conduct. Counting as "submissive" those patients whose problems at referral could be so designated, follow-up studies —eight cases—reveal that in every instance they did as well, or better, than their capacity in terms of I.Q. would indicate. The same would hold true if we added to the original number those cases whose original problems in aggressive behavior represented, according to our theory, inflated aggression in predominantly submissive personalities (Cases 1, 3, 11, and 14).

Of the twelve cases in the same group—Cases 1, 3, 5, 6, 7, 11, 14, 15, 17, 18, 19, and 20—seven are at work. All but one show evidence of work stability. One has had a steady job for four years (Case 5); another has worked at his first job for five years, and his second job for five years (Case 18). Another is supporting his family and finishing college by going to evening sessions (Case 11). Of the others, one is self-supporting, although he shifts jobs frequently because he says he has not found the job he wants as chauffeur (Case 6). Another is really a steady worker, satisfied with his job as errand boy, but stimulated to change to something better, although beyond his capacity, by his ambitious parents. At the latest follow-up, at any rate, the group represented as "submissive" had a stable and satisfactory record at school and at work.

Eleven patients were included originally in the indulged overprotected group—Cases 1, 2, 3, 4, 9, 10, 11, 12, 13, 14, and 16. The special feature in their relationships was in the aggressive phase, especially with the mother. Thus, unlike the dominated overprotected, their demands were not only in the form of a nagging dependency, but commanding, impudent, disobedient behavior, including teasing and striking the mother. Typically, also, in relation to friends their difficulty was in the form of bullying, showing-off, quarreling, and the like. In four of these 11 cases, follow-up studies revealed early diminution of the aggressive phase. Thus in Case 1, the patient's temper outbursts, assaults on the mother, and imperious demands, gave way rather quickly. His docility in the classroom, timidity with the psychiatrist, and early mixture of aggressive and withdrawing behavior with children which ended in shyness, all gave proof of a generally submissive adaptation. This was proved also by the investigation made 11 years after the patient was referred for treatment. The four cases were regarded as examples of prevailingly submissive personalities with aggression inflated in the overprotective milieu.

There remained seven cases whose aggressive behavior was consistent. They furnish the most noteworthy examples of success and failure in school or career. Thus in Case 4, the patient, age 15 years at the time of the latest follow-up study, was in third-year high school and doing brilliant work in all subjects except mathematics. He also showed special talent in music. In Case 9, the patient was likewise excellent in all subjects except mathematics; at 14 years of age she was in third-year high school, had numerous outside interests, and special dramatic ability. In Case 12, the patient graduated from college with special honors and was a candidate for a higher degree. Meanwhile he is very successful in a teaching position.

PSYCHOPATHOLOGY

The four others in the group represent all the examples in the series in which the problem of severe psychopathology arises. In Case 2, the patient, seen when age 25 years, had quit more than six jobs, because each one bored him. He had quit high school at the end of the second year. He gambled. His parents often got him out of trouble by paying his debts. He married at 24, and lived off his wife's wages. The marriage was held together by his mother, who persuaded the wife to return on the two occasions when she left him. The old problems of temper tantrums, and disobedience, remained unchanged. Dependency, irritability, and parasitism represented the main features of his maladjustment.

In Case 10, the patient, seen at 23 years of age, loafed through college, was "conditioned" in a subject in his fourth year, and refused to continue to his graduation. His mother begged, cried, and bribed, and finally prevailed on him to return and satisfy the requirements for his degree. Thereafter in a period of two years he had over eight jobs. He made a good impression and managed to get a new job very readily, but had no intention of holding it, changing quickly for something more interesting or profitable. He was, according to his mother, as irresponsible as ever, getting everything and giving nothing, although he had improved in regard to temper tantrums and sullenness. The patient expressed his philosophy of life quite frankly as a striving for pleasure and easy success. His ambition was to amass wealth quickly, entertain lavishly, and have numerous servants. Like the previous case, the selfish, demanding, dependent, and irresponsible behavior remained, although with more evidence of modification.

In Case 16, the patient, the only criminal in the series, was in a state penitentiary at the time of the latest follow-up study. He was then 25 years old and had spent the previous ten years inside a penal institution or on parole. His delinquent career had started long before his fourteenth year when he was first referred to the Institute. The case differs from the others in its mixture of indulgent overprotection and neglect. Due to the fact that the mother had to support the family, her indulgent overprotection had definite limitations. Unlike other mothers of that type she was unable to supervise her boy's schoolwork or his social life; hence she was unable to use her influence in stabilizing his school life and protecting him from a delinquent environment. Like the others, the patient had great charm in conversation, and special advantage in his studies through verbal facility. His intelligence, according to tests, was, however, only "high average." His early delinquencies in the form of stealing and truancy began when his schoolwork became difficult for him. In his case the truancy was consistent with the reaction of an aggressive indulged boy to an unsatisfying school situation.

The reader is referred to the case abstract for further details of the patient's career. It offers an interesting picture of that type of psychopathic personality in which the patient can so readily convince others of his good intentions. Actually, despite his record, the psychiatrists who first saw him were optimistic in their prognosis. Essentially, the basic pattern of his personality is similar to the previous cases (2 and 10) in regard to the parasitism—selfish, dependent, demanding, irresponsible behavior, social charm, and self-indulgent, undisciplined behavior—or, in general, to the fixity of the pattern of infantile response to maternal indulgent over-protection.

In Case 13, the patient died at the age of 25 years. The cause of death is unknown. It was either murder or suicide. Attempts to unravel the mystery were unsuccessful. The unstable career, however, was clearly revealed. It was featured by irresponsible, self-indulgent behavior, inability to adjust to routine or authority, truancy, and later work-instability. He married at 19, had a child, never supported his family or worried particularly about it. On occasions in which he earned some money he spent it for gifts or good times, without regard to the family's needs. He charged things in the grocery store and never worried about the bills. According to his wife, he never felt responsibility. He was always sure help would come. He made definite preparations for long trips with his wife, although he had no money. He knew he could get anything he wanted from his mother, and had the same knack of getting things from other people. To use his wife's expression, he lived all his life like a child. He was nevertheless intelligent, well-informed, a reader of serious books, very popular, polite, good natured, and made "loads" of friends.

In his case the overprotection was of the "purest" form. The mother remained indulgent throughout his life. She lost completely the power to discipline him or deny. She remained his uncritical defender in spite of his glaring maladjustment. The boy remained as fixed in the pattern of response to the mother as she was to him. With his wife he continued the relationship of an indulged, dependent, irresponsible child. Like the others in this group, similar features are revealed. There is an interesting difference in regard to the vagabondage and the numerous friendly relationships. He was the more charming ne'er-do-well. He seemed also to have a genuine feeling for people and gave as irresponsibly as he took. In his experience with the mother there was almost a complete absence of contention. The remarkable maternal complacency with the son was noted by several workers.

The four cases cited are diagnosed ordinarily as psychopathic personalities. In that classification, they conform to the egocentric type, in terms of exaggerated interest in gratifying personal desires, scholastic and occupational instability, and inability to modify any basic behavior difficulties through experience. Dr. Herman Adler's description of the egocentric psychopath [5] fits remarkably three of the four cases cited. It fits the fourth in essentials—egocentricity, chronicity, unmodifiability. Psychiatrists who rely for the diagnosis of psychopathic personality primarily on the presence of instability in social life [6]—especially job instability and antisocial behavior —would likewise agree.

The deviation from normal behavior in the examples cited is usually not revealed until adolescence or later. This is due probably to the fact that egocentric behavior of children is more or less taken for granted. It becomes clearer when more responsibility is anticipated from the older child; the condition is realized the sooner the adult forms of behavior become necessary in terms of self-maintenance or economic aid for others. Theoretically, also, the lower the intellectual capacity the earlier is the difficulty manifest. Put in another way, the greater the requirements of routine and acceptance of authority, the more difficult the adjustment for the indulged overprotected.

The two groups of three successes and four failures can be demarcated by a line of stability in school and occupation. A review of the case records indicates that despite overindulgence, the mothers of the successfully adjusted, in contrast with the others, used consistent pressure to keep their children working up to ca-

[5] Herman M. Adler, "A Psychiatric Contribution to the Study of Delinquency," *Journal of Criminal Law and Criminology*, VIII (1917), 45.

H. Douglas Singer, and William O. Krohn, *Insanity and Law: a Treatise on Forensic Psychiatry* (Philadelphia, 1924), Chapter IV.

[6] See George E. Partridge, "Current Conceptions of Psychopathic Personality," *American Journal of Psychiatry*, X (1930), 53–99.

pacity in school. Their efforts were expended on children who had superior intelligence and who obtained definite satisfaction through school success. The importance of this experience as a modifying influence on self-indulgent and impulsive behavior cannot be overestimated, since it represents a stabilizing influence preparatory to the later requirements of the job and of family responsibility. In Case 12, for example, after the patient's success in the primary grades, he regarded the school as his own domain to be protected against any intrusion by social workers or mother. He assumed full responsibility for his work and was regarded as a model pupil and a credit to the school. Success in his vocation followed. Assuming in his case failure in school or vocation with resulting dependency on his family, it is easy to surmise that the infantile response would be truly dependent, and would naturally use those parasitic devices with which he was so well equipped.

The various experiences that modify the infantile pattern seen in indulgent overprotection will result naturally in a great variety of forms, from extreme examples of psychopathic personalities to the slightly self-indulgent normal. Thus, Case 16 would be regarded as the most severe, Case 10 probably the least severe, of the four example cited.[7]

Psychopathic personality resulting from the severe emotional privation in primary affect hunger is characterized particularly by shallowness of affect. It is revealed clearly in early childhood. Dr. Lauretta Bender states[8] that aside from the "organic cases," every preadolescent psychopathic personality she has seen at Bellevue Hospital has a history of severe emotional privation.

Psychopathic personality resulting from indulgent overprotection is "earmarked" chiefly by school and occupational instability, and therefore not clearly recognized until adolescence or adulthood.

[7] Theoretically, a successful psychopathic personality may be envisaged. He would have the good fortune, or intelligence, or both, to find an occupation in which routine requirements would be minimal, and of which irregular hours, creative or imaginative work, and social talents, would be features. His wit and his charm would make up for difficulties in social relationships. His considerateness would balance his possessiveness. His temper outbursts would be assuaged by apologies and remorse. All in all, he would be an example of the less severe forms, and with increasing age would be capable of gradual modification of the early irresponsible, indulgent, and demanding behavior.

[8] A personal communication.

The contrasts in the two forms of psychopathic personality are striking. The "deprived" psychopath is presumably unable to adjust to life because of his inability to form a close human relationship, close enough for the purpose of emotional influence. He appears to be unaffected by a basic principle in maternal influence on the child, namely, the need to be loved. The mother's love of the child represents, from this point of view, an equilibrium in the mother-child relationship, that becomes disturbed whenever the mother withdraws love—disapproval. The child is rendered uncomfortable, struggles to regain the old status. Actually he may use desperate maneuvers to be restored. The situation is especially favorable for modification of any activity which the mother chooses to correct. The magnitude of the offense becomes measured by the child according to the degree of his mother's overt expression of disapproval. The varying degrees of sensitivity to the mother's behavior range from excessive concern with her slightest disapproval to indifference. In all close relationships a similar psychology prevails. The emotionally deprived psychopath is assumed to be so defective in his response to the feelings of parental figures that he is unable to build up that sense of social values which arises through the process of "identification." His original defect is related to the absence of any experience of maternal love in infancy, or to its absence for a long period of time after it was once experienced.

In indulgent overprotection the child presumably has been allowed free development of his early aggression to the point of a more or less fixed pattern. Put in another way, he has been allowed to hold the royal scepter too long, he has become too secure on his throne, to be affected by the mother's threat of withdrawal of love. The mother has never "turned away" from the child, as in Case 13, or has done so too late, or ineffectually. The child remains unmoved by threats of punishment. He holds the reins securely, and for the most part knows that the threats he hears are empty words. The mothers are baffled. They "have done so much for the child," they have "never crossed his wish," "have sacrificed everything for him," and lament the child's failure to respond with appreciation and good conduct. Typically they cite examples of mothers "who have done nothing," who have really neglected their children, and yet the results have been real appreciation and good behavior. They end with a typical conclusion—"the more you do for them the less they appreciate it."

In terms of "superego" structure, it is weak in the deprived psychopath because of a deficiency in the process of identification. It is weak in the indulged psychopath because the identification is so strongly represented by the indulgent loving mother. In the former, the person is defective in the capacity to develop "standards." In the latter, standards are well understood, but taken lightly. Theoretically, the prognosis is less unfavorable for the latter, than the former.

In those cases in which early emotional privation is manifested in strong attachments, a similarity with the indulged overprotected appears in the form of excessive demands, possessiveness, jealousy, intensity of feeling, and the like. The burdening of the relationship arises from the struggles of the "poor" in love, among the former, and of the "rich" in love, among the latter.

In all cases of psychopathy "constitutional" factors are assumed as intensifying the response to the particular influences exerted on the person. It was previously indicated that vasomotor instability, for example, might conceivably enhance the explosive phenomena among the indulged overprotected. So also other factors in the make-up would alter the picture. According to the conceptions advanced in this chapter they would represent secondary determinants of the types of psychopathic personality described.

CLASSIFICATION OF OUTCOME

Classification of outcome presents a number of problems requiring careful consideration. The threefold classification is the simplest, since it requires really but two determinations—success and failure. All other cases are allotted to the partial group. Failure is more easily defined than success, but when the latter term implies "a brilliant success"—that is, all symptoms gone, a happy patient, good adjustment in all spheres—it offers little difficulty. However, the majority of cases are lumped all together in the mid-group, and the nearly successful and the near failures are given equal weight.

With the aid of 21 students, Witmer [9] studied the classification of outcome and various factors pertaining thereto, at the I.C.G. In matching changes in the behavior of the patient against classification, Witmer found that the disappearance of symptoms determined the notation "satisfactorily adjusted," in the vast majority of cases—66 out of 72. Next came "change in the mother's attitude toward the patient." In most cases, however, even where no such change occurred, the case was regarded as successful, provided only the symptoms—problems—were absent. It is easy to understand why symptom cure was weighted so heavily in determining outcome, since the symptoms included, besides the problems for which the child was referred, problems found during investigation. Hence they included all the problems in major adjustment—in school, at home, and with friends. Our Case 19, for example, was closed 25 months after referral and classified "satisfactorily adjusted." The problems of dependency on the mother, submissive behavior to a younger brother, thumbsucking, enuresis and fear of dogs were absent after 20 months and remained absent for four months, when the classification was made. There had been no difficulty in school. If that had been the case, the difficulty would have been considered a "problem," hence the word symptom, as used at the Institute, had a broader meaning than usual.

On this basis, since "problems" included everything in the case that could be so labeled, change in regard to "problems" alone should have been an adequate classification of outcome. Under "problems," as in the example cited, all the difficulties of the patient were listed—subjective complaints, social maladjustment, intellectual, physical, or emotional deviations.

Nevertheless, after studying the factors determining classification of outcome at the I.C.G., Witmer worked out a scale of four categories, with "problems" as Number One, adjustment at home Number Two, school or work Number Three, and "social ad-

[9] H. L. Witmer, and others, "The Outcome of Treatment in a Child Guidance Clinic: a Comparison and an Evaluation," *Smith College Studies in Social Work,* III (1933), 339–99.

justment" Number Four. It was found, presumably, in studying case records that some "problems" were not classified under that category, though included under other headings. Witmer used numerical ratings, in her scale, in effect a threefold classification for each of the four categories—3 for satisfactory, 2 for partial, and 1 or 0 for "no better or worse"—with an extra division in the first category. Thus, the old classification "satisfactorily adjusted" would be represented by a score of 4 for problems, and 3 each for the "adjustments," making 13 points in all. There was a close matching of ratings with a similar scale based on subjective evaluations, and classified in five groups, from A to E.

However the final outcome was determined, whether at closing or in follow-up investigations, it was done in as thorough and systematic a manner as possible, utilizing numerous informants, and as much or more time as in the original social investigation. Physical and psychiatric rechecks, however, were not generally employed.

Although Witmer concludes that her classification of outcome is based exclusively on social adjustment, defined in terms of behavior, she errs in so far as the symptoms considered in the first category contain subjective complaints. The latter were also considered in evaluation of outcome.[10] When subjective criteria are

[10] Three follow-up studies of psychoanalytic institute cases are available. Of these the latest is to be found in the *Five Year Report, 1932–1937—and Supplement*—of the Chicago Institute for Psychoanalysis, pp. 30–40. Five classifications are used: "apparently cured," "much improved," "improved," "unchanged," "aggravated." The terms are not defined, but since diagnostic and subsidiary classifications are rated, one may infer that symptoms, and social adjustment in various relationships, are included. Thus, in C.I.P. Case 4, ratings are made on "hysterical anxiety state," and "character disturbance (inhibited personality)—sexual and occupational." From the captions we surmise that the patient suffered from anxiety states, difficulty in work and in sexual relationship. In essence this corresponds to the rating of symptoms or problems. The determination of cure of the hysteria in terms of its basic psychological roots remains the exclusive province of the psychoanalyst. In the Chicago study, material for ratings was derived from two sources only, analyst and patient. Other informants were excluded on the grounds of their emotional bias. An example was given of the wife of a patient who may have married him because of his neurotic traits. She would then presumably resent his cure. This is a far cry, however, from actual falsification of the known facts about a patient's social adjustment. However resentful of the cure a wife might be, in the example given, she would recognize a change from inability to work to steady employment, from avoidance of social life to active participation, from sex impotence to potency. Actually, although the patient is the best source of knowledge of change in inner feeling, he is not the best

left out of consideration, modification of subjective complaints is revealed only when the change is manifested behavioristically —which very likely occurs in most cases. Thus, "shyness" of a severe degree is to be found in Witmer's fourth category, as "no friends, solitary, seclusive," and the proof of its modification in "many friends." However, the patient may still feel shy despite being well liked and having many friends. "Fear of the dark" is seen objectively in "refusal to sleep without the lights on"; its cure in willingness to sleep with the room darkened. Nevertheless, the patient may still feel afraid despite social conformity. If in the instances cited the patient's statement of feeling is in agreement with the change of behavior, that is, he says he is no longer shy or afraid, then psychic and social criteria are in agreement. However, since the patient is always part of the investigation, his feelings are elicited. In general, it may be said that the feelings of children are much more likely to be manifested in social behavior than those of adults.

Classifications of outcome are usually fivefold. The first category represents success, the second and third measures of improvement, the fourth and fifth measures of failure.

The need of more than three categories was realized when near successes and near failures had to be lumped together. In the work of classifying in three groups, it seemed a pity not to classify a near success as success, or a near failure as failure. By splitting the group of partial success into two—much improvement and slight improvement—it was hoped to remedy the difficulty. Failures were split also into two groups—a group who showed no change after treatment, and a group who were worse than ever.

The division of the "partial" group into two was never quite satisfactory. The "much improved" were usually regarded as proof of therapeutic modification; the slightly or somewhat improved as very close to failure. It would seem to be advantageous to include an "improved" group that is neither close to success nor failure. Since "worse than failure," as a subdivision of the "failure" group,

judge of his social adjustment, since the latter is determined by criteria not necessarily his own. Moreover, psychoanalysts who do not use a definite scheme of classification may have varying individual evaluations of cure or improvement, although when presenting case studies they invariably utilize social criteria as proof of success.

seems superfluous as a separate group, it would seem more practical to put all the failures, however bad, together. We would then have five groups, one representing a measure of success; a second, third, and fourth representing three measures of improvement, and a fifth representing failure.

The criteria of adjustment used by Witmer were described by her as "absolute" [11]; that is, the scoring was made without considering the patient's limitations, environment, or any other factors except age and sex. This was done to avoid the peril of subjectivity. It fails, however, to consider values as the psychiatrist conceives them in relation to a given personality. Actually by the use of rigid normative standards, it may lead to inaccurate scoring. Take for example our Case 3, a boy who failed at the end of his second year in high school. According to the classification, he would be rated as unsatisfactory—a score of 0—in his quality of work in school, and also unsatisfactory in his attitude towards school. However, in terms of his I.Q.—85—and consistent difficulty with schoolwork, his ability to continue through the second year of high school despite dissatisfaction represents a high degree of stability. Various factors are discussed in the treatment summary to explain a rather unusual achievement despite his limitations. In terms of the patient's capacity his school achievement was high. Contrast Case 10, in which the patient failed to graduate from college because he refused to take his final examination. He had superior intelligence, and finished high school at age 16 despite meager effort. Until his fourth year at college, he passed all his subjects, although he showed poor application. Actually he manifested instability in his schoolwork as he did in his jobs later on. His school rating would be high in Witmer's classification of outcome, whereas, despite attaining the fourth year of college, it was low, in terms of his capacity. By a "relative" classification the first patient would be scored higher in school achievement than the second.

A further weakness of "absolute" classification lies in the weighting of values in the different categories. In Case 10, for example, the status at age 14, and at 16, was unimproved. At 23, distinctly favorable change in behavior as applied to the various categories had occurred. Temper tantrums and impudence were greatly diminished. Social withdrawal had changed into sociability; in fact, into pleasure and initiative in making friends. There was less friction with mother and increasing respect for father. Distinct favorable modification occurred in every aspect of the patient's behavior. He would be classified in the group of "much improved." However, the patient's work record was very unstable. He left numerous jobs for inadequate reasons—dislike of routine rebellion against authority, and the like. The seriousness of work instability in his case is obvious, since its continuance would result, of necessity, in full dependence on his parents, and a generally parasitic existence. A grave weakness in one of the categories may therefore throw out all the gains in all the others; or render them, for practical purposes, of little value. Hence, classification of outcome which represents, at its best, a summary picture of the changing personality over the course of time, must be judged not only according to a schema, but also according to our available knowledge of psychiatry.

Utilizing some of the points elaborated, a classification of the status of our patients was made according to the following scheme. Determination of severity in all categories is based partly on subjective consideration and on normative standards for each item when they exist. It is hoped that in time all problems will be measured by well-defined discrepancies from a norm. "Normal" is intended to mean within the range of normal, as determined by frequency studies and, in their absence, by personal judgment—an evaluation which, after all, is a daily task of the psychiatrist.

The degree of maternal overprotection, for example, has been estimated as severe or mild, as a necessary evaluation, in order to comprehend the effects of the relationship on a given patient. A detailed study of the four criteria of the relationship allows a more accurate measure of the relationship. The same development— subjective measurement, classification into categories, at first two, then three, then finer divisions, and finally a range of values—is a typical historic process in scientific investigation. The classification to be presented here contains elements of all three, and in time, it is hoped, will be superseded by measurements approaching the optimal procedure.

Degrees of severity correspond to degrees of modification. Thus a change of any symptom from very severe, or other category, to normal, represents a cure or successful modification. A change of severe or very severe to mild represents "marked improvement"; to moderate, "improvement"; very severe to severe "slight improvement." Any symptom or problem or relationship, regardless of severity, that remains unchanged is so characterized. A change of any category to normal is rated as "cured." There are thus five degrees of severity—from o or normal, to very severe—and five degrees of change—from o or no change, to cure. When the status at the end of treatment is changed, but only for the worse, it would be separately considered, according to this classification, or listed numerically as minus 1. Zero would then mean no change; plus 1, slightly improved; plus 2, improved; plus 3, much or markedly improved; and plus 4, cured. The symptoms or problems would have corresponding enumeration.

Before considering the classification of problems and spheres of adjustment to which the schema is to be applied, it will be well to utilize illustrative case examples. The problems of the four-year-old boy cited in Case 20 were summarized as oversensitivity to his mother's moods, attempts to be babied by her, submissive behavior to his younger brother, thumb-sucking, enuresis, and fear of dogs. They represent the problems presented when the patient was referred and those found on subsequent investigation. The first three of the six problems listed may be considered "relationship" problems, that is, difficulties in social relationship with mother, brother, and other children. The other problems—thumb-sucking, enuresis, and fear of dogs—are ordinarily described as "symptoms." Now each one of these problems may be considered separately in terms of severity. The psychiatrist, however, would first get a detailed description and arrive at a "general impression." He would regard the "symptoms" thumb-sucking and enuresis at age four as a common occurrence; and the fear of dogs at that age as rather frequent. He would not consider the dependency on the mother as very severe. In fact, the only discrepancy from the normal that would engage his attention is the fact that a four-year-old runs for protection to a two-year-old brother. That would stamp the act as evidence of severe timidity. He would, of course, want to know details of the thumb-sucking and enuresis, for example, but all in all, the case would strike him as a mild to moderate discrepancy from the normal, presenting no instance of severity except in the sibling relationship. He would regard the case as an example of mild to moderate submissive dependency in an infantilized child, and would anticipate some display of fears. He would consider the symptoms of thumb-sucking and enuresis, in this case, definitely as symptoms of a mild character.

Since the foregoing represents a subjective classification based on clinical experience, a determination of its accuracy would involve the pooling of numerous independent judgments of psychiatrists, applied to the same series of cases. If they were in agreement, one could conclude, at least, that the psychiatrists concurred, or psychiatrists in general have similar opinions in regard to severity of symptoms. More objective methods of evaluation would consist in carefully describing the criteria of severity in the different categories, or better, developing statistical indices of each type of problem based on children seen in various child guidance clinics, or in the general population. Thus, nocturnal enuresis occurred in 50 percent of the three-year-olds referred to the I.C.G. Whenever definite statistics are available they are utilized. Actually the psychiatrist feels fairly comfortable in evaluating severity, or unusualness, whether or not statistics are available, much like any other physician.[12]

A gross numerical evaluation of the problems in Case 20—without including any others would add up to 9 (1 + 1 + 2 + 2 + 3). Divided by 5, the number of difficulties studied, the result would be less than 2, or in the mild to moderate group. Thus any problem would be represented by a mark on a line divided into four parts. The determination of the location of the mark would be based on degree of severity qualified by type of problem, age, sex, intelligence, and certain cultural data. Thus nightly enuresis, which is a normal problem in our culture at 12 months of age, is a mild problem at age three years, a moderate problem at age ten

12 When, for example, a presenting problem is regarded as severe—that is, suicidal attempts in a child—he weights all "problems" as severe, disregarding a series of minor complaints.

years, and a very severe problem at age 18 years. If it occurs but once in several weeks at age ten years, it falls in the range of milder problems, and probably, at that frequency, in the range of moderate to severe at higher age levels. Further, the problem has varying aspects depending on special group attitudes. Depending on the problem, one or the other of these factors may determine our evaluation of its severity. Thus frequent epileptic seizures represent a very severe problem in our culture regardless of other considerations. Occasional major convulsions, however, are given much greater importance than their effect on the person warrants, because of group attitudes.

Enough has been written to illustrate the complexity in the evaluation of symptoms, when we think of them in terms of "individual" personality. To escape this dilemma Witmer has proposed an "absolute" standard. On that basis, a person with subnormal intelligence would be rated against the same scale of value as a person with superior intelligence. Its justification is chiefly in terms of simplicity and a higher rate of agreement among the observers. Furthermore, the method could be supplemented by another scale of relative values, of the type proposed in this section.

The scale of relative values, however, has the special merit of consistency in terms of actual thinking about a given patient. The complexity of procedure in evaluating severity for a particular symptom is more apparent than real. Further, within the limits of our culture, the criteria of change utilized in any given case requires slight modification for the majority of cases. Until there is a higher degree of exactitude in the determination of status it seems reasonable to use a relative scale of values that tells, as well as perception allows, what is happening to the patient at different periods from the beginning of treatment to the latest follow-up investigation.

The scale is related to problems, social relationships, and studies or work. Under "problems" are included all symptoms, including physical, for which the patient was referred, and those discovered through investigation. They include also problems in physical, sexual, and emotional development. Excepted are problems belonging to other categories. Under family relationship are included problems related to parents, sibs, and servants. "Behavior problems" in the home are included under "problems." It is obvious that symptoms or "problems" become "relationship" problems when any other person is affected by them, directly or indirectly. For convenience, however, they are best treated separately, since they have varying ranges of impact in social life; some residing closely within the personality, others expressed overtly in social behavior.

Under "friends" are included social relationships with members of one's own sex and age, and also heterosocial relationships. Sexual problems and sexual development are included under the first category.

Under "school" or "work" are included relationships with teachers or employers, and schoolmates or fellow employees, besides problems in scholarship or job or profession.[18]

The method, in brief, is an evaluation of difficulties in terms of discrepancies from a known or assumed norm. Applied to Case 1, for example, the problems at referral when the patient was eight years old were infantile dependency in the form of constantly nagging the mother to do things for him; defiance and disobedience at home, striking and spitting at the mother when thwarted; temper tantrums; shyness with everyone but the parents; lack of playmates; fear of the dark; and, fussiness about food. In school the patient was excellent in his studies and received "A" in conduct. In this case there is a sharp contrast in the aggressive behavior at home and the submissive behavior outside the home. The "symptom problems," shyness, temper tantrums, fear of the dark, and fussiness, when studied in detail, were classified as moderate; the problems in family relationship, with the mother as central figure, were classified as severe to very severe; [14] adjustment at school, normal; [15] problems in relation to friends, moderate.

[18] For patients who are married, family relationships include primarily relationship to spouse and children.

[14] Consider details in the case summary of this child's tyrannical behavior with the mother.

[15] In terms of discrepancy from the "norm," excellent work in school is not normal. As a discrepancy, however, it is a virtue, a "better than" normal, judged by our cultural standards. In a purely statistical sense, however, it is as abnormal as any other departure from a norm. Hence in all classifications of behavior or "symptoms," a distinction is made between variations that presumably are in the direction of maladjustment and variations that aid in adjustment. Thus a variation may be

On the whole, the problems in Case 1 are classified as moderate to severe—numerically, symptoms 2, family relationship 4, school 0, friends 2, average 2. At age 11, definite improvement was found. The patient was dressing himself, eating well, no longer tyrannical; his relations with his mother remained difficult but definitely improved with his father and with other children. Actually this improvement had been achieved by the third month of treatment and was maintained at that level when the patient was seen at age 11. A detailed study of the problems presented at that time determined the classification of "mild to moderate"—1 to 2. At 19 years of age further improvement was evident. The patient was doing well at college, had a number of friends, although no intimates, and was engaged to be married. Temper tantrums and fear of the dark had disappeared years earlier. Relationship with his father was distinctly improved. He was still finicky about food, still rather bashful, and too dependent for service on his mother. The latter, however, remained overprotective. At the latest follow-up the problems were classified as "mild," and the status of the case as "much improved."

Applied to the 19 cases available for this study, the results may be tabulated as follows.

CASES CLASSIFIED AS SEVERE OR VERY SEVERE AT REFERRAL—10 CASES

CASE 2. At 14 years, 3 to 4; at 17 years, 3 to 4; at 25 years, 3 to 4. Status: failure.

CASE 5. At 13 years, 3; at 14 years, 3; 15 years, 1; 16 years, 1; 24 years, 0 to 1. Status: much improved.

CASE 6. At 10 years, 3; at 11, 12, and 13 years, 1; at 19 years, 2. Status: slightly improved.

CASE 10. At 12 years, 3; at 14, 14½, 15 years, 3; at 23 years, 4. Status: failure.

CASE 12. At 15 years, 4; at 17, 18 and 20 years, 2; at 26 years, 1 to 2. Status: much improved.

---

supernormal—for example, a high I.Q.; another, abnormal—for example, perversion. Many of these distinctions are culturally determined, and the "abnormal," as a departure from usual behavior causing difficulty for a person at one time, place or group, may, at another time, place, or group, be normal or "better than" normal. On the other hand, certain difficulties remain in any culture. When a departure from the norm in terms of personality "assets" occurs, it is rated in our classification simply as normal.

Case 13. At 14, 15, 17, and 25 years, 3. Status: failure.

Case 14. At 5 years, 3; at 7 years, 2 to 3; at 16 years, o to 1. Status: much improved.

Case 15. At 7 years, 3; at 8, 9, 10 and 17 years, 1. Status: much improved.

Case 16. At 14 years, 15 years, 4; at 16 years, 1; at 18 years and 25 years, 4. Status: failure.

Case 18. At 16 and 19 years, 3 to 4; at 28 years, o to 1. Status: much improved.

Cases Classified as Mild or Moderate at Referral—9 Cases

Case 1. At 8 years, 2 to 3; at 11 years, 1 to 2; at 12 years, 1. Status: much improved.

Case 3. At 6 and 8 years, 2 to 3; at 16 years, 1 to 2. Status: improved.

Case 4. At 4 years, 2 to 3; at 6 years, 2; at 7 years, 1 to 2; at 15 years, o to 1. Status: much improved.

Case 8. At 7 years, 2; at 8 years, 1; at 16 years, 1 to 2. Status: slightly improved.

Case 9. At 4 years, 2; at 8 years, 1 to 2; at 14 years, o to 1. Status: much improved.

Case 11. At 10 and 12 years, 2; at 13 years, 1 to 2; at 21 years, o to 1. Status: much improved.

Case 17. At 13 years, 2; at 15 and 16 years, 1; at 24 years, o to 1. Status: much improved.

Case 19. At 12 and 13 years, 2; at 22 years, 1. Status: improved.

Case 20. At 4 years, 2; at 6, 7 and 15 years, o. Status: cured.

A difference in the results in treatment of the two groups is clearly discernible. In the first, where problems were rated as severe or very severe, half the cases turned out badly or only slightly improved—4 failures, 1 slightly improved. In the second, all but one turned out "improved," "much improved," or "cured"—2 improved, 5 much improved, 1 cured.[16]

The obvious conclusion derived from the tabulations is that good results are more likely to occur when the initial problems are less severe. But they show also that an initial measure of the difficulty is necessary in order to evaluate results properly. In that way, for example, a clinic in which severe cases predominate may com-

[16] Applying the method of classification to the entire group, and using the three divisions previously described—with groups "much improved" and "cured" as "successfully adjusted"; "improved" and "slightly improved" as "partial"—the results would be 11 cases successfully adjusted, or 58 percent; 4 partial, or 21 percent; and, 4 unimproved, or 21 percent.

pare its results with a clinic in which mild cases predominate, by classification in terms of initial severity.

If the results in the 19 cases are divided according to the classification of indulgent—Cases 1, 2, 3, 4, 9, 10, 11, 12, 13, 14, and 16—and dominating—Cases 5, 6, 8, 15, 17, 18, 19 and 20—overprotection, we find a relatively higher score in the latter, one cured, four much improved, and two slightly improved. The four failures are all in the indulged overprotected: one improved, six much improved, and four failures. If the consistently aggressive children are selected for comparison—Cases 2, 4, 9, 10, 12, 13, and 16—they contain all the failures in the group.

We have seen that efforts in therapy were directed largely to modification of the mother's overprotecting attitude and development of greater independence in the mother-child relationship. Direct psychotherapy of patients was directed to an understanding of the relationship, to demonstrating its influence on responsible and independent behavior, and encouraging the child in that direction. Numerous variations in technique were used, although the results were uniformly unsuccessful.

Psychotherapy of fathers was utilized to secure coöperation for the entire treatment, and strengthen the paternal role. Of 16 fathers seen, a beneficial effect was secured in four cases, and in very few interviews. Psychotherapy of mothers aimed at an understanding of the overprotective process, especially the mother's own contribution to the problems of the child. In the treatment of mothers the typical experience was some modification of the mother-child relationship in response to advice and environmental change, and little or no response to direct psychotherapy. There was, however, some evidence of initial success, although followed by the mother's struggle against further diminution of the protective relationship. They never accepted in any instance the role of patient—to social worker or psychiatrist.

Included under the heading "educational therapy" were giving advice and information to parents or patients, demonstrating to the mother methods of handling the child, tutoring, and books. Under "environmental" therapy the use of camps, boarding school, and group contacts were included, besides the encouragement of parents in various activities outside the home.

Usually therapy of the children, other than psychotherapy, was almost entirely "environmental" or manipulative. It consisted of trips, play groups, boys' clubs, dancing classes, camps, and boarding school. The purpose of such activities was to enable the patient to make contact with others, develop interests of his own, and to be separated for long intervals of time from the overprotecting mother. The response was generally favorable. Similar methods with mothers were used to help them develop other interests and improve the marital relationship. Mothers were encouraged to play golf, bridge, join classes, enter settlement-house activities, and the like, as well as to get help in the care of their children, attend movies and join in social activities with their husbands. These methods also were generally beneficial.

The "educational" therapy consisted in helping mothers to ignore the child's attention-getting behavior, to change nagging into direct commands and direct refusals, to stop coaxing, babying, waiting hand and foot on the child—in short to stop infantilizing behavior and surrendering to the child's domination. Mothers were encouraged also to utilize the father's authority and strengthen his role.

All the patients received physical examinations and were treated medically when necessary. In two cases the treatment of organic conditions was probably a most important modifying factor of the maternal overprotection.

In evaluating the therapies in these cases it would appear that all efforts to separate mother and child for periods of time, and enabling each of them to make social contacts outside the family were of first importance; that utilization of the father's role as a therapeutic agent has been neglected; that demonstrations of child care to the mother in the home were a most convincing performance; and, that psychotherapy of mother or of child was useless.

The reasons for the failure of direct psychotherapy were thought to be a lack of incentive on the part of the child, who had no wish to change his favored state, or on the part of the mother, to surrender her maternal overprotective attitude; and, the psychiatrist's failure to recognize the task as a serious and intensive undertaking.

Of the 19 cases under treatment, successful termination occurred in two—11 percent; partial, in nine—47 percent; and unsuccessful, in eight—42 percent. The same cases studied 9 to 12 years after referral showed two instances of success—11 per cent; 15, partial—77 percent; and two unimproved—11 percent. As compared with similar studies of large groups of I.C.G. cases, the results indicated a lower adjustment score at the time of closing, a higher adjustment score during "follow-up."

The high degree of later improvement was explained as due possibly to cumulative gains once a spurt toward independent activity was achieved, at times aided by the father; willingness of the mothers to yield ground on feeling a lessened burden in the relationship; maturation; and, cultural and accidental factors. A number of case studies indicate that patients' improvement occurred despite the mothers' attitude.

In follow-up studies definitely improved relationship of father and son was found in 11 cases. The change was ascribed to the same influences operating in usual family life.

As a whole the group showed a normal growth in heterosexual interests and activity.

Difficulty in making friends, a problem in every member of the group, with one exception, improved to such a degree that at the latest investigation, all but one of the 19 studied had friends of his own age and sex. An explanation for the favorable change was attempted in Chapter VIII. Seven members of the group had, however, no close friends. The early problems that prevented friendships, namely bullying, showing-off, selfishness, and withdrawing behavior were apparently modified into more acceptable forms.

Late follow-up studies indicated a general consistency in school attitudes and success. The dominated overprotected—12 cases—continued as stable plodding students regardless of I.Q. With one exception, those who were at work showed the same evidence of stability—seven cases.

Of 11 patients originally classified as aggressive, four revealed early diminution of aggressive behavior. Studies of their records seemed to demonstrate that they were prevailingly submissive personalities with aggression fairly limited to the maternal overprotective milieu.

Of the seven cases whose behavior remained consistently aggressive, three were successful in school and career, two of them outstanding.

The remaining four showed evidence of instability in their occupations and conform to the description of psychopathic personality, egocentric type. All give evidence of irresponsible, selfish, dependent behavior. In general, the pattern of infantile response to maternal indulgent overprotection held firm, with the least degree of modification in these cases.

Since the diagnosis is dependent especially on the degree of egocentricity, it is usually delayed till adolescence or adult life, since egocentric behavior and school difficulty in children is so common.

The successes and failures in the aggressive group were demarcated most readily by the stability in school and occupation. When, despite overindulgence in other spheres, school stability was achieved, through parental pressure and school satisfaction, it was explained that the maintenance of such success was in itself an important modifying influence on self-indulgent and impulsive behavior. Failure in school or work would of necessity result in the utilization of the infantile pattern of adjustment in these cases.

A contrast was made of psychopathic personality arising from emotional privation. In the former the psychopathy was related to a breakdown or deficiency in the ability to form a strong emotional bond in human relationship—a pathology in the process of "identification." The pathology of the indulged and overprotected psychopath was related to the lack of response to the mother's corrective influence—withdrawal of love—because of the exaggerated security in the overprotective relationship. In both types of psychopathy quantitative variations were recognized, besides constitutional factors.

X. CASE STUDIES OF TREATMENT
AND FOLLOW-UP

I N THE studies that follow, numerous details have been omitted. These have been covered in previous sections and in the case summaries, which should be read in connection with this chapter.

Follow-up studies made at the Institute usually ran from one to three years after termination of active therapy. These are summarized and the case "status" classified in terms of degrees of improvement as used at the Institute. There follows a comment representing in the main a critical evaluation of the therapeutic methods employed.

These comments were written before a decision was made to interview the patients for a follow-up study and have been left unaltered. The later follow-up was made with the help of Dr. Blume Brind, who was indefatigable in tracing the whereabouts of patients, obtaining interviews, and in most cases getting their coöperation for appointments in the office. These studies follow all but one of the 20 patients into late adolescence or adult life. They are recorded in detail. In the comments following the latest investigation an attempt is made to evaluate the entire case study especially in terms of the psychodynamics of maternal overprotection. Final comments in nine cases are omitted.

CASE 1

Age 8 years, 1 month: An only child, a boy, was referred through a settlement worker because of infantile dependency on his mother in the form of constantly nagging her to do things for him; also giving her orders, teasing and striking her, and temper tantrums.

The psychiatrist had one session with the boy, one with the father, and nine sessions with the mother. Social workers had 41 sessions with the mother and 14 with the patient. There were also several interviews with a settlement worker in contact with the case.

A definite plan of treatment was evolved early in the case. When attempts to induce the boy to come for psychotherapy were given up, a shift in the plan was made, and the social worker used her time, in the second year of treatment, chiefly in making trips with the patient, alone or in the company of another boy.

In her attempt to enable the mother to overcome the infantile attachment of her son, the social worker demonstrated in the home with the boy present how she could protect herself by not giving in to him. The worker had the advantage of dealing with a mother whose patience with the boy, when treatment began, was exhausted and who was desperately in need of help. Suggestions were given and related to specific situations of the value of ignoring excessive demands; of stopping threats and spankings; of stopping the constant conversation about the boy's bad behavior in front of him, telling him how he gave her palpitation, sinking sensations and the like. The mother kept a record of the situations productive of difficulty. Within three months she was able to demonstrate definite gains. In certain situations where she had previously coaxed and nagged she gave him definite directions. She met his old trick of firing a cap pistol repeatedly by acting as though he were not in the room. She watched him fight it out with another boy without interfering. When he refused to eat certain food or complained, she told him he did not have to eat it. In a neighborhood movie-house performance, there were only single seats available when she arrived with him. He refused to sit anywhere unless he could sit next to her. Thereupon she got a seat and let him shift for himself.

For these and similar episodes which the mother reported, the worker commended her highly. She gave her a book to read on the subject of child rearing, to add authority to her suggestions. Further progress ensued, and the patient was encouraged to play with boys, and stay at home nights when the mother left.

At this time, with evidence of early success in lightening the burden of the relationship, the mother acknowledged a partial change in feeling toward her son. She said, "I don't say that I hate him, but he has made such trouble."

Some further progress ensued. By the fourth month of treatment the mother took "the chance of her life" and let him go on an errand with another boy. By this time he was playing with other boys without trying to hit them; he was eating without fussing, and showing his mother more respect. He was still dawdling, however; still getting help in dressing. His mother was still walking with him to school, although by this time the patient protested. At this stage of the treatment the mother stated that she waited for him when he returned from school with the same feeling of anticipation, and the same activity getting the house looking orderly, as in her childhood when her father returned home from work.

The patient had his first camp experience during the summer, and after a period of refusing to enter the play with others, made a good adjustment.

By the fall—about six months after the beginning of treatment—the mother was complaining bitterly against all the contending forces in treatment, especially her husband, the boy's grandmother and aunts, all of whom were trying to counteract her efforts by babying the patient and spoiling him with gifts. As a reaction to a visit the social worker made to the school, thereby exposing the case study to the principal, the mother became antagonistic to the I.C.G., and claimed that the camp alone was responsible for the improvement that occurred. Furthermore, she now attributed the boy's dependency entirely to her husband's influence, and canceled a number of appointments with the worker.

At this time the worker took the patient on trips with another boy. The purpose of the trips was to observe his reactions with another boy, to demonstrate to him that the boys who go to the I.C.G. are not "bad," thereby to get him to keep appointments with the psychiatrist, and to enable him to make a friendly relationship with another woman and help weaken the mother-dependency. Such trips continued throughout the rest of the period of treatment and became the primary activity in the case. Museums, parks, movies, group activities of various kinds were utilized. The growing relationship with the worker gradually cooled down, and cancellations became more frequent. The trips ended as rather formal enterprises, in which the worker was relegated to the position of someone who merely took the boy to a place where he might be amused.

Meanwhile the influence of the worker, the mother, and an interview with the psychiatrist, helped to change the attitude of the father. His friendly interest in the boy was engaged. He developed a close relationship, helped with a stamp collection and, in fact, aroused the mother's jealousy and complaint that their activity was preventing the patient from playing with other boys.

In the psychiatric interviews the mother spoke more freely of her difficulty with her husband and of her problems with the patient. She told about her sterility and her wish for another child, whom she would "bring up differently." A gynecological examination was arranged. For her difficulty in managing her finances, the mother was given advice by a worker who helped her budget her accounts. In general, the psychiatrist tried to give the mother some knowledge of how her overprotective attitude made for dependency; thereby aiding and strengthening the efforts of the social worker.

In his single interview with the psychiatrist the patient refused to enter the examining room without his mother. He would respond to no questions, merely sitting quietly and grinning. The psychiatrist had the mother leave despite the boy's protests, and locked the door. The boy banged the door a bit and then made no protest. The psychiatrist used this as a demonstration to the mother how she could do likewise when he became unmanageable. According to the psychiatrist, the patient showed no overt evidence of resentment at this procedure.

Age 10 years, 4 months: The mother's second pregnancy was well in evidence towards the end of the second year of treatment. At this time she frankly stated she was hostile to the patient. "I only do my duty by him, what I have to—he is so mean. I hate him." The patient was still tagging after her, shouting, "Ma! Ma!" incessantly, and was freely impudent. His response to the coming event of the baby was expressed as follows: "No, I don't want one. I'll take it out of its bed and throw it away." The baby was born 2 years and 4 months after the patient was referred. The mother reported that the patient was delighted.

Age 10 years, 10 months: The case was closed 2 years and 4 months after the first interview, and followed up 6 months later. The status at closing and at follow-up was "partially adjusted." This classification was based on the patient's symptomatic improvement in regard to eating problems, self-help in dressing, and evidence of better social relationships with boys; on changes in the attitude of the mother, since she was able to ignore certain bids of the patient for her attention; and in the attitude of the father, who developed, in response to the therapy, a friendly relationship with his son, sharing and developing several hobbies with him. The major portion of the improvement occurred within three months of "opening." After that, results were meager and discouraging. However, a growth toward independence had been started, even though the patient was left at the end of treatment with the problem largely unsolved. Further, he could never be induced, after one interview, to return.

Age 11 years, 4 months: Six months later the improvements originally noted in regard to eating, interest in hobbies, a closer relationship with the father, were maintained. There were added notations of "going to school alone" and "dressing without help." The boy's attitude toward the baby varied from love to saying frankly he would like to choke it.

He was getting along well in his studies. However, although he had one friend, he still had difficulty making contact with boys. For all the improvement noted the mother said, "He is as bad if not worse than he was before." The father noted slight improvement, chiefly in regard to eating. The parents' attitude during the follow-up investigation was friendly and they expressed a similar feeling towards the I.C.G.

Comment.—The patient was referred at a favorable time, namely when the mother, for her own protection, was trying to overcome her son's infantile dependency. Theoretically one may infer that the younger the child when the overprotecting mother shows this shift in attitude, and the less severe the overprotecting behavior, the better the prognosis. In other words, it is obvious that success in treating maternal overprotection is more likely to occur when the child is young, the symptoms not too severe, and the mother feels strongly the need of help.

The plan of treatment was in the form of direct instruction and encouragement of the mother in meeting typical situations and encouraging him in the exercise of more independent behavior. The father, whose role as parent had been considerably weakened by the mother, was encouraged to play a more active part.

Dilution of the overprotecting relationship was continued by enabling the boy to make contacts with other children and with the worker, besides helping him to develop interests of his own, and by sending him to a camp.

As the burden of the patient's constant demands on the mother was lightened, her hostile attitude became more outspoken, as though with lessening of the problem and greater freedom of her own, her resentment at what she had endured could, with the help of the social worker, express itself. Freed from absorption in the problems of her son, she could also more readily respond to other difficulties in her life.

There was evidently an initial spurt in therapeutic progress and then a more or less static phase. The relation to the mother changed chiefly in the aggressive phase of the relationship; the dependency remained, with a lessening of the demanding phase. The quick diminution of the aggressive behavior would indicate that it was a highly artificial product of the maternal indulgence, operating only in relation to the mother. The boy was docile in school. In the interview as described by the psychiatrist we get no picture of the behavior typical of the other aggressive children in this group. His problem with the psychiatrist was due to his timidity and his fearful clinging to the mother. His aggressive behavior, when forced to remain with the psychiatrist, was of very brief duration. He had a generally submissive tendency. When the mother received support in her attempt to battle with the boy's tyranny, results were achieved. The boy's aggression seemed to be artificially fostered in a highly indulgent relationship. The fact that his aggression was limited so completely to one relationship would indicate that the submissive adjustment was the prevailing tendency. In other cases studied, even where the school adjustment was good, the aggressive reaction prevailed in all relationships, and especially with the psychiatrist.

The therapeutic method evolved will be found frequently in other cases. Psychotherapy with the boy breaks down quickly. The mother receives advice and some form of insight therapy, but somehow it is recognized that any kind of intensive psychotherapy or psychoanalysis will not be tolerated. A quick change is produced in the attitude of the father, since he is given support in greater self-assertion and prestige in the family life. In addition to any attempt at modification of parental attitude, the need of environmental aids is perceived. This takes the form of increasing the social life of the patient, of getting him out of the home for periods of time, as in camp or boarding school. We would expect also an attempt to increase the range of the mother's interests—all of which is an attempt to break up a mother-child monopoly, and restore those various interests and social contacts that make for the equilibrium of normal family life.

The therapeutic values in this case, besides strengthening of the paternal role, appear to be derived from the relationship between the mother and the social worker, for in this relationship the mother was able to develop sufficient courage to express her bitter feelings against her son, and to utilize suggestions leading to some freedom from a maternal burden, a freedom she could utilize to a limited although beneficent degree.

The mother's statement that she waited for her son's return from school with the same feeling of anticipation as for her father, indicates an identification process that may well have reinforced an overprotecting attitude. It is rather unusual to get a conscious expression of such feeling, although by no means rare in the case of mothers strongly attached to father and to son. Since psychoanalytic studies of these cases are not available, we can only assume that processes of identification and unconscious incestuous conflict must exist as factors in the overprotection. If they were the main factors then we would conclude that the overprotection is not "pure," but compensatory. If the maternal tendencies are regarded as primarily biologic, identification processes and sexual conflicts are in the nature of contributing factors.

Psychoanalytic investigations reveal the following psychodynamic processes that may enhance maternal behavior in a more or less direct manner: identification of the child with a beloved person; narcissistic gratification in a child of either sex; overvaluation through masculine fulfillment in a male child. Compensatory maternal activities may be derived indirectly through unconscious hostilities towards the child—seen chiefly in maternal apprehension—or unconscious sexual impulses, with resulting unconscious rejection, or overprotection through guilt of rejection. On the question of conflict and "guilt" overprotection, refer to Chapter VII, section on "Period of Anticipation."

Age 19 years, 7 months: Interviews were arranged with the mother, father, and patient. There were also interviews on five occasions in the home by an assistant.

Mother—interviews with worker and psychiatrist. When she looks back she thinks that the boy was not as bad as she thought. Four years after she was at the Institute she went to a child study club and found that other children were much worse. Her boy became bashful and then all at once he got a girl for himself. When, at this point, some of the case study was read to her, the mother recognized that there was a problem, only that as she looks about her she sees that people grow out of them. She thinks there was something wrong with her, that she needed the treatment, but what she means by treatment becomes really rest from the responsibilities of household care. She attributes all her difficulties to the fact that she had responsibilities too early in life— it made her take life too seriously, it made her old before her time. She spoiled her husband the way she spoiled her first son and is now spoiling the second. Her husband now has his friends, his club, and his hobby. She has to curb his extravagance in regard to his hobby. Otherwise they would all "go broke."

She was always very maternal. She took it for granted that she had to stay at home and devote all her time to her children. As the oldest, she used to take care of the babies in the family. She had almost exclusive care of them. She said, "If I had ten children I'd be the same way unless I had some help." By help she means servants. She also liked to take care of old folks as a child, even more than babies. When she was age seven to ten she used to go voluntarily to an old lady's house to take her for walks and bring her things. It always upsets her when a child makes a little noise or refuses food. When she is nervous she has to eat. She usually munches bread; even now when her son does not get home on time she keeps eating bread. Actually, as she recounts her maternal behavior, it seems clear that she resented her child-caring responsibilities. As she said, she was "fed up." There is, apparently, a strong maternal drive in her case, although not as strong as in many others in the group. This is shown by the fact that she did not have a strong response to pretty babies before marriage, when she saw them on the street. Further, she never had active phantasies of being a mother. The wish for a large number of children, typical of highly maternal women, is not present in her case. If she had all the help she wanted, she said, she would have three children. She had the patient at the breast 13 months and the second child 11 months. This long breast feeding is typical of "true" overprotection. We can summarize by saying that the mother of this patient had more than the average maternal drive, and that it was strongly reinforced by such factors as privation of love in her childhood, tremendous ambitions for which she sought fulfillment through her child, and other factors previously considered in the summary of the case.

She has fond memories of the I.C.G. "The doctor and the workers were like friends to me."

Observed in the home, the mother still looks after her two boys as if they were still children. She encouraged the patient's relation to his girl.

Father—interviews with workers and psychiatrist. The father is a very conscientious, stable, sweet, submissive man whose status as father has, however, increased from an almost negative factor to a rather important one. He has held his present job for 24 years. He says that his wife has changed in relation to her family. She is much less devoted to her mother than she used to be. Their sexual life was very unsatisfactory until recent years. She always tried to get out of it by claiming illness. She accepts the act better now than she used to. There is definite response, whereas previously she was completely passive—a change that occurred in her late 30's. The father was his mother's favorite and was always catered to. His mother is now 70 and still brings him fruit. She used to do it every day but now that she is older she brings it once a week. He was himself the obedient son of a very dominating father. He described his wife's behavior in regard to the nine-year-old child—the only other member of the family—as exactly the same as it was with the first born. The second child is more "a regular boy" than the patient.

Patient—interviews with worker and psychiatrist. The patient is well nourished and has good weight. He is 6 feet tall. In spite of the fact that his intelligence is no higher than average he has finished the second year at college, taking an engineering course. It seems clear that he will never get through, although he has been a plodding student. Shortly after he was seen he quit college and got a job. As the psychiatrist read to him the evidence of overprotection from the record, he said that it was the same way now with his brother, although not as much that way with him. He thinks it stopped very gradually. He has a number of friends, but at present not one close friend. He used to have one very good friend until he was about 14 years old. This boy stole money from him.

He has a steady girl and has been engaged to her for two years. If he could earn a living he would marry her. There is nothing unusual in his sex history. He masturbates once a week and obtains an emission from sexual contact with his girl, although he has not yet had coitus.

He has no memories of the problems that I read to him and does not remember why he went to the Institute except that his mother told him it was for bashfulness. He has no explanation of his defiance at home and docility in school. He is interested in sports. He remembers that he did not like the Institute. He remembers going on trips with the social worker but does not remember what she looked like, nor the psychiatrist. He talks about his shyness with people and how long it takes him to get acquainted.

His relation with his father is distinctly improved. His father taught him to row in his adolescence, took him on hikes, and taught him photography. There is little conversation between them, but the feeling is friendly.

He still quarrels with his brother, is finicky about food, and according to his mother, still excessive in his demands upon her.

Classification: He would still remain "partially adjusted," although on a higher level than the previous classification.

Comment.—Over a period of 11 years the relationship with mother and brother remains essentially the same; the relation with the father distinctly improved. Despite the close relationship with the mother, psychosexual development appears within normal range. The general submissive traits and stability of character resemble the father. Difficulty in making friendships remains. Despite a relatively long follow-up period, the test of marriage and parenthood are still wanting, for a more "comfortable" evaluation of the personality development. The patient may be described as a normal, submissive, shy, stable personality.

Age 14 years: An only child, a boy, was referred through a visiting teacher because of "extreme impudence and defiance of authority" at home and at school; also difficulty with schoolwork, especially arithmetic, temper tantrums and gambling.

Over a period of 24 months, the patient had 23 interviews with four psychiatrists in succession. The last psychiatrist also had two interviews with the mother and two with the father. A social worker had eight interviews with the father, nine with the mother, and seven with the patient. Besides these, she had nine interviews with schoolteachers on behalf of the patient.

The major problem was considered to be indulgent maternal overprotection; with parental quarrels over discipline. The early plan of treatment was psychotherapy for the boy, chiefly to give him insight into the relationship with his mother, and to encourage the growth of responsible behavior. It was planned that the social worker have interviews with the father to aid him in understanding the mother's attitude, and to overcome the friction between them in handling the boy. The father took a very active interest in the treatment and was available for conferences. It was planned also to enlarge the scope of the mother's activity outside the home, and encourage her to give a greater measure of independence to the patient.

In spite of the fact that four psychiatrists treated the boy, he made an easy relationship with each one of them, repeating essentially the same patterns of behavior. In general, each psychiatrist explained to the patient the necessity of treatment and, to help overcome the dependent attitude, placed on him the responsibility of keeping appointments. With each psychiatrist, there followed, after a period of late arrivals, usually one-half to one hour, cancellations of appointments. The patient would then be prodded to return by his mother. The first psychiatrist tried the method of free association in the third session, but gave it up since the patient seemed unable to use it. Thereafter a direct interview method was used. The patient described to the psychiatrist his exploits in the classroom, and showed how he tried to irritate the teacher to the limit. He would refer to himself as "yours truly, the worst in the class."

By the sixth session, it was decided that difficulties in the home were so intense it would be advisable to send the patient to boarding school. The subject was broached in the sixth and seventh interviews, but he refused to consider it. In the fifth month of treatment the patient was placed in a boarding school because, at that time, the school authorities, after several threats of expulsion, were about to transfer him to a probation school. A plan had already been in force of daily visits to the principal of the school, but after an initial period of improvement, the patient relapsed into his old difficulties. Problems of impudence, clowning, breaking the rules, continued in the boarding school, and expulsion followed after six months. The patient was then transferred to a city high school where the same problems occurred. The psychiatrist in charge of the case at this time used an "educational" procedure, in the form of talks about the development of dependent, irresponsible behavior with strong dominating tendencies, of a hypothetical boy. The patient showed great interest in the discussion, and eagerness to come for several interviews. The psychiatrist used this method because he noted that previous attempts to illustrate to the patient the effect of his own behavior were always met by accusations of the parents, by a series of questions for the purpose of evading the issue and of getting the psychiatrist as an ally in order to get more money and privileges from the parents. However, when the hypothetical case was brought into the patient's own life, he started coming late and canceling appointments as previously.

The treatment of the parents was left exclusively to the social worker, except for four interviews with the psychiatrist. For some reason it was decided that psychotherapy for the parents, if indicated, should be handled outside the Institute. The worker explained to the father the problems of the patient and urged him to help the boy develop more independent behavior. Each parent had interfered with the other's discipline. At the time of referral the father was more indulgent than the mother. The latter recounted to the worker her great difficulties with the patient, and tried to impress the need of making the father "firm" with the boy.

The worker attempted to ameliorate the marital disharmony. The father worked at night and the parents seldom went out together. The father had insisted that the mother stay at home in order to look after the patient and wait on him. The attempt to encourage outside activities for the mother was more successful than the attempt to establish social harmony between the parents. The mother took up golf and bridge and did have, at least, an occasional escape from the home situation. The worker encouraged the mother to talk at length about the patient in order to get more "relaxed" about him. As time went on, the mother was less emotional in talking about the patient, and dwelt largely on her marital problems. By the seventh month, the worker noted that no change in the parental attitude had been brought about and that the marital difficulties remained unaltered.

The first psychiatric interview with the mother was held in the tenth month of treatment. She had previously been able to express to the worker her growing hostility to the patient. Now she told the psychiatrist she had no affection left for him. She recounted her ten years of waiting and her hope of having a model boy—her belief also that she would be a very successful mother. Then she recounted her sufferings and told how she dreaded his visits home from the boarding school. She spoke also of her bitter feelings towards her husband.

A psychiatric interview with the father revealed the sexual difficulties of the parents. Although apparently well satisfied in the first few years of marriage, the mother thereafter used every pretext to avoid sex relations. She became frigid about the third or fourth year of marriage. She resorted to refusing sex relations as a means of punishing her husband. When the patient was away at school there was decreased marital tension and a developing relationship between husband and wife. An attempt to refer the mother to an outside psychiatrist failed. All therapeutic efforts with the parents likewise failed. Towards the end of the second year of treatment they became "more estranged."

The patient left school after five months, repeated the same behavior at another school, and elicited the same attitude from his teacher. The latter was rather indulgent at first, because he thought the boy was bright, although mischievous, and would, after a while, settle down and give evidence of his real capacity. After leaving school the patient got a job as usher in a movie. He held this job about three months.

Age 16 years: The status "partial adjustment" was recorded at the end of the treatment.

Age 17 years, 6 months: A follow-up 18 months later showed that the difficulties of the patient remained essentially the same as at the end of treatment. He had had a job playing drums with an orchestra for several months. He had a girl he was seeing regularly. His general behavior remained unchanged.

Comment.—This case should be studied in connection with Case 12. In both, the mother tried to maintain complete control over the patient to the end—and with similar response on the part of the patient. There are two striking differences. In this case the patient was poor in schoolwork and a disciplinary problem in the classroom. In Case 12 the patient was well behaved in school and very good in his studies. There is a contrast in the parent-child relationships. In Case 12 the mother was exclusively in charge, as in most of the other instances of maternal overprotection. In Case 2 the father was much more assertive both with the mother and with the child. The contrasts are cited in order to consider the role of school success in the possible outcome of this case. If the patient had been successful in his schoolwork, there might have been a measure of satisfaction that would render the steps parallel to those of Case 12. If the mother had been left solely in charge this might have been effected. One of the psychiatrists interpreted the boy's school failure as a revenge on the mother. Although such a mechanism has been well established in certain cases, the data of the psychiatric interviews furnish no proof of it. His behavior at school was quite consistent with his behavior since early life at home; the selfish, aggressive, and irresponsible activity of the type seen in indulgent overprotection. In retrospect, one may say that an attempt at psychotherapy was a questionable procedure. Further, placing the responsibility of keeping appointments on the patient was certainly an optimistic measure, in view of the general irresponsible behavior. Why should the patient, on his own, keep appointments when he did not have to? For the patient, the problem was chiefly how to get more privileges and more things from the parents. Psychotherapy might well have been delayed until the patient had actually suffered from the results of his behavior, when a motive for treatment might be present.

Age 25 years: Patient—interview with worker. The patient was tall —6 feet, 2 inches, handsome, well nourished and in good health. He was married one year. The worker arrived at 11 A.M. The patient was still undressed. His wife was at work away from home. He was obviously annoyed when the worker explained her reasons for an interview. Nevertheless, he responded to questions and elaborated his replies, becoming more friendly as time went on—2¾ hours.

He claimed very good relationships with his father, praised him highly as a steady responsible person who kept to himself and went nowhere. His father was not satisfied with him because he was not earning money.

His mother, in contrast, was nervous, restless, vivacious, and constantly on the go. Both parents, he said, still considered him a child, gave him advice, even woke him up in the morning when he stayed at their home.

He spoke highly of his wife, of his marriage, of his home, and displayed every piece of furniture in the house for the worker's admiration. He spoke of the many guests they invited to dinner and of his host of friends. He used to gamble and get in debt, he said, but had not done so in some time.

He regretted the fact that his wife had to work, and was sure he would get a good job quite soon and then keep her at home.

After marriage he worked as a salesman, the kind of job he liked best since he was so good at influencing people; but the work was dull and he quit. He spoke freely of his talents, his artistic ability, his knowledge of people. The trouble was, he said, that he never stuck to anything. He should have gone to college. He has had quite a number of jobs but they all bored him; that is why he stayed at home mornings and slept.

His parents were too easy on him. They should have forced him to finish high school and go to college. He was the only child and they did not force him to study. Nevertheless, everything was fine; he had a nice home, a wife he adored and better than anything else—his independence. Reading was still his hobby. He liked swimming, dancing, music, and night clubs best of all.

He still had bad temper tantrums, but that could not be helped. Like his mother, he explained, he was nervous.

According to the worker, the patient was handsome. He was decidedly trying to make an impression, and observing the effect he made on his listener. He flatly refused to keep an appointment with a psychiatrist, saying majestically, "I am not a child."

Mother—interview with worker. The mother was 56 years old, neatly dressed, short, plump, large-breasted, gray-haired—height 5 feet 2 inches, weight 150 pounds. She was at once friendly and confiding. She spoke quickly, excitedly, volubly, at times rising from her chair, and crying.

Her son, although married, was still a problem, she said. "My husband is a wreck, I am a wreck, and the boy is a wreck." He never wanted to learn. He never worked. He gambled. The parents were often compelled to pay his debts. His wife also was worried about his gambling. She left him twice, and twice he went to her mother's home and persuaded her to return. The wife has kept steadily at work. No, he never changed at all. He is the same as he used to be. He still has temper tantrums, and then shouts and swears at his mother, even when his wife is present. Afterwards, as usual, he apologizes, and says he is so nervous.

He reads a great deal, goes to bed at any hour, gets up late in the morning. He has had a number of jobs, but never held one for more than a few months. He is talented, speaks well, plays an instrument, has learned a lot without trying, and has stuck to nothing.

The mother recounted in her old manner the sacrifices she made for her son and his ingratitude. She rented an apartment in the country for both son and daughter-in-law during the hot summer months. They accepted it all and never said thank you. She furnished their home, sent her maid in to help them out; she herself supervised the work. She invited them to her own home for meals. They were both selfish, her son as mean and demanding as ever. Yes, she was always too good and her reward was always the same—ingratitude. Now things are different. She will not be a slave any longer. They are both grown-up people, responsible for themselves. She will treat them that way. She told them a few weeks ago they could not have their meals in her house any longer. She would invite them to her home once a week, as guests. They were quite surprised. They did not like it, but she does not want to be a slave any longer.

Her daughter-in-law is really a good child. She loves her. She hopes she will change her son. She has good sense and knows the value of money.

The mother said she received no help from the Institute, her son likewise. "They only let her talk." Maybe it was her fault. She never followed their advice.

She asked the worker to call again and willingly gave her son's address.

Seen a month later, the mother asked all about the interview with her son. She spoke again about the boy's gambling, since she had just paid off another one of his gambling debts. She was going to advance money to him, so he could open a business of his own. She could not stand it. He had no money. He was looking badly. He needed help.

Her greatest pleasure was to see him look well. Really, she had so much fun with him. He was so entertaining. He told jokes so well. He was such wonderful company. He amused everybody. True, he did not want to work. He gambled. He had a nasty temper. He treated her badly. Nevertheless, she had moral obligations to help him. Again the mother promised to keep an appointment with the psychiatrist, though she did not know, clearly, why she should.

Seen two months later, because she had not kept her appointment, the interview proceeded along previous lines. Now the mother expressed fear that her son's wife would leave him. She added numerous complaints about her husband, who would never go out with her and fell asleep in theatre or movie on those occasions when she forced him to go.

Mother—interview with psychiatrist. The mother was quite co-operative, enjoyed telling her troubles, and seemed quite willing to elaborate any topic that was proposed.

She did not consider herself an indulgent mother. She gave her son no more than he required, she said. She kept him on the bottle five years, but she had made many attempts, unsuccessfully, to stop him. Besides, he was so overactive, she found it was the only way to quiet him down. Various details of the hyperactivity were given.

Yes, she dressed him long past his time, but otherwise he would never get to school. He would stay in the bathroom a long time. He still does. He would do anything to kill time.

She loves children to this very day. She can stand around and admire any baby. She can still fuss with a doll. She has always been a "baby-carriage peeker." She loves infants until they are unruly, at five or six, "when they're out of infancy and are like little boys." She says she has no sex preference; possibly she favors girls. Various inquiries made at this point concerning her maternal behavior throughout life indicated a very high degree of maternal behavior since childhood.

She resigned herself to sterility in the eighth year of her sterile period. She had wondered whose fault it was. At the fourth or fifth year of marriage a doctor wanted to examine her husband's semen, but she did not allow it. She attributes her pregnancy to a suggestion given by a friend in regard to coitus. She tried it and became pregnant. The doctors had diagnosed "infantile uterus." No, she never felt sterility was due to any sin on her part. She felt clearly entitled to a child. She never thought of adopting one. She wanted her very own. She used to mother her sister's baby as though it were her own. At first she blamed the sterility on her use of Lysol douches the first year of marriage. In her third year of marriage she had an appendectomy and thought the appendix might have been the reason. Then she thought maybe it was her husband's fault. By the fifth year of marriage she had been told of her infantile uterus. During the period of sterility she felt an intensification of her need for a child.

When her son became such a trial, she began to doubt that she wanted more children. Then she started douching again, maybe as long as eight months. Then she stopped entirely, but no pregnancy came.

She denied any panicky feeling when her son was ill, except when he had scarlet fever at 13 years. He had an abscess in his ear and she was afraid of mastoid because she heard of several fatalities from that condition among boys in the neighborhood.

She regards her son's difficulties as due in the main to her husband, who spoiled him, and would not coöperate with her. She had the feeling that the boy was ruining her life when he was about 12 years old. She denies that her love for him ever turned to hate. She thinks of her husband, as of her son, "if he'd mind her, he'd be all right." She tried to prevent her son's marriage. But she could do nothing about it. They were married two years before they announced it, and that was a year ago.

The boy is just as he was. His main difficulty is "lack of ambition, self-indulgence, lack of consideration, and impudence." Whenever he is with her, there is bound to be trouble. He will always beg for money. He is always trying to suck something out of his mother or father. She tries to shame him. Then he loses his temper and gets moody and irritable. Yet he has lots of friends, friends who like him and want his company. He is full of the devil, a good entertainer, and has a marvelous personality which fools everybody.

Her husband is still the same steady responsible employee, who has no life outside of his work. He has been with the same firm over forty years. In business he is too good, too submissive. She states she had normal sexual response in the early years of marriage, but, through dissension over the boy, sexual difficulty increased. Nevertheless, until about age 45 years she had some sexual response, if not orgasm. Since then she has had no sex feeling.

She has never had a "nervous breakdown," has never been in a sanitarium. But she considers herself very nervous. She used to be a fussy housekeeper, always rearranging furniture, but "broke away" from all that years ago. There was no evidence in this or other interviews of psychosis or "classical" neurosis. She would be described as a tense, excitable although stable, responsible, dominating personality.

Maternal uncle—interview with worker. The patient's uncle was present during the first interview with the mother. He said it was true that his sister, the mother of the patient, was really too good, she did too much for her family, and therefore the people were so ungrateful.

He described the patient as socially brilliant, a show-off, in love with night life, the crowd, the easy way of living, and schemes for quick financial success. The parents both spoiled him, and were now reaping what they sowed.

He described the father as a man who was excellent in his work, but without any other interests.

Comment.—The closing status when patient was 16 years old was "partially adjusted," since at the time he was at work and showed some diminution of temper tantrums and generally rebellious behavior. At 17 years, 6 months, the status was changed to "unimproved." At 25 years, he remains "unimproved."

The "symptom problems" of temper tantrums, disobedience, clowning, impudence, and laziness remained unchanged. Of the relationship problems, the mother-son difficulties were unaltered. There was evidently a change towards the father—less impudence and a more respectful attitude. Towards his wife, the patient maintained the same demanding, dependent attitude as with his mother. In spite of verbal denials, he made little effort to get a job and was willing to be supported by her. He also had temper tantrums with her, as with his mother. Selection of his wife seemed to be determined largely by her good looks—she was a professional model. His wife was apparently maternal to him, still willing after three years of marriage to continue his support. She was not interviewed, hence the determination of choice by identity with the all-giving mother could not be weighed. Most consistent with the psychology of the overindulged appears the taking on of a wife, regardless of ability to support, regardless of parental criticism or denial, and with a happy optimism that everything would turn out well—meaning that someone else would take up the burden.

The patient was unstable in school and in work. He was constantly in difficulty because of his undisciplined behavior. In school, as in his numerous later jobs—more than six, he was unable to stick to routine, accept any kind of humdrum, or remain in solitary work long enough to develop mastery of a trade, despite intelligence and talent—at 14 years, I.Q. 113, marked superiority in language tests, and, later, talent in singing. He needed social contact constantly, especially to show off to an audience.

Difficulty in making friends, a problem up to the age of 14, when for the first time he had a chum, was distinctly improved. He had loads of friends, although there was no proof of intimate relationships. However, evidence on this point is meager.

No details about the patient's sex development were secured, except that, according to his statement, sexual activity in marriage was very satisfactory.

The dependency, instability, and parasitism are the main features of the patient's maladjustment. They represent the most dangerous outcome of indulgent overprotection—a mastery of all essential human relationships by the one experienced with the mother. The psychiatric diagnosis of such cases is psychopathic personality. They are regarded as fundamental disturbances of personality structure, quite resistant to psychotherapy.

In line with the patient's difficulty, the maternal attitude remains inflexibly sacrificial. Efforts on the part of the host to shake off the parasite, sometimes quite desperate and pathetic, are always abortive. They indicate the extreme need of external help to save either partner in this relationship.

CASE 3

Age 6 years, 1 month: A boy, an only child, was referred through a settlement worker because of overactivity, destructive behavior, fighting with children, impudence and disobedience at home, and enuresis. "Peeking" and lifting girls' skirts at school, also a referral problem, cleared up spontaneously in a short time.

The psychiatrist had five interviews with the patient. The social worker had ten interviews with the mother, of which several were visits to the home. She also had four interviews with schoolteachers, two with other social workers in contact with the family, and one with the father. A psychologist had one tutoring session with the patient because of a special reading difficulty.

Overindulgence by both parents was recognized as the major problem. A plan of treatment, besides the care of symptoms revealed in the physical examination—a moderate degree of myopia and dental caries —involved interviews with the parents by the social worker for the purpose of giving specific advice to help the patient develop self-reliance. Since the boy's intelligence was below average, the parents were aided in recognizing his scholastic limitations and overcoming their educational ambitions on his behalf. The patient was also treated by the psychiatrist to give him insight into his infantile dependency and encourage more independent behavior. Besides these measures, contact with other children through some form of group play was advised.

The social worker visited the school, urged the teacher to accept the necessarily slow progress of the patient, and obtained permission to have him leave during school hours to keep his appointments with the psychiatrist. The mother was grateful for this service and apparently also for the opportunity to complain to the social worker about all the difficulties she had to endure. She was encouraged to let the patient do things for himself. He was not even undressing himself at the time of treatment, and was often taken into the mother's bed. In treating the mother, the social worker found that her attitude was difficult to modify because of her strong tendency to overprotect and also because of her ignorance. Attempts to get the patient into group activities, even into a hospital clinic for visual and dental treatment, were unsuccessful. The patient's interviews with the psychiatrist were not effective.

Age 6 years, 10 months: Because of the mother's lack of coöperation the case was closed, status unimproved, nine months after referral. At the time of closing it was noted that the mother was still overprotecting, "waiting on the patient hand and foot," taking him to and bringing him from school, watching and protecting him in his play, dressing and undressing him, still washing his hands.

Age 8 years: Visited 14 months after closing, the same conditions were found, except that the patient had had visual correction.

Comment.—This example of indulgent maternal overprotection is complicated by the illiteracy of the parents, paternal overprotection, and the patient's low average or subnormal intelligence —I.Q. 85. The father was probably more indulgent than the mother, a fact which usually elicits maternal discipline. This "discipline" on the part of the mother consisted of spanking the boy when he irritated her beyond endurance.

The patient was showing difficulty in the first grade. Since both parents were illiterate and especially sensitive about it, they were very eager that the patient do well in school. The mother, who was ambitious for her son, naturally and unfortunately had intellectual ambitions for him. In spite of the high degree of parental indulgence, the parents exerted strong pressure to keep the patient in school.

The effect of illiteracy on the overprotection in this case is readily comprehended. Besides important factors in her period of anticipation and "extra hazard," the need for a child is greater in the case of the illiterate mother than the literate. The parents "sat very lonely"; they had little to talk about. A child widened their range of interest, overcame the drabness of their existence, to a degree naturally greater than to the literate.

The typical problem of the overindulged—aggressive, undisciplined, selfish behavior—is present. As compared with other cases in the indulged group we miss the tutoring activities of the mother, as well as her utilization of medical advice. Both factors may be attributed to ignorance, the latter also to apprehension. There is nothing in the record denoting the boy's charm or winning ways. This may be due to his relatively lower intelligence.

The protective behavior of the mother almost precluded all therapeutic efforts. Typical of all other cases in the series, the boy saw no need for treatment, nor could there be any need, from his point of view. He was happily indulged, given in to, helped at every step. To expect a boy to overcome his mother's overprotection and modify behavior highly satisfying to him was certainly expecting too much. Efforts to enable recognition of his scholastic limitations were probably the most rational steps taken. It is not clear why in a case of this type, in which coöperation for psychotherapy is not to be expected, more energy was not expended in utilizing other social contacts, especially group play—this was advised but not achieved—and temporary separation from the mother, as in camps.

Age 16 years, 6 months: Mother—interview with worker. The mother was a short, stout, vivacious, neatly dressed woman of about 50. A bit on the defensive at first, she recalled that there had been no need of taking her son to the Institute, because he was quite normal. As the interview went on both parents became friendly and eager to talk about the patient. They were seen together on one occasion, later separately. In another interview the mother and son were seen together.

The mother said that her son went to high school for two years, and then refused to go any longer. That was six months earlier. A few months later he got a job as usher in a movie. He liked this job very much. He read little. She urged him to read books but he would not. He read only the newspaper comics. In the presence of her son, the mother told how she taught him to keep clean and to wash frequently. She told also how she discouraged him from going with girls outside his own faith, because that would be unfair to them. The patient did not protest when his mother spoke about him.

Seen alone, the mother told how she warned her son never to do such a thing when she noticed that he touched his genitals. He slept with her no longer. He was even ashamed to appear before her in pajamas. He was still wetting the bed, although only occasionally. She told him that his wife would never sleep with him if he wet the bed. She tried to guide him in all things, telling him what to do and what not to do, she said.

It was clear that the mother tried at first to minimize her son's difficulties. The husband corected her many times. When asked why she altered the facts, she replied that a mother had to defend her son.

Mother—interview with psychiatrist. A short, stout, large-breasted woman, the mother was voluble, quite friendly and coöperative. Her son was seen in a previous interview. She wanted to know everything, he said. He had lost his job at the movies and wanted to go to a C.C.C. camp, a decision which I favored. The mother refused on the basis that he is an only child.

She always loved children and hoped to have two or three. She always liked to take care of her younger brothers and sisters, but after age 13 she went to work and had little time for them. Before marriage she never had active phantasies of being a mother, nor did she peek in baby carriages. She does not remember how she responded to a pretty baby before marriage. But after marriage the need of a child was felt intensely and her period of sterility difficult to bear. She said, "After marriage I used to sit at the window and cry. I used to cry terribly, why can't I have a baby like other women, why can't I wheel a baby carriage?" A doctor told her it was hopeless. She went "here and there and everywhere." Finally an operation was performed—dilatation of the cervix?—and she became pregnant. The mother said at this point,

"I was going to cut myself—do anything to get a child." Contraception was never practiced.

Further material served merely to confirm data previously recorded. She repeated the story of the maternal role played by her husband and said of him, "He can raise a child better than a woman. He diapered and bathed the baby. He raised him—not me."

Her reason for bottle feeding her son up to four years of age was his refusal to drink from a glass.

Sexual difficulty with her husband had not been modified. The mother presented the same picture in all her relationships as described ten years before.

Father—interview with worker. A man age about 55, short—5 feet, 5 inches, rather halting in his speech, the father was more defensive at first than his wife, and tried to deny that his son was ever at the Institute. He wanted to know how the worker got his address, and would not offer her a seat. Later he became very friendly, and corrected his wife when she tried to minimize their son's difficulties.

The father complained about his difficulty in making a living. He attributed it to loss of "nerve," by which he meant aggression, a quality which his wife, unlike himself, had in abundance. He had had a difficult life, he said. He was pushed around here and there until finally he came to this country, where everybody has a chance. But he did not have "the nerve." His son also lacks "nerve." The father attributed this lack in himself to lack of education. That is why he wanted his son to study, and was so disappointed in him. He would gladly spend everything he owned, to his last shirt, if only the boy would study. He told him many times the consequences of laziness in school. The uneducated man becomes a slave like himself—a slave to his little store. The father complained that for all their efforts the boy did no better than the work of an usher in a movie. For this he received $6 a week and spent $2 for cigarettes and trifles.

The father told of his care of the boy in infancy; how he used to bathe and dress him. In fact he did more for him in that way than his wife.

His voice became tremulous when he said his boy was a liar. You could never trust what he said. One day he claimed his boss was a millionaire. The next day he said his boss had no money. The father gave other instances of this sort—all of them boastful lies.

The father's store was the front room on the first floor of the house. He left to take care of a customer; then he returned and continued. He said the mother spoiled the boy. If they had more children it would not have happened. He repeated his woeful tale of hard luck, of his lack of initiative, of his fear that his boy would share his fate.

The father was still the steady, responsible provider, somehow making both ends meet, and presenting much the same picture recorded ten years previously.

Patient—interview with worker. Patient was a strong looking, blond, pimply-faced boy of 16 years, 6 months, of good average height. He was not spontaneous in conversation but seemed willing to answer questions and elaborate his replies.

He finished junior high school, he said, with passing marks. In his first year he took up French, but dropped it soon and switched to auto mechanics, which he liked. He mentioned other courses he took in mechanics. He went to a vocational high school. He was never interested in studying and was glad to quit. He had a quarrel with a teacher in his last year and was glad of an excuse not to return.

He spoke about his job as usher. In his free time he played ball and went out with his friends. He disclaimed any interest in girls. He said he had no problems, excepting to get rid of his pimples. He knew they came in adolescence and disappeared by themselves, but all the same he would like to do something about it. He seemed unworried, unafraid, optimistic.

Patient—interview with psychiatrist. He was a sturdy, muscular boy, weight 169 pounds, height 5 feet, 7 inches. He wore glasses, starting at age 7, because of myopia. He was left-handed and changed to the right when in the first grade at school. He now wrote with his right hand; used his left for baseball and mechanical work. He went around with the boys in his neighborhood. There was a good bit of fighting. He avoided fights if possible, but "when he had to, he had to." He was so successful that on two occasions he fought in the ring and won each time by a knock-out. The main blows were with his left. He thought of making fighting his career, but his eyesight prevented it. When a hand swings close to his face, it scares him because, he said, he sees it blurred.

At school he was on the track and handball teams. He is short-winded, he says, and also gets "heart pains," which he attributes to excessive smoking. In a number of physical examinations, the latest six months ago, no abnormality was revealed. He had a job for a while carrying loads of bananas and had no difficulty.

He complained also of getting excited easily, chiefly when sitting at home. It made him nervous. He thought he ought to learn a trade, get away from home, then his mother could not nag him. He asked me if that was a good plan. I told him it was. He used to get nervous, too, when he shot craps with the gang, at 13 and 14 years of age. He used to win a lot, but he would spend it all. After hours of gambling he used to be "a wreck—nervous and cranky." It's a good thing, he said, they moved out of that neighborhood.

His mother was right, he thought, when she said he was easily influenced. They never could influence him to steal, or break slot machines.

When they did, two years ago, he had to fight to get out of it. They called him "yellow belly," but he would not do it. They could influence him only to do something like going to a basketball game when his mother did not want him to.

He quit school at the end of his second year in high school because he flunked. He did well only in subjects requiring mechanical work. His hobbies were sports and woodwork.

After leaving school he got a job helping at a fruit stand. He worked at it two months and liked it, but his father decided there was no future in it and made him quit. He lost his next job as usher in a movie after two weeks. He was fired for letting a friend in without a ticket. The other fellows did it often, he said, but never got caught. He was caught the first time he did it.

He thought he got along with the parents very well. His mother still had arguments with him for not going back to school. He had more respect for his father and obeyed him at once. He obeyed his mother, too, but after she nagged him a lot. He wanted to go to a C.C.C. camp. His father agreed with him, but his mother would not have it and, of course, she would have her way.

He masturbated, he said, about once a month. However he frequently had mutual sex play with girls, with resulting orgasm. He had actual sex relations three times in his life, he said, at age 12, 15 and 16. He has girl friends and hopes to get married some day.

With girls, as with strangers, generally he was shy, although much less so than at 13. Belonging to a skating club, football teams and the like, helped to get him over it.

During the interview he gave the impression of a bashful, stupid, friendly, submissive boy.

Comment.—The interesting problem presented in this study lies in the change of the aggressive features. The original picture appears typical of the indulgent overprotected—disobedient, impudent, aggressive behavior. Ten years later the picture changed to that of a shy, submissive boy quite well dominated by his parents. He wanted help to get into a C.C.C. camp, but knew it was up to his mother. They succeeded in keeping him at school long after he wanted to quit, and despite his poor marks. At school he was obedient and shy. When his mother complained about him in his presence he held his peace. In the interview he answered questions put to him, elaborated replies, but was never spontaneous. It is interesting also that despite dissatisfaction at school, he never joined in the delinquency of his companions. His revolt at home consisted of minor infractions of the mother's rules—not getting home on time, or going to a basketball game. The account of his impudence, fighting, even sexual aggression at the age of six, was in marked contrast with the submissive picture he presented at 16. In his brief work history he was willing and obedient. He quit his first job in obedience to his father. He was discharged from his second job because of poor judgment rather than aggressive behavior.

Assuming that his position of behavior remained consistent, we would have anticipated selfish, aggressive, dominating behavior, in line with most of the other cases of indulgent overprotection. An attempt to explain the inconsistency of the findings in his case at 6 and at 16 years involves the following considerations. Assuming that our patient was "naturally" submissive, or in other words, that generally submissive or aggressive behavior is influenced by constitutional—inherited or hormonal—factors, we would say that the aggressive phase of his personality was given unusual incentive to growth because of indulgent overprotection by both parents. We would then have a generally submissive boy with an artificially dilated aggression. The aggression would yield readily, however, with increasing age, and his "true" submissive adaptation become more evident with life experience. This theory involves a concept of aggression and submission as quantitatively varying components of personality, constitutionally and experientially. It would imply that the aggressive response of our patient, though sufficient to allow stimulation to a high degree in the home environment, was not sufficient to weather the storm beyond the nursery.

A second consideration involves special stress on external influences, disregarding the problem of constitutional make-up. From this point of view we would submit the type of overprotection to further scrutiny. Unlike other instances of overprotection in this series, there is a strong paternal influence. The father's indulgence was followed by constant pressure on the patient to make good in school. The mother likewise struggled with the patient in the same direction. The indulgence of both parents was punctuated, after the infantile period, with scolding and spanking. Hence we may have a ready explanation for the patient's submissive turn in the form of parental discipline. The factor of below-average intelligence would operate in the same direction, since the patient was compelled to conform, willy-nilly, to a situation in which he had to accept distinct frustration. His dissatisfaction with school, although frequently expressed, was of no avail. He had to keep up his studies. It was not until the age of 16, when he failed in a number of subjects, that his self-assertion finally carried the day.

A third consideration would involve primarily the factor of inner emotional response. His own compensatory devices in the form of a long continued struggle against an intellectual handicap; his attempt to placate with good work the, presumably, feared parent; a wish to present his mother with the gift she earnestly desired— the gift of intellectual attainment; atonement in the form of good schoolwork for the guilt of incestuous attachment; an attempt to outdo the illiterate father on the basis of rivalry—all these inferences would be tested under our third line of attack on the problem of his turn from aggressive to submissive behavior. Since they would require psychoanalysis of the patient, for verification, they remain, as inferences, purely speculative. Even if the patient had been psychoanalyzed, and his unconscious motivations revealed, the question would still remain unanswered, since the turn to aggressive or submissive behavior would still involve the factors of make-up and the stress of external pressure.

The mother's premarital maternal history shows a feeling for children higher than average, although by no means as high as some other mothers in this series. After marriage, especially during the period of "sterility," the longing for a child was intense. Yet the fact that in this case the mother allowed her husband to perform a number of her maternal functions during the patient's infancy, would lead to the conclusion that, although higher than average, she was not "naturally" very maternal. Her high degree of overprotection would have to be explained as secondarily reinforced through such factors as the period of anticipation, extra hazard, illiteracy, thwarted ambitions, and sexual dissatisfaction.

CASE 4

Age 4 years, 9 months: An only child, a boy, was referred through a settlement worker because of marked dependency on his mother, temper tantrums, disobedience, impudence, hyperactivity and thumb-sucking.

Psychiatrists had 17 interviews with the mother, one with the father, and seven with the patient. Social workers had 33 interviews with the mother—a number of these were visits to the home, three with the father, four with the patient, and one each with a schoolteacher and a settlement worker. The treatment covered a period of 2 years, 8 months.

The problem was thought to be due primarily to maternal overprotection, reinforced by relatives living in the home. The plan carried out in the first year and a half of treatment consisted of direct therapy with the patient, advice to the mother in handling definite situations, in enforcing discipline, ignoring attention-getting behavior, avoiding fussing or the like. She was to keep a chart of the patient's behavior. A camp was also recommended.

There were numerous delays and broken appointments due chiefly to illness and to the death of the grandmother.

Psychotherapy with the patient was unsuccessful. The latter coöperated in talking about his day-to-day events, but dodged attempts to get at any of his problems. The worker noted the patient's behavior in the home on numerous occasions. She developed a friendly relationship with the mother and gave advice based on situations she herself observed. After a few months the mother spoke freely about her difficulties with the husband, who seemed as dependent as the child, and played no role at all as a father. By the seventh month, the mother was making efforts to have her son play with other boys and to do more things for himself. In the eighth month of treatment she reported with pride his improved behavior with other children and his gains in independent activity. The mother herself was taking an active part in settlement-house activities and showing more initiative in handling her son's problems. She entered him in a kindergarten. After an initial period of difficulty, including regressive enuresis, the patient adjusted well.

Age 6 years: Fifteen months after referral, the notations of the staff conference were summarized as follows: "In spite of improvement in the mother's understanding of the constructive value of the school experience, the patient's behavior when in the home remains essentially unmodified." This "failure" was attributed to the mother's sexual maladjustment, financial problems, and the presence of a maternal uncle and aunt in the home. The patient was getting attention daily from five adults. There was "always a pandemonium when the patient was around." Although he was doing well in school, he was still quite a problem at home.

It was decided to change the stress in treatment, and concentrate on the mother. Beginning with the 21st month following referral, the mother was to be seen frequently by the psychiatrist. Only four interviews were held, however, due to the mother's cancellation of appointments. Nevertheless, improvement in the relationship of mother and son continued. The patient was left alone for longer periods of time. His temper tantrums diminished and his demands were less insistent. It was thought that the mother's increasing interest in club activities had been of special value since it prevented excessive contact with the patient, and also made up for some of her dissatisfactions at home. She became president of several clubs and enjoyed a dominating type of leadership.

Age 7 years, 5 months: 2 years, 8 months after referral the mother reported further improvement. The patient was going to school alone, playing nicely with other children, dressing himself and showing no evidence of the difficulties present at the time of referral. She "saw no reason for continuing contact." The case was practically, though not officially, closed at this time. The mother had kept up a sporadic contact with the Institute. On one occasion the psychiatrist challenged the mother with her attitude in treatment, showing how she refused to enter any of her own problems and would have to decide to accept treatment or stop coming. The mother tried to change the subject, and then insisted that she had come only to cure the patient of his thumb-sucking and nose-poking. The psychiatrist concluded that progress in the case was due to the mother's outside activities, and the patient's own demands for independence, rather than to any direct aid from the Institute. The status at closing was not recorded. Since the referral symptoms were diminished, the status would be classified as "partial adjustment," in spite of the failure of direct psychotherapy.

Comment.—It is interesting that despite definite improvement in the patient's behavior, the staff was dissatisfied with the progress of the case. This was evidently due to the fact that improvement was related to environmental and educational treatment, rather than to direct psychotherapy. There was a tacit assumption that unless therapeutic efforts succeeded in penetrating the psychic life of the mother, nothing "real" was accomplished; that it was all external and impermanent, since no inner change of attitude was ever demonstrated. Yet the mother's efforts in overcoming her son's dependency, in helping him form friendships with other children, her coöperation also in following the worker's specific suggestions, including her own activities outside the home, indicate a definite willingness to modify her overprotective behavior. She chose to limit the area of treatment to the problems of the child and refused to "enter into her own problems." The insistence on formal psychotherapy appears, in retrospect, rather dogmatic. Valuable gains were looked at askance because they did not favor a particular formula.

Yet, however they are brought about, certain changes in behavior carry their own momentum, and may produce a change in attitude. When our patient does achieve a certain independence in behavior, he is rewarded with praise, and also with a certain pleasure of mastery from his own performance. If his mother can aid in this direction, he may propel himself toward greater success. Assuming that his mother can accept such gains, and that her reward, aside from the knowledge of their value to his future growth, lies in immediate release from a nagging dependency, she also may modify her overprotecting attitudes. In this modification she may be aided by the patient when he fights against her renewed infantilizing tendencies.

There was evidence in the patient's infancy of an episode of "independence." At the age of three years, when he entered kindergarten, he would not let his mother come near him when he was at play. But during the summer vacation, he was with her constantly. When the fall term began he refused to return to kindergarten, leave her side, or play outside the home alone.

This instance suggests the value of determining, in cases of overprotection, if periods of temporary growth towards independent behavior have occurred. The inference would naturally be made, for the purpose of therapy, that a previous accomplishment of this sort might be repeated more readily than if it had never taken place.

Age 15 years: Mother—interviews with worker. The mother was a short, stout, large-breasted woman of about 40, who spoke quickly, fluently, and with a good sense of humor. She accepted the worker's explanation for the interview and immediately launched forth on the history of her recent operation, in which her uterus was removed. Thereafter she had numerous hot flashes. She went on to tell in great detail of previous operations and illnesses, and recounted the Caesarian operation for the birth of her son. She still had only one child. She told of her son's illnesses, necessitating treatment of the antrum, and on another occasion, an appendectomy. In her son's presence she told of his success in school. He was then in his third year of high school.

She told of the great change that had taken place in her husband. For years he was sociable, went to movies and on visits with her. He even encouraged her own social activities, and was proud of her importance. He was also on good terms with his son. They would go bicycling together week ends, where previously they had no contact. His father was proud of him and liked him immensely, although he still quarreled with him about his extravagant habits.

Her husband still held his old job as a clerk. He used to detest this job and wanted to quit. He is now quite satisfied and appreciates the fact that his wife encouraged him to keep it.

The mother gave evidence of the old overprotecting tendencies. She postponed going to the hospital because she was afraid her son would not get proper food. Finally she was able to get a friend to cook for him. When her son would try to answer the worker's questions she would invariably answer for him. She still made certain about his bowel movements. Interviewed on another occasion, when the boy was absent from home, the mother spoke of the patient's stubbornness, his bossy manner, his insistence that he knew everything. He was the same way with his father and his uncle. He still expected the mother to wait on him at table, sucked his thumb while reading a book, and also poked his nose, as in the days when he went to the Institute, although not as frequently.

In a third interview, the mother explained for the first time what she had hoped to gain at the Institute. At that time her husband used to beat her, because he believed she was unfaithful. He insisted she had many lovers. It was purely imaginary, she said. Her son was exposed to their quarrels. He often cried at night, afraid his father would kill her. He swore he would get revenge on his father, but she would calm him down. He resented his father's stinginess and told her he would buy her a fur coat when he could earn money.

She explained that her husband's improvement was due to "three reasons." First, he had great difficulties with his mother, who became senile and very troublesome. She protected him from all contact with her, making all the visits herself. A second reason referred to an accidental brawl that landed him in jail. A crazy woman on the street who said he was looking at her, spat in his face. He spat back and was arrested. The mother helped his release. Her third reason was ascribed to the expense of her operation, six weeks previously. Her doctor persuaded him to spend generously on behalf of his wife. He was always so stingy. When they insisted at the Institute that she tell her story, she simply could not tell them the truth.

She made little of the fact that her husband accepted her brother and mother as boarders in the home, and insisted that it was much better to have them.

Regardless of the past, things were quite different now, she said. Her husband was a pal. They both appreciated each other and loved to go places together. Again, at a later interview, her attitude to the husband became quite critical. She had grave doubts that the great change in him would last.

Mother—interview with psychiatrist. Problems concerning the patient as given in the previous interview were confirmed. Her son excels in all subjects except mathematics, in which he failed. His highest grades are in language. His main outside interest is music. "He knows almost every symphony by heart." He has friends, but is never intimate with them. He is very popular. He charms people. She thinks he dislikes his father. Yet they do go out together and the father comes to him often for information.

She had only one child, she said, because doctors thought it was dangerous for her to have another. Her husband was strongly opposed to another child; nevertheless, she told the doctor that if he thought she could survive another major operation she would force her husband to make her pregnant. The method of contraception was coitus interruptus.

She was always very maternal. She made friends with a neighbor she disliked just because the neighbor had a baby. As a child she voluntarily mothered her sister's children. She hoped to have six children of her own. Friends have told her they never met a person so maternal as herself. She loved children so. Before and also after marriage her heart went out to any baby. "You'll always find me at a baby carriage." When a child, she was too poor to have dolls, but she used to make dolls out of diapers and play with them.

As a girl she was always a leader and in adult life the president of a society. When her boy, at the age of seven years, refused to come to a settlement club because they did not make him president, the director said he was just like his mother. Her ambition was to be a professional woman.

Other phases of the interview confirmed the original investigation which is abstracted in the case summaries. Sexual adjustment was in the form of passive acceptance of the act without orgasm, although with definite pleasure. There was no evidence of psychosis or classical neurosis. She was somewhat hypochondriacal.

Maternal uncle—interview with worker. He and his mother, the patient's maternal grandmother, have lived in the home for some years. His relations with his sister were apparently very friendly. He had helped the patient with his schoolwork until it became too advanced. He thought the patient was very witty and would make a great success on the stage. The boy was "pretty good and friendly," yet "a problem child," always used to having his way.

Father—interview with worker. He was 41 years old, 5 feet, 4 inches tall and rather plump. He was friendly and polite.

He spoke proudly of his son as a very bright boy and of good character. There was not a smarter boy around. Although taller than himself, he worried, nevertheless, that his son was too short. He thought also he was too thin, and too much interested in calories and vitamins. He was too serious. He was not wild enough or playful. He read too much. He thought also that the boy had no sense of shame. He would undress in front of his mother and think nothing of it. His father had to shame him.

The father contrasted his own boyhood when such a thing was impossible. He told also of his ambition to have his family live out in the country. It would be a healthier life. He would come out week-ends. His wife was always opposed to this idea. "She thinks I'll leave her," he said. He spoofed at the idea that he would ever leave her. Since her operation, he explained, she was afraid she would lose sex desires.

He expressed satisfaction with her social activities and also with his job which he had once detested. He wanted no more children because of the danger to his wife of Caesarian birth.

He dwelt at length on the subject of health, food, and home cooking. He went into details about his life insurance and the duty of every man to make his family secure in case of death.

Patient—interview with worker. He was 5 feet, 5 inches tall and weighed 120 pounds. His voice was still unchanged. He was friendly, interested and answered questions quite willingly. However, in the first interview, his mother was present, and constantly interrupted. He accepted these interruptions without protest.

He was able to say that he was in the third year of high school and attended a "rapid advance" class, that he had very good marks in English and history and failed in mathematics. Biology was his favorite subject. He was able to tell something about his friends, and confirmed what his mother had said about his having very good friends, but no intimates. He elaborated this subject when seen alone.

He read a great deal, chiefly modern literature, and preferred the "better" movies, like *Pygmalion*. He said he was coöperative at home, quite willing, but his mother did not want him to do things. He went out with his father on week ends. He used to go to camp and liked it very much, but quit in recent years because the food was not to his liking. It was too coarse. When he refused to eat, the boys called him "sissy." He was fond of baseball, however, and swimming.

Patient—interview with psychiatrist. Apparently at ease in the interview, he sat down with knees widespread, legs sprawled, "quite at home." His face appeared distinctly adolescent with growing facial hair. He was good looking. His manner was free, self-assured, and rather cocky. He remembered nothing of the Institute. He was then only four or five.

He thought his mother had done a lot for him, sometimes too much. The effect of her great love for him was largely as an "inspiration—a mental bucker-upper." He could think of no ill effects. His father was more critical. He thought the patient was not self-reliant and much too sloppy in his habits—having other people pick up his things. On the subject of his father his replies were distinctly guarded. He went out with him. He respected him. "Well, of course, he's my father." He spoke of him without evidence of affection or admiration.

He could think of no problem for which he wanted help except to be better in mathematics. He had one good friend, a jitterbug like himself and interested in baseball. They never talked about personal things. He was interested in mechanical things and dissection. In his studies he was "excellent" in languages and biology. His plan was to go to college. If he should not be able to on account of his weakness in mathematics, he did not know what plans his father had for him, he said.

He played baseball with some girls but never went out with them. He dated the onset of his nocturnal emissions at 12 years. He felt an urge to masturbate, but never did, insisting his emissions took care of that. His erotic dreams were all of nude women. He hoped to get married some day but that was way off.

He did not regard himself as moody. He would "get blue before a math exam and that's about all." He was not shy, "not even with the females," and "decidedly not" in the classroom. He recited before the class with ease. That he inherited, he said, from his mother, who was always class valedictorian and speechmaker. He recognized that he had a bad temper but he knew how to control it in front of a teacher. "They should know the urges I get." He could concentrate well in a subject that interested him. A teacher told him he did not concentrate when people talked to him. That was true when he was not interested. He just would not pay any attention. He wanted a teacher in mathematics who would "pump it into his head."

He regarded his life as very happy. He did not miss having a brother or sister. He said he would rather have it that way.

Comment.—The original problems at the time of referral were still in evidence, although in reduced form. Dependency on his mother was seen especially in relation to service at the table. It operated no longer in dressing, washing, getting to school, having mother always at his side. Temper tantrums were much better controlled. Kicking and scratching when thwarted were merely historical notes, as also such items as "refusal to come to meals," and "runs out to the street before he finishes his meal."

Disobedience and impudent behavior at home were now seen in the form of stubborn insistence in arguing a point, bossy attitudes, and "preaching at" his parents.

In relation to his mother there was evidently a protective feeling and the wish to play the role of provider. A period of increased hostility to his father which intensified the attachment to his mother was apparently curtailed by the improved relationship of the parents. In this connection, data bearing on the period of the father's jealousy and his brutal treatment of his wife are too meager to allow inferences of his motivation. It is interesting that the father tried for years to get his family to move to the country, an attempt which his wife frustrated. In any case, the relationship of the two greatly improved, a change in marital relationship to be noted in other cases of this series.

The boy's relationship to the father evidently contained a strong element of hostility. The fact that they went on trips together, and that the father went to his son for information, indicates social contact potentially favorable to an improved relationship.

The difficulties of the parents may be seen in terms also of a salutary influence on the patient. In that period, when hostility to his father mounted and his anxiety was manifest, he tried to console his mother. He represented the father as a man who was just excitable, not really vicious. It was a period in which his complacency was shaken. He was forced to play a more responsible role. His protective feelings towards the mother were then aroused.

In relation to friends, the patient made considerable progress. Originally, it will be remembered, he was despised by other boys and considered a pest. His mother bribed a boy to play with him. In time he became popular, developed steady friendships, although he never confided in anyone.

His educational progress was very favorable, excepting in mathematics, which, as previously noted, is a special problem for the indulged overprotected. His interests in reading continued, and his tastes in music and the theater became more discriminating.

There was a beginning interest in girls and a denial of such

interest, as in very early adolescence. Erotic imagery was heterosexual. The patient claimed that nocturnal emissions were the
sole outlet for sexual tension. There appeared no evidence of sexual pathology.

Evidence of change in relation to the parents and especially to
other boys, besides control of emotional outbursts, determined the
classification of "partially adjusted." Dependent, demanding behavior, and the lordly attitude at home remained, although in
reduced form. Acceptance of his father's plans for his future,
steady application in schoolwork, development of intellectual interests, acceptance of certain aspects of his mother's dominating
behavior, may be cited as factors that operate against the instability of severe indulgent overprotection.

Despite a symptom-picture identical with certain others in this
series that developed into severe maladjustment, the prognosis appears favorable. As an explanation we may first consider the overprotective relationship. Judging from the fact that the patient attained a temporary spurt in independent behavior at three years
of age, that the mother utilized the advice of the social worker so
readily, and from the general aspect of the maternal relationship,
it would appear that the overprotection consisted of periods of
overindulgence followed by periods of recoil. It happens commonly enough in family life, that after giving in to her child too
readily a mother becomes strict, yields again after a while, and
repeats the cycle. In the overprotective relationship it occurs likewise. It would appear in this case, however, that the recoil from
the indulgent relationship was more forceful.

Paternal behavior appeared more assertive in this case than in
others. The father was "stingy to the mother" for a long period of
time and brutal to her. His behavior was unlike the typically submissive behavior of the other fathers in the group. Without further consideration of the influence of the parental relationships
on the patient, it is clear that he was not exposed exclusively to
maternal indulgence, with the father playing a negative role.

Another factor relates to the patient's response to a change in
maternal attitude. He went through periods in which he fought
for the gains he made in independent behavior. He was proud

when he could dress himself without help and go to school by himself. We do not know what factors in the patient's personality explain this behavior. One may venture to guess that, although aggressive in response to maternal indulgence, he was less so than the patients described in, for example, Cases 2 and 10. A constitutional factor is, however, an explanation too convenient. It rests on an inference derived in the interview with him. In spite of the self-assured manner, the cockiness and the rest, he seemed distinctly less aggressive than the patients referred to.

CASE 5

Age 13 years, 4 months: A boy, the second of two children, was referred through a settlement-house worker because he was shy and timid, afraid to assert his rights, to play with other boys, and because he malingered illness to avoid going to school.

Over a period of four months the psychiatrist had three interviews with the patient. The social worker had three interviews with the mother, one with the patient, one with the father, and one with a settlement worker.

The difficulty was attributed to maternal overprotection, but before a treatment plan was completely formulated, the patient was withdrawn. However, from the material presented in the record, the plan of treatment was clearly indicated. The psychiatrist tried to give the boy insight into his behavior but recognized that psychotherapy would be of little avail, because of the patient's "absolute lack of enthusiasm or of responsibility or of ambition." The patient's indifferent, lackadaisical manner was never altered. He broke the second and third appointments, evidently with the mother's consent. The social worker in her one interview encouraged the patient to go to school, and tried to show that he was using illness as a pretext. It was indicated to the mother how she contributed to the difficulty of the child by her solicitude and her lack of firmness. The father was encouraged to play a paternal role. He told the worker how his wife had never allowed him to use discipline or enter into the rearing of the child in any way.

Evidently as a result of interviews with the worker, the mother became firmer with the patient and, when he refused to go to school, using illness as a pretext, administered punishment for the first time in her life. She also told the patient how he was wrecking her life.

Because of the mother's later refusal to coöperate the case was closed as "unadjusted" in the fourth month of treatment.

Age 14 years, 4 months: 12 months after referral a follow-up interview was made and the same status classified.

Age 15 years, 5 months: 25 months after referral there was open marital difficulty. The parents, although not separated, had little to do with each other. Meanwhile the mother had taken in a niece; the patient had a job at which he was working regularly. He was a member of a club and was generally improved. Observations made at this time of the older son showed that he was very fearful and timid.

Age 16 years, 3 months: 35 months after referral further improvement in the patient was noted. Both boys were "gradually breaking away from home." The patient had made a number of friends.

Comment.—This case is an example of follow-up studies in which the investigator learns that after "a failure in therapy" the patient did very well. Such cases stress the importance of "after-studies," not only as an empirical test but also as an aid in understanding the process of therapy.

Although the follow-up investigations do not include the particular events to which this patient responded with increased initiative, the general features of the case allow certain inferences. The problems presented appear understandable as correlates of the dominating overprotective relationship. The patient remained in an infantile dependent state, was insecure when at a distance from the protecting mother, and used the typical weapons of submissive adaptation; namely, of helpless status, of illness, to avoid the difficulties of the external world and to ensure the nearness of maternal security. At the time of treatment the patient seemed without energy or enthusiasm, completely untouched by psychotherapeutic effort. One apparent effect was scored in the interviews with the mother. She became vocal in expressing her hostility towards the patient and actually administered punishment. The effect of her change in behavior towards him was not investigated. We are told only that he remained as shy and dependent as ever until one or two years after the close of treatment. Thereafter his social activity is noted. He made friends, joined a club, went to school regularly and did better in his studies. Later he landed a job and did well at it. The closing notation, three years after treatment, gives further evidence of growing responsibility and independence.

The data available furnish a clue to the understanding of his improvement. Starting with the treatment, the patient's secure relation with his mother was jolted by a series of events. Through her interviews with the social worker, the mother was able for the first time to "attack" her son. Assuming that the critical attitude toward the patient continued, we have the picture of a chick pecked by the mother hen at every attempt to get back under her wings. The estrangement of the parents and the addition to the family of a niece, especially the latter, represent events potentially shattering to the complacency of the patient in the old relationship. We are unable to determine how the mother was enabled to pursue a consistent attitude of loosening the patient's infantile hold on her. We can only conjecture that the events that occurred in relation to the boy's growth were timely and propitious.

Age 24 years, 8 months—Summary of worker's interviews with mother and settlement worker: The patient is about six feet tall and in good health. He is not shy, but still lacks initiative and needs "pushing."

He still is very close to his mother and confides everything to her.

He prefers to stay at home. He has made friends at the office where he works and they occasionally visit at his home.

He did not finish high school. He took a special course in a trade school. He has held his last job four years, and has steadily advanced.

He is engaged to be married, to "a very nice girl," of whom the mother approves. He and his girl are saving money to buy a home. However, he goes out with his girl very little. His entertaining is chiefly in the form of taking his mother to the movies.

His outside interests are reading and listening to the radio.

Status: partially adjusted.

The mother is still the dominating member, resisting any interference with her role. Both sons have been engaged to be married for years. She tried unsuccessfully to prevent their engagements, but has been able to postpone their marriages. Her husband is still living at home, although his relationship with his wife is distant and strained. The mother has spied on her husband and sons.

CASE 6

Age 10 years, 1 month: A boy, an only child, was referred through a school teacher because of fears of the dark, of other boys, of being left alone, shyness, and insomnia.

Over a period of five months he and his mother had two interviews each with a psychiatrist. A social worker had two interviews with the mother, one with her friend, and one with the boy's teacher. On two occasions the psychiatrist visited the home.

The difficulty was attributed to maternal overprotection. The fears were explained in terms of infantile dependency and of poor physical health. Medical treatment was instituted early to overcome malnutrition, poor vision, and dental caries. The patient gained in strength and weight in a few months. The plan of treatment included psychotherapy for the mother, to enable "weaning her son away from her"; and for the patient, to overcome his fears and his preoccupation with himself. The stepfather was interviewed to convince him of the need of giving the boy more freedom and less authoritative handling. The boy's school-teacher was interviewed with the object of gaining more recognition for the patient and aiding in his contact with other children.

The mother coöperated in fulfilling recommendations made for the patient's physical health, but not for psychotherapy. The stepfather acted on direct advice and was less harsh with the boy. After the social worker and psychiatrist had two interviews with the mother, they gave up further contact because of her lack of response. The mother was herself a submissive woman, rather fearful and suspicious. She relied largely on the judgment of a friend, a church worker in her neighborhood. Besides, since the boy showed improvement in health, school behavior, and became more aggressive with children, she saw no further need for treatment. At the time of closing, besides the gains noted, there was also less evidence of fear, and the classification "partially adjusted" was made.

Age 11 years, 5 months; 12 years, 6 months; 13 years, 1 month: Three follow-up studies were made, 16, 29, and 36 months after referral. In all, improvement in health, behavior in school, and general social relationships was noted, especially in the few months preceding the latest investigation. The patient was fighting his own battles and making a good relationship with a baby girl, taken in as a boarder about two years after referral; and with a new baby sister, born about 30 months after referral.

Comment.—The mother of this patient has been described previously as the one example in the group of overprotection in which submissive, anxious maternal behavior was featured.

She lived in fear of her first husband. The child was born after his desertion. She then feared he would return to kidnap the boy —a fear based on real circumstance. The child was left as her only object of love. Her maternal behavior was featured by anxious clutching of the child, in a period of social isolation. Her relation to her second husband, as to a church worker, was typically dependen⁺ She was a stable, steady worker, and managed to earn a comfortable living as a seamstress. In her second marriage, she ran her home and helped in her husband's business.

The dependent attitude of her son, and his identification with her fears, are readily explained. The puzzling question remains, why was a favorable result so easily effected? There was practically no psychotherapy, contacts were very few, and yet early improvement was evident. The answer can only be surmised, since no one at the time attempted to study the progress made from this point of view. The improved health of the child is the first consideration. There was distinct growth in health and strength, correction of myopia, besides better care of the teeth. The interviews with the psychiatrist apparently increased the patient's self-esteem. He responded certainly to being the center of attention, a response fostered by his schoolteacher. The material leads to the inference that the patient thrived as soon as he was relieved of various stresses and strains, in the form chiefly of malnutrition and severity in the paternal relationship. He apparently needed little help to encourage the development of aggressive behavior. A follow-up ten years later would be of interest, to see if the boy could throw some light on his development.

Age 19 years, 10 months—Summary of worker's interviews with mother; of psychiatrist's and worker's interviews with patient: Patient is 6 feet, 1 inch tall, weighs 148 pounds, and is in good health. There is no evidence of shyness. His fears had disappeared after his treatment at the Institute.

He finished second-year high school and took up auto mechanics. At that time, when he was 14 years old, he had an accidental injury to the skull, was unconscious for an hour. Since then, he said, he was unable to do any heavy work. For that reason he quit auto mechanics and got a job. He has had numerous jobs since, the longest of only five months duration. He gives various reasons to explain their temporary nature, all of them based on external circumstances. A year ago he got a job out of town just to get away from his mother. In a few months he was out of a job and returned to the city. For several years he had had a room away from home. He visits his mother about once a week. He says she picks on him, worries about him too much, and always hovers around. He manages to support himself and, when he has extra money, he gives some to his mother.

He has a few male friends, one especially close, though he disapproves of the fact that the friend gambles and goes to prostitutes. He disapproves of sex relations before marriage although, he says, he has necked a lot. He gives the usual history of adolescent masturbation.

He had a steady girl whom he loved for some years. She died a year ago. Since then he has had girl friends. He hopes to get married by age 25.

In general, he shows little feeling of responsibility for his family, overrates his abilities, decries his hard luck, and is an unstable worker. His reputation in the neighborhood is that of a handsome, polite person who is somewhat of a bluffer, and a disappointment to his mother who hoped he would be a scholar.

Status: "Partially adjusted."

CASE 8

Age 7 years, 4 months: The patient, an only child, a boy, although selected by the usual criteria for this study, was originally not referred to the Institute. He was one of a series of children of parents with manic-depressive psychosis, part of a special research project. His problems were found to be poor schoolwork—although he had adequate intelligence—difficulty in getting along with other children because of bossy behavior, and overattachment to his mother.

The psychiatrist had four interviews with the patient, and one with the father. The social worker had seven interviews with the mother, five with the father, four with the patient, and five with various people concerned with the family.

It was decided at the initial conference that the mother, who had always overprotected the patient, was in need of psychoanalytic treatment. After four months in a psychopathic hospital she recovered from her first attack—manic-depressive psychosis, manic phase—a month before the patient was studied. The attack was precipitated by her son's failure to make more than a passing mark in his studies. She went to the school immediately on receiving his report card, became violent, made a physical attack on the principal, and was soon committed to a hospital. There she told the doctors, towards the end of her stay, that she tried to make up through her son the love and affection she missed. She was reported to have recovered with good insight.

Direct treatment of the patient was considered to be unimportant. Until psychoanalytic treatment could be arranged, it was planned that the social worker have interviews with the mother, in order to help her recognize the limitations of her son's intelligence—he was adequate, I.Q. 97, and not a genius as the mother claimed—and develop interests outside the home, especially to give expression to her talent in music.

The mother was told that her son was a good average boy, and encouraged to accept him on that basis. Much effort was expended to get her an opportunity to develop her interest in music. After an initial enthusiasm she stopped her lessons, saying they were too expensive. Thereafter she did voluntary work in an agency for children.

The father was interviewed to engage his coöperation, originally for the purpose of persuading the mother to come for treatment. Later, as the possibility of the psychoanalytic treatment for the mother seemed remote, he was interviewed with the hope of clearing up the marital difficulty—chiefly sex incompatibility. Again when further direct observations of the patient—at home, in school, and at a children's party —indicated that he was clearly a "spoiled child," wanting more attention than other children, and a bad loser, the father was called on again to help in getting the patient into treatment. Although both parents were very coöperative in early interviews, they became increasingly resistant; and, largely through the father's influence, appointments were canceled.

In his interviews with the boy, the psychiatrist tried to get into his difficulties, especially in relation with the mother, but without success, because of the patient's timidity. The psychologist tutored the patient on two occasions because of a reading disability.

In the third month following referral, the mother had her second manic attack, precipitated also by worry over the patient. Meanwhile the father refused to let his son continue treatment.

Age 7 years, 11 months: The case was closed seven months after referral, status "unadjusted." A prognosis of "ultimately unfavorable," was made.

Age 8 years, 6 months: Seven months later—one year, two months after referral—a follow-up visit was made to the school. The patient was making good progress. He was as usual obedient and overly polite. According to his teacher, he was playing well with other children.

At that time the mother had already been nine months at home, following her discharge from the hospital. She seemed quite normal. She complained that her son wasn't eating what he should, or wearing the clothes she wanted him to. She appeared generally less solicitous about him than previously.

Status: "partially improved."

Comment.—There is a mixture in this case of problems in aggressive and submissive behavior in keeping with the mixture of dominating and indulgent maternal overprotection. The patient's difficulty with children is typical of the indulged child—boastful, bossy behavior, overly competitive in games, using any method in order to win, and a poor loser. Yet in relation to his "exacting" mother and his aunt, he was very obedient. To his grandmother, who was a mild person and indulgent toward him, he was insolent and disobedient. He was definitely anxious in the psychiatric interviews and very guarded about expressing his feelings. At school he was quite obedient.

The balance veered distinctly to the side of dominating overprotection. The first follow-up indicated an improved adjustment along submissive lines, an expected modification in such cases. It will be noted also in examples of dominating overprotection in this series, namely, certain difficulties in aggressive behavior in early childhood, readily solved by the presumably basic submissive adaptation in later childhood. They are easily differentiated from the indulged group, as in this case, by their behavior during the interviews, in school, and by symptoms of anxiety.

The grave prognosis was made presumably because of resistance to therapy on the part of mother and patient, and the mother's psychosis. Yet it was purely a conjecture, based on the assumption that the mother's psychosis must ultimately affect the child deleteriously, and that only psychotherapy could possibly prevent such an outcome.

The difficulty of getting the mother into psychoanalysis or any other form of psychotherapy was typical of the other cases in which it was tried. The psychogenesis of her manic attacks was not disclosed at the Institute or at the psychopathic hospital in which she was confined. Precipitation of the manic attacks by her son's failure with schoolwork, although not evidence of etiology, indicates the powerful blow to her self-esteem occasioned by that episode, and her defense against it by projecting the difficulty onto the teacher.

In centralizing her neurosis on her son, the question of the "purity" of the maternal overprotection arises. Was this direction occasioned by naturally maternal tendencies? On this point, the record is incomplete.

Age 16 years, 6 months: The parents and patient were interviewed singly and together by the worker. The school principal was also interviewed. The parents refused to see the psychiatrist.

Father—interview with worker. The father, a tall, well-built, healthy-looking man of 61 seemed friendly and willing to have the interviews. He regarded his son as a normal boy and disparaged his wife's exaggerated estimate of him. The boy lacked initiative. He had to be pushed, otherwise he would not do his work. He was having difficulty with Latin, but that was not so important, said the father, as the fact that he had no initiative, no opinion of his own. At the same time, however, the father pointed out that his son was normal and had no problems; there was no point in seeing the psychiatrist.

The father spoke rather cynically of his wife's breakdowns, most of them resulting from the boy's "flops" in schoolwork. It was evident that his attitude towards her had not changed since the time of the original investigation.

He had been out of work five years, dismissed to make room for a younger man. He bore no resentment. He had saved money and also received rentals from a few tenants. He worked around the house, took care of his garden, read books and stayed at home. He aired his political opinions with animation. He was strongly opposed to relief, government spending, grafting unions, and help for all the beggars who refused to help themselves.

Seen at a later day, his wife also present, a quarrel started about differences over the boy. The father resented his wife's insinuation that he left the whole job of educating the boy to her. He brought forward the point that although the boy was always much more influenced by her, he tried to help him in every way. The mother launched into a tirade against her husband, bitterly assailing his lack of interest in the boy, his general lack of sociability, sticking to the house, never taking the boy anywhere. What did he mean, helping the boy? The father, in his defense, claimed he used to go to dancing parties, once he took the boy to a museum, and that right now he was trying to help him form an opinion of his own instead of just spouting what his mother said. The father's points were countered with sarcastic retorts. In the battle, the father tried to show that the boy was completely unchanged, and showed the same lack of initiative and dawdling at meals. When the mother rose to defend her son, the father quickly withdrew his accusations. He apologized to his wife and asked the worker to bear witness that in his interview with her he said his son was a normal boy and very satisfactory.

In the ensuing conversation it was clear that husband and wife had markedly conflicting views, and that whenever the argument rose to a high pitch, the husband withdrew. He explained later to the worker that he was careful not to upset his wife.

Mother—interview with worker. The mother was 59 years old, tall, rather stout—height 5 feet, 8 inches, weight 148 pounds—and large breasted, well dressed. She was very friendly and inquired about the worker she had seen at the Institute. She spoke of her manic attacks and hospital experience without embarrassment.

According to her, the patient was bright, much brighter than any other boy in the school, despite the teachers' opinions. She was unable to understand why they made Latin so difficult for him. Their behavior was strange. She was glad her son was not selfish like other boys. He was not interested in making friends. A neighbor's boy paid him a visit sometimes, but her son never returned it. She had been too careful with him. That came from reading psychology books. She learned her lesson, she said, and would not try again to bring him up by rules. She was averse to visiting the psychiatrist. It might make him feel different from other boys. She was ambitious to have him become a diplomat.

When she spoke about her husband, she indicated her dissatisfaction with him, his lack of appreciation of her interests. She evidently felt superior to him. Their relationship was the same as it had been when they first brought their son to the Institute.

As in former times, also, she had her cultural enthusiasms. Previously it was music; now it was poetry. Her interest in religion became stronger. She hoped to overcome her difficulties by religious devotion. Husband and son were religious too.

In the past eight years the mother had been admitted to the hospital twice for recurrence of attacks of manic-depressive psychosis. The most recent followed the death of her mother and was of short duration— five months.

An interview was devoted to a study of the mother's maternal attitude. She was particularly fond of dolls and played with them until age 13. In her play with other children, "mother and baby" was her favorite. She always took the role of mother. She always had a strong feeling for babies, hoped to have three or four children as quickly as possible, and take care of them without help of nurse or governess. When a child, she found a stray dog, took sole care of it and spent her last cent to buy a dog biscuit. However, she never voluntarily took care of other children, although she had many opportunities to do so. On a scale of maternal feelings toward children, she rated herself "above average," instead of "very maternal," explaining that she did not "hanker after taking care of other people's children," and therefore could not take the high score.

School principal—interview with worker. According to the principal, the patient was never a good student in the private school he had been attending the past three years. His poorest subjects were Latin and mathematics. He would undoubtedly fail the final examinations. He lacked initiative. He never showed any ambition. He was obedient and reserved. The principal stated that the father often visited the school to inquire about his son.

Patient—interview with worker. The patient, tall—5 feet, 11 inches

—slim, pale and shy, spoke only in answer to questions and without elaborating his replies. In the presence of his parents he kept silent. When urged to express his political views, he said nothing. When urged by his mother, he repeated in a few words what his father had just said. Persuaded to say something at another time, he repeated an opinion of his mother.

When seen alone, he seemed friendly, although never spontaneous. From his replies it appeared that he had some friends in the neighborhood, never went with girls, disliked Latin, preferred history, and liked baseball. He said he was more influenced by his mother than his father. He gave the impression of a passive, obedient immature boy of ordinary intelligence. He had no girl friends, a point his mother confirmed. No information about masturbation was elicited. He was religious, attended church services faithfully. He was still as obedient as ever to his mother. Like his father, he was a stay-at-home.

He seemed distinctly on better terms with his father than in previous years. There was evidently a rivalry of parental influence exerted upon him.

Comment.—The overprotection is of the dominating type. The patient's adjustment is submissive. In spite of school failures and retardation he remained regular in attendance, obedient and unprotesting. Although handicapped for scholastic success in high-school subjects by mediocre intelligence, he seems to have no recourse but continuous half-hearted attempts to master subjects beyond his capacity. His lack of initiative appears consistent with the infantile, dependent, passive attitude seen in dominating overprotection. His obedience, however, would aid in the acceptance of authority, hence, in work stability. Judged by the other examples of the dominated group in this series, in which obedient daily application to school tasks is the rule, we would infer that his difficulty is primarily related to scholastic intelligence. On that basis, it would be fair to predict that in work within his capacity he would be a stable, steady worker.

The ambition of the parents made it difficult for the patient, since each tried to push him along intellectual lines. The mother's exaggerated estimate of his capacity required brilliant success in school. The father was self-cultivated, read serious books, and had a definite political philosophy of the self-reliant, independent person, a philosophy that ran counter to the son's entire mode of existence. The father tried to fill the boy's head with his political philosophy, and thereby also had an opportunity to attack his wife. In her presence, he was always timid, after initial outbursts of assertion. With the boy he had an opportunity to fight against her, and also protect him against what he believed was a vicious influence. But his fight also ran along intellectual lines. It is understandable, then, that all these efforts, at school and at home, would enhance the boy's defense against a too difficult situation. His type of defense was of a passive variety—reserve, silence, and withdrawal.

The only change from the picture of this family when the patient was seven years old appeared in the growing relationship with the father.

More information about the mother revealed that she was always a maternal person, certainly higher than average. Factors especially significant in intensifying her maternal attitude appear to be the following: an emotionally deprived childhood, heavy family responsibilities, late marriage—age 39, "one child sterility," and marital dissatisfaction. The cause of her psychosis is unknown. It seems probable however, that since her whole existence became maternalized, her psychosis would be reflected in that sphere.

CASE 9

Age 4 years, 5 months: A girl, an only child, was referred by a physician because of night terrors, fear of the dark, fear of going outdoors alone, also—and these became the major problems in the case—aggressive attention-getting behavior, disobedience, constant demands for attention, including striking and spitting at the mother when she could not get her own way.

The period of treatment was 3 years, 9 months. The patient had 39 sessions with the psychiatrist and 26 with the social worker. The psychiatrist also had three interviews with the mother. The social worker had 30 sessions with the mother, one with the father, two with the family physician, one with the school teacher, and five with officials of various agencies. The worker's sessions with the mother and child were chiefly in the form of home visits and in accompanying the child to and from the Institute. Much time was also spent trying to get the mother a widow's pension, in the second year of treatment.

Maternal indulgent overprotection, reinforced by numerous relatives, was considered the major problem. Besides the treatment of certain minor medical problems, the plan was to give specific advice to the mother for the child's feeding and sleeping problem; also insight therapy for mother and father. It was decided not to treat the patient directly, on the assumption that her behavior would be modified through treatment of the mother.

The case was carried along these lines for about six months, and closed when the mother moved out of town. During this period of treatment the mother told the social worker about her childhood experiences, her difficulty with her husband who had, she said, little understanding, and left the entire problem of training the child to her. She made numerous complaints also of the child's disobedience, incessant teasing, and tricking her out of any discipline.

Age 5 years, 3 months: About ten months after referral the father died. The mother was then in the seventh month of pregnancy. Treatment was resumed. It was arranged to have the child promoted from kindergarten to the first grade to keep her out of the home a longer period of time. This idea originated with the mother. After the father's death the patient's difficulty increased. She was "lost, morbid, would not eat or go to bed, and prayed to her father to come back." After several months of this behavior and a period of regression, in which she climbed into the baby's carriage and sucked the bottle, her hostility to the mother and the baby increased. There was at this time an increase also in temper tantrums of a destructive type—biting, kicking, breaking dishes—also attacks on other children.

Shortly after the case was reopened for treatment the patient was taken on for psychotherapy. There was a succession of three psychiatrists. The pattern of behavior was similar with each except that she made many attempts to hug and kiss the third psychiatrist. In the interviews she dawdled, teased, and was capricious, behaving as she did with the mother. She dodged any attempt to discuss her own problems and used the play material as a means of distracting attention. Every attempt to engage her in conversation about her own difficulties failed. "She absolutely refuses to discuss anything which remotely bears on her environment." She was typically impudent with each psychiatrist, would freely say, "You crazy man"; yet she remained in a very friendly relationship and wanted to come. She would get to her appointments very late, however, often a half or three-quarters of an hour. Much of her behavior was showing off and attention getting. She often refused to leave when her time was up.

After the death of her husband the mother became dependent on relatives. Her interviews with the social worker were full of complaints against the child, against her relatives, and against the Bureau for questioning her right to a pension. She used her real problems to resist any attempt to get into a "therapeutic relationship" with the worker. She showed in many ways that she felt guilty about being "a bad mother," and refused to listen when any criticism was made of her relationship with the patient. In time she learned to depend on the Institute for the care of her child. She relied on the Institute to make contacts with teachers, to get the child into camp, and for various medical and other services. She "poured out" her difficulties to the worker and blamed everyone but herself. It was clear that after the death of the father and the birth of the second child, the patient was really rejected. It was in this period that the child showed great hunger for affection, quickly embracing any adult.

The patient did well at school, was bright, and throughout the period of treatment was promoted regularly. The complaints by the mother were not apparent at school, excepting a tendency, not serious, to engage the teacher's attention. In the two summers in which she was at camp, there was an initial period of about four days in which showing off was a problem. After this stage she adjusted very well, was popular, in fact, and praised as a good camper by the counselors.

Notations from the record reveal that the problems at referral remained fairly consistent throughout, with some diminution towards the end of treatment. In the second year it was noted that she was worse if anything, stubborn, willful, throwing dishes, breaking things, hitting and kicking the mother, also hitting other children. At this time it was noted that the mother "resigned herself" to the bad behavior of the patient. In the third year of treatment the problems were still present although not as marked as in the period following the father's death. They now included jealousy and fighting with the baby. In this period also the mother remarked that when she went out visiting people would say that if they had such a child they would kill it.

Besides camp as a method of separating the child from the mother and increasing her range of social life, the patient was entered in a dancing school and engaged in a number of trips to parks, and museums, with the worker and another patient. It was clear that the child was getting more love and recognition at the Institute than at home in the period following the father's death. Attempts to broaden the mother's social interests were partially successful towards the end of the period of treatment, when she joined a mothers' club.

Age 8 years, 6 months: In summarizing the treatment, the staff regarded summer camp and dancing classes as helpful, also a period of some months during the second year of treatment when the worker maintained consistently that the mother was a good mother. The status was classified as "partially adjusted," the prognosis "uncertain, with expectation of acute problems in adolescence."

Comment.—The early picture is quite typical of indulgent overprotection. As usual, direct psychotherapy failed with both mother and child, whereas some success was achieved with environmental methods. The child's operative experience at 30 months, with its consequent anxiety, evidently increased the child's dependency and thereby control over the mother. Favorable features in adjustment were her good behavior in school and at camps.

An interesting turn in the case started with the medical treatment. It helped to overcome maternal apprehension. A tangible help of this type is often more convincing than any psychological procedures, and lends prestige to every worker in the case. On the other hand, however, once an organic problem is solved, it may be followed by loss of interest, when the parent utilizes the physical care as proof that the difficulty in the child had no relation to his own behavior.

Circumstances favored exploitation of the Institute on behalf of the child. After the death of her husband the mother was dependent on relatives and happy to turn to the workers for every aid. Since the patient suffered displacement by another child and also the loss of her father, besides maternal rejection, the therapy naturally changed into maternal support. At the same time it was decided not to burden the mother with any critical appraisal and to assuage her feeling of guilt. The reason for the unfavorable prognosis is not clear.

Age 14 years, 5 months: Maternal Grandmother—interview with worker. The grandmother was friendly at once, praised the Institute, told how the patient was before she was treated and how the treatment improved her. Patient was still going to the same camp the Institute had chosen. The grandmother thought that the patient's difficulties had been due to her father's death. She was surprised when the worker reminded her that all the difficulties preceded the father's death by a year. Grandmother went on to tell that the patient was now quite grown up, helping with the housework, and going to high school. She had only praise for her granddaughter.

She told also how wonderful the mother was, how successful in her work before marriage, and how now she was president of a mother's club, and supplementing her widow's pension by various jobs.

Mother—interview with worker. Mother, a short, stout woman of over 40, rather carelessly dressed, was friendly and confidential. She complained a great deal about financial worries and about her despotic mother, with whom there were frequent quarrels. She complained about her sisters, who still were burdens for her to bear. She complained also that her daughter would offend people by asking them impertinent questions. The daughter was good natured, however, and did not mean to offend. She showed little initiative in helping her mother.

At this point the younger daughter, now age nine years, entered, begged the mother for a few pennies and, when refused, kept nagging until she got a promise from her mother. In response to questions the child told the worker that her older sister helped with the housework and was taking her to a movie that evening.

The mother continued her account of the patient, told about her omnivorous reading and refusal to go out with young people. The patient was very good at school, interested in art, music, and dancing. She recited in public. The child's reason for not going out, according to the mother, was sensitivity to obesity. At one time the obesity was treated with medicine but, mother said, she could afford it no longer. She was sleeping with both children in the same bed, although an inspection of the house showed that it was unnecessary. It appeared that the mother indulged her claim of misery. She refused to allow either the grandmother to cook for the children or the children to cook for themselves. She still insisted on serving them.

Mother—interview with psychiatrist. Short, stout and large-breasted, the mother was dressed neatly when she appeared in the office. When told she was selected for study as a mother who showed a high degree of maternal love she denied being overly maternal. She had to indulge her child after the mastoid operation, to save her life. Otherwise she never overprotected her.

She told about her family difficulties and asserted that she maintained the same responsible attitude in her family now as always. Her numerous friends also relied on her for important decisions.

As a child she used to take care of the two younger children, bathe and dress them. She taught her younger sister to recite. She never resented having to take care of the young ones. She always loved dolls, even to this day. Whenever she would see a pretty baby on the street she had a strong impulse to hug and fondle it, and a longing—before marriage—for one of her own. As an adolescent, she used to organize parties for her little sisters and their friends. She hoped to have four children after marriage.

At the time of her marriage she was very popular. She held herself aloof and finally married her most persistent suitor. When in school she was a very good student and took prizes in English.

She confirmed the findings in regard to the items satisfactory sex adjustment, social incompatibility, and thwarted ambitions, as recorded in the original investigation. Although obviously disappointed in life, a complainer, indulging in self-pity, she remained the energetic, aggressive, stable breadwinner for her family. She revealed no evidence of psychosis or classical neurosis.

Patient—interview with worker. A rather short, obese girl—weight 110 pounds—the patient was pleasant and friendly. She described her school subjects in detail. She was excellent in all subjects except mathematics. She belonged to a number of clubs at school. Her chief outside interest was reading.

She confirmed her mother's statement about the difficulties with grandmother and was evidently strongly sympathetic with her mother's point of view.

She confessed shyness of people. Her trouble, she thought, was that she offended people by telling the truth. A girl would ask, "Do you like my dress?" She would reply, "No, it makes you look old." She also asked too many questions. With boys, she said, she just refused to pet. She had a boy friend, one whom she liked more than anyone else. They read together. She said the girls called her baby because she did not use lipstick, did not wear curls and did not know the modern dances; also because her mother insisted on her being home by nine o'clock. She was liked much more by the girls' mothers than by the girls themselves. She was also favored by the teachers. She preferred boys to girls, except when they got mushy.

She was fond of all sports, also music, art, and reading. She knew many poems by heart. She was fond of her sister and liked to take care of her.

She admitted her shame of all the service her mother gave her. Mother washed and ironed her clothes, and shined her shoes. Her mother was her friend and her pal. She taught her to play and to recite. She saved pictures for her scrap book. Her mother, she said, is "a marvelous woman," "a compelling personality," and "respected by everybody." She defended her mother against all the criticism of the aunts and the grandmother with vehemence.

She hoped to get married some day and have lots of children.

Patient—interview with psychiatrist. Short, squat, large-breasted, expressive, the patient apparently enjoyed the interview.

She remembered going to the Institute when she was four years old. She recalled the name of her psychiatrist and the nice time she had. She had no idea why she was sent there. I read her the list of problems for which treatment was requested. She laughed and said her sister was the same way now. The patient said she still has a fear that something will happen to her sister, when they are both alone in the house. She imagines then that someone might kill or kidnap her.

When I read about her problem of being so bossy with children, she said "what a brat I was." She could not imagine being that way now, she said. She recounted her difficulty with girls, as she had to the worker. It appeared that for her bossiness she substituted what she described as "insulting them unintentionally."

Her temper tantrums, she said, were still present, but only at home. Sometimes they took the form of just simply crying. She was impatient and argumentative with her sister but "the sisterly love" was all there, nevertheless.

The patient returned again to the question of bossiness. On the contrary, she said, she let people walk all over her; she did everything for her friends, even writing compositions for them.

She accepted the Institute's version of "too much mother." Nevertheless she found nothing to criticize and did not want her mother to change. "With such a mother you don't need any friend," she said.

Her resentments were chiefly of her grandmother whom she frankly hated.

Her own menstruation started at 13 years, was fairly regular, about every 28 days, although she did not keep count, and lasted three or four days. There were no special difficulties. She expressed a fear of sex, of venereal disease, and she said, "of what women go through. It fills me with fear right now. My heart goes pounding." She has "an insane passion about children." She still liked to play with her sister's dolls. She used to play especially the role of mother in her games with girls.

Her father died when she was five years old. Her memory was of a kindly man with a nice smile, who once spanked her with a strap. Her mother came to the rescue.

Her relation to boys was as described by the worker—"early adolescent."

Comment.—After a period of indulgent overprotection the patient experienced a period of rejection, and was then restored to the previous overprotection. The case study is complicated by the transient rejection and also by the sex of the patient. She is the only female in the series.

Her response to the birth of her sister was quite severe. She had, for her age, a strong regressive reaction, actually climbing into the baby carriage and sucking at the bottle. In a previous study on sibling rivalry it was determined that the reaction to the new baby was, theoretically, as strong as the dependency on the mother. Statistical data were used to demonstrate that in general the older the child at the time the next younger is born, the less demonstrable was hostile and jealous behavior.[1] When dependency on the mother does not diminish with age, however, reactions of the infantile type occur. Although highly modified, the patient's hostility to the sister was revealed even at the age of 14 years, in recurrent anxiety about her death. The rather morbid reaction to her father's death is difficult to explain. In the case of a young child, especially one whose emotional life was so centered in the mother, we would anticipate minor reactions, if any, to loss of the father. Besides, up to the time of his death, the father showed little affection or interest in the patient. He died within two months of the birth of the baby sister. In the absence of psychoanalytic data we can only raise the possibility that the patient's severe reaction to her father's death was intensified by anxiety over her strong hostility towards him, an anxiety requiring the strong defense of deep mourning. This hostility was presumably displaced on to him from the mother, as it was later displaced to the grandmother. It is interesting in this connection that after several months of mourning for the father and infantile regression, there was increased overt hostility to the mother and baby, destructive temper tantrums, and attacks on other children.

The patient's free and impudent relationship to the psychiatrist was typical of indulgent overprotection. Her special demands for affection from her latest psychiatrist occurred in the period of maternal rejection. The mother's complaints about the patient were typical of other overindulgent mothers. It would seem that the period of rejection, even though followed eventually by overindulgence, had some effect in reducing the dimensions of aggressive, impulsive, and attention-getting behavior.

The question of sex in relation to indulgent overprotection is of special interest in this case. The choice of the male as the object of overprotection has been considered previously. The problem to be considered relates to the dimensions of aggressive behavior in the indulged overprotected girl. As compared with the boys in this series, the patient's aggression appears highly modified. Although

[1] David M. Levy, *Studies in Sibling Rivalry*, American Orthopsychiatric Association Monograph No. 2 (New York, 1937).

impudent to her mother, she responded readily to requirements that seemed infantilizing and exacting to her friends. In relation to other girls her bossiness was modified into making impolitic remarks. She used also submissive devices, helping out her friends to a degree unnecessary, even letting them "walk over her." The modification of aggression towards her sister has been described. The hostility was distinctly repressed.

In general, the requirements of submissive adaptation are stronger for girls than for boys—at least in their outward manifestations. In our culture, aggressive behavior in girls is not well tolerated, especially in relation to boys. The latter are allowed the liberty of boasting, showing off, impudence and authority-rebellion to a much greater degree. It is interesting that the patient did have a good relationship with a boy. It remains a question whether her refusal to allow any physical contact was determined primarily by her need of maintaining the aggressive role, or by a prudery derived out of some sex anxiety. Further complications in this problem are the period of rejection, and the patient's naturally strong maternal feelings.

The mother was apparently highly maternal. Her rejecting phase was due to unusual circumstances, and overprotection of both her daughters was reëstablished. Yet, it seems, the giving phase of her maternal relationship never assumed the proportions it had originally when the patient was first referred. Reasons for this modification were given in terms of expanding interests of both mother and daughter, resulting from therapy. There is the probability also that in this case as in others, although the essential pattern of indulgent overprotection remains unchanged, the mothers are able to retract some measure of their indulgent attitude.

Final status: partially adjusted.

CASE 10

Age 12 years, 5 months: A boy, the oldest of four children, was referred through a friend of the family because of disobedience, impudence, and dominating behavior at home, excessive demands and dependency on his mother, "utter selfishness," marked jealousy of the siblings, and hypochondria.

Over a period of 22 months, he had four or five interviews with the psychiatrist. The social worker had two interviews with the patient, nine with the mother, and five with the father.

The difficulty was attributed to maternal overprotection. The treatment plan had three objectives: to enable the mother to give the boy more independence, to strengthen the father's role, and to give the boy insight into his dependent and tyrannical behavior.

The patient broke many appointments with the psychiatrist, and after four or five interviews refused to come. In these interviews he made various defenses of his behavior, when prevented from escaping the subject, by typical distracting conversation.

The mother was told of the special need of greater independence for an adolescent boy. Her protective attitude, especially her close supervision, was reviewed. She was also given specific advice, for example, the importance of not requiring the boy to account for every cent of his allowance, telephoning him every afternoon, even when she knew where he was. "In a generally charming manner she opposed every suggestion made." Her complaints were chiefly about the patient's lack of consideration. Despite her oppositional tactics, she reported towards the end of her first year of treatment, that she was having the patient do more things for himself.

Modification of the father's attitude was more successful. He became friendlier with the patient, assumed responsibility for attending to problems of discipline previously left entirely to the mother, and spent much more time with him.

At a staff conference one year after referral it was stated: "There is a question as to whether the boy's problems are really very important. He appears to be making a fairly adequate struggle in a difficult environment."

Age 14 years, 3 months: The case was closed 22 months after referral and the status classified "unimproved."

Age 14 years, 5 months: Two months later the father telephoned by arrangement and reported that the boy had "vastly improved." The father and mother had taken a vacation away from the family for a month. Improvement was attributed to that fact, also to the patient's joining the Boy Scouts, and to the Institute, who "did more for the parents than for the boy." The patient was more independent and less demanding. The father said the parents had learned when to be firm and when to be lenient. Some difficulty in the mother-son relationship still remained. The father was apparently quite pleased and ended by saying that the Institute had now lost a patient.

Age 15 years, 11 months: Twenty months after closing, interviews were held with the patient and the mother by social worker and psychiatrist. The improvement after the parents returned from their trip was short-lived. The problems revealed at the time of referral were unsolved. The patient was still arrogant, disobedient and selfish. The mother regarded the value of her interviews at the Institute chiefly as a way of "clarifying" her thinking. This led her to conclude that the Institute was wrong in its advice. She had given the boy too much freedom and therefore decided now to be more strict. This change, she said, had already produced results in making her son more obedient.

Comment.—Therapy was limited to advice and giving "insight." No attempt was made to modify the patient's environment. An attempt at psychotherapy with the patient failed. It was seen early in the treatment that the mother's attitude would preclude efforts to enable her to accept the role of patient. It is of special interest that with a few interviews the father-son relationship was improved. The same result was found in other cases. Apparently where the father retains an affection for the patient he is able, when aided, to improve his status in the home. Since the challenge of the treatment is in the form of raising the father's self-esteem, the results are well comprehended; moreover, the problem as revealed to the father is easily understood and advice is specific. The father is to do definite things with the boy, to spend more time with him. Actually, in each instance where the father has changed, few definite suggestions were necessary. Although the father is helped to increased self-assertion, the mother is asked, when the overprotection is indulgent, to give up a relationship, to create a distance between herself and her child. Her task is to surrender her previous maternal function, evidently a more difficult problem than to make the contact closer.

It is significant that at one point it was the staff's decision that the boy's problems were rather unimportant, that he was an adolescent boy showing typical revolt against adult authority. The whole account of the indulgent overprotection and the problems of the patient in terms of selfish behavior and excessive demands might have been evaluated quite differently. Certainly the patient's difficulty in conforming to the requirements of discipline was a serious problem at the time, and since there was little if any modification of it, it was bound to be serious in the future. The fact that he was very bright and was doing pretty well at school may have mitigated this prognosis. Nevertheless, at school also there was some evidence of the same difficulty as at home, although never as serious.

Although hypochondria is given as a complaint at referral, it is not mentioned later on in the case record. A number of physical examinations were made and the patient was reassured during the period of investigation. Since the mother was voluble in her complaints it is very likely that if this problem had not abated she would have mentioned it.

It would appear in reviewing the problem that various aspects of the case were not regarded with sufficient seriousness; for example, the strong dominating phase in the mother's overprotection, the boy's overt sexual conflict in relation with the mother—mentioned in a previous chapter—the patient's refusal to continue with the treatment, and the sexual adjustment of the parents. Indeed, it may be stated generally that the problem of the over-indulged child is not treated with the seriousness it deserves.

Age 23 years, 1 month: Mother—interview with worker. The mother, a short plump woman in her 50s, was neatly dressed and spoke in a rather slow, modulated voice. She was quite friendly and spoke freely of herself, her children and her special problems with the patient. She was still very active socially and president of several organizations.

She gave the details of the patient's school progress and told of her great disappointment when he would not graduate from college. She cried, begged and bribed him to continue. Finally he did return to graduate but would not go on to a professional school because he wanted to marry. She told of the various jobs he had—he always managed to get a new one because of the fine impression he made. However he had no intention of holding such jobs steadily, changing always for something more interesting or profitable. Since he decided to marry, however, he was trying to find something steady.

The patient had his first girl at sixteen. The affair gradually waned. The mother "cautiously" managed to bring this about since she did not think it was a good match. His present girl was sweet, simple, and very submissive—so much so that the mother asked if she should try to make her more aggressive.

The mother has done everything for her children, yet the patient is still a problem. She always encouraged him to bring his many friends to the house, let them stay week ends. The patient, as previously, never wanted to help and was very careless with his room. The mother showed the worker his room. It was quite disorderly. According to the mother, the patient still would not eat at the table unless his mother served him. He still presented the same problem. He got everything and gave nothing. All the mother's attempts to make him more responsible at home failed. His temper tantrums, his "sullen and morose moods" were improved, especially since his friendship with the girl. That improved him a lot. In the course of time he had also become less impudent to the mother, in fact he was usually polite; and she must admit, though he never offered to help, he took part in all events at the home. He has been confiding in her, telling her all his problems.

Her relation with her husband, she said, remained as it was. She still regards him as the most interesting man she knows. They have many interests in common.

It was clear from the mother's account that she still watched over the patient's every step, tried to make all his decisions for him and steer him in the direction of her ambition.

In considering the work of the Institute, she expressed great admiration for its objectives, but thought, however, it was of no value to her in bringing up the patient; in fact, she regretted that she ever came because of the stigma. She admitted, however, that she never coöperated in the treatment.

Mother—interview with psychiatrist. The mother was coöperative and friendly. No evidence was revealed of psychosis or classical neurosis. She was still an active, ambitious woman, a type of community leader, organizer and president of societies, working as though driven, as overly concerned about her societies, she said, as about her children. Marital relations had not altered. She still accepted her husband's sexual demands with unpleasurable passivity, and still spoke of her husband in glowing terms.

She explained her solicitude toward the patient as a compensation for paying so much attention to the younger sister who was desperately ill for years during his early childhood—patient was age 4 to 9 years during this period.

The mother has always somehow taken care of people. In her own family, too, she took care of younger brothers and sisters. She was "always grown-up." She had no childhood of her own. She never played with dolls. She never protested against her duties. She loved the little ones. As she elaborated this theme, however, she revealed her inner protests. She wanted to be free. She resented the fact that whenever she went to see a friend she had to drag the kids along. Yes, she had enough of taking care of children. When she thought of marriage, she thought always that she did not want children. Nevertheless, she always needed to take care of people. As a child she used to bring all kinds of tramps to the home and got her mother to get them clothes and food. She always preferred children to babies. She was never a carriage peeker. When she would see a pretty baby on the street before marriage, she never felt a wish to have one of her own. She was "surfeited." Really, she said, "I never got what I wanted." Her ambition was research or art or music. She laughed, "I'm a frustrated woman. But regardless of what you do," she said, "you have to love children." As for men, she used to think they were all brutes. She had a number of proposals and refused. She had men friends, of course, but allowed no hugging or kissing.

Further elaboration produced very little material that differed essentially from the case summary written ten years earlier. There was in her case a strong father attachment and idealization, and powerful "masculine" strivings, especially along intellectual lines. Idealization of her husband, her sexual attitude, and intellectual ambitions for her son, are seen as derivatives of this relationship. She was frankly hostile to her mother. Her husband was similar to most others in the group in being kindly, submissive, responsible, and stable. He held an important position in a factory over thirty years.

The maternal behavior in this case had a more dominating than giving quality, although the latter was distinctly present. All in all, it appeared more compensatory than "pure," as evidenced by the weak response to babies as babies, the wish to have a childless marriage and the feeling of surfeit with the care of siblings in childhood.

Patient—interview with psychiatrist. The patient was well nourished, handsome, neatly dressed, tall—6 feet, 1 inch, well mannered, and a persuasive talker. He appeared eager to tell his story and was coöperative in taking a number of tests given by the psychologist. He had attained scores indicating marked superiority in intelligence tests at the age of 12. Repeated at the age of 23, his scores showed the same high rating. In vocational tests he selected jobs in which he could act independently, keep his own hours, make decisions, lead men, and have high executive position.

In the tests, as in the interview, he appeared anxious to make a good impression, to give the perfect reply, and at times turned the interview about and asked personal questions of the examiners, although with a polite foreword, for example, "I don't mean to be personal, but—".

In his two years of work, he had over eight positions. In each he was apparently successful but left for something better, on one occasion, after working three weeks. He gave up a good chance for advancement to embark on a speculative business enterprise with a friend. It came to nothing. In a factory job in which his original ideas were appreciated and utilized by the boss, he was not advanced when such an opportunity arose, because he could not be trusted with the responsibilities of the new position—a criticism he accepted as true.

At college he did fairly well in his studies, despite a great deal of loafing. He found the routine of study hard, and hated subjects requiring simply steady application—like foreign languages. "Conditioned" in one study, he refused to take the final examinations. A year later his mother compelled him to return to college. He did and finally got a degree. As an undergraduate, in line with the family tradition, he organized and became president of a student club.

He was quite frank in expressing his philosophy of life as purely a drive for pleasure and easy success. He had numerous business schemes and inventions. None of them were fantastic, in fact, some of them interested people competent to judge, yet none were based on thorough knowledge or experience. In his work he found adherence to routine difficult, and carrying out someone else's orders most difficult of all. He hoped to amass wealth quickly, entertain lavishly, buy expensive cars, have loads of servants, and the like. In spite of numerous shifts in his work he remained quite optimistic, bolstered up by evidence of success based on actual social talent, persuasive powers, and good imagination.

His relation to his mother had changed somewhat. He used to think she did not like him, that she preferred the other children. Now he thought differently. As in his childhood, her influence was greater than his father's, for whom he now had greater respect than as a child. He complained, as in childhood, that they did not give him enough privileges, that they did not allow him full use of the car, or enough money for clothes.

He spoke highly of his girl, whom he intended to marry as soon as he got a steady job. He was quite willing, however, to marry at once and accept parental support. This they refused to allow. From his account of his fiancée, her admiration of him and love of serving him seemed to be important factors in their relationship.

He had many friends, entertained at his home and was quite the life of the party, contributing songs and stories. He spoke of how people tried to take advantage of him and borrow money. He gave the impression that among his numerous male friends he had no close relationship.

He was quite frank about his sexual development. The usual adolescent masturbation was followed by irregular coitus starting at 17 or 18. He never suffered from impotence. Gratification with his fiancée was effected through mutual handling.

He was still much interested in reading, and favored technical books related to his inventions. He was a good swimmer. He had worked a few summers as camp counselor, was very fond of children, and was thought to be very successful with them. He was interested also in parties, dancing, and amusements.

There was no evidence of the hypochondriacal complaints recorded in his childhood. There was a great deal of interest expressed, however, in illness and sex.

Comment.—The closing status when patient was 14 years old was "unimproved." Two months later, the father reported definite improvement, which he and his wife attributed to their firmness and to the boy's membership in the Boy Scouts. A year and a half later, it was revealed that the improvement had been short-lived. The status was recorded again as "unimproved"—patient age 15 years 11 months. At 23 years, although the personality problems remain essentially the same, there was sufficient improvement in external behavior to adjudge status as "partially improved."

This improvement is seen chiefly in diminution of temper tantrums, and of impudent, disrespectful behavior. He now has better manners, is polite and apparently anxious to have his mother's good opinion. There are fewer tirades in the home, less irritability and complaints. There is also less display of jealousy towards his siblings and some evidence of interest in their activities. Nevertheless the patient remains selfish, demanding, dependent, and irresponsible in his duties as a member of the household.

In regard to his social relationships there is much improvement. He has changed from a timid cowardly boy, afraid to fight or make contact with other children, into a very sociable being who entertains frequently and seeks the company of others. In relationship with his mother there was also less friction, more politeness and many confidences. There was increasing respect for his father, although he still made numerous complaints that his parents were not doing enough for him.

His school progress had continued as in boyhood—fairly good achievement with little effort. He finished high school at 16, went to college for four years, did not graduate because he refused to make up a condition; finally he returned to do so through his mother's urging. His easy surrender of a degree because of a little extra work showed an instability that became more apparent when he worked for money. He would leave a job after several weeks or months, in an unstable manner, even though he could defend each change on the ground of more salary or interesting work. Some of his jobs were terminated because of his dislike of routine or because of authority rebellion.

Nevertheless, in evaluating his career as student and employee, the fact remains that he was stable enough to finish college, and was possessed of enough initiative and intelligence to get employment. He indicated also that he was eager to get a job and this time stick to it because he wanted to marry. In favor of potential stability was his anxiety to have general approval and his disturbance when it was pointed out to him that his work record showed unstable tendencies.

His previous aggressive behavior was distinctly socialized. He was polite, responsive, self-assured in conversation, distinctly able to talk for himself. The boyhood showing off and clowning had also been modified into the more acceptable entertaining conversation. Nevertheless, there seemed to be a distinct difficulty in relation to people. He could not take them naturally. He had to do something with them all the time, entertain them, help them, make them his audience. His difficulty was similar in this regard to his mother's, who was unable to accept children or grown-ups functioning independently of her. They had to be brought within the orbit of her protection or domination.

The patient's sexual development was considered with special interest because of the early history. He slept with his mother until age 13 years, when he showed overt anxiety, turning pale and leaving her bed. At 12 years there was disclosure of sex play with a sister. At 2 years of age he was told that if he continued playing with his penis a black cat would bite off his finger.

Evidently the threat during infancy did not curtail or exaggerate adolescent masturbation. Frequent sleeping in the same bed with his mother until age 13 had apparently no deleterious effect on his potency. However, anxiety about sexual experiences was inferred from his tenseness during that phase of the interview.

Although he seemed quite frank and coöperative, it must be remembered that the follow-up investigations presented in these studies were based on interviews, not on psychoanalytic explorations. Hence they cannot reveal material unconsciously repressed. Concerning the sexual adjustment of the patient we would conclude that although he manifested anxiety about sex it did not render him impotent, or deflect a heterosexual direction.

The patient's general improvement—except in regard to friends —may be described as a quantitative diminution of egocentric behavior. This is seen chiefly in the elimination of temper tantrums when thwarted; also in lessening of imperious demands, impudence, and infantile tyranny. The personality structure remains, however, essentially the same. Most serious is the evidence of instability in his work. It is possible, of course, that due to his brightness, initiative, and imagination, he may succeed in some work in which routine requirements and discipline are relatively unimportant. But in spite of modification in the magnitude of egocentric behavior, his ability to make that adjustment to authority and discipline of routine required in most undertakings appears quite unlikely. A diagnosis of psychopathic personality is made rather tentatively.

The mother's attitude remains inflexible. The father had changed when the patient was age 12 from an indulgent to a somewhat more disciplinary relationship. This has continued. The patient has felt his father's disapproval. This may help in his acceptance of paternal values, especially stability in work.

CASE 11

Age 10 years, 11 months: A boy, an only child, was referred through a physician because of disobedient, defiant, impudent, selfish behavior at home, and temper tantrums.

Psychiatrists had 16 interviews with the boy, five with his mother, and three with his father. Social workers had 20 interviews with the mother, one with the father, three with the patient, and two with his teacher. Treatment extended over a period of 15 months.

Maternal indulgent overprotection reinforced by the grandmother was recognized as the basic problem early in the case. The treatment plan consisted of psychotherapy for the patient to give him insight into his infantile symptoms and encourage growth into responsible behavior; psychotherapy for the mother to improve the marital relationship and give advice in the case of the patient.

The mother was told how her nagging and yielding to the patient contributed to his behavior. She was advised to ignore his screaming tantrums. She was given an opportunity to complain to the worker about the patient's spiteful behavior and encouraged to talk about her marital problems and her early difficulty with her own parents. She confessed to feelings of inadequacy in handling the patient, and fear that when he would be older he would disregard her because of her poor education. The advice given to her dealt with specific situations as they arose. It consisted chiefly in demonstrating how to ignore his attention-getting behavior, and encourage independent behavior. When, through the service of the Institute, the patient was sent to his first camp for two months, the parents were delighted. The mother during her visit felt jealous that the camp was able to discipline him. The boy told his parents that he knew "now" they wanted to get rid of him. When he returned in the fall, the mother was able to say to the social worker, "It's that boy that causes all the trouble. Our home was happy when he was away." The mother's difficulty with her husband was "a gradual estrangement." She concluded that his change after marriage from a "jolly, fun-loving demonstrative man" into an irritable and depressed one was due to the fact that she repelled his advances.

As treatment progressed the mother was able to talk more freely of her hostility to the patient. Finally she asked that he be sent to a boarding school. Although she scolded him more vehemently and freely complained about his difficulties, she would never accept treatment for herself. She dodged any discussion of her own difficulties in the relationship, and although numerous efforts were made by the social worker and psychiatrist to get her into therapy, the attempts failed. She remained friendly, however, toward the Institute, utilizing their help to get the patient into camp and to boarding school. She liked to feel the Institute was there, ready to help her. She hoped at the beginning of treatment they would act as policemen to her boy.

Psychotherapy with the patient failed as signally as with the mother. Free association was tried in the third interview and quickly given up. The patient did tell about his various methods of spiting his parents, like staying up late, but efforts at developing insight into his dependent attitude, and his baby tyranny, failed. He evaded all questions dealing with his own problems and managed to prevent the sessions from developing into anything more than social chats or "question and answer" interviews.

The father was seen on a few occasions, chiefly to give him understanding of the methods to be used and to gain his coöperation. His business did not allow sufficient time for more than a few appointments.

Age 12 years, 2 months: The case was closed 15 months after referral, status "unimproved." A month afterwards the father returned to the Institute and urged reopening the case.

Age 13 years: A follow-up visit, ten months after closing, revealed some improvement. The patient was not as impudent or disobedient, although it was still difficult to get him to go to sleep or wake up on time. He still refused to help with the housework. The mother complained that he was shy and retiring with strangers. He invited no children to his home, nor accepted invitations from others. His chief interest was reading. The patient never asked to return to the Institute, though he had liked coming. The mother thought he benefited from the sex instruction and was eager to return.

Status: partial adjustment.

Comment.—Therapeutic failure in this case was complete, yet the mother was enabled to coöperate in sending her son to a camp, and to express some of her hostile feelings. She arrived at the point where she even requested that the boy be sent to a boarding school, a real achievement in this type of case. She realized also how far the absorption in her son had affected her marriage, and was apparently willing to take helpful measures in improving her relationship with her husband. Despite these favorable signs, however, the treatment ended in failure.

One explanation lies in the stress placed on direct psychodynamic therapy. Although distinct progress was made, the staff was apparently dissatisfied in the way it was made. There was evidence of change in the maternal attitude sufficient to enable coöperation in getting the boy away from home. Along such lines, including direct advice to the mother, further progress might have been made, as in other cases. With increasing independence on the part of the patient, his own handling of the mother's overprotective attitude would have been strengthened. Yet all efforts in therapy became an attempt to penetrate the mother's inner psychic life. When she remained quite resistant, interest in all other procedures was dropped. This was an unfortunate favoritism of therapeutic method.

An interesting contrast of the patient's shyness in the presence of other children and free aggression at home was revealed in the follow-up study. The easy surrender of aggressive demands during his first experience in camp is a similar form of discrepancy explained in other cases in this series as evidence of highly inflated aggression in an overprotected relationship of a prevailingly submissive type of boy.

Age 21 years, 3 months—Summaries of psychiatrist's and worker's interviews with mother, father, and patient.—Patient: The patient was a good-looking, healthy, very muscular, neatly dressed young man of 21 years. He was 5 feet, 10 inches tall and weighed 180 pounds.

His problems at present, he said, were the "reverse of aggression." He was not aggressive enough, except at home. He was not especially assertive. He recognized he was very much so as a child, but he was unable to indicate any special period in which the change occurred. "It must have been very gradual." He never volunteered to recite at college, but if called on he had no difficulty because of shyness. He felt uncomfortable in the presence of girls, was afraid to make a "date" and envied boys who could talk to girls and "kid" them. He has always had difficulty, he said, in mixing with people. He had four or five friends he saw every Saturday evening, for cards and movies. He was too busy at present to have much social life, he said. He never had any "intimate" friends. He had a girl friend, but "not a steady."

In his work, the patient said, he was assertive, stood up for his rights, and on one occasion lost his temper with a bullying boss and struck him. Nevertheless he was considered justified and held on the job.

At age 16 years, he weighed over 200 pounds. He attributed his reduction in weight to his job and to sports, especially swimming and handball.

He has continued his studies. Because of family reverses he had to switch to night school and work during the day. He has been a shipping clerk the past two years, a job involving much lifting and hauling. He was the sole support of the family since his father failed in business one and a half years ago.

He was a junior at college. He majored in biology. At high school his grades were low because he spent too much time playing baseball.

He saw his mother at breakfast and dinner only, and Sundays. She still took good care of him, and made sure that he ate enough, he said. His relation to both parents was good, he thought. He learned to have a great deal of respect for his father. He thought the change came at the age of 15 to 16 years when he helped in his father's store and learned something about responsibility.

He began to masturbate at 16 years, and quit after a few months. He thought it was something to be condemned and anyhow he found he had no need for it. He denied ever having nocturnal emissions, or other forms of sex experience.

The patient was evidently a reliable, responsible, stable, industrious person with evidence of repression.

Mother: A neat, well-dressed, rather obese and tense woman, the mother was quite coöperative. She no longer regarded the patient as a problem. Temper tantrums and impudence at home were highly diminished. Certainly he made no bid for her attention. She complained that his table manners were still bad and he read way into the night. She confirmed the patient's statement about his bashfulness.

The mother was insistent on correcting any impression that she ever felt hostile to her son. She, like her husband, concentrated all her hopes on him. She moved to a section of the town convenient to his school and arranged everything according to his wishes.

Mother and father were now quite harmonious. The mother stated that all her bickering with her husband in the old days was only on account of her son.

Questions related to her maternal attitudes since childhood revealed a distinctly higher than average score on "maternal feelings."

The father regarded his son's bashfulness as an inheritance from himself. He spoke admiringly and affectionately of his son. He still could not sleep evenings, he said, until the boy was home. He considered his wife an excitable and nervous type, not easy-going like himself. He regarded their marital life as quite harmonious. He spoke of his financial difficulties. Despite his age, he was starting on a new job and was not discouraged.

CASE 12

Age 15 years: A boy, the second of two children, was referred through a high-school teacher because of unruly and defiant behavior at home, to the point of striking his mother and sister and throwing food all over the floor.

The psychiatrist had 26 interviews with the patient, and 10 with his mother. The social workers had 35 interviews with the mother, of which about eight were with both the mother and father. They also had 12 interviews with schoolteachers, relatives, employment agency and social settlement workers; several, also, with the patient. The treatment period was 35 months, but few contacts after the first 23 months.

The overprotective features were obvious, hence a clearly defined program of treatment was instituted early in the case. Psychotherapy was planned for the patient, to give him insight into his dependency, dominating behavior, and incestuous attachment to his mother. It was planned also to give the mother insight into her strong infantilizing behavior, to enable her to release the boy from her domination, and provide outlets of interest outside the home. It was planned also to help the father play a more active role with his son, and to improve his relationship with his wife. In case the objectives to be derived from psychotherapy could not be reached, it was hoped to separate son from mother for long intervals of time through summer camp and boarding school.

As the case progressed it was revealed that the mother had been very indulgent and the patient had become very aggressive, dominating and demanding. At some point, some years before referral, the mother reacted to the growing aggression of her son; the latter reacted in turn to the mother's attempts at discipline, producing a stereotyped pattern of nagging. It consisted of maternal attempts to infantilize and of filial attempts at release from maternal domination, resulting in insults, temper tantrums, assaults and imprecations. For example, when he was 15, the mother was shining his shoes, waking him up in the morning, still attempting to wash him, trying to prevent him from reading detective stories or listening to the radio, or joining a boys' club, or making friends. She was trying to control every movement he made. On the other hand, he freely criticized her appearance, her manner of speech; he spoke openly of his wish for her death; he accused her of being pregnant and of sleeping with a strange man. He prevented her from sleeping with her husband; he struck her when angry, threw knives or dishes at her, and threw food he did not like on the floor.

The patient was referred when the mother was in despair. She wanted the psychiatrist to frighten her son, to threaten him with an institution, to shame and scold. She herself had previously and unsuccessfully tried to board him with a relative. The idea of a boarding school for the patient was considered, but abandoned because of the patient's refusal. Further, it was believed that the mother would pursue her previous pattern of preventing a separation after it was made.

The mother quickly responded to the social worker and psychiatrist in a friendly way. She tried to utilize them for the purpose of aiding in the discipline of her son, of having them listen to stories of her maternal sacrifices and the resulting ingratitude. She telephoned frequently in order to have the worker at hand when the patient was performing at the height of his bad temper. She begged for boarding-school placement, and demonstrated her genuine distress and loss of health as a result of the bad treatment she was getting.

Attempts to get the father interested in the patient were unsuccessful. The patient was derogatory to him. The father took a night job in order to avoid the field of battle, yet remained the stable and responsible provider.

Throughout the period of treatment the workers were unable to change the mother's attitude to her son. Numerous demonstrations of her attempts to treat a 15-year-old like a three-year-old were made without effect. An attempt to explain, after about two years of treatment, that his various accusations of pregnancy and the like meant that she had so bound him to her that in his adolescence he was clearly sexually involved provoked only her disgust. Yet she remained attached to the psychiatrist and worker because she needed their help so badly.

In the second month of treatment when she was told she must stop shining his shoes, and performing similar services for him, the mother said, "O, how you break my heart when you say that." In the fourth month of treatment the worker noted "the mother's determination to dominate the patient and subject him to her will." A job was secured for the patient chiefly to keep him out of the house afternoons. The mother's response to this respite was, "The hours he is not home fly away so rapidly." In the eleventh month of treatment the mother finally expressed her willingness to have her son continue treatment with the psychiatrist, a woman, saying, "I do not care if he loves you better than me." As pressure was brought to bear on the mother to make her realize the ill effects of her infantilizing behavior, she had recourse more and more to various excuses that the difficulty was due to her son's fatigue, nervousness, abnormality, and, finally, insanity.

The boy made a quick and well-maintained positive response to the psychiatrist, despite his suspicion, because of numerous physical and intelligence tests, that she believed he was queer or insane. He diagnosed his own problems as "spoiled," blamed the mother for doing too much for him and himself for acting so badly. The interviews were held to an "insight level" of a rather discursive type because the patient showed quick resentment—and cancelation of appointments—when he was brought face to face with the real situation. It appeared as though he was making efforts to control his temper and his impatience with his mother, to gain the approval of the psychiatrist. A camp experience, starting seven months after referral, was of distinct value. At least for two months thereafter his behavior improved at home, although the relapse for a time was fairly complete. At camp he was popular and coöperative. When his parents visited him he treated them both, to their great delight, with affection and respect.

Age 17 years, 11 months: He lost two jobs through arguments with his employers, an attitude of indifference, and refusal to work. A third job was maintained longer than a year when the treatment ended. The gains that determined the classification "partially adjusted" were greater control of temper tantrums—less frequent and severe; maintenance of his job; and, generally more coöperative behavior at home.

Throughout the years of treatment and before, the patient was excellent in his studies and, according to the principal, "the pride of the school."

Age 18 years, 6 months: Follow-up studies were made two, five, six and seven months, respectively, after closing. The classification of the results of treatment at closing and follow-up was "partial adjustment."

Age 20 years, 1 month: Two years after closing, the patient, then age 20 years, graduated from college, an honor student.

Comment.—The feature of this case lies in its approximation to the theoretically extreme tyrannizing-infant product of indulgent overprotection, described in Chapter VIII. The overt behavior runs the whole gamut of activities testifying that the family is controlled by the child—disobedience, impudence, verbal abuse, complete lack of respect for the father, dominating and striking the mother. Maternal attempts to handle the problem likewise represent an extreme measure—that of escaping the fearsome aggression by sudden and complete abandonment. All measures failed because the mother nullified her own efforts. Pampering followed discipline, love followed abuse, entreaties to return followed eviction. The marked passivity of the father favored the development of so remarkable a picture of maternal overprotection, since there were no inhibiting measures to constrict the boy's dilating aggression.

Aside from the sexual elements in the relationship, manifest at the time of referral, case data, in retrospect, offer sufficient grounds for a very definite therapeutic maneuver; namely complete separation of mother and son. Other therapeutic activity could then be utilized, but not until the separation had been effected. It was apparent, early in the case, that psychotherapy was ineffective, and it appears doubtful, in view of the rigidity of the relationship pattern, that the most skillful psychotherapy could have budged it. Actually the only therapeutic spurt was in response to a placement at camp. Separation, as a feature of therapy, was considered after about six months, but excepting for a summer at camp, it was given up because of the patient's refusal to leave home.

The sexual involvement should have made separation a paramount issue. The boy's accusation that his mother was pregnant might have been interpreted as his refusal to have a rival brother or sister. An accusation, fortunately transient, that his mother was having sex relations with strange men, throws a different light, however, on the relationship, since it represents a typical mechanism of projecting one's own sex impulses on to others. The boy's desperate efforts at release and, at the same time, his strong efforts to keep the mother bound to him, were no longer explainable as a simple extension of the mother-infant problem into puberty, complicated as the relationship became by an active and stormy Oedipus complex.

The rapid adolescence of the patient helped to stimulate a series of crises, in which the mother was also definitely involved. Hence the attempts to separate the pair, and keep them separated for a long period of time, might well have engaged the major efforts of the staff. Psychotherapy of mother and son might then have had a chance to operate. Witness the relief the mother felt when the patient was out of the home. Her attempts to bring her son back and precipitate anew the difficulties of the patient might have been prevented by reinforcing the son's efforts at release.

In general, also, the improved behavior of a child when placed in camp or boarding school and the mother's feeling of relief during the separation give a measure of the "relationship-pathology," and a guide to therapy. There is quite a difference in this case from the relief of presumably normal mothers during a vacation from the burden of family cares. Other instances will be seen in these records, similar to this case, in which the mother's first experience of freedom from her indulged overprotected child is experienced as a wonderful respite.

Age 26 years, 10 months: Mother—interview with worker. A short, stout woman, with wrinkled face and gray hair, the mother looked at least ten years older than her actual age. She spoke with strong feeling, at times cursing, threatening, weeping bitterly. It was difficult to stop the torrent of words. She dominated the interview, brooked no criticism, repeated endlessly the refrain of the ideal mother, enforcing proper rules of conduct on her children, giving her life in the process and suffering only martyrdom.

She spoke of the Institute and the workers there with great affection. She wanted them to threaten her son and make him obey her because she knew what was best for him. Although he was a very successful college instructor, and a wonderful boy whom everybody loved, she said, he was still a problem at home. He graduated with honors and was working for a higher degree. He was still "nervous," still biting his nails. She believed a proper marriage was what he needed. Many girls were crazy about him, she said, but he took none of them seriously.

She complained that he was still stubborn and disobedient. He still wanted to be the boss. He spent money freely on himself, but gave little to his parents. Yet she saw to it that he ate the best kind of food and received every service. Even when he was in high school she used to bring his lunch for him every day. She still had to wake him up in the morning, caution him about going to bed on time, about reading too much, about reading detective stories. She gave definite indications that she was still completely informed about every detail of his life. He was still fighting hard against all her admonitions and requirements. She resented his having a car because in that way, she said, she could not always know where he was. She could not run after his car.

He was still threatening to leave home. He had left on a number of occasions but always came back. At this point the mother sobbed. She recounted the story of her moving into another apartment without his knowledge, as she had told it in the original investigation.

In the next interview the mother continued a similar refrain, complained of being the most unhappy mother in the world, and then stated that her son had moved out of the home.

The mother refused to keep an appointment with the psychiatrist, claiming she was ashamed of her appearance—so wrinkled and old.

In a third interview, limited to an investigation of maternal behavior she was quite willing to answer all questions. She had always been motherly since childhood. She often voluntarily took care of neighborhood children. Her favorite play with other girls was "mother and baby." She always responded very strongly to any baby she saw on the street. She hoped to have a child as soon as possible after marriage and as many as the Lord would provide. In her relations with men she was also primarily maternal. Her own rating of "very maternal" was consistent with all her replies.

Father—interview with worker. The father was seen in the presence of his wife. He was a tall, well-built man who looked quite young for his years. When he spoke critically of his son, his wife stopped him, and when he protested and tried to show how inconsistent she was, she stopped him nevertheless, and tried to change the subject. At this time her main concern was the fact that her son had moved. The father was able to say that his son was disorderly in the care of his room and showed him little respect. Because of the mother's insistence the father was still sleeping in the same room with his son, since the latter did not like his parents to sleep in one bed (see case summary, Appendix).

The father gave the impression of a resigned, intimidated, discouraged, and submissive husband. He claimed, nevertheless, and despite his wife's strong objection, that his son was on better terms with him than with her, and at times even complimented him.

Both parents praised their 22-year-old daughter. She was a good, obedient girl, who would marry according to their wish. She had a job in a distant city and helped support her parents. Her brother, they said, was mean and always fought with her.

Patient—interview with worker. The son, a very tall—6 feet, 3 inches —good-looking, well-mannered person, was quite friendly. He had fond memories of the Institute. They helped him a lot but he was still a problem, he said laughingly. His difficulties with his mother were the same now as then. Outside his home he had no difficulties. He spoke about his teaching, and his outside activities.

His mother still nagged him, he complained. She still tried to run his life; nevertheless he liked her very much and realized he was "a bad boy." He liked his father. He never had any trouble with him. He realized his father was under his mother's thumb. He told of the numerous attempts he made to please his parents. When he treated them to the theater his mother never stopped nagging him for his extravagance. He was engaged to be married, he said. He kept his fiancée from visiting his mother because of the numerous questions to which she would be exposed.

He knew, he said, he had an Oedipus complex. That is what he was told at the Institute. He really never had a home. His mother spoiled his childhood. Her authority alone, he said, ruled the household. Father dared not say a word. His protests were feeble and quickly ended. Sister frequently rebelled and was now living outside the home. He liked his sister and was going to visit her soon. They quarreled at home, but no more, he thought, than other brothers and sisters. No, he would not let his mother spoil his future, as she had spoiled his past. At the end of the interview he left to see a football game.

Patient—interview with psychiatrist. It was interesting to note the mannerisms of the patient compared with those observed when he was fifteen. Seen in the waiting room, he was sitting down with knees spread far apart, smoking a cigar. He rose to greet me affably. He had grown considerably and weighed over 250 pounds. He was friendly during the interview; said he knew he was the worst kid on earth. When an attempt was made to explain how this came about, he said, "Don't tell me. I know. It was my lack of will power. Many kids with the same upbringing came out all right." When I tried to demonstrate that his reply was another version of his idea that he was just bad, his reply was, "Well, you're the psychologist. You know more about these things than I do." Unlike the fifteen-year-old behavior, he was not contentious. There remained a similar assurance, a similar "I know better than you" attitude, general freedom of gesture; nevertheless a more flexible use of the aggressive tactics with modification through politeness, admission of ignorance, and the like. What appeared clear was the socialization of the early adolescent impudence. He gave the impression that as a teacher he would be very effective, since he would be direct, incisive, verbalize in an interesting manner, never vague or wobbly in expressing his opinion.

In regard to his mother he had solved the problem, he said, by just keeping away. He went there for mail and ran out as quickly as he could. He just could not take it any more. She would start to nag, to holler, and abuse him. She upbraided him constantly. Whatever he did was unsatisfactory. He gave her many gifts. She found fault with all of them, even household utensils, which he thought would appeal to the "home body." He had thought of saying, "Tell me, what do you want? I'll give you as much money as I have if you'll stop nagging. What's the price?" But he knew it would do no good. He had himself insured for a large sum so that in case of his death she would have enough money. When he marries, next June, that policy will not be altered. He will take on new insurance for his wife.

He showed me a letter written by his father, which he received yesterday. It was full of abuse. It said, in effect, no son has treated his parents so badly, that he hopes when he has a son he will get his just dues; but it ended with a line reminding him that tomorrow is election day and he should not forget to vote. The patient said this was a typical pattern of all the letters he receives. Of course, he said, it was his mother's letter, written at her dictation by the submissive husband. The note at the end was also typical. No matter how far the abuse went there was always that loving note at the end—"don't forget to take care of your cold," and the like. This letter as a specimen was a mild example and that was why he was willing to show it to me, he said. The others were terrible. He felt guilty about his mother every so often, but it passes off. In response to a question, he said that he had a fear at the Institute that he must be crazy because of all the tests they gave him. He could not accept their assurance that he was not. Evidently he still had that feeling, and in that connection I asked if his feeling of guilt was a problem to him sufficient to be treated. "Not at all," he replied. He was perfectly satisfied. The feeling of guilt he had about his mother—"Oh, it comes once in a week or so and it always passes off"—he considered he could do something about. He felt so obligated to her, knew all she had done for him, and how bad he was, and how ungrateful. But what can you do about it? He could not stand her nagging. He just could not take it.

The only nervous thing about him, he said, was his nail biting, which he still does. He has done it since he was a kid. With his sister, his relations were friendly, at least cordial, He believes she went out of town to get away from home. Mother ruined her, too. She shows, he thinks, traits similar to his own. The mother tried to run her life in every detail as she did his.

Fortunately he has gotten out of it. Time has helped. As for the treatment at the Institute, it did little for him. However, there was one point he wanted to stress. It did a valuable thing for him by sending him to camp. That was the first really "social" experience he had in his life and he was sure it helped. Also as time went on he realized that the doctors were really interested in him, that they were really trying to help him. That he felt keenly.

He has a large number of acquaintances, especially fellows who borrow money from him. As for friends, he regards three as intimate.

He still plays chess and reads a great deal as he did in childhood. His old chess companion has become quite an expert.

As for his scholastic success and his honorary key, he discounted their value. He went in for his specialty because he happened to write an unusually good paper and the professor commented so favorably on it that he took more courses with him. That was always his best subject. He was also good in mathematics, he said. He was poor in biology. He thought of going into medicine at one time because by chance he got 100 on a biology examination, when students far better than he got 70s and 80s. He is considered a successful teacher, he said, and an authority in certain phases of the subject he teaches. He will soon get his Ph.D.

In response to questions, he said he was sexually potent. He had his first experience in sexual relations at 21 years and it was successful. Coitus has occurred at regular intervals since. He was now engaged and intended to marry in a few months. There was not sufficient time to elaborate the determination of his choice.

He left in a very friendly manner, thanked me very much for giving him this time, said there was a great need for psychiatry and that if he ever found someone with problems he would send him over. He recounted how parents came to him and told him how badly their children behaved at home whereas in college they were all right. This statement was in response to a question I asked as to his own explanation of his obedient behavior in school in contrast with the rebellious behavior at home. He was not especially interested in any explanation I had to offer, because he was quite sure that any explanation was false. "You never can tell," he said, "sometimes it's one way and sometimes it's the other."

Comment.—Problems of special interest in this case appear to be success in a career despite severe overprotection; presumably normal heterosexual adjustment with a history of incestuous conflict and a powerful mother-son attachment; and, rigidity of the maternal overprotective attitude.

The protection of his school experience from the inroads of maternal overprotection was shared in this case, as in others, by mother and son alike. It has been demonstrated previously how mothers, indulgent in every other way, exempt the child's schoolwork from that type of behavior. They utilize the protective relationship in ensuring the child's success by disciplining and assisting in homework, and visiting teachers. Maneuvers on the part of the child to get out of responsibility, likewise, may fail completely, in regard to studies, although succeeding in other directions.[2]

The patient had superior intelligence. He enjoyed a great deal of satisfaction in his school success. He regarded the school as his own domain, one in which neither parent nor social worker was allowed to enter. He protested violently against any contact between the Institute and his school. After the early grades he assumed full responsibility for his work. His mother's nagging was unnecessary, although she tried to prevent him from reading to all hours. Teachers regard him as a model pupil and the principal at graduation exercises spoke of him in terms of highest praise. His vocation as teacher was a continuation of work in which he felt most secure.

This success is probably the redeeming feature in regard to the patient's stability. It will be noted in cases of indulgent overprotection that the breakdown in work stability occurs when intellectual discipline is weakened by the self-indulgent behavior. Success in his vocation evidently had also a general stabilizing effect on the patient. He learned to think in terms of his career and guard his behavior accordingly. An explanation of his apparently normal sex development is attempted in Chapter VIII.

The control exerted in this case, explained in part as a development out of work stability, has apparently included also the patient's decision about marriage. He has provided for his parents. His selection of a wife is deliberate. His guilty feelings about his mother are, in a sense, evidence of a responsible attitude.

The mother's completely unmodified attitude is something to marvel at, but difficult to explain. It indicates the remarkable tenacity of heightened maternal behavior, and probably its generally primitive and elemental quality. In this case, besides the "reinforcing" factors referred to, the binding quality of the incestuous conflict is noteworthy.

[2] Besides various competitive drives on the part of parents, and the need of self-esteem through the child's success, there is frequently a feeling in regard to schoolwork that it is a necessary life adjustment.

CASE 13

Age 14 years, 6 months: A boy, the older of two children, both boys, was referred through a "guidance teacher," because of failure in school-work despite superior intelligence. To this problem the patient appeared quite indifferent. He truanted frequently, always alone, and spent the time away from school reading books. He was an omnivorous reader. There were complaints also of boisterous, undisciplined behavior in the classroom, talking, constant restlessness and disobedience. The younger brother was seven months old. Excepting for poor vision, well corrected by glasses, the patient had good health and strength.

He had 10 interviews with the psychiatrist, 12 with social workers. The latter had also 12 interviews with his mother, seven with his father, one with his uncle and nine with school teachers, over a period of 15 months.

"Evidence of spoiling by the mother since the beginning" was noted as obvious by all those in contact with the case.

The treatment plan began with an attempt to solve the school difficulty by urging his promotion to a higher grade, despite failure, since tests of intelligence and scholastic achievement indicated that he was placed two grades below his proper level. It was thought that work in a higher grade would overcome his boredom and stimulate him to greater achievement. Since his father had practically no contact with him, it was thought advisable to exploit the relationship to an uncle in order to establish paternal influence. Contact with other children through play groups or a boys' club was also recommended. As for contact with girls, the mother was frankly prohibitive and said she wanted to hold on to him, as her boy, until he reached the age of 30 or 35. Psychiatric interviews were arranged, in order to give the boy insight into his behavior, and encourage the development of a responsible attitude. For the summer vacation, a plan was made to place him in a tutoring camp. to make up his deficiency in arithmetic, his weakest subject.

The main difficulty in treatment, summarized in a case conference four months after referral, was related to the mother's "complete satisfaction" with her son. Since attempts to change the attitude of mother and son had failed, it was decided to shake the maternal complacency, and indicate clearly that she was the source of the patient's irresponsible behavior.

The social worker, a male, took several trips with the patient and his friend. On these trips the patient was inconsiderate, and relied on the others for most of the work. On a trip to Coney Island he was a nuisance, interfering with the amusement of others, rushing from one place to another. Numerous attempts to get him to accept a camp experience finally succeeded. During his two weeks at camp, he showed off a great deal but was well accepted by the counselor and boys. He was especially good in swimming.

His promotion to a higher grade was accomplished. However, he truanted as previously and also failed to keep appointments with the psychiatrist. In the fifth month of treatment, the mother acknowledged her helplessness with the patient. She said she had no control over him. He did as he wished, going where he pleased and coming home at any hour. She confessed also her fear of the Institute study, a fear that they would try to find insanity in her son, as her neighbors warned her. This attitude was consistent also with her earlier belief that the school teachers were especially opposed to her son and failed to appreciate his real merit. During this period, the mother revealed to the workers the difficulties of her childhood, her strong maternal feeling for all children, her sexual and social difficulties in marriage.

In the next month—the eighth month following referral—the school authorities transferred the patient to a probationary school, because of his repeated truancies. The patient did well in his studies at this school "because of fear" of their disciplinary measures. Although urged by the Institute to keep him there, as a necessary experience in meeting a "reality situation," the mother tried her best to get him out. She gave up her educational ambition for him, and had her husband use influence to get him his working papers. During the probationary school period the patient had frequent attacks of headache and vomiting spells, for which the mother tried to keep him home. During a psychiatric interview, at this period, the patient was told clearly "the severity of his problem." Psychotherapy with more frequent interviews was recommended. Meanwhile, however, the mother enabled her son to get working papers, and his school experience was ended—18th month following referral. The headaches and vomiting spells disappeared.

In looking over the working papers it was found that the mother had concealed from the Institute—and the patient—her son's true paternity. She confessed she had made a runaway marriage at the age of 15 years, was divorced a year later because of her first husband's neglect and alcoholism. She married again when her son was less than one year old.

Meanwhile the patient was lax about getting work. He held a few jobs for short periods of time. The family moved on two occasions and left no forwarding address, although apparently friendly when contacts were reëstablished. The patient kept up a desultory contact with the psychiatrist, trying to get his help in securing a job with the merchant marine. He maintained a friendly attitude. The mother strongly opposed the patient's wish to get a job as a sailor. He threatened to run away from home. But the mother was adamant and the patient kept his word. When visited at home the mother seemed less disturbed about him than the worker anticipated. Since neither mother nor patient ever really accepted therapy, the case was closed.

Age 15 years, 9 months: The status, 15 months after referral, was classified as "unimproved." During the next two years, five attempts to locate the family failed.

Age 17 years, 10 months: Two years and four months after the case was closed, the patient came to the Institute to visit his psychiatrist. Although the latter was no longer in residence, the patient was quite willing to interview another. He revealed that he had kept in contact with his mother, although he no longer lived at home. She supplied him with funds. His reason for remaining away was not the job, he said, but a love affair he wanted to forget, knowing it could not end in marriage because the girl's family was opposed. In the intervening two years he had held various odd jobs. One of his "real reasons" for interviewing the psychiatrist in previous years, he said, was the chance it gave him to skip school. When asked what his goal in life was he replied, "Yes, I have a goal—everyone has it—that's death. We all have to die." Later he changed his reply to "an urge for travel."

Status: unimproved.

Comment.—A high degree of indulgent overprotection was manifested. The mother stated frankly her aim of continuing to mother her son until he would be 35 years old. The tenacity of the relationship cannot be expressed more clearly. The father, or rather the stepfather, as he later turned out to be, entered the relationship only to add to the indulgence. He had so little influence that the workers in the case decided it was hopeless to engage his interest in developing a paternal role. The mother at times recognized her plight, wished her husband could exert more influence, but was apparently unable to modify her behavior, fighting against all therapeutic efforts.

It is difficult to tell from the record in how far the patient's special difficulty in arithmetic was related to the truancy. Refusal to remain in a classroom in which an unpleasant task was at hand is quite consistent with his behavior elsewhere. He was never able to adjust to ordinary classroom discipline, to keep from wandering about the room. Home and school behavior were more consistent in his case than in the other overindulged boys with high I.Q.'s. The truancy was not of the usual delinquent variety, since he spent the time out of school chiefly with books.

His sexual behavior is difficult to appraise. It may be understood as an incestuous conflict with his mother; a theory that would explain the instance of sex experience, the smutty talk, the attempt to marry so early in life and get away from home. The difficulty could be explained also in the light of his undisciplined behavior and self-indulgence. On that basis, conflict would assume a secondary role to "instinctual" gratification.

The markedly unstable school and work record, the high degree of self-complacency, and the continued experience of life with a mother fighting off the possibility of modification through reality experience, makes for a doubtful prognosis.

Age 25 years, 6 months: The patient died at the age of 25 years, 6 months. The worker had interviews with his widow and his mother.

Mother—interview with worker. The mother was a tall, large-breasted, neatly dressed, dignified woman of 49—height 5 feet, 11 inches; weight 146 pounds. She was friendly and coöperative. She talked slowly and calmly. When speaking of her son her eyes filled with tears. He was everything to her. She gave the impression when talking about him that he was still alive.

He died two years ago. He was found lying on the sidewalk unconscious, taken to a hospital in a police ambulance, and died there in 45 minutes. His death remains a mystery. The police record noted a fractured skull, received through a fall from the roof of the house where he had been visiting friends. On the night of his death he had been visiting an old man, whom he used to see frequently, and a friend of his own age. Accident, suicide and murder were all considered as possibilities. The mother believes it was murder.

Indirectly she attributed the murder to his wife, who would not share his interests, who lived her own life and led him therefore to seek friends of whom they knew nothing. Her daughter-in-law missed her son as much as she did, she said. She is a nice, intelligent girl, but she never should have married. Her son was unable to support a wife, especially the kind of wife she was—a child, totally unprepared for life, ignorant of the duties of a wife, unable to fight for a man or stimulate him to live a decent life. He married at 19. She was 18. They kept it a secret, each living in their own home. One day the mother discovered their marriage certificate. Then she had them both live with her. Their baby was born soon afterwards, five years ago. Later they moved to their own apartment, although her daughter-in-law knew nothing about managing a house, or anything else. Her son helped a lot. He used to clean the child, take it to the park, and really bring it up. When the wife went out evenings studying voice, he would stay at home with the baby. When she finally got a job on the road, he came back with the baby to live with his mother.

He never reproached his wife, although he must have suffered very much. His condition at this time was revealed by a poem he wrote, a poem in which he expressed his longing for death, which he depicted as a benevolent woman.

When his wife returned they lived together in a furnished room. The mother never visited that room, because at that time she was not on speaking terms with her daughter-in-law. This came about because her daughter-in-law said very critical things about her son.

The mother told her story in a quiet, rather factual manner. She went on to say that her son never had a steady job. He worked with his father for short periods of time. He got a W.P.A. job for a while but quit in a few months because the work was too hard for him. He was on relief most of the time. The mother also gave him money. She does not regret it. She could never refuse him. Why did that girl ever marry him?

He had loads of friends. Everybody liked him, and his nice manners. He made acquaintances easily, associated with everybody. He was generous to a fault. He would give away his last cent. But his quick friendships did him no good, as his end proved.

The mother then dwelt on her son's virtues, his delicacy, his talent for art and poetry. If he had had a good education he would have become a creative artist. He just could not look for a job, not that he was lazy or that he did not feel badly about not supporting his family. He was a child. He was never responsible. He never worried about the daily problems of life. He never should have married.

For her, he was the best son in the world. The severest punishment she could give him was refusal to kiss him goodnight. He used to tell her everything. He was always so charming. He always brought her gifts.

Her husband was still the steady worker and provider. He was always good to his stepson, treating him like his own.

The younger son was quite different from her first-born. He was sturdy, good at school, not confidential like the older, and ambitious to be a football player. Just a regular boy.

Seen on two other occasions, the mother confirmed the material elicited in the original investigation.

An inquiry into her "maternal feelings" revealed strongly maternal behavior since childhood. She always selected the role of mother in childhood play. She took a doll to bed with her up to adolescence. She had a keen interest in babies. As an adolescent her ambition was to be a mother, have a large family, and get her first child as quickly as possible. In her relation with men she also played chiefly a maternal role. She rated herself as very maternal, and knew no one who, more than she, "put her own life" in her children.

In relation to her grandchild, she wanted to assume full care. But her daughter-in-law fought against it.

Wife—interview with worker. She was a small, thin, fragile woman of 23, rather reticent at first, later quite friendly.

She idealized her husband when she first spoke about him, describing him as a kind of saintly bohemian. She was 18 when she married, and as childish as her husband. Whenever he earned some money he would spend a good part of it to buy her presents, without regard to their needs. He had no trade. He never worked steadily, yet he never worried about money. He spent very little on himself for clothes, but always had enough to buy candy and liquor for himself.

Her marriage changed her considerably. She learned to manage a household, take care of the child, and manage as well as possible with a small budget. But her husband never changed at all. He would charge things in the grocery store, get everything he liked and never worry about the bills. He never felt responsibility. He was always sure help would come.

At first he expected his mother to help them. Later his wife took on the mother's role. When he would be really up against it, he would sit down and read. He read a great deal. Funny, he was not really lazy. He accepted work when it was offered to him. He seemed strong and willing, but he never could look for a job, and could never find one. For most of their six years of married life, he was on relief. He had a job for a little while with the W.P.A. When they fired him he was heartbroken. Then he felt altogether useless.

His wife praised him for his intelligence, his information, and his artistic talent. He kept on educating himself and felt inferior to others who were better educated than he.

He was quite popular. He made friends easily and had a good word for everybody. He was polite, good-natured. His ease in making friends probably caused his death.

She tried to explain the cause of his death. They had not quarreled for a long time. She had nagged him earlier in marriage, but gave it up as hopeless. She knew he had thoughts of death, thoughts, he said, she could never understand. But for months before he died he had shown no evidence of morbid thinking. It could not be suicide, she said, yet it was hard to believe that anyone killed him. Everybody liked him. He had no enemies. It was all so puzzling.

When their child was born, he was quite jealous. He thought she gave the baby too much attention. Later when she went out with both of them, each quarreled to be near her. He thought the boy was too wild, and that she was too indulgent.

Her husband was often as gay as a child. He liked to travel and planned a long trip, although they had no money. Yet he made all preparations and was always on the look-out for an old car.

Their sexual life was normal in the first year of marriage. Both enjoyed sex relations. Although passionate, he was considerate of her. As time went on, her desire for sex relations was less frequent. In general, she concluded that her husband had been childish and completely unprepared for marriage. He lived and died as a child.

She knew that he could get anything he wanted from his mother. He had the same knack of getting things from other people too. People somehow "felt compelled" to help him. She blamed his mother for spoiling him, and keeping him so irresponsible. She knew, of course, that his mother never wanted him to marry.

She is now having trouble with her son. She does not know how to handle him. He disobeys and even though only five years old he does not get to bed until eleven. She would like to get a job but has not the courage or the energy to make the rounds. She would rather live on relief as she is now doing.

Six months after the interview reported above, she wrote to the worker requesting help for her mother-in-law. The latter "loved her grief." She wanted her daughter-in-law and husband to keep in perpetual mourning for him. She surrounded herself with his pictures and belongings. Going to her home was a constant reënactment of his death. The mother-in-law chided her with "getting over" her grief. She was also constantly insinuating that the baby would be better off with her. She wanted her son's baby, and tried to instill fear of the future in her. The daughter-in-law's question was simply, should she desert her mother-in-law on behalf of the child and her own mental health?

Comment.—Maternal overprotection is represented in this case in "purest" form. As far as possible the mother made the relation to her son her sole *raison d'être*. To use her expression, she put her life in her son. The same outpouring of feeling continued after his death.

In the difficulties that ensued, the mother was completely helpless. She lost the power to discipline or deny. She could only give. In spite of his irresponsible behavior, school truancies, failure in work, and a foolhardy marriage, she could readily find excuses for him. When she first came to the Institute there was a period of critical reaction on her part. This passed by. As in the case of other mothers in the series, it was forgotten or denied. In her defense we perceived also a necessary defense of her own being, which was invested in him.

Psychoanalytic investigation, as explained previously, was not possible in these cases. The patient's suicidal impulses could have been understood in the light of that procedure. Nevertheless, their relation to the incestuous attachment may be inferred. The first inkling of a suicidal trend appears in the record when the patient was 17 years old. Then he stated that his goal in life was death. His morbid thoughts were well known to his wife. She believed he was in need of treatment on that account. In his poem he depicted death as a benevolent female, obviously a mother-figure. His escape from home and his impulsive marriage indicate the turbulent adolescent struggle to solve the problem of incestuous attachment. Since his poem greeted the female figure of death as his love, and extolled her virtues of kindness and generosity, it would appear that his suicidal impulses represented a wish to die in order to attain eternal union with his mother, as in the paradise of infancy, rather than a murderous revenge against reality, turned inwards.

He never changed; he remained a child. This observation repeated by mother and wife is well confirmed. With his wife he continued the pattern of dependent, indulged child, and remained throughout his marriage in close contact with his mother. His response to frustration was not vindictive. At such moments he would bury himself in books. The entire picture lends support to the inference that his suicidal trends were determined more by regression than revenge.

Facts about his death are too meager to allow speculation about its cause. His ready association with any person he met, a probable contributing factor, is in keeping with his experience from early childhood that everyone would play the role of kindly parent. His wife spoke of the fact that everyone he knew felt "compelled" to help him, like his mother. He had evidently a winning way with people, consistent with findings in the other cases of indulged overprotected—the disarming and immediate confidential, appealing behavior of the young child.

The manifestations of his personality that appear in others of the indulged group are complacency, optimism, self-assurance charm, conversational ease, ready dependency, irresponsibility, selfish behavior. He differs from the others in showing a greater sensitivity, less impudence, aggression and initiative.

Of special interest in this case, as in others, is the fact that the remarkable attachment to the mother did not apparently affect his sexual potency. There was also no evidence of homosexuality. A possible explanation for this finding, on the basis of the need to gratify one's impulses as exerting a prior claim to conflict, has been stated in Chapter VIII.

CASE 14

Age 5 years, 11 months: A boy, the elder of two children, was referred by his father, because of quarreling and fighting with his sister and other children, impudence, disobedience, and attacks on the parents.

The psychiatrist had two interviews with the patient. The pediatrist examined him several times because of sinus infection. The latter also had two interviews with the mother, two with the father, and one with the family physician. The period of treatment was 15 months.

The difficulty was attributed to maternal oversolicitude, and marital disharmony. The treatment plan was habit training for the patient and work with the mother to diminish maternal anxiety and encourage social contacts outside the home. The father, who kept at his work constantly, was to be encouraged to spend more time with the children. To ease the problem of sibling rivalry the four-year-old sister was to be sent to a nursery school. The maternal oversolicitude was mitigated chiefly by the pediatrist, who was able to demonstrate that the patient had good health, and that the difficulty with the sister was a usual family problem. The pediatrist gave the mother advice that enabled her to expect more "self-help" from the child, in the way of putting on his clothes and other items. She explained her overprotective attitude on the basis of her own bitter experience in childhood. She swore if she ever had children they would never suffer from lack of love. A particular problem had to do with her fear that when the children were educated they would be ashamed of her difficulty in speaking English and her foreign ways.

The problems that the mother presented, of affect hunger and anxiety over possible rejection by her own children, the marital difficulty which involved sexual frigidity, were not utilized in therapy. The reason is not clear from the record, which is somewhat contradictory on this point. One may infer, however, that after her anxieties about the child's health were allayed—there was a history of several severe infections of infancy and much warning by the doctor to give special care—she showed little interest in further treatment. In general, the method used in the treatment of this child is of a type that any general practitioner utilizes; namely, reassurance about the child's health in view of the absence of organic pathology, further reassurance that the child's behavior is much like that of other children and that the mother's worries about the future were unfounded, and advice that she should not baby the child.

Age 7 years, 2 months: The status at closing was "partially adjusted." There was no follow-up. The details that determined the classification "partially adjusted" are not given, excepting that the mother presumably became less apprehensive about the child. A closing note states that the mother was satisfied that she obtained all the physical examinations and information she wanted, and was grateful. Evidence that there was any change in the behavior of the patient is not given. Since, for whatever reason, the case was treated chiefly on the basis of advice and reassurance, a follow-up study would have been of special interest. However, this was not done.

Comment.—It is difficult to evaluate the factors in this case. The mother said in one of her interviews with the social worker that she was much relieved to find out that there was nothing organically wrong with the child and that his behavior with the sister was nothing unusual. The fact that she did not care to go on with the treatment after such reassurance may be due to the fact that very little pressure was brought to bear upon her, or that the workers on the case were satisfied with the results obtained by their method. Since there was tremendous apprehension about the child's physical condition, it is easy to understand how a solution of this problem would in itself release sufficient tension to change the mother's attitude towards the whole problem. On this point there is evidence of strong external factors. The child had a severe infection of the cervical glands in infancy, with high fever and convulsions. Illnesses occurred over a period of 10 months; the physician was himself apprehensive. He advised the mother to keep the child out of drafts because of his tendency to run high temperatures so readily. The examinations at the Institute were thorough; much time was taken with the mother in the examining room. After she was relieved about the child's health she apparently had little interest in going on. The difficulty in evaluating the severity of the overprotective attitude lies in the determination of the extrinsic factors involved, since under the circumstances given, a presumably normal maternal attitude would be intensified. There is other evidence, however, that we are dealing in this case with maternal overprotection (see case summary).

Age 16 years, 3 months—Summary of worker's interviews with mother, father, patient, and sister. Patient is 5 feet, 11 inches tall, well nourished and in good health. The general problems of aggressive behavior were apparently modified towards the end of treatment. He has been obedient, submissive to his mother, and distinctly shy. His relation to his father is cordial and respectful. His relation to his sister is very friendly. She twits him about his shyness and tries to encourage him to make friends. His parents likewise encourage more social activity, but he prefers to stay at home, and uses various pretexts to keep out of the company of boys or girls.

When first examined at the Institute, he was a model child in kindergarten, although difficult at home. He remained a very obedient and successful student in school. He graduated from high school at 15—I.Q. 117—and is now at college.

He is a hard worker, always busy with his studies, and has no time for hobbies.

A history of his sexual development was not obtained.

Status: partially adjusted.

The mother's attitude remains unchanged. The old observation that "she watches her children as though through a microscope" remains true today. She directs the patient's choice of subject, vocation, and encourages him socially by inviting boys and girls to the home. A strong and very friendly relationship exists between all members of this family, including husband and wife. The father remains the same reliable, steady, shy, submissive soul, and his wife's great admirer. The wife says she cares for him in the same way as her other children, and knows all his wishes before he expresses them. The sexual difficulty has remained unchanged.

A "maternal history" of the mother was secured. It shows a consistently very high "maternal score" since childhood.

Case 15

Age 7 years, 5 months: A boy, the older of two children, was referred by his mother because of difficulty with school work, lack of aggression, clumsiness, difficulty with other children because of fear, and "mental retardation." Intelligence tests at the time of referral and eight months later yielded a rating of "low average intelligence."

Over a period of two years, two months, psychiatrists had 19 interviews with the patient and one with his grandmother. Social workers had 31 interviews with the mother, five with the father, 15 with schoolteachers, and two with relatives of the patient. The psychologist and pediatrist had 16 sessions with the patient and his mother.

Maternal overprotection was recognized as the major problem. A plan of treatment was outlined which had as its objectives a change in the mother's attitude, to enable the boy to become less dependent on her; a change in the father's attitude, so that he would stop making unfavorable comparisons of the patient with the brighter son; also to cure the patient of malnutrition and correct his myopia. Congenital syphilis was considered at the initial examination, because of slight incoördination and twitching of eyelids, lips and fingers during the Romberg test. This was confirmed by laboratory tests. The mother was also examined. Both had syphilis, and took treatment until repeated Wassermanns were negative. The mother showed no clinical evidence of the disease. Placement at camp was considered, only to be rejected, since it was thought to be too drastic a step at the time. The main reliance in treatment was placed on a change in the mother's attitude.

The social worker gave the mother specific advice in handling the patient: for example, to have him shine his own shoes, dress himself, to wait on himself at table, and cut his meat; and to be more casual with him, stop coaxing and babying, and explaining everything. The worker also gave the mother books to read on the subject of "growing up." By the seventh month of treatment the patient was dressing himself, going to school alone, and showing other benefits of that type. Examined in the eighth month of treatment, improved coördination was noted, and attributed to the antiluetic treatment.

The schoolteacher was interviewed. She coöperated in helping the patient by private instruction after school hours. A better visual correction of his "moderate" myopia was achieved. Interviews with the father resulted in a greater display of interest in the patient, and a growing companionship. The father aided also with the patient's schoolwork. He did carpentry with him, and promised to get him a dog.

Age 8 years, 7 months: Physical improvement in health, strength, and coördination was noted in a summary of the "case status" at the 14th month of treatment. By this time the patient was going places himself, and having friendly play with boys. The mother was less protective of him and apparently willing to accept the fact that he would always have difficulty with school subjects because he lacked scholastic aptitude.

Throughout the life of the patient, an interfering paternal grandmother was a constant problem, frequently visiting the home and attempting to dominate the household. On one occasion, about a year after referral, when her mother-in-law was more insulting than ever, the mother slapped her face and, according to her accounts, with good results.

Meanwhile the patient showed evidence of increasing independence, social activity and school progress.

Age 8 years, 10 months: By the 17th month of treatment the reaction of the younger brother became difficult, probably in response to the improved status of the patient. The latter was now considered easy to handle, the former difficult. The mother was gradually overcoming her oversolicitous attitude. She was no longer watching him from the window until he got into the school house. Her boy was better able to take care of himself, fighting back if attacked, no longer called a "sissy." As he advanced in the grades, school work became increasingly difficult for him, and outside tutoring was necessary. He was the dullest boy in his class.

Age 9 years, 7 months: The case was closed two years and two months after referral. The mother attributed his change to his physical improvement. He was bigger, stronger, healthier, less dependent, and getting along well with other children. He presented no difficulty in the home. His only difficulty was schoolwork. The father read with him every evening. The staff noted "considerable success through manipulative treatment," and established the status as "partially adjusted," with a "partially favorable" prognosis.

Age 10 years, 6 months: Follow-ups one month, and 11 months after closing, revealed that the patient had failed to pass his school grade. The alignment of mother and patient, father and younger son, was again evident. The interfering grandmother was interviewed. She spent the entire session upbraiding her daughter-in-law, calling her "lazy, a gossip, no brains, from a low-down family," and urged that the children be taken away from the home. The psychiatrist regarded her as a paranoid aggressive woman, trying to disrupt the household.

Comment.—The influence of medical treatment on the general improvement in this case, as in Case 6, is an important consideration. With a variety of influences operating on the patient— change in maternal and paternal attitudes, special instruction from the schoolteacher—it is difficult to evaluate each factor. Obviously the visual correction and improvement in strength and coördination were of sufficient therapeutic values in themselves, regardless of other considerations. Yet it appears logical that this improvement in health would have definite psychological importance; theoretically it would raise the prestige of the Institute in the mother's eyes, enable her to accept more thoroughly the social worker's advice, and also be less protective of the patient because of his lessened value as a stimulus to protective feelings. The boy would also be aided in his social adjustment through greater self-esteem and in the esteem of other boys through improvement in sports and self-defense; and in better condition to accept the mother's efforts at his emancipation. It is readily understood also that without a change in maternal attitude, or in his own, the improved health and strength might have had no effect at all on his social adjustment. It must be remembered also that the success achieved in this case occurred in spite of continued difficulty in schoolwork, and an interfering grandmother constantly attempting to create difficulties in the family.

Influence on the mother was exerted almost exclusively through specific advice. Favorable change in the father's attitude was brought about by the same method. The psychiatrist's 19 interviews with the patient were spun over a long period of time and seemed to have little if any therapeutic value. When an interview technique was used it was in the form of a chat with the child about day-to-day activities and occasional remarks about fighting his battles and relying on himself. When a play method was used, the patient became engrossed with the play and quite oblivious to anything else. The most frequent notation by the psychiatrist was that patient was hyperactive and "it was difficult to get his attention to discuss anything with him for any length of time."

Age 17 years—Summary of interviews of worker and psychiatrist with patient, grandmother, aunt, and two neighbors: Patient was a tall—6 feet —dull-looking boy, 17 years old. His mother died two years previously —carcinoma of liver, according to hospital record. Six months after her death his father was adjudged insane and committed to a state hospital.

After his mother's death the patient first lived with his grandmother, later with his aunt. His last series of negative Wassermann tests was taken when he was 15 years old.

He finished Grade VIII at 16 years. He was always a poor student but received special merit for good behavior. After grammar school he went to vocational high school, disliked it, and quit after a few months. At the time of the interview he had been working as errand boy for two months.

He had a number ot friends, chiefly much younger boys in the neighborhood. In fact two of his good friends were aged, respectively, eight and ten. His aunt wondered how he managed to keep out of a bad gang. He was a good boy, however, and kept out of trouble.

He was fond of all sports and a member of a neighborhood baseball team. His ambition was to be a life guard. Actually he had once saved a boy from drowning.

He masturbated about once or twice weekly. He had no other sex experience. He was interested in girls, particularly in one whom he took to the movies occasionally.

He was apparently adjusting well in his aunt's home. The aunt accepted him as a stupid good boy, requiring little attention.

Grandmother: The grandmother was seen. She spent the entire time of the interview reviling the mother of the patient, her daughter-in-law, with an unmitigated hatred.

Two neighbors who saw the mother in her final illness recounted her kindness and devotion. They confirmed the Institute's description of the grandmother's personality.

CASE 16

Age 14 years, 4 months: The patient, a boy, was referred for stealing, truancy and incorrigibility. He had already been twice committed to a "protectory."

The psychiatrist had seven interviews with the patient, one with the father—who was released from prison during the period of treatment —and one with the mother, over a period of seven months. A social worker saw the mother on one occasion. A worker in a coöperating agency also had interviews with her.

The difficulty was related to maternal "spoiling," the factors being: a first-born child, absence of the father through repeated prison sentences, and estrangement of the mother from her family.

The plan of treatment was to give the boy insight into his irresponsible and dependent behavior, to play the role of father to him, and keep in a supervising relationship. It was planned also to get him a job in which he could attain a measure of satisfaction not possible in school, because of his poor scholastic achievement. It was hoped through the coöperating agency to enable the mother to alter her constant protective attitude toward the patient, and enable him to become mature.

After several interviews the psychiatrist was impressed with the boy's frankness, charm, punctuality in keeping appointments, and his coöperative attitude. He decided it would be necessary to see the boy no oftener than once in three or four weeks, just to keep in touch with him. The boy had also coöperated in getting dental treatment for pyorrhea which had been diagnosed in the routine physical examination. A change of psychiatrists took place after the seventh interview. Thereafter the patient came late for the two appointments he kept, and failed to appear for several others. However, he had already shown evidence of delinquent behavior.

Age 14 years, 11 months: The closing entry in this case was "status unadjusted," since the patient had been apprehended a second time for stealing, during the period of treatment, and was committed to an institution. Furthermore, there was no evidence of any change in the mother's attitude. She remained to the end the protecting mother, ever ready, like the boy himself, to explain his misconduct through the evil influence of others, to regard it lightly, or to insist on his innocence; and always to attest to his goodness and assurance that he had learned his lesson and would never be in trouble again.

Age 16 years, 3 months: Followed up 16 months after treatment, it was found that the patient ran away from the institution and was brought back. At the time of the follow-up study he had been released six months. In this period he was earning money and was regarded as "unusually satisfactory" by his employer. He was going with more desirable companions, adjusting well at home, and keeping company with a girl his age. The follow-up status was put in the C category—partially adjusted.

Age 18 years, 2 months: Less than two years later—23 months—the patient was awaiting sentence in court following his conviction for robbery.

Comment.—A striking feature of the case is the optimistic outlook on the part of the psychiatrist. In spite of a previous record of delinquency involving two commitments, bad companions, a criminal father, and a blindly overprotecting mother, he was satisfied, after a few interviews with the patient, that the prognosis was good.

Since this optimism appears typical of psychiatrists—as of laymen—in their early contacts with, especially, intelligent delinquents (the psychiatrist in the case was having his first year of training as a Fellow), it is worth considering. The charm, good looks, and frank and friendly behavior of the patient were so convincing that the temptation to consider the boy as he appeared in the office, instead of viewing the whole picture of the case, could not be resisted. However, other elements were duly considered by the psychiatrist. He laid stress on their "constructive" aspects. The mother's role was seen as that of stable provider who kept the home together regardless of poverty and her husband's incarceration. The father had always been friendly with the boy, and in relation with him, played a good paternal role. Since the prison sentences were due mostly to crimes relating to his drug addiction, these were regarded by the boy, and by the father, as evidence of abnormal weakness rather than viciousness. The father utilized his prison record as a warning to the patient to keep away from bad companions. As an influence the father was regarded, therefore, as having potentially positive values. Reinforced by supervision of companions, a summer-camp experience with normal boys, satisfying employment, a social worker in contact with the mother, besides the psychotherapeutic efforts, it was thought, naturally, that the patient's behavior could readily be deflected from a delinquent direction. The early period of freedom from delinquency during the course of therapy helped to confirm the favorable aspects; likewise the first follow-up investigation.

In evaluating the case data, apparent weaknesses were revealed in estimating the boy's past record, in failure to appraise the meaning of his "charm," or the powerful forces involved in the mother-son relationship. Considering the record of truancy and stealing, within the limitations of the material presented, it could be said that the behavior was consistent with the indulgent overprotection, especially if the factors of maternal neglect and exposure to delinquent companions are added. For, as an example of indulgent overprotection, this case differs from others in the group in that the mother was earner for the family and absent from the home a good part of the day. Hence the typical protection of the boy from companionship, good or bad, and coaching in school subjects, features of "pure" maternal overprotection, could not be put into effect. Further, his easy success in school subjects could not be attained in the higher grades, since his intelligence, according to tests, was no more than "high average." Actually, there is a consistency with his truancy and difficulty in school subjects, which came when he was about 10 years old. The truancy, therefore, a typical response of the aggressive boy to an unsatisfying school situation, was consistent with the aggressive features developed in indulgent overprotection. The difficulty of bearing any frustrating experience is especially severe in the indulgent overprotected. This fact, if it had been considered, would have made the psychiatrist quite guarded in his prognosis.

The boy's charm, an asset frequently seen in the overprotected child, may be explained by a special background of experience in wheedling the mother. The overprotected child's skill in verbalizing has been previously described. That it is put to the service of getting out of responsibility, is natural enough. Also all the winning ways of a child would be highly fostered in an overprotective relationship in which the mother is so ready to respond. When it happens so frequently in the indulged group that the child is not made to fulfill his promises or take the consequences of his behavior, a general pattern of opportunistic verbalization is easily developed. This pattern has been ascribed also to the optimistic outlook of the overprotected, originating in excessive love and protection and resulting in the unrealistic expectation that the world, like mother, will always provide. Thus, the patient carried a convincing story that his previous difficulties would never be repeated, that he could explain everything, and that he was most eager to coöperate with the psychiatrist.

Belief that the maternal attitude could be changed was held without full appreciation of the powerful forces involved. To the end of the case study, the mother maintained the belief that the entire difficulty was explained by the influence of bad companions on a good boy. Besides the usual dynamics of maternal overprotection, there were unusually strengthening factors in the case. The mother made a marriage against the strongest opposition of her parents and was eager to prove, through her husband's success, that they were wrong. Her hostility towards them was to be satisfied in this way, as well as her strong need for increased self-esteem, which was lowered by complete separation from her family. Her husband's incarceration was a blow so great that, for a while, she contemplated suicide. Through her son she hoped anew to regain all she had lost. As far as the record goes she never altered in her uncritical attitude towards him, in spite of the facts. The need of maintaining her illusion is seen clearly enough in the material revealed in the comment, aside from the maternal overprotection factors described in previous summaries.

The patient is the only one in the entire group referred because of stealing. His delinquency must be considered also in relation with a criminal father and delinquent companions. As a direct influence, the latter may be considered the more important, since the patient lived in an environment in which delinquency was a readily available outlet for his dissatisfactions. Since the case represents a combination of indulgent overprotection and neglect, that is, overprotection in which the protective phase became highly diminished, the lapse into delinquency as an easy way of gratification in regard to theft and the satisfaction of gang leadership is well comprehended. In a sense, the parasitic relationship to society in general, represented by this case, is similar to the others in which the parasitism, in the form of taking without giving, is confined within personal relationships.

Age 25 years, 6 months: The worker had four interviews with the mother, and interviews also with father, daughter, son-in-law, and probation officer. The patient was in prison. He was not interviewed. Information from the Division of Parole reveals a number of arrests for hold-ups, in one of which the patient with two other boys knocked a man unconscious. The patient had spent most of the past ten years in a reformatory or penitentiary. The parole officer considered him a dangerous criminal who would probably meet his end in the chair. A physical examination made when the patient was 20 years old revealed no evidence of disease. He was well nourished and strong. His height was 5 feet, 9 inches. On intelligence tests he scored an I.Q. of 103, a result similar to his performance when age 14 years—I.Q. 109.

The patient was still the great center of interest in the family, who spoke continually about him. The mother wrote him three or four times a week, sent him packages of food, and visited him whenever possible. She would let the family starve, she said, to send him the things he asked for. She was firmly convinced he was innocent. She believed he was framed by the police. In the next sentence she blamed his difficulties on evil companions. He was a good boy. He just never had a chance.

He used to give her all his money, call her sweetheart, kiss her a great deal, and tell her everything. The mother, a short, stout woman of 45, cried freely as she told her story. She described in detail her son's charm, politeness, his dream of buying her a house and garden, of making her rich. He was very strong. He used to pick her up high in the air and swing her around. He often fought in the ring and hoped to become a prize fighter.

Of course, she gave in to him very easily. He could change any attempts at discipline into another extra indulgence.

He was not interested in girls, she said, though he went out with them. He promised her he would not marry until he had her well established in a home. When he did earn money, he gave her all he earned, and she gave him an allowance.

The mother confirmed her defense of her son. She used to write letters frequently to the judge who had last sentenced him. The judge died, she believed, as retaliation from God, and, as she warned him, for sending an innocent boy to jail.

She also defended her husband. He was no longer using drugs. No, there were no longer any sexual problems. She was resigned to the fact that her husband was a weak, sick man who could not work.

She herself was employed as usual, and held her job many years.

Her daughter and son-in-law were living with them, for which she was happy.

Mother—interview with psychiatrist. She was short—4 feet, 10 inches, stout, large breasted. She was eager for the interview in order to leave no stone unturned to get help for her son. She wanted a letter to the warden proving that rightfully her son's sentence could be shortened by giving him credit for time spent at a previous incarceration.

When the main facts of her history were reviewed, she said, "I'm right back where I started from, always in trouble."

She loves her son evidently as much as ever, gave further evidence of his lover-like relationship, his embraces and kisses, his compliments about her cooking, his beckoning through a shop window when she could buy a dress, to tell her which one to choose.

Before marriage, however, she was not especially maternal. She never enjoyed caring for children, never responded to babies, nor cared for dolls. She used to say she would never have any children. After marriage she decided to have no more than two. When her son was born, however, things were different. She was "crazy" about him. She could deny him nothing. No, she has no idea why. He was just as crazy about her, too. She never thought keeping him on the breast 18 months was too long. She thinks maybe his swollen glands may have had something to do with her strong feeling for him. They were cut open before he was a year old. She had to have them dressed for two weeks.

Her daughter's feeling that the boy got more affection was no doubt true, she said.

Her husband was the first and only man she was ever serious about. She met him at 14 and married just before she was 17. She reconciled herself long ago, she claimed, to the absence of sex gratification.

Apparently a proud, aggressive, and stubborn woman, very hostile to her mother, she made a suicidal attempt, although half-heartedly, when she had to accept the fact that her mother was right about her bad marriage. At the time of her son's trial she wrote letters to the judge threatening to kill herself if he did not release the boy. She remained a stable, responsible worker and managed to keep a home ready for husband or son.

Interviews with father, sister, and brother-in-law served chiefly to confirm the mother's statements about her relation to her son. Father, sister, and brother-in-law offered the same defense of the patient. The father's record with the Department of Welfare was investigated. He refused employment at his old trade, claiming his tools were too old. He had had irregular and short periods of work with the W.P.A. The father said he was too weak for any kind of outdoor work, and criticized the W.P.A. severely. He made the same type of excuses for himself as for his son. He blamed policemen for arresting people just to get a promotion. Innocent people get arrested for murder. His son's case, like his own, was a matter of hard luck. He elaborated this theme vehemently for an hour. The father was also seen by the psychiatrist. He was short, thin, sallow complexioned. His manner was obsequious, his conversation designed to arouse pity for a poor man who never had a chance, and the like.

He says his wife could never deny her son anything. But she always liked to please everybody. She cannot say no. He recognized the fact that the boy had been badly spoiled.

An attempt to get some light on his own addiction to morphine was met by a series of stereotyped defenses—his hard luck, letting bad people influence him. A month following this interview he was imprisoned again for possession of morphine.

Comment.—In relation to the patient, there is little more to add to the comment already made at the end of the earlier follow-up studies. The pattern of behavior has become fixed, and a diagnosis of psychopathic personality is established. The attitude of the family that he was a sweet, charming boy, very convincing about his good intentions, was shared by the workers who had contact with him earlier in the case. The remarkably uncritical devotion of his mother, for whom the patient remains ideal son and lover, was well determined when the patient was first seen at the age of 14 years. The picture at present is that of a dangerous criminal, with a devoted family completely influenced by the maternal attitude, and ready to protect him against the consequences of his behavior.[3]

[3] An analogous case appears in a series of psychiatric studies of murderers, once collected by Commissioner Woods of the Rockefeller Foundation. It was the case of Martin Durkin. There was a similar history of a combination of indulgent overprotection and neglect, and delinquent companions. As in the present case the early crimes were robbery and assault. The murderer also had charming manners and showered his mother with gifts. He had a fascination for women, several of whom he married. They were apparently maternal types, who, in spite of his crimes, his infidelities and neglect, appeared at the trial on his behalf. In time the mother became involved in his crimes, because when he insisted on using the home as a

An interesting finding in the mother's history is the lack of evidence of maternal feeling before marriage. It is evidently not a true, but rather a compensatory type of overprotection, presumably based on neurosis. In her early history the bitter hostility to her mother and the early marriage in spite of tremendous opposition, even including commitment to a protectory, are the most significant events. This fight characterized her whole life, the fight to prove her success, to prove her superiority to her mother. It is not difficult to understand how this battle, after acceptance of defeat in acknowledging the failure of her marriage, became focused entirely on the son. Her father was a hard-working, undemonstrative man, who saw very little of his children. He died when she was eight years old.

It is difficult to make a psychiatric diagnosis. Obsessional neurosis seems a likely term, if it can be utilized to describe a relationship that is obsessional, in spite of the absence of obsessional symptoms. For in her case there was no evidence of obsessional thoughts, or behavior, or ritualistic protective devices, or of the typical overconscientiousness. In common with the obsessional neurotic is, probably, the aggressive, stubborn, stable personality. A psychiatry of relationship pathology does not yet exist. When it does, "obsessional relationship" may be one of its classifications.

CASE 17

Age 13 years, 9 months: A boy, the oldest of three children, was referred through a vocational guidance teacher because of eye-blinking, sniffling, temper tantrums and difficulty in school.

Psychiatrists had 27 interviews with the patient; seven with his mother. Social workers had 20 interviews with the mother, ten with school teachers, five with the patient, and four with a boys' club and the family physician. The treatment extended over a period of 20 months.

The patient's difficulty was interpreted as, primarily, a dependent at-

---

warehouse for stolen goods she could not refuse him. He was the first-born child and only son in a family of girls, spoiled by his mother and sisters. The father played no role in the family life. Maternal overprotection was intensified by her son's scar from a birth injury, infantile convulsions, two severe illnesses, and the death of the next sibling. His exploits were characterized by the attitude that he would always be protected, that an exception would always be made for him, that he could marry and remarry at will.

titude to a dominating overprotecting mother. After ruling out organic difficulties, the blinking and sniffling were diagnosed as tics, related to the birth of the second-born, and interpreted as a bid for the mother's love and attention. School difficulties were attributed to an irresponsible attitude and attention-getting behavior. The temper tantrums turned out to be limited chiefly to the school, and consisted in throwing objects, or attacking boys who teased him because he was "sissy." At home he was generally obedient to his mother and jealous of his brothers.

The psychiatrist planned to aid the patient chiefly by giving him advice and insight into his irresponsible, dependent behavior, and his difficulty in making friends. Plans were made also to have him join a boys' club. In the 20 months of treatment, the patient had three psychiatrists in succession. He was friendly and chatty with each, came late at about the third or fourth interview, then omitted a few, and then after a mild scolding became punctual again. After the first few months of treatment it was decided that the psychiatrist play also a paternal role since the boy's own father, although friendly, assumed no authoritative responsibility. It was agreed that although some improvement was manifested it had little to do with direct psychotherapy, to which the patient was indifferent.

The patient's response to a boys' club was at first enthusiastic; later indifferent. After the first year's membership expired the mother decided it was not worth the trouble of nagging him to go.

The social worker tried to give the mother insight into her boy's dependency, to enable her to ignore his tics and give him more responsibility. The schoolteacher was interviewed and shown the value of giving the patient more recognition, and of being more tolerant of his intellectual achievement.

Along these lines some improvement was made. The patient was chosen class monitor. At home he was asked to help the younger children with their work. He was allowed to go on errands alone. Progress in school was noted, his tics were less in evidence, his temper tantrums were diminished, and he showed signs of making friendly relationships with boys. Nevertheless, the staff decided towards the end of the first year of treatment that progress was slow and unsteady, and concluded that the difficulty was basically the mother's refusal to yield to the boy's growth in independence. It was decided, therefore, to have the psychiatrist take over the major problem in therapy with the mother. Hitherto she had been seeing her family physician, who was also a friend of the family, and had been discussing her various problems with him, including her husband's infidelity. The psychiatrist in his first four interviews with the mother tried to show how her early starvation for love was a strong feature of the case, how she longed through marriage to gain everything she had lost in childhood, and how also her husband's infidelity reinforced the overprotection. Further, from the material she produced in the second interview, it was explained that the husband's infidelity was in part due to her own sex prudery. To this she protested strongly, and refused thereafter to come to the Institute.

Closing status: partially adjusted.

Age 16 years, 5 months: A follow-up study was made a year after "closing" and the classification "partially adjusted" was confirmed.

Comment.—As in Case 11, the question of pursuing lines of therapy already proved of value and letting well enough alone became an important consideration. In all the cases of this series, it was naturally taken for granted that direct psychotherapy of the mother was a primary necessity inasmuch as the maternal attitude was the basic problem. Hence, regardless of favorable progress it was thought that the outcome of the case would be jeopardized unless the mother's basic attitude was changed. Further, there was at that time, as now, a strong predilection for a psychoanalytic form of therapy, the therapy of choice for modification of "inner" attitudes. In this case, especially, since part of the problem was a compensatory overprotection resulting from sexual difficulties in marriage, a solution of that problem was sought. The difficulty of modifying maternal overprotective attitudes was not sufficiently realized. Attempts made in several cases to refer mothers to psychoanalysts were unsuccessful, so that the test of psychoanalytic modification of "true" maternal overprotection was not at hand; nor did the literature furnish any examples, other than compensatory forms.

Since the various forms of therapy were not appraised, the value of direct aid to the mother in attaining a freer relationship through advice, through demonstration in specific instances at home, and direct building up of independence in the child by using external factors, were assumed to be of minor importance. Actually, they have turned out to be the major therapeutic values of this series of cases.

The problems presented by the patient may be regarded as primarily "submissive." There was no problem of disobedience at home or of discipline at school. Aggressive behavior in the form of temper tantrums was elicited only when boys teased him by calling him "sissy." Jealousy of his brothers did not occasion fight-ing so much as bids for the mother's attention. His general adjust-ment to his difficulties was in the form of dependency and symp-tom formation—tics. Where problems in submissive behavior are the rule, the prognosis for adjustment at home and at work is fa-vorable in this series of cases.

Age 24 years, 1 month—Summary of worker's interviews with mother, father, patient, two siblings, and family physician: The mother, a short, stout woman, was at first vehement in denouncing the Institute for "meddling in her private life." Later she joined in the interview but remained suspicious. At the age of 53 years, she was still suffering from the menopause, she said. She was still playing a strong maternal role to her children, watching over all of them, especially the patient, whose dependence on her she defended as "something that was not wrong." She denied that the patient ever had any problems, except tics. She criticized the methods of treatment used at the Institute and said they had been of no value either to herself or her son. She resented especially their taking notes. The whole thing was misrepresented to her by a bad teacher who was unable to tolerate her son's grimaces. She leveled fur-ther criticism at another schoolteacher. The patient, who was present during this part of the conversation, defended the Institute. His mother seemed rather pleased at his remarks and commented proudly on how well he expressed his thoughts.

The patient's tics and temper tantrums had disappeared years ago, according to the mother. He was still quite a reader, and was interested for some years in books on mechanics, a field in which he had worked steadily for years. He was friendly with his brother and had one good friend outside the home. He had some girl acquaintances, although no special interest in any one of them.

A study of the mother's attitude towards children revealed consist-ently high maternal feelings from childhood.

The patient was tall—6 feet, thin, and apparently in good health. Like his mother, he blamed the school for his early difficulties; that is, his failure in mathematics. He made the point that he managed to make up this deficiency later on. He generally minimized the problems for which he was sent to the Institute. He proudly exhibited his diploma in engineering, and spoke interestingly of his work as a mechanic, and of general labor problems. He was a member of the National Guard for three years, and at the time of the interview was still unemployed in his own field. Meanwhile he was working as an elevator man.

He spoke highly of his mother to whom he was still quite obedient. He praised his father likewise. He had one friend, besides his brother.

He was on the whole rather seclusive. His interests were all serious. He confirmed his mother's statements about his relations to girls.

The father and brother confirmed the statements recorded and noted the patient's continued dependency on the mother.

It was learned from the family physician that the father became reconciled to his wife, after a period of infidelity—see case summary. It was obvious that the relation of the father to the family was strained, and that the mother and sons comprised the true family unit.

CASE 18

Age 16 years: The patient, a boy, was referred by the principal of his school chiefly because he was so unpopular with his classmates.

He had four sessions with the psychiatrist. His mother had eight to ten sessions with social workers over a period of 17 months. Many appointments were canceled.

It was evident after numerous examinations, including X-ray of the skull and several Wassermann tests—all negative—besides the usual procedures, that the problem was primarily overprotection, in which the dominating aspect occurred in the highest degree. The psychiatrist tried to give the boy some insight in regard to the antagonism he evoked in his classmates through his supercilious manners. Attempts were also made to get him interested in activities that would widen his social contacts—tennis and dancing. Interviews with the mother were of no avail since she used them only to show how the schoolteachers were in league against her son, how they refused to appreciate his genius. When she failed to bring the worker to her side in this controversy, she lost all interest, and regarded the experience at the Institute simply as a waste of time.

At its close, the status of the case was classified as "unimproved."

Age 19 years, 1 month: A follow-up interview 1 year, 8 months later —three years from the date of referral—resulted in the same classification. There was no change in the presenting symptoms, mother-son relationship, friends, outside interests, or attitude toward the Institute.

Comment.—This case has been described in previous chapters as an example of an "impurity" in a "pure" overprotection series, since the dominating aspect outweighed all other maternal considerations. Besides the general paranoid coloring, the interviews revealed latent homosexual tendencies in the mother. In retrospect it appears reasonable to conclude that if efforts were to be expended in this case at all, they should have been used to enable the mother to get psychoanalytic treatment. Such efforts most likely would have failed, yet an attempt might have been made to enable the mother to realize that she was a mentally sick individual, in need of treatment.

Age 28 years, 4 months—Summary of psychiatrist's interviews with mother and with patient: A handsome young man of good height and weight—height 5 feet, 10½ inches, weight 158 pounds—the patient remembered his experience at the Institute very well. He said he was "a bad case, a complete mama's boy, grade A example, a complete void and under the domination of a headstrong and powerful lady."

He started "breaking away" about six years ago through the aid of friends who kept constantly encouraging him to get away from his mother's influence. Three years ago he started living apart from his mother. He said, in relation to his mother, "I pulled myself up by the roots, in my way of thinking, in my sex life, and everything else." He visits his mother once a week. He regards her as "completely static," yet admires her independence and ability to get along. She takes complete credit, he says, for his success; and he continues not to disillusion her. He helps to support her.

He saw the father occasionally until the latter's disappearance 15 years previously. "I never had a relationship with my father," he said.

After leaving school at 18 years, he got a job which he held five years. Now a salesman, he has worked steadily the past five years, although he much preferred a job "with social value."

There was nothing unusual in the history of his masturbation. Onset of coitus was at age 20. Excepting for a period of six months, sex relations were intermittent. His first experience was with a woman who "awakened" in him a knowledge of sex and took him in hand. There was no history of impotence or homosexuality.

At the time of the interview he was engaged to be married.

He dated his "social adjustment" as of five years' duration. Previously he was shy, used to "sit in corners at parties with that nervous feeling in your stomach." His friends took him in hand. He was a good dancer, he said, and that helped. Gradually his shyness "wore down." He finds it easy now to make contact with people. He has many friends. In the interview he appeared quite at ease.

No evidence of neurosis or psychosis was revealed.

An interview with the mother disclosed the same attitudes expressed 12 years previously—the same resentment about the school, the same defense of her son, the same attitudes toward her husband. She denied that she was ever possessive or dominating in relation to her son. She tried only to guard him from the danger of bad people, she said.

At 69 years of age she was still self-supporting and in good health.

Questions about her maternal behavior revealed strong mothering activities from childhood, chiefly in the form of protecting people from illness or hardship, especially from death. She attributed her choice of the nursing profession to the illness and death of her mother when she was seven years old. She never tried to "mother" men; in fact she avoided that type. She never had thoughts before marriage of the number of children she would like, or any maternal phantasies. Her maternal behavior was of the aggressive, protecting, apprehensive variety.

CASE 19

Age 12 years, 10 months: An only child, a boy, was referred by his family physician because of difficulty with schoolwork, ascribable to "lack of concentration," and marked dependency on his mother. He was still demanding that she accompany him to school. He had a right spastic hemiplegia, attributed to an encephalitis—not epidemic—when he was nine years old. There was distinct limitation of movement in the right hand and some disability in walking, although he was able to manage fairly well without crutches.

The psychiatrist had two sessions with the patient and one with the mother. The social worker had three sessions with the mother and one with the family doctor, over a period of four months.

Although the treatment was incomplete because the patient moved out of town, a definite plan was worked out. The method was largely manipulative; that is, the use of a boarding school to separate the mother and son, besides interviews to give the mother insight into the patient's dependency. The mother had already sent the patient to a camp the previous year because she had been told that she had babied him too much. The father died when the patient was age ten years. During the period at the Institute the patient also received massage and exercise of the affected muscles in a swimming pool.

Comment.—It was clear that the relationship was one of dominating maternal overprotection. The patient apparently accepted the relationship thoroughly, was quite happy in it, and tried to prevent any change in his infantile dependency. Although this case may be considered questionable since an organic factor was involved, in itself a strong stimulus to overprotection, it was clear that the maternal attitude had been consistent since the patient's birth. Such a relationship is difficult to modify, especially if both mother and child are not made uncomfortable by it. The patient was cheerful, pleasant, and distinctly unworried about his future. The reassuring quality of the overprotection was very well marked. The organic problem enabled the mother to regard it as the entire difficulty, and hence to minimize the overprotecting feature of the case. Lack of concentration and similar school complaints seemed consistent with the general irresponsible attitude, with the attending lack of initiative and general inability to take a serious attitude towards any problem. The patient remained sweet, compliant, unworried. If the treatment could have gone on, it would seem very doubtful that the status "unadjusted" would have been altered.

Age 22 years, 10 months—Summary of psychiatrist's and worker's interviews with mother and patient—Patient: The patient walked well with a brace, and without a cane. He had a right-sided paresis of arm and leg. He could shake hands as well with his right hand. He was not handicapped in his work as a student of commercial art. At age 12, he was diagnosed as Fröhlich's syndrome. He started shaving at 17 years. When seen at 22 he had a steady girl. He was then 5 feet 6 inches tall and weighed 185 pounds, fully dressed.

He gave the usual history of adolescent masturbation. He had not had coitus. He was still evidently quite obedient to his mother, who still regarded him as a child. He remembered feeling like running away from home when he was 14 years old. He quarreled occasionally with his mother for treating him like a baby.

Occasionally, too, he worried about not having a job, and hoped we would help him get one. He had tried seriously to get employment. He had been away from home on two occasions, once for six months at age 17, and again for a year at age 20. He was in a special school for the physically handicapped. In those periods he saw his mother only once a month.

He never liked school. He finished high school at the age of 20. He was interested especially in physics and chemistry. He was very fond of reading, especially medical books. Once he took a course on photography. He sang weekly in the church choir. Though he had no intimate friends, he was well liked.

He gave the impression of a very good-natured, lazy, genial fat man. He presented the same optimistic unworried complacent attitude. He felt sure that in good time a job would be forthcoming. Someone surely would help him. He would get married some day when the right girl appeared. He never had "a case of blues." "Life," he said, "is a pretty place."

Mother: The mother, an obese, large-breasted woman—height 5 feet, 7 inches, weight 180—of 57, gave the appearance of a stern, dominating figure. She devoted all her life to her son and felt bound to do so, she said, as long as she lived. She never thought she gave him too much attention, although after his illness she became "doubly devoted." She recognized that her son was too close to her, "much too much for his own good."

A history of her maternal attitudes showed above average "maternal feelings" since childhood. She lived a rather secluded life with her son, and managed quite well on a small income. Somehow she felt the community was to blame for her son's lack of employment.

Status: partial adjustment.

CASE 20

Age 4 years, 5 months: The patient, a boy, was referred because of oversensitivity to his mother's mood, attempts to be babied by her, submissive behavior to his younger brother and other children, thumb-sucking, enuresis, and fear of dogs.

Social workers had 28 interviews with the mother and her friend, a settlement worker; one interview with the father. The psychiatrist had five interviews with the mother and five with the patient.

The treatment of the child was highly "manipulative." He was taken on a number of trips with children and the worker, without his brother, and the two boys were sent to different schools. Both brothers were also sent to camp. The dependency on mother and younger brother was thus treated by separating the patient from them for varying intervals of time, and enabling him to make new contacts. The five interviews with the patient served no therapeutic function, nor yielded new information.

The treatment of the mother consisted in "environmental" therapy, advice, information, reassurance, and some insight therapy. She was encouraged to broaden her interests by taking courses in English and domestic science; to get a young woman to care for the children afternoons; and to go places together with her husband. It was hoped thereby to lessen her absorption in the patient, and give her more time for her husband, who, by the time of referral, had very little social contact with her. The mother responded to these changes and regarded the summer, when the children were away at camp for the first time, as her "second honeymoon."

She was given information on the importance of independent growth for the child, advised specifically on how to get him to dress himself, how to allow certain problems to take care of themselves. She was reassured that she could do the job successfully and praised for her cooperation. Attempts to allay her anxiety were made by informing her that certain tendencies she regarded as hereditary were environmental.

Problems of her early privations and her sexual difficulties were taken up with the psychiatrist. She was encouraged to speak freely about these problems, was told of their relationship to her role as mother, and of the importance for her sake as well as the rest of the family of developing a good marital adjustment. She brought out the fact that she could and did deny, at times, the patient's wish to be fondled. She also stated that she felt "relieved" after each interview with the psychiatrist.

Age 6 years, 6 months: The case was closed 25 months after referral with the status "satisfactorily adjusted." This status had been reached five months previously. Improvement in behavior was manifested within two months of the onset of treatment.

Age 6 years, 10 months: A two-hour follow-up interview was held with the mother four months after closing the case—29 months after referral, and the status "satisfactorily adjusted" maintained, even after the birth of a third sibling—12 months before closing.

The results were strikingly good. Attempts to explain it were made by the staff and various theories advanced. The mother was also asked to give her version. Her explanation was simply that she had faithfully followed the suggestions given her to make the child more independent, and it worked.

Comment.—A fairly easy and rapid success was achieved in this case. The patient's development of initiative, increasing independence; diminution of bed-wetting and finger-sucking were in evidence after a few months of treatment, and a satisfactory adjustment was maintained.

The feature of the therapy was the use of an environmental method. Various social resources—camp, group activity, and settlement house—were used to break up the mother-child monopoly, enabling each to make other contacts and develop other interests. Psychotherapy was used largely as an aid to the "manipulative" therapy, in order to get the mother's coöperation with the methods used, to overcome her anxiety over the, to her, drastic steps that were taken, chiefly by means of reassurance and persuasion. In several interviews certain events of her early life, as well as her marital relationship, were considered with apparently beneficial abreaction of anxiety, judged by her own account of the benefit of the interviews. The psychiatrist showed how her personal difficulties were related to the overprotection.

Significant is the revelation that at times she withheld affection from the patient in infancy. In connection with the rapid success achieved in this case, it raises the question of the type and intensity of the overprotection. It would point to a compensatory rather than a pure form—compensatory to her unloved and deprived childhood. But this transformation of an unhappy childhood through her own maternal activities was in conflict with apparently a revengeful attitude, as her denials of love to the child indicated. The guilty feelings arising therefrom were abreacted in psychiatric interviews, judging by her statement that after each one of them she felt greatly relieved. The successful therapy is explainable by the fact that the measures employed to overcome the mother-child monopoly were not circumvented, as in so many other cases, by a powerful maternal overprotecting attitude. For these considerations further data are necessary—data revealing the maternal feelings in premarital life.

Age 15 years, 3 months—Summaries of interviews by psychiatrist and worker with mother, father, and patient—Mother: A short, rather plump woman of 36, she recalled the "wonderful job" the Institute did for her boy. She recounted the referral problems in detail, and how they "were all cured at about the same time." When the boy had his sixth birthday both she and her husband remarked how different he was. His thumb-sucking and enuresis had stopped by that time, too.

In the last few months the boy had changed. He was seeing more of his friends and less of her. He used to run home right after school to talk to her. She was missing that. She did not want him tied to her, never expected "any of his dark secrets," yet she missed his companionship. He was still considerate of her, however, and had also a good relationship with his father. He liked to boss his brothers, regarding them all as "kids." The mother was proud of her son's success—he was an honor student—and proficient in sports.

She praised her husband as an ideal husband and father. She seemed completely absorbed and happy in her household activities and her role as mother. She maintained an easy discipline in the management of her home and appeared devoted to her husband and all her children. She had six, all boys, at the time of the follow-up interview.

Inquiry into her maternal feelings revealed a curious discrepancy. As a child she took care of her younger sister, feeding and dressing her quite happily. She also mothered every child she knew. Yet she would never fight to defend her child. In fact she regarded herself as lacking in maternal feeling because she did not have that part of it "like fighting for your young." She felt also that she was not "passionate" about children like other mothers, getting excited when they took sick. Yet she knew she managed children and took better care of them than others.

Men meant very little to her, she said. One was as good as another. She married to get away from home, but she never thought of getting love from a man, because her father was so mean. After marriage she wanted many children, and as quickly as possible. She nursed all her children at the breast.

Father: He confirmed all the material presented in the original investigation. He believed that none of his children presented any special problems at the time of the follow-up.

He confirmed the statement about his wife's sexual adjustment—passive acceptance without display of passion.

He stated also that she did not have "a very strong feeling" for children. She loved them, but was not demonstrative.

He gave the impression of a very polite, submissive, reliable, friendly person.

Patient: Of good height and weight—5 feet, 10 inches, 140 pounds —and strength, the patient was quite coöperative. He remembered little of his experience at the Institute. He was sent there, he thought, because of thumb-sucking.

He thought he was still "a little shy." He had no difficulty reciting in front of his class, but he preferred not to. Although he had a lot of friends, whom he saw at a swimming club, he was not really interested in them. He saw them, however, three times a week. He still preferred to be alone.

Until two or three years ago he was shy with girls. Now he had a steady girl, his third. She had some experience "necking." He masturbated but twice in his life. He felt it was sinful, he said, because "no one ever said it was right."

He was up to his class in school, and doing good work. His ambition was to be a "dairy herdsman," and he was taking a course in agriculture. He wanted to finish college and then start farming.

He was an excellent swimmer. He liked to read, chiefly agricultural and other technical books. He was also fond of riding horses.

He never missed doing his homework, went to bed at ten, and generally liked regularity. He was always obedient but in recent months he felt, he said, the need of more independence. He does not know how that happened, but it did.

In general, his demeanor was quite like that of his father.

APPENDIX: CASE SUMMARIES

Institute for Child Guidance contact: February, 1928, to May, 1930. Patient is an only child; male, age 8 years, 1 month. Average intelligence; grade III. Physical examination: overbite, caries, mastoid scar, error of refraction; well nourished; good strength; tall—five inches above median; good weight.

BASIS OF SELECTION

Mother always gives in to him, does everything for him. She is dominated by him. "Extreme dependency"—opinion and observation of school teacher, physician, psychologist, and father.

EVIDENCE OF OVERPROTECTION

"When he was an infant, mother could never leave him for an instant, and when he was two years old she was so despondent because she needed to get away from him that she had moods in which she wanted to die, and others in which she deliberately broke dishes."

Mother says she feels worried and unhappy when patient is out of her sight.

Mother dresses him every day, takes him to school in the morning and calls for him in the afternoon. At school, mother pays for the patient's lunch and tells the waiter what to give him.

Mother has been sleeping with him the past six months—because he has called her. She lies down with him at night and leaves a light burning until he falls asleep. The patient goes to bed at 10 P.M.

Patient has one friend whom mother takes him to see every two weeks.

Mother does not allow him to help with the housework for fear he will fall or break a dish.

Breast fed 13 months.

Mother fed him the first five years.

Mother still goes to the bathroom with him and waits for him.

Mother takes the patient with her wherever she goes, even to Mothers' Meetings and Child Study Class.

PERIOD OF ANTICIPATION

No unusual event.

EXTRA HAZARD

Patient is an only child.

He was a sickly baby; had "croup" when teething; bronchial pneumonia at 14 months; frequent colds and sore throat to age six, when a tonsillectomy was performed; a mastoid operation at five; measles at five and a half; chickenpox when age six years.

MATERNAL FACTORS

Marital: Mother has always been averse to sexual activity. Since the birth of the patient she fears having another child. She is sexually frigid and blames her husband the next morning after the sex act, if she does not feel well. The husband is apparently submissive to his wife.

Social: Mother has many friends and is well liked, but complains that she has no common interests with her husband. Father likes to walk; mother hates walking. He can go out with her or the patient only on Sundays. She sees her mother or relatives every day.

Background: Mother's early life was one of responsibility and hard work. Her mother was ill and even at the age of six she had much housework to do. She had to care for the children—she is one of seven; and at age 14 nursed her mother during confinement. Even now her whole family depend on her and "never do anything without consulting her."

She attended evening high school three and a half years, and is very anxious that her child have a good education.

She had a dominating father whom she still obeys. "Even now all the children fear him when he speaks."

Mother constantly complains of her health and makes frequent visits to a gynecologist, who advises her to have no more children. She has had occasional fainting spells in the past two years.

Mother wanders around the house at night, trying the windows for fear of burglars.

PATERNAL FACTORS

Relation to patient: Father sees little of the patient, as he has worked nights most of the time since the patient's birth. He sees the patient only on Sundays. Father holds the patient while the mother whips him —past six months. Father, like the patient, "expects mother to do everything for him." If the patient bothers him he says to the mother, "Take him away. For God's sake, can't you do anything?" He aids in infantilizing the patient by insisting that the mother accompany him to school.

Background: Father was the youngest of three and is still being "spoiled" by his mother, who brings him a bag of fruit daily.

He constantly complains of his health, although he will not visit a physician.

PATIENT

Behavior problems: Patient opposes everything the mother asks. She says, "He acts as though he wants to get even with me." He delights in teasing her, in "making her miserable." He annoys her; for example, he continued shooting a cap pistol until she wept. He has struck the mother during anger, and spits at her if offered something he dislikes.

When patient does not like the food set before him, he has thrown it angrily on the floor. He is very finicky about food.

He throws his clothes around.

He orders his mother about peremptorily and she obeys his commands until she is exhausted, when to "relieve her feelings" she whips him.

Delinquency: None.

Sex: The patient has asked questions but mother has given him no information, since she feels he "wouldn't understand."

Friends: He quarrels with other children and will not play with them unless the mother is nearby. When other children do not give in to him immediately, he cries.

School: He is an excellent student and receives "A" in conduct. He skipped Grade II B. He is very fond of school and anxious to be on time. He is docile at school, although defiant at home.

Interests: He rarely indulges in spontaneous play and avoids sports. He is very fond of school.

Developmental history: Normal birth. First tooth at five and a half months. Walked at 14 months. First words at eight months; talked "plainly" at one and a half years.

Habit problems: The patient has always been constipated; he will not eat fresh vegetables, and is not regular in his toilet habits. Nocturnal enuresis stopped at two years. He has always had food fads. He goes to bed late and is restless at night. He is careless about personal cleanliness, neglecting to brush his teeth unless watched, and washing only the back of his hands or his wrists.

Case 2

I.C.G. contact: December, 1929, to June, 1930. Patient is an only child; male, age 14 years. Grade VII. I.Q. 113; marked superiority in language tests; special arithmetic disability. Considerably taller than the average—68.4 inches; well developed; good muscle power; periostitis left leg; acute otitis media.

BASIS OF SELECTION

Father thinks that mother has always been overanxious about patient. Social worker and psychiatrist regard mother as very overprotective.

EVIDENCE OF OVERPROTECTION

Mother gives as the reason for moving to her present home the fact that it is now possible for her to "watch her son go down the street for a considerable distance."

Patient was weaned from the breast at 11 months, but kept on the bottle until age three and a half because "he did not want to give it up."

From the time he suffered a fright at the age of six, until about age 14, the patient has not "permitted the parents to go out in the evening and leave him at home."

Mother bathed and dressed the patient until he was six years old, and helps him wash and dress even now.

PERIOD OF ANTICIPATION

Mother was anxious to have a child. She was examined because of "sterility" and received treatments for several years to make possible her pregnancy. Both parents became increasingly worried and anxious because of this situation. The pregnancy occurred in the tenth year of marriage, when the mother was 33 years old. The sterility was attributed to an infantile uterus.

EXTRA HAZARD

Patient is an only child. There has been no other pregnancy, although no contraceptives were used.

Patient had a diphtheritic sore throat at 14 months. Mother states that she was afraid he would choke to death and since that time she is "always panicky" when the child is ill. Mild mumps and chickenpox at six; tonsillectomy at six; scarlet fever at 13. Otherwise there is nothing unusual in the medical history.

MATERNAL FACTORS

Marital: Mother has always been averse to coitus, using various pretexts and evasions to prevent it; father has "always had to fight" to have intercourse with her ever since they were married, and has complained to her mother on that account.

Social: Father and mother do not enjoy doing things together—walking, or going to the theatre. He prefers to remain at home, doing his office work there in the evenings. Mother was very sociable before her marriage, but went out very little afterwards, remaining "cooped up in the apartment." She visits her invalid mother very frequently.

Background: Her mother was the dominant family figure and ruled the household despite the father's violent temper. Mother, the fourth of ten siblings, is more devoted to her family than to her husband. She left school at the age of 11 to help support her family and worked in the same factory until her marriage at 23. All her brothers and sisters still consult her about furnishing their homes, and look to her as the one naturally in charge of the family situation. Mother is an aggressive, dominating person.

PATERNAL FACTORS

Relation to patient: Father also "overprotects" the patient. Mother accuses him constantly of excessive leniency—which is true—and spoiling her discipline. Father enjoyed helping with the care of patient during infancy, and is very fond of the patient.

Background: Father was strongly devoted to his mother and was antagonistic to his father for marrying within a year after the mother's death. His own mother, father said, "depended on him a great deal." He never accepted the stepmother. He was the oldest son and his mother's favorite. Father left home to work when he was about 14 because he could not stand the stepmother any longer. A very steady, overconscientious worker, he has been with the same firm for over 15 years. He is strict with his men, and fairly successful. He married during a period when he was afraid he would lose his job because the original firm was liquidated.

PATIENT

Behavior problems: Patient is disobedient and impudent at home and at school; he is "always" disobedient to the parents. When angry at mother, he shouts, "I hate you," and "Go to hell." He is less impudent to the father because "he—father—always yields to him." At school patient says "Shut your mouth" to teachers and disregards the requirements for homework.

At school there is attention-getting behavior through defiance of rules and authority. He teases girls, throws paper wads across the room, pushes the line in front of him, interrupts examinations, and has been the school's "general nuisance" since Grade I.

He has temper tantrums at home, although not at school. They began when he was about 12 months old and have occurred especially in the last two years; they now consist of yelling at the top of his voice if crossed. Mother then loses her temper and yells back at him. In the first year of life he was a quiet baby, never "fretful."

He is inattentive at school. He rarely pays attention to what is going on, although when he does he is able to make up his work quickly and keep up with the class.

Delinquency: None.

Sex: Mother has warned the patient against self-abuse since "he could not understand anything," and has pointed out that cripples are caused by masturbation. She occasionally uncovers him when he is in bed to determine if he is masturbating. There is no evidence of masturbation. Patient told father he learned everything he needed to know about sex matters from books.

Friends: Patient has no friends at school; he is "an isolated figure." According to mother, patient has always played with smaller boys. Recently, patient has cultivated a friendship with a boy of about his own age, who is, however, in senior high school. Patient was never a member of a gang.

School: Patient has been "in hot water" since the beginning of his school experience. The teachers are united in regarding him as a bad and incorrigible boy. He has been denied promotion three terms, although the wide range of knowledge he has acquired from reading has taken him far beyond most of the other children. His chief disability is in arithmetic.

Interests: He reads a great deal; remains in the bathroom over an hour at a time reading. He entertains the family with stunts, dancing and singing. He is a good swimmer.

Developmental history: There was rapid infantile development; he walked at 11 months; was a "precocious talker," making sentences by 22 months that astounded the family and neighbors; cut teeth early.

Habit problems: Toilet habits were established before age two years; no enuresis. There were no sleep disturbances until the age of six, when at a summer boarding home with the parents he was frightened by a "big, dark insect." Since then his sleep is restless; he complains occasionally of nightmares and it has always been "necessary that someone be near when he retires." Patient has a good appetite but is "prone to pick and choose his food, criticizing the mother severely if she does not prepare what he likes." He is very untidy and throws books and clothes around.

CASE 3

I.C.G. contact: May, 1929, to December, 1929. Only child, male, age 6 years, 1 month. Grade I. I.Q. 86; all other psychological tests consistent with this rating on Stanford-Binet. Physical examination: moderate myopia; dyslexia; sinistrality; carious teeth. Adequate height; 8 pounds above median weight. Deep scar of forceps injury on forehead. Rather jerky movements of extended fingers and poor on steadiness test, but coordination generally good.

BASIS OF SELECTION

Mother is considered over-solicitous by teacher and relatives. She is always watching the child and interfering with his activity by much questioning. He was always "given his own way."

EVIDENCE OF OVERPROTECTION

Patient was bottle fed until age four.

He sleeps in a crib in the parents' room. They are afraid to let him sleep alone.

Mother always protects him against the neighbors, who blame him for every fight. She takes him to school daily, although he protests.

PERIOD OF ANTICIPATION

Mother was very anxious to have a child, and was disappointed when she was not pregnant at the end of the first year of marriage. Both she and her husband are illiterate and "sat very lonely," with no interests in common. She became "nervous and upset over it" and finally agreed to have an operation, two months after which she conceived. The child was born in the fourth year of marriage; mother was then about 31 years of age.

EXTRA HAZARD

An only child. No other pregnancy. Before conception another operation was necessary which mother did not wish to undergo.

Serious illness in early infancy. Forceps delivery; born asphyxiated. In the first six weeks had boils all over his scalp. Visitors to the ward would say, "Look at that poor baby. I doubt if he will live." Mother afraid the baby was not getting enough attention, cried and begged to have the baby sleep with her. She would lie and watch him in her arms most of the night. The patient was bowlegged at 2½ years. Braces were prescribed, but refused by mother. Measles at 4; tonsillectomy at 6.

MATERNAL FACTORS

Marital: The parents are sexually incompatible; mother finds sexual intercourse difficult and unsatisfactory. The parents quarrel and disagree regarding the management of the child.

Social: Mother sees the members of her family about twice a week.

Background: Mother is illiterate, the only uneducated member of her family. She is very ambitious for patient's education. She was a factory worker before marriage and there was much economic struggling. She is regarded as "aggressive and a climber."

PATERNAL FACTORS

Relation to patient: Father aided his wife in the care of the child. He used to bathe and dress the patient and was "more like a mother than a father to him." He never accepted his sister's suggestion to give the boy more independence. He quarrels with his wife over the management of the child. Each neutralizes the other's discipline. Both have resorted to strapping the patient.

Background: Like his wife, he is illiterate and the least successful member of his family. He was ashamed of his illiteracy, tried to learn to read, but was unsuccessful (dyslexia?). He has many difficulties in hiding his illiteracy and has concealed the fact from his son. He goes to lectures and is very ambitious for the patient. He says, "I am dumb but my wife is a climber."

PATIENT

Behavior problems: The patient is destructive, disobedient, and impudent at home. He is a "peeper," and attempts to peep under girls' skirts at school. He also peeps into drawers of desks and closets at home and when visiting. He is overactive and fights with other children.

Delinquency: None.

Sex: Precocious sex activity; patient tries to lie on top of mother, strokes her skin; constantly kisses and caresses her. At the age of four, he made a "suggestion" to an older girl. He is very curious about sex; mother evades his questions.

Friends: He prefers to play with girls. He constantly hits other children and the neighbors refuse to let him play with their children.

School: Patient is easily distracted and slow. Has difficulty in arithmetic and reading due to subnormal intelligence. He is left-handed; reverses letters and figures in writing.

Interests: He apparently enjoys reading and writing.

Developmental history: Breast fed nine months—one breast, because of scarcity of milk—with occasional bottle; bottle to age four. Teething at 9 to 12 months; walking at 13 months; talking at 20 months. A very heavy baby; bowlegged. Mother refused to consider his wearing a surgical appliance.

Habit problems: There is little information regarding toilet habits. He has nocturnal enuresis. He is restless at table, grabs food, eats a great deal between meals. His sleeping hours are irregular; he is restless in sleep.

CASE 4

I.C.G. contact: January, 1929, to June, 1931. Only child, male, age 4 years, 9 months. I.Q. 133; very superior in all tests, especially language. Adequate height and weight, flabby muscles. Pronated feet; arch-supports worns since age two.

BASIS OF SELECTION

Father thinks mother is too much concerned with the patient. Mother says everyone tells her she pays too much attention to patient. Psychiatrist, physician, and social worker indicate abundant evidence of maternal overprotection.

EVIDENCE OF OVERPROTECTION

Patient will not leave his mother, nor will he allow her to go out unless she says she must go to the doctor. At age three, he developed independence of the mother in kindergarten, not allowing her to come near him at play. However, after the summer vacation when he was with mother constantly, he refused to leave her side, to return to kinder-garten or play outside the house alone.

Early psychiatric examinations were made difficult because the patient refused to leave his mother. Later he would run out to his mother in the waiting room.

Patient rules the household by his screaming and imperative voice. Mother will always comply with his demands rather than hear him scream. He comes in for lunch whenever he pleases, and although mother protests, she always feeds him.

When the mother accidentally knocked over his blocks, although he had refused to move them from under the sink where she was washing dishes, he swore at her and the mother weakly replied, "You musn't call mamma a bad name."

During the patient's psychological tests, the mother, being interviewed in an adjoining office, sat tensely on the edge of her chair, frequently asking, "Is that Johnny? Is that Johnny?" and was sure that he was calling her. After the examination she had him read aloud nursery tales in the waiting room where children and adults were present.

Observed at a meal, the patient pushed back his plate of potatoes and said, "It stinks." When mother put him back in bed, after his getting out, he kicked at her and struck her in the mouth.

OTHER FACTORS IN OVERPROTECTION

In his early years, the maternal grandmother also "lavished affection" on him and gave him things to eat. She still indulges him, brings him a great deal of candy and "likes to be ordered around" by him.

PERIOD OF ANTICIPATION

Mother became pregnant three months after marriage. Abortion was considered because of nephritis; mother's ankles were swollen and she had difficulty in walking throughout pregnancy. Caesarian birth.

An only child. Caesarian birth.

The medical history shows no serious illness, but numerous colds, much nursing care by the mother and much attention to his feet because of pronation due to rickets, for which arches were worn since age two. Diarrhoea from three weeks to five months of age; rickets diagnosed at eight months. Mild diphtheria at three years; mild measles at four years; tonsillectomy at 19 months.

MATERNAL FACTORS

Marital: Both parents state that they were in love when they married but are much disappointed in "the reality." In regard to sex life, mother states that father is "the most considerate man in the world, as he never bothers me." Father, rather than mother, employs contraceptives, although he says they have a bad effect on his health and prevent orgasm. The parents have no common recreation or interests outside of immediate family problems.

Social: Mother has frequent contacts with a neighborhood settlement house, and is active in a parents' club. There is much quarreling with the paternal grandmother, who nevertheless visits the home.

Background: Mother describes the maternal grandmother as mentally backward, still unable to cook; hence much of the household responsibility was left to the patient's mother. Grandfather was absorbed in books; very domineering and strict in religious observances; described as the "patriarch." Mother idolizes him and was favored by him, yet says she believes she married to get rid of his tyranny. There was early poverty. After graduating from high school, mother worked as a clerk for two years until her marriage. "Always a leader," she is active in mothers' clubs and the president of one. "She is the kind of a woman who looks after other people's troubles and does not attend to her own." Mother is a poor housekeeper. She had a tic of the right shoulder—onset at age 10 to 11 years—which lasted about two years. It returned again when she left high school but diminished greatly after marriage.

PATERNAL FACTORS

Relation to patient: Father did not want children because of economic pressure. His night work keeps him out of the home and allows him but little contact with the patient. He leaves the discipline of the child entirely to his wife, as he does all the problems of the household, even plans for moving.

Background: Father is a very steady, low-salaried worker as a government clerk, although he "loathes" the work. He took this job when the mother became pregnant because he felt the need of stable employment and was afraid to take a chance with other types of work. He is opposed to having children because he is a poor man; "it's a crime to bring them into the world." On vacations, he takes hitch-hike trips alone. A short man, he is worried that patient will be as short as he. Father's family is much less educated than mother's. Paternal grandmother was the dominant parent, paternal grandfather unassuming and submissive to her.

PATIENT

Behavior problems: The patient is disobedient, hyperactive, impudent to the parents; calls them names, kicks and scratches when not given his own way, will not come to meals and runs out into the street before he is finished.

He refuses to go to kindergarten without his mother; makes constant demands that the mother be near him, to help him dress, to get her attention.

He makes constant bids for attention from adults, by making noises, for example.

He has screaming tantrums when the mother does not give him what he wa ts.

The mother's chief complaint is the patient's thumb-sucking, with an accessory movement of poking his nose, onset in the first half year of life.

Delinquency: None.

Sex: Patient has inquired about the facts of birth but mother did not tell him the truth. At age 5 years, 4 months, the patient was involved in a doctor game with a girl in which he tried to give her an enema with a stick.

Friends: Patient has very few friends, attributed to his unpopularity with children. Mother bribed a boy, when patient was age five, to play with him and bring other boys to the house. Rejected by boys his own age because he is "a pest," he tries to play with older boys, who do not want him.

School: He is interested and anxious to go to kindergarten although he resents it all as baby games and wants to go into Grade I.

Interests: Patient likes to hear stories, to copy words from school-books, and to play the usual nursery games.

Developmental history: Caesarian birth. Breast fed five months. First tooth at 13 months; walking at 13 months. A few words at eight months; nursery rhymes at 18 months. Patient has always been left-handed.

Habit problems: Toilet habits were established at 10 months; no enuresis after two and a half years. Patient has never slept well, is restless. Has an irregular bed time—6:30 to 8 P.M.; has refused to take afternoon naps since age three.

He dawdles over his food and must be coaxed, though he eats sufficient amounts.

Case 5

I.C.G. contact: February, 1928, to March, 1930. The patient is 13 years, 4 months old, male, the second of two siblings. The older brother is 18. I.Q. 114; all tests indicate superior intelligence. Grade IX. Height 58.5 inches; weight 103 pounds. He is somewhat shorter and about 13 pounds heavier than the median. Has a high-pitched voice, large hips, well cared for fingernails, hair perfumed with brilliantine. Genitalia well developed; fair growth of pubic hair. Slight external strabismus of the left eye; wears glasses for slight hyperopia; mild hypospadias. Strength average.

BASIS OF SELECTION

Father and mother state they have been too lenient with him. All workers note maternal oversolicitude and constant mothering.

EVIDENCE OF OVERPROTECTION

Mother says he was very close to her as a baby—that is, to age seven —since she never let him go out without her, not even with his father or another adult.

At age 15, he had been sleeping with his mother the past three years.

His schooling was delayed until he was seven, because the mother did not like him to leave her.

"She has always kept him in very closely and was afraid to have him mix with other children for fear of diseases and the things he might learn from them."

Mother responds to his pleading and walks to high school with him —patient age 15. When father wanted to make him go to school— Grade I—after patient pleaded not to, the mother interfered, kept him at home several days and said he was not feeling well.

When patient is disobedient, mother puts him to bed in the afternoon, even now.

Mother's plan of overcoming his unhappiness in school—the present problem—is to "simply sacrifice everything and take him out of school and go with him some place where she could be with him all the time . . . and maybe next fall he would be able to come back to school."

Mother always blocked father's attempts to discipline the boy.

Mother blocks the plan of sending him to boarding school by saying that if she visited him and he were homesick, she would bring him home—patient age 13.

When patient was sent to camp—at age 14, mother became anxious, visited him the second day, found his feet were wet and took him home.

Patient got a job selling candy at a theater and liked it. He did not want his mother to interfere but she insisted on telling the "chief boy" that her son was being cheated on commissions.

Mother still prepares special food for him since he is always a fussy and finicky eater.

PERIOD OF ANTICIPATION

Patient was born five years after the birth of the first child. No contraceptives were used, but mother hoped to avoid pregnancy because of a very difficult first labor. When pregnant, mother was very happy and hoped the child would be a girl. There was a difficult, prolonged labor and instrumental delivery. A five-month miscarriage occurred five years after the birth of the patient—the last pregnancy.

Mother has always been very fond of babies and wants to adopt a female child.

EXTRA HAZARD

None. Patient was a healthy baby. Had mild measles and pertussis in infancy. Mother is overly concerned about illness, she says, because he always looks pale.

MATERNAL FACTORS

Marital: There is no quarreling. The husband "is easy to get along with and a good provider." Mother has been sleeping with the patient the last three years. Father is "estranged" from the mother and does not speak to her, although he has given good economic support the past year and a half—that is, to March, 1930. Mother was ignorant and ashamed of sex activity in the early months of marriage; there has been a gradual decrease in frequency as "they didn't care about it."

Social: Mother always had friends as a girl, and although she "liked a good time," was more serious than the others. Since her marriage she has no desire to go out but "sacrifices everything to stay at home and give her children what she feels is proper care."

Background: Mother was the seventh of eight children and the youngest of four girls. Her father left home when she was two years old. He lived in the neighborhood and she saw him weekly. As a child, she was fond of her father, but fonder of her mother.

She quit school and went to work at about age 13 to help support the family. Her first job was taking care of a baby. She worked in a store for over five years. Her final promotion was to a job as cashier, which she held until marriage.

She is an aggressive, dominating woman who resisted all treatment of the patient and finally withdrew him from the I.C.G.

PATERNAL FACTORS

Relation to patient: The paternal role is weak. Father's attempts to be firm with the patient are frustrated by the mother. He decided to use strict authority when the patient was 13, and tells how the older boy was encouraged by the mother to quit jobs, whenever dissatisfied, but he was able to keep him at work.

Father has taken patient to the movies once or twice a week in the past year.

Background: Father was the youngest of five children. He was timid and seclusive as a boy, like the patient, he says. He is a "home" man, a very steady worker and "never happy" when away from the shop. One New Year's Eve when all the other workers in the shop took time off, he stayed and worked all night to finish a job.

He provided for and lived with his mother, not marrying until after her death, when he was age 35. He was his mother's favorite and strongly attached to her. He was antagonistic to his father, who was alcoholic and never supported the family. He himself is a teetotaler.

PATIENT

Behavior problems: The patient is timid, shy, and reserved. He never plays on the street with other boys, lacks any social initiative or ambition, and prefers to stay home all the time. Boys call him "sissy" and tease him.

He is very dependent on mother and insists that she walk to school with him. He wants to help her with the housework, although mother discourages it.

He is fussy about food and still needs coaxing to eat, as in infancy.

When he could not get his own way, he threatened to jump out the window.

He fakes illness to keep from going to the present school.

He usually whines and sulks, although he never has temper tantrums and never even uses cross words with his mother.

Delinquency: None.

Sex: Psychiatric interviews revealed that the patient is ignorant of primary sex differences and has childish conceptions about birth.

Friends: Patient had none until age 13, when he started going out with boys.

School: There is now much difficulty in getting him to go to school; two years ago he liked going. He skipped several grades and finished Grade VIII at 13. He is now failing in high school.

Sibling relationship: There is no evidence of sibling rivalry or jealousy. The older brother gives him spending money. They are apparently fond of each other.

Interests: The patient's only interests are reading and music. He likes to do housework but the mother discourages it.

Developmental history: No delay. Taken off the breast at five months by advice of physician because of inadequate supply of breast milk. On bottle until 11 months. Walked by 13 months; talked by 15 months.

Habit problems: No enuresis. No sleep disturbances. Very neat and clean. Feeding difficulty discussed under "Behavior problems."

Case 6

I.C.G. contact: May, 1928, to April, 1931. Patient is an only child, male, age 10 years, 1 month. Grade III. I.Q. 88, rated as low average intelligence; scores are adequate on performance tests; some language handicap. Patient is of medium height; seven pounds underweight. He appears pale, undernourished, and weak. Carious teeth. Testes are incompletely descended and the penis is small. Correction advised for myopia.

BASIS OF SELECTION

Stepfather states that the mother kept the patient too close to her; all workers in the case, including teachers, regard patient as pampered by the mother.

EVIDENCE OF OVERPROTECTION

He was breast fed for three years whenever he cried and twice nightly. Mother explains the prolonged time by saying, "You know he was all I had." She enjoyed nursing him and quit because advised to do so on account of her health.

Because patient complained that he was molested by boys in the first grade, mother hired an older boy to accompany him to school. Although patient belonged in one school district, mother sent him to another school because it was a shorter walk.

Mother never allowed him to play with other children because he would learn bad habits from them and they were rough. In the last few years he has been allowed to play with children in front of the stepfather's store, and now also plays with a cousin in the store.

Mother slept with him until he was about six years old.

He still clings closely to the mother, is loath to leave her in the morning, is very anxious if he is a little late returning from school and explains why, being very responsive to mother's anxiety. He is very concerned about the mother's worries; her slight disapproval is very effective in making him mind, although she has punished him for disobedience by making him go to bed early and occasionally by spanking.

PERIOD OF ANTICIPATION

Mother was emotionally upset by the desertion of the father during the period of pregnancy. She worried and wept a great deal; her appetite was poor and she lost a great deal of weight; she wanted to die.

EXTRA HAZARD

Difficult birth and immediate worry after the birth over the fact that the child's head was imperfectly molded.

Only child and only pregnancy.

Mother fears that the father may come back and claim his son.

In his early years patient was one of a few Chinese boys in a white neighborhood.

MATERNAL FACTORS

Marital: Mother's first husband was her employer; she worked for him four years before marriage. After obtaining possession of her dowry he deserted her when she was pregnant. The first husband is considered a very unscrupulous, tyrannical person. He arranged the marriage with the mother's family, who were taken in by his devotion and apparent wealth. Mother was 27 at the time of her first marriage. She fears that her first husband will kidnap the patient, on the basis of actual threats.

The present marriage appears to be happy. For advice, the mother goes to a social worker who has befriended her, rather than to the husband. There is no sexual incompatibility. No contraceptives have been used, yet there has been no pregnancy in the second marriage. Mother spends much time helping her husband in the store. There is occasional disagreement over the patient, whom the mother protects from the stepfather's chastisement. He is described as very kindly to his wife and stepson.

Social: Family life is at present restricted to home and store in which, however, there are many social contacts. During the first five years of the patient's life, the mother lived practically alone with him.

Background: Mother was the youngest of four siblings and the only daughter. She had little contact with her father, who died when she was nine years old. She was very fond of her mother, "worshiped" her, and was sheltered by her mother and older brothers. The latter are now all married and successful businessmen. As the only girl, she was kept at home to do the housework, although she worked irregularly in factories until about age 23, when her mother became paralyzed. After this, she cared for her mother for several years until a brother married. The sister-in-law then took her place in the home and the first marriage was arranged. After her first husband's desertion, she was left stranded in New York and earned a good living sewing. She had learned fine needlework from her mother. Always dependent on her family, she is now dependent on a social worker who says, "She will do anything I tell her." Mother has always been thrifty, industrious, and conscientious.

PATERNAL FACTORS

Relation to patient: Patient had no contact with his own father. The stepfather is affectionate with patient and much interested in his welfare. He occasionally spanks the patient and then makes up with him by taking him to a movie or Coney Island. He is ambitious to have the child go through college. He often disagrees with his wife's overprotective attitude. Patient is apparently quite fond of the stepfather.

Background: Data on stepfather are incomplete. He is six years younger than the mother and of smaller stature; thin, very neat and tidy in appearance. He was always industrious, ambitious, fairly successful in business, and anxious for education.

PATIENT

Behavior problems: He is very dependent on mother, afraid to be at home without her, he is over-responsive to her worries, disapproval or approval; wanting to do just as she does, helping her with housework. He is loath to leave her in the morning and cried many times when she left him at kindergarten. In his earlier years, if anyone helped the mother to remove her coat or took her things, he would cry, grab the hat, and say they were his mother's.

He has always been fearful of strangers. Onset of acute fears was placed at the first grade when he was molested by boys, who teased him and stole his candy. Patient has exaggerated these difficulties; he has told of boys lying in wait to chase him. When molested he never fights but threatens to tell his mother. He recounts fears of the dark, of dogs, and monkeys.

Had breath-holding temper tantrums until about age six, also feet-stamping tempers which the stepfather cured by spanking him. The temper tantrums occurred when he couldn't have his way.

Delinquency: None.

Sex: Stepfather noticed some toying with genitals, punished him and threatened it would make him sick. Patient says he has never masturbated.

Friends: Patient had no friends until he started to school at age six. He has played with boys only in the last year or two. He selects only boys younger than himself. He will throw snowballs at a boy and then walk along innocently; gets some revenge by this form of deceit. He is afraid to fight.

School: The patient gets poor grades in all subjects except drawing and arithmetic, in which he is excellent. He has repeated several grades. He makes some play for attention and tattles; there is some mischief making like tickling the boy in front of him and then putting on an innocent face.

At kindergarten—age five to six years—he refused to play with others and never shared his toys or possessions. This type of selfishness is still present.

Interests: His interest now is chiefly in play with companions. He likes to be read to, but is not interested in reading. He likes to draw pictures and shows some artistic ability. He likes to take mechanical toys apart, although he cannot put them together.

Developmental history: The patient walked at 18 months; talked at 16 months. Mother was not worried over the delay.

Habit problems: Mother made no effort to train the patient in the first two years. Bowel and bladder control was established by age four years. Patient's sleep is irregular; he is not put to bed until 10 P.M. when mother quits work in stepfather's store, and he then lies awake "worrying," often until midnight. No night terrors or other sleep disturbances. Good appetite; no feeding problems. He is very neat and clean.

CASE 7

The patient, 11 years, 3 months old, is a male, the second of two living siblings. The older sister is age 13. Grade 5 B; one of the best students in school. No intelligence tests recorded. For physical data, refer to "Extra hazard."

BASIS OF SELECTION

The patient's dependency was shown at the time of examination when he held the mother's hand and begged her to come with him. When taken to the examination room, he opened the door several times to see where his mother was. The mother asked to be taken to the examining room, saying that all doctors allowed her to be present at the time of examination and giving arguments as to why it should be permitted.

EVIDENCE OF OVERPROTECTION

Dependency noted at the time of examination.

The patient was breast fed 11 months. Mother had to quit because of sickness and cried when she weaned him because "you feel that they are taken away from you."

Mother still sleeps with the patient, who will not fall asleep unless she is with him.

Mother often examines the child's genitalia—"It is all right for him to be naked before me. He is still just like a baby."

She takes the patient along wherever she goes, even now.

PERIOD OF ANTICIPATION

Mother had a fear of sterility. She was always anxious for a boy; she would write the name "Marty" in the sand in the first year of marriage. She said: "I waited four years for Marty."

A child born after the first year of marriage was stillborn. The second child, a girl, now 13 years old, had infantile paralysis at eight months, and is now in an ungraded class. The patient was born two years after the birth of the second child.

EXTRA HAZARD

Patient is the only boy.

He had colic during the first year of life and much medical care was necessary. There was developmental delay—late walking and talking. Mother did not worry about the delay in talking because the patient had given indications of brightness before that time. At three and a half years he had double pneumonia followed by empyema for which a thoracotomy was done; the child's life was despaired of. At four years he began to take on enormous weight and the genitalia appeared to be very small. The mother has taken him to various clinics and he has received glandular therapy since—his present weight is 123 pounds; height 57 inches. The penis appears very tiny; however, when the suprapubic fat is pressed backward, it appears normal for his age— penis four centimeters in length and testes large peanut size. The patient was used as a demonstration case of Fröhlich syndrome at a local hospital about four year ago. Mother sat in the back of the auditorium and heard the doctors say the child would die by age 17 years. The boy also heard it and repeated it to his mother. She assured him that he heard wrongly, and said that she made up her mind after that that she would give him his way more than ever.

MATERNAL FACTORS

Marital: Mother says she was always "cold"; never liked the sex act and very often would feign illness to get out of it. She would be irritable when she had sex relations with her husband. He was disappointed at this and would ask if she really loved him. Had she allowed it, she thinks he would have had sex relations every night. She would rather have had no sex relations at all: "maybe I am abnormal that way." She says she was more a mother than a wife. Throughout her married life, she never appeared naked before her husband.

The husband played a submissive role; mother was the dominant member of the household. He was very modest and very kind to his wife, often making breakfast for her. She contrasts her husband with her father, who was the dominant person in the home. The husband was very stable; held his last job 32 years. He died when the patient was eight years old.

Social: Mother never went any place with her husband without having the children along. She does not go out with neighbors or members of her family; she has stuck entirely to the house since her marriage. Mother says that she was very devoted to her husband; she was so in love with him that she would have left her own mother to nurse him if he were ill, before her marriage. She broke her engagement to another man to marry patient's father, even though her father opposed it because her husband was so much older than herself. She preferred older men, and had been engaged to a man 15 years older than herself. She was 26 at the time of marriage; her husband was 47. He was a widower, his first two wives having died. He had had no children by either marriage and mother was willing to sacrifice having children in order to marry him.

Background: Mother was the third of ten children. Her father was a farmer and she had hard work to do on the farm. She was fond of her mother but antagonistic to her father because he was stern and cruel and punished them severely When her father beat her, she would go out on the farm and beat the animals. She thought she would be severe with children, as her father was, but says, "When they come you just can't help loving them all the time." Her mother died when she was 17. She nursed her mother two years before her death, "not taking her clothes off for the last seven days." Since the death of her husband, patient's mother has done sewing and is apparently competent to make a living. She takes the children about from clinic to clinic, and is regarded as coöperative, patient and careful, faithfully following the advice of physicians.

PATERNAL FACTORS

Relation to patient: Father never disciplined the children and left everything to his wife. Mother says, "I would never let anyone touch the children." He was very good to the family, bringing gifts, for example.

Background: No information other than stated elsewhere.

PATIENT

Behavior problems: Note that mother makes no complaints.

The patient is afraid to fight. He keeps away from boys and has no friends. Mother has urged him to play with boys and he has several times played baseball, only to run back to mother.

Delinquency: None.

Sex: He is completely ignorant. No evidence of masturbation.

School: He is very obedient in school, always receives "A" in conduct, and is "one of the best boys in school."

Sibling relationship: He is jealous of his sister and comes in between them when mother kisses the sister. The sister "idolizes" him.

Interests: Patient spends his time chiefly with mother but reads a good deal.

Developmental history: There was developmental delay; he walked at 17 months. First words at about the same time.

Habit problems: No enuresis since age 18 months, after about three months of training. He has food fads; will not eat vegetables, dislikes meat, but is very fond of fruit. Sleep is noted under "Evidence of Overprotection."

CASE 8

I.C.G. contact: October, 1930, to April, 1931. The patient is an only child, male, age 7 years, 4 months. Average intelligence, I.Q. 97. Grade II; doing fairly well at school. The present schoolteacher says he is not doing well in arithmetic but is excellent in reading and language ability. Good health, strength, and coördination; about three inches above the average height for his age, and somewhat below the average weight for his height—9 percent. "Fatigue posture."

BASIS OF SELECTION

Father says the mother is "completely wrapped up" in patient, considers him a genius and devotes all her time to him. Social workers and psychiatrist regard mother as highly overprotective and overdevoted. Patient is a very much wanted child by both parents, especially the mother, who, however, preferred a girl.

EVIDENCE OF OVERPROTECTION

Patient was breast fed 11 or 12 months.

Since his birth mother has always insisted on staying home with him and has stopped much of her previous social activity.

She continually watches him from the window.

Mother considers the patient, who has average intelligence, "a genius." She comes to the school frequently to protect the patient against supposed discrimination and whenever he receives poor grades.

PERIOD OF ANTICIPATION

Both parents, especially mother, strongly desired children. Contraceptives were never used. There was a miscarriage two years preceding the birth of patient. After this, she was "doubly anxious" about the second pregnancy. She grew "so fearful lest she lose him." There was much abdominal pain in the last three months of pregnancy. Another miscarriage followed the patient's birth. Mother accused her husband of having syphilis because she was unable to carry her pregnancies to term, and insisted that he be examined.

EXTRA HAZARD

Patient is an only child. The possibility of more children is very remote.

Patient was in hospital at two years of age for phimosis, circumcision, and excision of a lipoma. At four and a half he had German measles; at about six the school doctor advised a heart examination; at seven he had measles while the mother was in hospital.

He is generally in good health. No developmental delay.

MATERNAL FACTORS

Marital: Mother is "repelled" by sex relations and feels "revolt" against her husband after the act. She referred to her husband as "a stick-in-the-mud." There is a general conflict in interests.

Social: The husband does gardening in his spare time and tinkers with his automobile. Mother is interested in things of a more "intellectual and abstract" nature. The family have auto rides together. Mother describes her evenings at home as deadly monotonous; the husband "knows nothing interesting to talk about." They "just sit; there is nothing but heavy silence."

Mother led an active social life before marriage but quit her friends when the patient was born. In recent years she has gone to the movies with her mother almost daily.

Background: Mother is the second of eight children, born in Ireland of poor, uneducated, religious parents. Father died in her childhood. Her mother was easily excited and often depressed, required much "petting up" by the children. Mother had a hard early life. When a girl, she worked as a housemaid for wealthy neighbors. She came to the United States at the age of 20 and took training in a hospital, receiving her nurse's diploma at 23. She worked as a nurse until her marriage at 39. The husband was then 41. At the hospital she was cheerful, efficient and had many friends; she enjoyed social life before marriage.

She was ambitious to be an actress. In school she studied hard and made high grades. She used to sing in a church choir and now would like to take music lessons. Her strong urge for cultural attainments was never gratified.

When the patient was seven years old, she was confined in a hospital for four months with manic-depressive psychosis. She had a second attack when the patient was eight. The first attack was precipitated by the patient's report card showing a low mark in arithmetic. Mother immediately went to the school and manifested very excited behavior and definite psychotic symptoms. The husband attributed his wife's difficulty to her fear of sterility—for which at first she blamed him and then became overly attached to the patient.

PATERNAL FACTORS

Relation to patient: Discipline of the patient is left largely to the mother. Although the father disapproves of his wife's method of shouting, sometimes slapping, then apologizing to her boy, he does not interfere. In his own relations with the patient he is consistent, "expects less from the child," and is not very firm. Mother varies from "nagging, shouting and criticism to considerable indulgence."

Background: Father was one of eight children. His father was a farmer and in poor circumstances. He was very attached to his mother and remained at home longer than any of his siblings. After his father's death, he stayed at home, working for his mother. He did not marry until after his mother's death; he was then age 41. His sister, to whom he is strongly attached, lives in the home.

Father is a steady, responsible worker. He has held his last job as a clerk seven years. His active social life before marriage was curtailed after the birth of the patient because mother then insisted on staying home. In his spare time he works in the garden. He spends very little money on himself.

PATIENT

Behavior problems: He does not get along well with other children because he is boastful and tries to boss. In the past six months, however, he has had two playmates. Observed in play with other children he differed from them in being overcompetitive and using unfair methods in order to win.

Mother is worried about his masturbation. Patient is unable to talk about it to the psychiatrist or repeat any nasty word he has heard; in general he is "overly fearful about exposing any of his experiences."

His attitude toward the mother's condition, even toward the episode in which she manifested manic behavior in his classroom, is to act as though it never occurred.

Patient is excessively religious.

There is some evidence of infantile behavior, for example, playing and dawdling at meals. He is very demonstrative and likes to be kissed and petted.

Although he is insolent and disobedient to maternal grandmother, he obeys his paternal aunt implicitly, and is very obedient to "an exacting and nagging mother."

Delinquency: None.

Sex: Father does not think he has any sex information. See "Behavior problems."

Friends: See "Behavior problems."

School: His progress is regular. He is quite obedient and makes fair grades. Is now in Grade II A. His recent report card showed B+ in reading, A in deportment, and C+ in arithmetic.

Interests: He usually plays around the house. He has no special interest in gardening or mechanics—father's interests—or in reading.

Developmental history: He was a good baby, neither too quiet nor hyperactive. First tooth at nine months; several teeth by 12 months. He talked and walked at 12 months.

Habit problems: Toilet habits were established by 13 months and there has been no wetting or soiling since. He has always slept soundly and has a fair appetite, but dawdles and plays while he eats.

CASE 9

I.C.G. contact: May, 1929, to June, 1933. Patient is an only child, female, age 4 years, 5 months. Very superior intelligence, I.Q. at age four 117; at age five 128; consistent with test scores and conversational level. Adequate height, weight, and strength. Acute otitis media and sinusitis at time of first physical examination.

BASIS OF SELECTION

Father says that mother and grandparents spoil patient, the patient's problem is "too much mother"; family physician thinks likewise. The child is spoiled. All staff workers emphasize the problem of overprotection.

EVIDENCE OF OVERPROTECTION

Patient was difficult to wean from the breast when it was tried at 10 or 11 months, and was therefore breast fed until 16 months.

Mother cooks several different kinds of cereal each morning to please patient.

Mother would not let anyone share the care of the child when the latter was ill after an operation—suspected mastoid—and stayed up with her all night.

Patient often refuses to eat at meals, whereupon the mother still feeds her and coaxes.

The patient refuses to come in from play at supper time and it is often 11 o'clock before she can be put to bed.

Mother used to spank the patient until warned not to do so because of the child's illness after an ear operation when she was about 30 months old. Since then, the mother has used false reasons to get her to do things, for example, to get her to change her seat in the auto, asks her to "see the lovely trees on this side," a method which the child usually sees through. Patient pays no attention to mother's calls to come in when she plays outside, is generally very disobedient; mother's occasional direct insistence is met with prolonged crying.

Patient sometimes commands the parents to turn off the radio and if not obeyed, will turn it off herself.

Observed at the I.C.G., mother gives in very quickly when the child refuses to obey.

OTHER FACTORS IN OVERPROTECTION

The patient is much admired by all relatives and is the favorite of all four grandparents, although contacts are not frequent.

PERIOD OF ANTICIPATION

None. Pregnancy and labor were apparently normal. Mother says she was very ill after the third month of pregnancy; nevertheless she worked willingly in husband's store until the last month of pregnancy.

EXTRA HAZARD

Patient had colic and cried a great deal in the first six or seven months of life. She had mild diphtheria at two years; a tonsillectomy at two years, four months; and within a few months a paracentesis of ear abscesses on several occasions; also treatment for ear and sinuses weekly since that time.

Following an operation at 30 months, the patient was sent from the hospital to the home of her grandmother. She screamed when anyone came near her, trusted no one, was sure the water contained medicine and was taken back to the hospital on the pretext that she was going to a hotel. There she quieted down and returned home in several weeks.

Patient screams nightly in her sleep. Onset, according to mother, followed the tonsillectomy; according to the father it preceded the tonsillectomy. The child shouts as if in terror, calls for her parents, at first fights them off, then later accepts their reassurance and implores them not to leave her. They remain until she falls asleep. Sometimes they take her into their bed and remove her to her own when she is asleep. There has been sleep-talking since infancy.

At 3 years, 3 months, patient was badly scared in an auto accident, after which she was afraid of the dark and has had a light in her room at night since.

Patient is an only child and first pregnancy; a seven-month miscarriage, due to an auto accident, occurred when the patient was 3 years, 3 months old.

MATERNAL FACTORS

Marital: Father rarely shows affection to mother or child. Mother resents the husband's business failures and the fact that he is financially the least successful in his family; she refers also to his lack of education. She feels very much "alone" because she cannot discuss her worries with her husband and she has no close friends. She has little social life in common with the husband, who works most nights.

Mother says their sex relationship is satisfactory. She was never in love with father, but married him because of his "kindness." She never expected him to understand her "real feelings or interests."

Social: Mother sees the maternal grandparents weekly. She was very active socially before marriage and went to many parties. She has much less social activity now, although she is active in a woman's fraternal order of which she was president. She says she has no close friends because of difference in financial status, and will not visit most of her old friends because she can't dress as well as they.

Background: Mother was a weak child, although actually confined to bed very little. She blames her parents for not sympathizing with her artistic ambitions as a girl. Her father, a carpenter, was a very irregular worker because of ill health. Her mother had to take in boarders. Mother is the third of five children and had an affectionate relationship with her parents, who, however, did not have much time for the children. The two younger siblings now live with the parents and support them. Mother was the only one who was not made to study a commercial course immediately after finishing the eighth grade. Although they were poor, the family were ambitious for education and managed to keep mother in high school until the fourth year. She held various jobs for several years after she left high school. She worked six years in one place, until her marriage, and says she was imposed upon to do extra work because she was too timid to assert herself.

After marriage mother helped her husband run a store, or, rather, ran it for him while he got jobs elsewhere. The husband says he wishes his wife would stop being "too much mother," and had other interests or would take a job again.

Mother's friends still come to her to ask her advice, especially on matters of "home etiquette and decoration." She had a number of "artistic jobs." Her friends respect her highly and "what she can do to them if they get nasty is a shame."

Mother is a meticulous housekeeper. She complains constantly of ill health, is dissatisfied with her lot in life and feels that fate has been unfair in preventing the development of her artistic career. Yet she wants another child, though her husband is opposed to it.

PATERNAL FACTORS

Relation to patient: As regards the patient, mother says the father "does whatever I tell him to." Yet he showed much impatience with the child and spanked her for crying when she was age four or five. He rarely accepts the patient's "advances." He says he is fond of children but does not like to have anything to do with them.

Background: His own father was very undemonstrative, though kind. Father is the second of seven children. Of his siblings he says, "We didn't hate each other, we just didn't have any love for each other." Father rarely visits his parents. As a child he was much attached to his next younger brother. Father was his mother's favorite, very mischievous as a child and the "family fighter." In Grade VI, he disliked the teacher, truanted, and was expelled from school. He then went to work—age 13. He enlisted early in the war, and since then has failed in business twice. He is now an insurance agent. Social workers regard the father as an ineffectual person who plays a minor role in the home; yet he is a steady worker at his present job, a good provider and careful to take out considerable insurance for the family. The father died 11 months after the initial social examination.

PATIENT

Behavior problems: Patient is aggressive, disobedient, and attention-getting in her behavior. She ignores mother's calls to her and always gets her own way—refer to "Evidence of Overprotection." She is very self-assertive and very free during office interviews. Screams when her will is crossed. She refuses to feed herself and mother must feed and coax her. She constantly talks and asks questions.

Night terrors and fear of the dark began at about age three years, following an automobile accident, a collision in which two people in the other car were thrown into the car in which the patient was riding. The patient's ear operation followed one month after the auto accident. The onset of fears is related to both events. Note data under "Extra Hazard."

Delinquency: None.

Sex: Occasional masturbation noted since infancy.

Friends: She was very free with children and not at all shy, going up to any child and sharing her toys until about age four, when the mother of some children with whom she played shouted at her. Since then, she has refused to go on the street and play unless one of the parents accompanies her, and even then keeps close to parent. This later improved. When observed with other children patient was rather bossy and argumentative and "could not endure to be teased or outdone in any way." She will cry if a child crosses her will. She cannot bear to have a child dispute her opinion.

School: At five patient was sent to kindergarten where there was no problem except for occasional screaming "for no apparent reason."

Developmental history: No delay. A precocious talker; first words at eight months, sentences at 12 months, walked at 14 months.

Habit problems: For sleeping and eating problems, refer to "Behavior problems." Bowel and bladder control was established in infancy.

CASE 10

I.C.G. contact: February, 1929, to March, 1930. The patient, male, age 12 years, 5 months, is the first of four siblings. The next younger children are girls, age nine and four; the youngest is male, age two. Patient is in Grade VIII. Alpha score 151, equivalent to I.Q. 140; on a Stanford-Binet test at the age of nine he rated I.Q. 160. Achievement test scores are above Grade X. Height 61 inches, weight 106 pounds— 5 percent above median height and weight. Very good muscular strength and coördination. Has a rather short penis and wide hips. Complains of bodily illness, especially his heart. Previous physical examinations were negative, except myopia.

BASIS OF SELECTION

Social worker thinks that during the child's infancy mother "watched every breath he drew." Staff workers regard mother as excessively concerned over and attached to the patient. Mother states that she and her husband have been too lenient with the boy.

EVIDENCE OF OVERPROTECTION

Patient was breast fed 12 months because mother "hated to start" weaning. She very frequently kisses and fondles him.

Mother practically never left him alone during infancy. She kept him away from all but a very few people for fear he would get an infection. She used different vessels to bathe him—a basin for his head, one for his hands, and one for his genitalia.

Patient still sleeps with mother when father is out of town.

If he does not get the "largest piece" at the table, he leaves and refuses to eat.

At the age of nine, patient made many complaints because a new bedroom suite was bought for the parents' room and not for his own; he still complains about it.

He constantly demands mother's attention; had a temper tantrum at age 12 because she did not butter his bread for him.

He is disrespectful to the parents; for example, he resents giving up his chair for mother when reminded to do so.

PERIOD OF ANTICIPATION

None.

EXTRA HAZARD

When the patient was four years old, his sister had meningitis resulting in mental deficiency. Mother took her to a doctor daily for several years and yielded to advice on private institutional placement five years after the onset of the child's illness. As a result, mother's overconcern about patient's health was intensified.

Patient had a mild case of measles at five and pertussis at seven years. He has a very good health history.

MATERNAL FACTORS

Marital: Mother considers her husband ideal and still the most interesting man she knows. They have many cultural and social interests in common. She has "never had any pleasure in the sexual relationship." She submits passively to his sexual demands.

Social: Mother has an active social life with friends and family.

Background: Mother was the third of five children. Although she was the father's favorite she felt jealous of her other siblings as a child. She was frankly hostile to her mother and strongly attached to her dominating, although kindly, father, on whom her mother was very dependent. In childhood, mother was apparently happy and well-off until about age 12, when the family came to America. After her father's death, when she was 14, the family suffered financial difficulties. Although mother was very fond of school, she had to give it up and work. In her younger days she was active in labor movements and socialism. She is now president of a women's club.

Mother has always "loved to look after people." Her brothers and sisters always rely on her, especially for advice and help.

She wanted to be the "leader" of patient's friends, taking them to art museums and the like, but her husband dissuaded her.

She tried to dictate methods of examining the patient at the I.C.G., telling how the child should be approached.

PATERNAL FACTORS

Relation to patient: Father joined in early devotion to the patient, but now strongly resents the patient's lack of respect for him. He was very lenient with the patient in earlier years, but has now become irritated with the patient's lack of consideration. He rewards the patient for ordinary courtesy, for example, paying him a dollar for carrying his suitcase. Father started stricter discipline when the patient was about age 12, scolding and yanking him out of bed in the morning, instead of coaxing. The wife contrasts her husband with her dominating father who, although friendly, got respect and obedience from his children.

Background: Father was the third of five children, very respectful and obedient to his "authoritative" father. He was very stable, a good student, and is now a graduate engineer and successful in his work. He is a short, slight man weighing 120 pounds.

Father is very fond and proud of his children, but has become irritated with the patient and speaks of a constant "barrier" between them.

Father is very devoted to his wife. During her pregnancy with patient, for example, although she was in good health, he persuaded her to lie on a couch all evening while he did the housework.

PATIENT

Behavior problems: Patient is disrespectful and impudent to the parents, lordly to servants, and tries to dominate everyone at home. "The parents have lost a good many maids because of patient's treatment of them." He complains about the food, the other children and the routine of the home.

The patient demands mother's attention on all matters such as eating and dressing. When he resented the fact that she did not butter his bread, he answered mother's question as to what he would do when a man: "You'll butter my bread until I'm a man and then I'll get a wife to butter my bread."

He is snobbish, expresses his superiority and is very derogatory of other people, "imputing unworthy motives" to their actions.

He is selfish, wants the best of everything and resents the fact that the sister has a larger room than his, that parents bought new bedroom furniture for themselves and not for him.

He is very timid and cowardly with other children, afraid to fight, and would run away until about age 12—after many boxing lessons with father.

He constantly complains of pains in different parts of his body and exaggerates fatigue, despite a negative physical examination.

He has temper tantrums and still throws himself on the floor and cries when angry, although this has improved in the last three months.

Delinquency: None.

Sex: Mother noticed masturbation when he was two years old, and threatened that a black cat would bite his finger off if he continued. She once pinched his finger and said it was the black cat. Since then he does not touch his genital while urinating.

One instance of sex play with sister when age 12.

He slept frequently with his mother during the absence of the father until age 13 years, 1 month, when after coming to her bed he turned pale and left. Mother asked him why he would not come in and he answered: "It makes me sick."

Friends: Patient had no contact with other children until he went to school at six. He had no friends until recently—age 12. He "clowns" for them and goes through many antics to provoke their laughter. Note "Behavior problems."

School: He has made good school progress but does not make grades consistent with his ability. He behaves well in the classroom.

Sibling relationship: He is jealous of the younger children and annoyed at any attention they receive. He is quarrelsome with them, and sarcastic in his remarks.

Interests: His interests are largely intellectual. He is a voracious reader.

Developmental history: Normal birth and pregnancy. No delays; first tooth at four months; first words at seven months; walked at 14 months; had eight teeth at 12 months. Healthy infancy.

Habit problems: Bowel and bladder control was established by 18 months. He is critical about food, wants the largest piece, and occasionally refuses to eat to get attention, but is coaxed back to the table. Has a good appetite. He is late in going to sleep and in rising; otherwise there are no sleep disturbances.

CASE 11

I.C.G. contact: September, 1929, to February, 1931. An only child, male, age 10 years, 11 months. I.Q. 146; superior in all tests, including school achievement. Grade VII B. Physical examination negative except slight knock-knees and lordosis; average height 56 inches; weight $93\frac{1}{2}$ pounds—10 pounds overweight.

BASIS OF SELECTION

Mother states that he was spoiled by herself and maternal grandmother, and later she gave in to his demands for the sake of peace. Father says the patient's difficulty is due to being spoiled when he was small. "My wife lost one, a miscarriage, when he was 10 months old, and another, a stillbirth, when he was two years old. We both felt terrible and made more over the one we had." Father feels that the grandmother is largely responsible for the spoiling. "If my wife would correct him, she [grandmother] would say, 'Don't hit my child.' If she heard him cry she would pound on our floor and just give my wife hell."

Social workers and psychiatrist confirm the statements made by parents.

EVIDENCE OF OVERPROTECTION

Patient was bottle fed to the age of 21 months.

Mother still wants to bathe him. He locks the bathroom door and will not let her in. She stays outside and gives him directions for bathing.

She always gets his hat and coat for him when it is time for school in the morning; he angrily snatches it from her, but is very cross if she does not get it. "He is so slow he would be late if I did not constantly keep after him; then he gets mad because I do," according to mother.

He was always given his own way in infancy, if not by mother, then by grandmother; whenever refused, he always commanded obedience by screaming, and now by persistent repetition of his demands for toys or money.

He sleeps either on a single bed in the parents' room, or on a couch in the living room, as he wishes, regardless of mother's desires. He turns off the radio when his parents turn it on, regardless of their wishes.

He is disobedient always, defies his mother in the street, refusing to go home when she calls, so that the children in the street say, "Go with your mother." When mother attempts to punish him by denying meals, he goes to the icebox, gets foods, and cooks it for himself.

The parents have always bought expensive clothes for him because he demands them, but he is very careless and when chided, says, "Why don't you buy me cheap clothes, then it wouldn't matter." However, he refuses to wear cheap clothes.

He refuses to stay home nights and leaves at will, returning usually at 10 P.M.

PERIOD OF ANTICIPATION

The child was wanted; born in the second year of marriage. Mother had doubts as to the husband's ability to impregnate.

EXTRA HAZARD

Mother had a spontaneous miscarriage when the patient was 10 months old, and a stillbirth when the patient was two. She wanted at least three or four children, but has had no subsequent pregnancies. Never used contraceptives.

Patient is an only child.

Patient had measles at one year, a "polio" scare when he was two, pertussis for three months when he was two and a half. He has always had frequent colds. Tonsillectomy at three, chickenpox at three, mild scarlet fever at 10 years. An undescended testicle caused mother much worry.

MATERNAL FACTORS

Marital: Father has psychic impotence. Mother once accused him of being at fault because she wants more children. He has had various medical injections to aid erection without success. Venereal disease is denied. Contraceptives were never used. Mother cried when telling of her husband's impotence. Hymen was not ruptured until the fifth or sixth month of marriage. The husband says his wife frequently cries because she "does not receive satisfaction."

Social: Father works very hard, often until late at night, and has no time for social life. He and mother belong to neither clubs nor social organizations. Mother once belonged to a women's club where she had a chance to be elected to an office, but she made excuses so that the members would not find out how uneducated she was. The parents have few social contacts, now attributed to the patient. "He is ruining our home and our lives." The parents occasionally quarrel, mostly about the patient. There are contacts on Sunday with maternal or paternal aunts or uncles, but none during the week.

Background: Mother had a hard early life due to poverty. Her education was limited to night school. She came to America at the age of 13. Here she was successful in factory work, working ten years in one factory. She was frequently promoted, a "forelady" and "not afraid to talk to the boss."

Maternal grandmother was the dominant parent. "She was the one who went ahead. My father followed her." She handled the money and made all the decisions. Patient's mother was strongly attached to maternal grandmother and turned over all her salary to her. Mother had a strong educational drive, although discouraged by maternal grandmother. Mother met her husband at a lecture and passed herself off as an intellectual, and has since always struggled "to appear intelligent."

PATERNAL FACTORS

Relation to patient: Patient's early training was left entirely to mother and maternal grandmother. Father says the patient is not chummy with him and does not care about him. When listening every night to his wife's stories about patient's bad behavior, he says at times, "Why did I ever come back when we quarreled before we were married."

Background: Father was sickly until 10 years of age, and never active in games or sports. He was a very obedient boy; his father's word was "law." He is patient, has a "good disposition," is friendly with everyone, and runs away from fights. He has no time for recreation and describes himself as "rushing all day and being tired out at night and Sunday." He is very responsible, a steady and serious worker, successful in business, and a good provider.

PATIENT

Behavior problems: Patient is disobedient and impudent at home. He is disobedient in regard to homework and bedtime, leaving home and coming in at will, or reading hours after bedtime, eating meals when he pleases, refusing to answer when spoken to. He is sullen and impudent to both parents, taunting and teasing them.

Ever since infancy he has had temper tantrums in the form of screaming and shouting when he does not get his way.

He is very careless with his clothing.

Delinquency: No truancy. He recently took money from mother's purse when she refused to give him any.

Sex: Mother has seen the patient touch genital area over his clothing while reading and has brought this to his attention. She has observed no masturbation. In the past four months there was one instance of patient's embracing and kissing mother while she lay on a couch and a distinct sex proposal. Mother is very embarrassed and reluctant in allowing her son to have sex instruction.

Friends: Patient has no chums; although he is not barred from the group, he is not popular. "He hangs around on the edge of the group and talks a lot." When playing, he wants to be a leader and have his own way.

School: Patient presents no problem in school except a lowered grade in deportment for talking to other boys in the class. He is very fond of schoolwork and of tests. "I enjoy having examinations and seeing what marks I get." His teacher was surprised recently to learn that he was such trouble at home.

Interests: Patient's chief interest is reading, especially adventure and, recently, mystery stories. He rereads a book five or six times. Note bathroom reading.

Developmental history: Difficult labor. Breast fed until ten months; took bottle until 21 months old. Walked at 14 months; first phrase at 18 months.

Habit problems: Bladder control during the day was established by 12 months; at night by 24 months; bowel control by eight months, with a return of soiling at 18 months which lasted three or four months. He now locks himself in the bathroom with a book for an hour. He is a sound sleeper but restless and occasionally talks and laughs in his sleep. Keeps his own hours. He has no food fads, but overeats and has slovenly table manners. Nail-biting and thumb-sucking in infancy.

CASE 12

I.C.G. contact: November, 1927, to November, 1930. Patient is 15 years of age, male, the elder of two siblings. The younger sister is 11 years old. Very superior intelligence—scores 141 on the Army Alpha test. H.S. II. Very tall, 71½ inches—6½ inches above average; weight 140 pounds—10 pounds below median for age and height. Fair strength. Myopia; corrected by glasses. Very restless and overactive. Slight postural lordosis.

BASIS OF SELECTION

Mother's extreme devotion to the patient and constant worry and solicitude over him. Social workers, physician and school teachers regard mother as excessively anxious about the patient. Patient "blames his parents because they have spoiled him and never made him obey." "The mother is entirely absorbed in the patient."

EVIDENCE OF OVERPROTECTION

Breast fed 14½ months.

Up to the age of 10, "if mother left him for more than ten minutes he cried and called for her."

Mother shines his shoes for him still, "otherwise he wears them to school unshined."

Mother "recounts endlessly how she served and watched over" the patient, prepared only "food that he liked," and spent much money for gifts and parties.

She never permitted him to play in the streets and guarded him from the influence of other children.

She has never allowed her husband to "touch" the patient.

She makes many trips to his room during the night to "see if he is sleeping quietly, or is restless."

PERIOD OF ANTICIPATION

None. Patient was born in the tenth month of marriage.

EXTRA HAZARD

None. Patient had mild pertussis at 18 months, measles at five years and a tonsillectomy at 12. No other illnesses. A healthy baby. Walking was delayed to 16 months, but first words at 9 months and phrases by 12 months.

MATERNAL FACTORS

Marital: Mother considers it disgraceful for a husband and wife openly to share the same bed, so that their children can say, "Oh, look, mamma is sleeping with papa." Patient shares a bedroom with the father; the daughter sleeps in a double bed with mother.

Social: Because she is "wrapped up in her child," mother does not participate in any club activities, she says.

Background: It was difficult to get facts about the mother's own life as in every interview she constantly turns to the subject of her son.

Her father died four months prior to her birth. Her mother died when she was 10 years old. She was brought up by an older sister, 20 years her senior. She was very unhappy and felt "jealous" when she heard other children say "father" and "mother." She told this with choking sobs.

Mother was always "extremely self-sufficient." She "listens to no one and takes no advice, not even from her husband." There is no friction between them because "he is always satisfied with her decision." Mother showed this same initiative as a child. She "was gay and active, entirely lacking in shyness."

PATERNAL FACTORS

Relation to patient: Father plays a very weak paternal role since the mother has taken "complete charge" and he yields to her decisions. On one occasion when the boy was hitting his mother, the father pleaded, "Don't hit her, hit me." Patient's attitude to father is derogatory, at times contemptuous. He never has friendly conversations with him, and refers to him as "the horse." Father attempted to thrash the patient several times when the latter was younger, but mother did not permit it. Now when mother calls on him to discipline the patient, he pleads exhaustion. Patient has never been spanked. Father has often told the boy how to behave, has expressed dissatisfaction with his excessive reading, pleading with him.

Father is a waiter and his relatives are waiters and salesmen; mother's relatives are successful professional people and college graduates. As a waiter father works 14 hours a day and sees very little of the patient. For long periods he is on night shifts and sees the patient only on Sundays.

Background: Father is a hard-working, plodding, conscientious person, a waiter who failed as a restaurant owner. He was the only worker who "got along well" with an "irascible employer." He was the only son and the favorite child of his mother. He was devoted to his mother, and is now devoted to his wife. As a husband, he is considered an "angel" who gives everything he has to his family.

PATIENT

Behavior problems: Rebellious, bullying and destructive at home, he loses his temper when his wish is crossed and strikes mother or sister.

He is openly critical and disparaging of them both, calling them names and criticizing their appearance and manners.

He accuses the mother of being pregnant and tells her she has no right to have more children.

He disobeys in spite of mother's constant entreaties. Mother nags and many of her requirements are obviously excessive, for example that he must not play chess, that he must not read detective stories. "His behavior towards the mother alternates between kissing and swearing at her." Mother has gone so far as to send him to a relative and move away during the night so that he could not return home; then she herself called him back. During quarrels with mother, he will throw crockery, frames, soil his shirts and cut his suits, tramp with muddy feet on the clean floor, and numerous other similar performances.

Patient has bitten his nails since about age seven or eight.

Delinquency: None.

Sex: Patient has never been given any sex information. He shows no interest in girls. Mother believes he is ignorant of the facts of pregnancy. He will never permit any member of the family to see him undress and covers himself with a blanket when mother enters the room. He complained to the I.C.G. examiner of his adult genitalia.

Friends: Patient has no friends. As a child he always wanted his own way, kept friends for a short while and then quarreled with them.

School: Patient is a serious student and "permits nothing to interfere with routine." He is ambitious to make high grades and insisted on going to summer school despite the parents' protests. He is never disobedient at school.

Sibling relationship: Patient quarrels with sister and hits and bullies her. He orders her about, states he has the right to do this, ought to do so, and gives this as a reason for staying when urged to live away from home.

Interests: Patient's interests are solitary, chiefly reading and chess.

Developmental history: Patient was a "large baby"; mother was badly torn at birth. No anaesthetics were used during delivery. Patient was breast fed 14½ months. There was no difficulty in weaning. He cut his first tooth at nine months. Walking was delayed until 16 months because the patient was heavy. First words at nine months.

Habit problems: Toilet habits were established by age two, although there was occasional wetting of clothing up to age four. Mother has always humored the patient's whims regarding food. For the past nine months—age 15— he has at times refused to eat. He sleeps well, but stays up late to read. Mother must remind him many times to bathe.

CASE 13

I.C.G. contact: March, 1928, to April, 1929. Patient is 14 years, 6 months old, male, the elder of two siblings. The younger brother is nine months old. I.Q. 110. Grade VII. He is a well-developed, muscular boy, slightly above the median height and weight. Internal strabismus of the right eye, corrected by glasses. Harrison's groove. Scoliosis.

BASIS OF SELECTION

Mother was always overindulgent. She insisted on rearing the child the way she liked, regardless of what her husband thought about it. "My Robert, he is my life." When the stepfather attempted to whip him in infancy, she threatened to leave home if he ever touched the patient; stepfather never did punish the patient, but "always gave in to him."

EVIDENCE OF OVERPROTECTION

Patient was breast fed to age two.

He is allowed to keep his own hours; he goes to the movies when he wishes and mother has his meals ready for him when he comes home. He is given an allowance of a dollar a day. He has no home responsibilities.

Mother told the worker it was hard for her to think of losing the patient, through his marriage. She "would like to hang on to him until he is about 30 or 35."

PERIOD OF ANTICIPATION

A first-born child, a year older than patient, died at the age of seven months.

EXTRA HAZARD

Patient's birth was preceded by a child who died of convulsions at the age of seven months.

Patient's birth was followed by a stillbirth, and mother was led to believe that she would then be sterile and the patient would be her only child. The second living child was born 14 years after the birth of patient.

Patient was "sickly and weak" up to age seven. During infancy he had vomiting spells and one convulsion. At four years he had influenza and pneumonia, after which he was "very restless."

MATERNAL FACTORS

Marital: "Had I realized what marriage meant," mother says, "I would not have married." Her economic status was lowered by marriage.

She married her husband "out of pity," she says. For advice she never turns to her husband, but to a brother-in-law. She says she regrets that her husband does not dominate.

Social: Mother has had no friends since marriage. She feels inferior as the wife of a building superintendent and tells how, for that reason, she refused to accept an invitation to visit a woman in her apartment building.

Background: Mother was the oldest of four daughters and "assistant" to her mother until the latter's death, that is, "manager" of the younger sisters. It was a very strict home and her childhood was unhappy. Before her marriage she decided if she had children she would be very lenient. Her parents tried to prevent her marriage because her fiancé was a Catholic and she a Protestant. She eloped despite protests. Her husband was a gambler and unstable. Mother was divorced and re-married when the patient was a year old.

PATERNAL FACTORS

Relation to patient: The stepfather has little to say about patient. He feels that the mother has always spoiled the patient and, although disagreeing with her, he leaves the discipline entirely to her.

Background: Stepfather is a good worker but afraid of being fired. He is superintendent of a modern apartment house with four men in his charge. He is quiet, retiring, and stable, and finally yielded to mother's insistence and moved out of New York.

PATIENT

Behavior problems: Patient is retarded about four terms in school. He is good in English, but very poor in arithmetic, and doesn't care. He truants, "but the parents do nothing about it," says the teacher. He does as he pleases in the classroom, is boisterous, leaves his seat to look out the window, and says he is bored at school, "the work is too easy."

He is disobedient to mother; goes out to play although she asks him to stay at home; wears sneakers to school although forbidden to do so; stays up late and gets up late.

He is cocky, boastful, and overly familiar; has an exaggerated ease of manner.

He masturbates in the classroom, exposed his genitals to girls—one instance.

He is regarded as a "sissy" and nicknamed "Mary."

On a camping trip with worker he was careless with things and insisted on throwing away a campfire grate instead of taking it home. Let his friend and the worker do all the work.

Although one or two hours late for I.C.G. interviews, he wants to be admitted at once. Both mothers and son show resistance to treatment in not keeping appointments.

Note is here made of the fact that mother refuses to breast feed the younger son because the patient "embarrasses" her.

Delinquency: See under "Behavior problems."

Sex: See under "Behavior problems."

Friends: Patient has no school associates. The teacher says boys stay away from him because he is "immoral and dirty." He has had one chum for years, a rich boy who goes to preparatory school. They visit each other very often and anticipate each other's homecoming. Patient is much influenced by this boy; latter has many girl friends.

Interests: Patient takes many walks by himself and is an "omnivorous" reader. He is interested in sports and shows leadership and initiative. He delights in letter writing.

Developmental history: Patient teethed and walked at the regular time. He has always been nervous and sickly, according to the mother.

Habit problems: Enuresis stopped at an early period. There are no sleep disturbances, although the patient keeps irregular hours. He has irregular eating habits, also, although no food fads. He is careless with clothes and possessions.

CASE 14

I.C.G. contact: July, 1928, to November, 1929. The patient is 5 years, 11 months old, male, the older of two siblings. The younger sister is age four years. I.Q. 117; superior intelligence on all achievement tests. Patient is in Grade I. He is tall—three inches above median height, and of good weight, although poorly nourished. There is some enlargement of the right anterior cervical glands. The physical examination is otherwise negative, except for extreme restlessness.

BASIS OF SELECTION

Both parents are markedly overanxious and solicitous, especially the mother. She feels that her anxiety is "something she cannot control." She states that she "has always watched over the children as through a microscope."

EVIDENCE OF OVERPROTECTION

Mother is exceedingly careful and watchful over patient's food. She dresses him now, although the child can dress himself.

The patient plays about under mother's eyes; if she is not on the street with him, he must be within sight of the window.

Mother takes him to school and calls for him every day, although the school is at a short distance. He was allowed to go alone, however, when the sister was ill, and patient was proud of this fact.

PERIOD OF ANTICIPATION

Mother was very anxious to have a child. Patient's birth was preceded by a miscarriage. Mother was afraid of sterility and had numerous gynecological examinations. She rejected the advice of several physicians to have a minor operation, but finally accepted the advice of a physician to go to the country for a rest; then became pregnant. She was much worried over the health of her child while pregnant. She was put on a vegetable diet and she felt "poorly."

EXTRA HAZARD

At the age of 14 months, the patient had three convulsions with cervical adenitis and high temperature. The physician warned mother against ever exposing the child to drafts.

Patient was very ill with croup at three and a half.

There are many visits to physicians.

MATERNAL FACTORS

Marital: Mother says she has never been passionate, but is willing to "satisfy" her husband. The necessity of contraceptives makes the sex act less pleasant.

Mother's economic status was lowered by marriage; otherwise there is no discord, no quarreling.

Social: Mother was very sociable before marriage. She now has little company due to financial status, devotion to the children and the husband's indifference to social life.

Background: Mother's childhood was unhappy. Her mother died in her infancy and she was brought up by maternal grandmother, not cruelly, yet not affectionately. She envied other children and longed for a mother. She was determined that her children would never suffer from lack of love.

Mother is much interested in education, has studied books on eugenics and biology, and continually consults physicians as to the care of the children. Mother came to the United States at 13, and worked before her marriage.

PATERNAL FACTORS

Relation to patient: Kept the patient on a vegetable diet until he was three. Sees the child only mornings and Sunday. Father enjoys playing with the children and used to take them out for walks; he has stopped doing this because they quarrel. He never uses force, "a timid soul."

Background: Father has "nervous indigestion" and is a vegetarian. He will not eat ice cream for fear it may contain poison.

Father works for a jeweler. He spends his evenings at home studying and inventing. He is strictly honest in business and gives in to customers for fear of any combat. Because of his poor physical condition, he sold out his own store after eight years. He is overconscientious about honesty and courage.

PATIENT

Behavior problems: Patient is irritable when corrected, calls his mother names, kicks, pinches and screams.

He often refuses food and has vomiting spells.

He shows off before company.

He is jealous of his sister, pinches and hits her, and takes her toys.

There is occasional nocturnal enuresis, which occurs, however, only after taking hot milk at mother's insistence before going to bed.

There is fanciful boasting, which he admits, when checked.

Delinquency: None.

Sex: The child is aware of primary sex differences. No evidence of masturbation.

Friends: Patient has no friends; he fights with children and tries to boss them.

School: Patient entered kindergarten this year—age 5 years, 10 months —and immediately adjusted to the school regime. The teacher considered him a model child.

Interests: Patient likes books and music; is less interested in toys.

Developmental history: Normal. Patient has a tendency to left-handedness.

Habit problems: Toilet habits were established at about two, with occasional nocturnal enuresis since—see "Behavior problems." The child lived on a vegetarian diet until age three, when because of anemia the physician ordered that he have meat. Patient is never forced to eat—note "Behavior problems." He is given an enema if his bowels are not regular. There are no sleeping problems.

CASE 15

I.C.G. contact: April, 1930, to June, 1933. Patient is 7 years, 5 months old; male, the elder of two children. The second child is a boy age four. I.Q. 85; consistent with performance test scores. Grade I. Teachers rate him below average in reading and arithmetic. Adequate height, weight, and strength. Very restless in all examinations. Slightly spastic gait. Slight intention tremor of hand. Poor in steadiness test. Enlarged cervical glands. Malnutrition. Positive Wassermann. Diagnosis: congenital syphilis.

BASIS OF SELECTION

The school principal says patient is coddled by mother; father says mother has kept the patient too close to her, Psychiatrist and social worker also stress this finding.

EVIDENCE OF OVERPROTECTION

Patient was breast fed 18 months.

He cried so frequently during the day that mother fondled him continuously after his second week. "I always had him around me; even when cooking I would have one hand on the stove, the other on the carriage; anything to stop his screeching."

Because of the patient's temper in infancy, mother would not allow father "to bother with the boy at this time because he would not understand him, so I took him everywhere with me."

In his sixth year he had a street-car accident in which he was not badly hurt; the car "just brushed" him. After this he was transferred to another school so that he would not have to cross the street-car tracks.

Mother visits the school weekly to check on the patient's progress, and when she cannot go she sends the father. The schoolteacher has refused to give her a reader with which she wishes to coach patient.

OTHER FACTORS IN OVERPROTECTION

Father's mother visits the home daily, constantly interferes with the mother's discipline, gives advice, and is frankly critical and hostile toward the mother. She lives close by and from the roof of her house where she often sits she can look into the back yard of her daughter-in-law. She screams at boys who make threats or fight with the patient, scaring them off. She also indulges patient.

PERIOD OF ANTICIPATION

Patient's birth followed a seven-month stillbirth and preceded a spontaneous miscarriage.

EXTRA HAZARD

Developmental delay. An accident at age six when patient was hit by a street car was significant only in frightening the mother. "To this day she does not remember how she got home," after being told about it by a neighbor while shopping. Tonsillectomy at three and a half years; mumps at seven.

MATERNAL FACTORS

Marital: The parents seldom go out; father usually visits paternal grandmother weekly alone; both parents occasionally go to the movies with the children. The husband complains that his wife keeps too close to the house. Paternal grandmother, who lives nearby, constantly intrudes and is regarded by mother as "catty" and a nag. The parents lived with the paternal grandmother in the first year of marriage. Father is very critical of mother's handling of patient. Mother is a meticulous housekeeper.

Social: Mother is not interested in her neighbors because "all they do is talk about you"—her neighbors are much better educated than she. She goes to night trade school twice weekly for lessons in sewing. Mother has no contact with her relatives.

Background: The maternal grandfather died when mother was two years old; the maternal grandmother, who was much loved by patient's mother, died when the latter was eight. Mother remembers how hard maternal grandmother had to work, doing washing to provide for the two children. After their mother's death, mother and her brother lived with her paternal grandmother and a paternal uncle. The latter she dislikes as grouchy and spiteful. This uncle had her taken out of school when she was ten, contending that women have no need of education. Until age 14, mother worked in the home; after that, in a factory. She ran away from home at 15, although she continued visiting her grandmother. As a waitress she saved money and in two years—age 18—she went to a hospital for a course as a practical nurse. She married after a year of training. Mother regrets especially her lack of education and is ambitious that her boys become doctors.

PATERNAL FACTORS

Relation to patient: Father regards the patient as too "babyish," a child "who is shy and cannot take his own part," and favors the younger son. Patient is constantly making bids for father's affection and is treated indifferently, in marked contrast with the affection given the second child. Discipline is largely in the mother's hands, particularly for the patient, although the father does slap the children when provoked by them. Mother brought the child to the I.C.G. without consulting the father.

Background: Father is the oldest child in a family of four children, with a very dominating mother who is still ruling her children and her submissive husband. Grandmother rents out rooms, decides to sell the house, and makes all important decisions. Father visits his mother's home weekly, seems quite happy to go there and to visit his father, whom he enjoys seeing although there is little conversation between them.

PATIENT

Behavior problems: Patient is immature in his behavior, plays with baby toys and smaller children. He still lapses into baby talk. He is aggressive in breaking up children's games and kicking them. When they fight, however, he is afraid, screams and runs away to his mother, who always watches from her window.

He cannot be depended upon to do errands at the grocery store, is delayed by distractions, and may forget the errand altogether.

Delinquency: None.

Sex: He has asked no questions and no information has been volunteered by the parents.

Friends: He is anxious to play with other children, but does not know how, according to the parents. He prefers to play with girls because they are not so rough. He has much trouble in school for picking quarrels, for which he is summoned to the principal's office—refer to "Behavior problems."

School: Patient is retarded in school, repeating the first grade. He is failing in all subjects. He has difficulty in adjusting to the classroom, is restless, and will not sit in his seat. He is regarded by one teacher as too docile.

Sibling relationship: Patient often yields to his four-year-old brother's lead, and latter has taken the patient's part against older boys. Patient is "led around" by younger brother, and fights with him.

Interests: Patient, unlike his brother, is not interested in father's activities. He likes to stay in school and do homework, and responds fairly well to school chores. He is interested chiefly in play.

Developmental history: Normal birth. Patient was breast fed 18 months; no feeding schedule—nursed to satiety. First tooth at nine months; walked at two and a half years—crept up to that time; talked at four years.

Habit problems: Toilet habits were established when the patient was two. There are no food fads. Little information in regard to sleeping habits.

Case 16

I.C.G. contact: January, 1928, to February, 1930. Patient is 14 years, 4 months old, male, the older of two siblings. The younger sister is 12 years old. Grade VI B. Adequate intelligence; I.Q. 109. According to achievement tests, patient could do VII A work. His scores are lower on performance tests. Patient is four and a half inches below the median height for his age; weight is inadequate for age and height. Good strength and coördination. Pyorrhea; error of refraction; postural lordosis.

BASIS OF SELECTION

All family case workers, including I.C.G. examiners, emphasize mother's overprotective attitude toward the patient.

EVIDENCE OF OVERPROTECTION

Patient was breast fed 18 months; not weaned before, as mother "did not wish to bother." There was no feeding schedule; he was fed when he cried.

Mother always makes excuses for his delinquencies, never blaming patient.

He is unmanageable at home. He refuses to do any chores. Mother depends on daughter for help in the house. She "would not think" of asking the patient to do any of these things.

He is "allowed to dominate mother and sister" and have his way in all things. He does as he pleases; mother does not know what he is doing when out in the street. He goes to the movies frequently regardless of mother's wishes.

Mother and sister pick up his clothes rather than precipitate a scene by asking patient to pick them up.

PERIOD OF ANTICIPATION

None. Pregnancy and birth were normal.

EXTRA HAZARD

Developmental delay.

Patient had infected cervical glands in the first year of life, requiring incision and drainage. Mild diphtheria at two years, chickenpox at two years, pertussis at six, appendectomy at 10 years.

MATERNAL FACTORS

Marital: Mother's love affair was "a neighborhood battle"; each family tried to prevent the marriage because of difference in religion—mother Jewish; father Catholic. They married despite strong opposition. The maternal family stopped all contact. Because of the husband's nonsupport and numerous terms in the penitentiary, several agencies have urged separation, but the wife remains loyal to her husband. She says their sex life was normal. The husband is a morphine addict.

Social: Mother's social life is now limited to job and home. She sometimes goes to the movies with her daughter. She has "only one person I call a friend."

Background: Her father was hard-working and undemonstrative with his children. He saw very little of them and died when the patient's mother was eight. After the father's death, two of the three younger brothers—mother is the eldest of four and the only girl—were sent to an orphanage, and she was left to herself a great deal since her mother had an outside job. Her mother, the family diciplinarian, was strict, authoritative, just, but unsympathetic, and continually wrangled with the patient's mother. She took the latter to children's court and had her committed to prevent marriage—commitment lasted about 18 months.

Mother left Grade VI to work in a factory. She was always regarded as self-willed, capable, anxious to handle her own affairs, and proud. She has held the same job for the last six years. Previously, she worked irregularly, when her husband was out of a job and economic difficulties were severe.

Mother indicates in the psychiatric examination her tremendous drive for family success and unity, concealment of her husband's record, her remarkable loyalty and energy in attempting to "show up" her family, to prove that she had not made a mistake as they warned her. Her suicidal attempt occurred when she had to face "the fact that her mother and relatives were right."

PATERNAL FACTORS

Relation to patient: Father is affectionate, patient, more devoted to the boy than is mother. He has little contact with his son because of penitentiary commitments. Patient is told that his father is in the hospital or on vacation. Patient's attitude toward the father—as expressed at age 14—is that he is "a weak man, gives in to temptation and is just no good." He knows of his father's penitentiary record.

Background: His father was a "heavy drinker," and died when he was age two. His mother remarried when he was five or six. The stepfather was unsympathetic, especially to his stepchildren, and had them quit school to go to work as early as possible. He is the younger of two children by his mother's first marriage, and was always her favorite. He has four half-siblings.

Father did not finish grammar school. He is an irregular worker. He started taking drugs at about age 25. There have been 11 arrests and seven sentences, totaling in all four years imprisonment. The charges were chiefly possession of drugs and larceny. Father is described as "decent but weak." He is devoted to his wife and very fond of his children. He is dependent on his wife, who alternately scolds and praises him and used to go to his place of work to make sure of his return home.

PATIENT

Behavior problems: "He is antagonistic to any person in an authoritative position" and unmanageable at home.

At 13 he was a leading member of a school gang which created trouble by disrespectful classroom behavior, calling teacher names on the street, and general undisciplined activities. He was transferred to his present school for bad conduct.

He refused to report for Grade VI so that he could loaf.

Delinquency: Patient steals and truants. At age 10, he stole stamps with another boy and, in the same year, money from the cash drawer in a store. He was sent to a protectory. The next year he stole packages from a truck. He was put on probation and there has been no stealing since.

Sex: Masturbation is denied. He is much interested in girls and tattoed his arms to attract their attention in school—age 14. Mother has not discussed sex with patient, feeling he has learned about this from outside sources.

Friends: Patient easily makes a place for himself in the group and belongs to a school gang. He is not a leader, but is outstanding in the group. His playmates are his own age. He is considered an attractive, polite, charming personality by adults.

School: Patient thinks school an unpleasant necessity. He is considered bright but not a student. He is extremely mischievous. There have been numerous changes of schools due to the family's moving and to his transfer to truancy school and protectory. Some promotions have been withheld because of his bad conduct.

Sibling relationship: Patient orders his sister to wait on him and when she refuses he hits her. In the morning he lies in bed and orders his sister to bring his clothes to him, shut the windows, and get his breakfast.

Interests: Patient likes reading, workshop, and especially movies.

Developmental history: Birth normal. Developmental delay; walked at 18 months; talked at two years; first tooth at nine months.

Habit problems: Patient has a good appetite and is not fussy about food. He had enuresis till age 9, for which he was scolded. Has no sleep disturbances, but keeps his own hours.

CASE 17

I.C.G. contact: April, 1929, to March, 1931. Patient is 13 years, 9 months old, male, the oldest of three boys. The second is 11 years, 9 months old; the third, 10 years old. Grade VII. Average intelligence as measured by the Army Alpha test, consistent with performance and educational tests. Three inches below median height for age; well nourished; good strength and coördination; tics—eye-blinking and sniffling; somewhat feminine fat distribution; small penis and testicles; high-pitched voice. Complained of pain over heart area. Heart examination negative. Error of refraction.

BASIS OF SELECTION

Mother says she has always been too easy with patient; that since her husband's infidelities she "has hugged the children closer." Staff workers note especially that mother has been overprotective and has kept the patient dependent on her.

EVIDENCE OF OVERPROTECTION

Mother says that for her "the door to the outside world is closed." She cannot live away from her children; whenever she goes out she must come back immediately.

Mother indulges the patient in his physical complaints and has him lie on a couch when he complains he is tired. She keeps the other children out of the room.

Mother is always afraid something will happen to the children, awakens easily at night, hears every move they make and gets up to see how they are.

She has always done things for patient. When the patient was 15, he requested a glass of water and she refused for the first time, telling him to get it himself. Mother says that patient tyrannizes over her.

PERIOD OF ANTICIPATION

Mother was ill with eclampsia; had loss of vision several days before the birth of the child. Full-term labor without instruments. Mother's illness continued several months after the child's birth. The child meanwhile was taken care of by neighbors.

EXTRA HAZARD

Patient "cried incessantly" as a baby. He had temper tantrums in which he ran "wildly" back and forth through the rooms.

Neighbors told the mother the baby was underweight and delicate, especially in the first year of life. She was afraid she would lose him.

Patient has had no serious illnesses; eye-blinking and sniffling tics at four years which have continued; mild measles, pertussis and chickenpox at five. Patient has had headaches—migraine?—since age nine. No faints, no loss of consciousness, no convulsions.

MATERNAL FACTORS

Marital: Mother makes a passive adaptation to sex role and "does her duty" by her husband. His infidelities started after the first year of marriage. Mother states she has always loved the children more than her husband, that she "discarded him after the first child was born," and that the husband was frankly jealous of all the children. The husband's evenings away from home are spent with other women.

Social: Excepting occasional visits to her own family, mother sticks very closely to home "on account of the children."

Background: Mother was the youngest of seven siblings. Her father deserted her mother and the latter died when patient's mother was four years old. She was placed in a home, then on a farm where she was punished severely and made to work hard. Through the help of a farm laborer she escaped, walked four miles to a station, took a train to the town in which her brother was placed and found him there. She was then eight years old. An older brother placed her in a convent which she greatly disliked. She describes with some emotion her one love object, a doll, which she had to give up to a sick child, and her shock and grief when she saw the doll thrown into the fire after the child's illness. The loss of the doll was her greatest grief in childhood. Mother remained in the convent to age 19, after which her sister's adoptive parents took her out. She then worked in a factory where she was very successful, doing fine sewing until her marriage. She has had much initiative, aggression and responsibility since early life. While at the convent, she did much phantasying about her father.

PATERNAL FACTORS

Relation to patient: Father has left all discipline to the mother. He gets easily irritated with the patient and says he sometimes walks out of the room to avoid punishing the boy as severely as he would like. He brings gifts to the children, plays with them at mechanical toys and takes the family for auto rides weekly, also to the movies. Patient complains that father is indifferent to him and places all responsibilities on the mother's shoulders, yet tells of a number of sightseeing trips with father.

Background: Father was the third of five children. Despite his infidelities, he is quiet, stable and now a good provider. He helps with the housework, spending his Sundays at home helping his wife. His mother was "a domineering woman who wanted to manage the entire family down to the third generation." Father was a happy child and proud of his parents, whom he still visits frequently.

PATIENT

Behavior problems: Patient is a disciplinary problem in school, punching the boys near him, tripping them in line, talking and being generally "irritating." He evades work with numerous excuses.

At home he is usually willing to do whatever he is told, and except for temper tantrums and periods in which he is disobedient and unmanageable, he is regarded as "sweet, affectionate, and considerate."

His blinking and sniffling tics, which are absent when he is quiet, are aggravated when he is irritated.

Patient has temper tantrums in school and at home, especially directed toward sibling. On one occasion he threw a heavy battery at his younger brother, just missing him and breaking a window.

He is very dependent on mother.

Delinquency: None.

Sex: Masturbation is denied. He still adheres to the stork theory of birth. He regards the whole subject as "dirty." Mother had early warned him against masturbation and urged cleanliness of genitals. In the past year, there has been sleep-walking to mother's bed.

Friends: Patient prefers to stay home and read rather than to go out with boys. He is prevented from making friendships on the street because the parents say the boys in the neighborhood are too tough. Boys call him names—"sissy" and "mamma's boy." He does not enter into sports; is excused from 'gym' because of his complaint that his heart is weak. Mother also uses the excuse of illness to keep the children quiet. When with boys of his own age, the patient is quarrelsome. He fights with boys younger than himself but is "afraid to take his part" with boys his own size. He recently played with some boys who were tying each other to posts as part of the game. When patient's turn came to be tied, he objected and refused to play.

School: Patient has always given trouble in school. Although he has been promoted regularly, his record shows consistent difficulty in arithmetic and oral expression in grades below VI A. Much consideration has been shown patient in school because of his physical condition.

Sibling relationship: At age two, he was placed with his grandmother for a time until the birth of his brother. On his return home, he cried himself to sleep in mother's room and for "his bottle." He asked if the baby was to have his bed, and one day slapped the baby on the head. He is quarrelsome and fights with his brothers; yet, on occasion, the next younger brother has fought his battles for him.

Interests: Patient reads excessively. He is interested in mechanical appliances and spends much time with mechanical toys. He avoids sports and competitive games. "He prefers to read than play."

Developmental history: First tooth at eight months; walked at 10 months; first words by 12 months. Considered a clever baby with "cute" ways, who said "cute" things—much more so than the others.

Habit problems: Bowel and bladder control was fairly well established by six months; no soiling or wetting after the ninth month. Breast fed four days. Mother used various methods of stimulating the breast unsuccessfully. He took the bottle well. There are no feeding problems. There has been sleep-walking in the past year, and also some screaming in his sleep, occurring about once a week. He keeps regular hours, he protests, through mother's management. He is very neat and clean; considered excessively so. Mother is the same, a meticulous housekeeper.

CASE 18

I.C.G. contact: February, 1928, to September, 1929. Patient is an only child, male, age 16 years, 5 months. I.Q. 105; achievement tests indicate average general intelligence. Grade X, private school. Patient is tall and thin, although well nourished and developed; height 69.5 inches, weight 132 pounds. Flat chest. Strabismus in left eye; wears glasses. He also wears orthodontic appliances. Female distribution of pubic hair; adult development of genitalia. He is concerned about his heart, which on examination was found to be normal. Several Wassermanns, done at mother's request, have been negative.

BASIS OF SELECTION

The teacher says mother "has fastened her clutches on the boy." Teacher and social worker say that mother permits him no independent existence and insists on sharing his every experience. The school has constantly criticized mother directly for her excessively close supervision of the patient.

EVIDENCE OF OVERPROTECTION

Mother constantly writes letters to teachers and principal, defending her son in his criticisms of the school. She has many interviews with teachers and is the "school nuisance."

She never permits patient to join in outdoor sports, except recently when she "accompanied" him to a baseball game in which he took part.

She has visited many physicians since his birth, "thinking he was developing every possible illness."

She has always taken him to movies and explained the subtitles in such a way "that there was no danger of his mind being poisoned."

Mother has always helped him with every school subject except geometry, which she has not studied. He is poorer in mathematics than in other subjects and has failed only in this.

PERIOD OF ANTICIPATION

Mother was unwilling to have children in the early years of her marriage because of her economic circumstances. She had several induced abortions. Later no contraception was used and by the age of 37 she felt certain she was sterile; yet she was not anxious for a child since her husband was "indifferent" to children. When she became pregnant at the age of 40, she felt "destiny ordained that her maternal urge should be satisfied by giving her a child late in life" and was very happy over the prospect of having a baby.

She was thrown from a horse during pregnancy and feared that something "must have happened to the foetus."

EXTRA HAZARD

Patient's medical history is not unusual; circumcision at 12 days; "colitis" and pneumonia at age three; tonsillectomy at six, adenoidectomy at eight; orthodontic treatment at seven for protruding incisors, attributed to thumb-sucking. At one time mother became "panicky" because the family had been using milk from a tubercular cow. She has constantly had patient examined since birth, and has also had Wassermann tests made on herself and the patient, for fear of his inheriting syphilis from the father. She had the patient circumcised at 12 days to prevent masturbation.

Patient is an only child and also a source of alimony for the past three years, since mother's separation from the father.

MATERNAL FACTORS

Marital: There were many open quarrels. Mother insisted that father had paresis, although a letter from a physician showed that he was in good health. She left him three years ago and receives a weekly allowance. She says that he was always jealous of her and claims that the patient is illegitimate.

Mother was averse to coitus on the basis of protest against the subjection of women to men. She has said to her husband, "It would be far better to put women out to stud like the animals than keep them in such slavery to good-for-nothing men, who think they own them, body and soul."

Mother prevented the I.C.G. interviewing the father.

Social: Mother has no friends. According to the patient, "Well, mother's just like I am. She doesn't make friends, and I've never been able to."

Background: Her mother died when the patient's mother was age seven. She was then brought up by her maternal grandmother; at nine she was cared for by an older sister, and later by a stepmother. She had an unhappy childhood and has been "on her own" since age 16 as a "nursery governess" and later a graduate nurse. She was a Red Cross nurse during the war.

Mother claims to have a beautiful voice. According to her story, she was always very successful but unappreciated. She talks about the great celebrities she knows, about her accomplishments and her medical knowledge. She now works occasionally as a model. Her son also works with her. Although successful in a play, she lost her job by "laying down the law" to the manager.

PATERNAL FACTORS

Relation to patient: When in contact with the patient, father was antagonistic, according to mother. Father was always occupied with business schemes and had very little to do with the patient.

Mother has always discussed father's weakness with the patient, and father is thought of by patient in a derogatory way.

Background: Unknown.

PATIENT

Behavior problems: Patient is unpopular with his schoolmates. He has never made friends; "they" do not like him, although he has tried.

Patient has a supercilious, critical attitude—like mother's—toward teachers and schoolmates.

Patient is considered a "sissy" because of his effeminate mannerisms and his refusal to join in sports.

He has excessive interest in body ailments and worries about tachycardia—physical examination negative.

Delinquency: None.

Sex: Masturbation is denied.

Friends: See under "Behavior problems."

School: Patient failed in algebra and later in geometry, although he is good in other subjects.

Interests: Patient's chief interest is reading. He avoid sports.

Developmental history: Nothing unusual except precocious talking and dancing.

Habit problems: No sleep, food, bowel and bladder problems.

CASE 19

I.C.G. contact: June, 1929, to November, 1929. Patient is an only child, male, age 12 years, 10 months. Grade VI. I.Q. 113. On achievement tests, patient rates best in language usage; arithmetic is on a par with other subjects. Patient is two inches below the median height, with marked obesity—20 pounds above median weight. Feminine fat distribution; large breasts, small genitals. There are other physical signs of "Fröhlich syndrome." Visual fields are normal. There is moderate limitation of movement in the right arm and leg, with slight atrophy of the right leg due to infantile paralysis at the age of seven.

BASIS OF SELECTION

Patient was referred by the family physician because of marked dependency on the mother. Overdependence on mother was observed by worker at lunch; mother fed him, asked many questions about the interview with psychiatrist, what he said, and so on.

EVIDENCE OF OVERPROTECTION

Mother still feeds the patient and helps him dress. She sleeps in the same room with him, although in a separate bed. She still slaps him.

Patient was breast fed to age 13 months.

PERIOD OF ANTICIPATION

One miscarriage preceded the birth of patient. Patient was a much wanted child; the parents were very happy during the pregnancy.

EXTRA HAZARD

Patient is an only child—born to mother when she was age 33.

The patient had poliomyelitis at age seven. The doctors did not expect him to live. There was much nursing care for 12 months, and since then numerous visits to doctors for treatment of patient's paralyzed right side. He uses his left hand almost exclusively, although he can whittle a stick by holding it in the right hand, using the knife with the left.

Tonsillitis at age two and a half; mild measles and chickenpox at six.

MATERNAL FACTORS

Marital: At 32, mother married a man 16 years older than herself. He was submissive to her and the relationship was apparently a very happy one; they had social interests in common. The husband's death was a shock and grief to mother.

Social: Mother does not go out on account of her son; she spends her evenings with him. Mother is now working part time.

Background: Mother's father died when she was four years old. After that her mother ran a boarding house to support the three children. Her childhood was happy, according to mother.

Mother graduated from high school and college. She took a secretarial course before marriage and was a valuable collaborator for a doctor, whose office she managed.

PATERNAL FACTORS

Relation to patient: Father was also overprotective of patient, "babied him more than mother," according to informants.

Background: Father was closely attached to his father. He is said to have had a very happy childhood. Father died when the patient was eleven years old.

PATIENT

Behavior problems: Patient has to be forced to do things for himself; wants mother to accompany him to school. He is irresponsible; has to be spoken to twice, for example.

Delinquency: None.

Sex: Mother has given him no instruction and believed him innocent of all knowledge until his camp experience, after which patient made remarks that led her to believe the boys had been talking of these matters. There is no evidence of masturbation.

Friends: Patient is friendly and popular, although he has no chums. Mother has discouraged friends by not allowing patient to invite them home.

School: Patient has a fairly good record. Mother thinks his slowness in writing with his left hand—before paralysis he wrote with right hand —accounts largely for his poor marks in written work.

Interests: Patient is fond of reading, although he reads poorly for his age. Father formerly read to him. Patient says, "I never had to read." He is also interested in drawing.

Developmental history: Normal. Walked at 12 months; first word at 13 months. Teething was normal but the first teeth decayed early and had to be extracted. He was on the breast until 13 months and weaned with no difficulty.

Habit problems: Toilet habits were established early. There has been no recurrence of enuresis. No feeding or sleeping problems. Patient is neat and clean.

CASE 20

I.C.G. contact: January, 1929, to February, 1931. Patient is male, age 4 years, 5 months, the elder of two siblings, the younger a boy age two. There is a foster sister age eight. Patient has very superior intelligence— I.Q. 132. He is in nursery school. At the time of the I.C.G. physical examination he had a slight bronchitis. He is well developed, slightly above the median height and weight for his age—height 42 inches, weight 40 pounds. He is pale, and has flabby muscles. "Overbite" of thumb sucker. Slightly impaired hearing.

BASIS OF SELECTION

Settlement workers and staff members note mother's babying of patient and complete occupation in the children, especially patient.

EVIDENCE OF OVERPROTECTION

Mother still dresses patient—until, when patient was age five, this was modified by treatment.

Patient refuses to leave mother alone for talk with examiner, holds on to her tightly, refuses to play with other children, preferring always to be where the mother is.

Patient sits on mother's lap a great deal. There is much fondling and general infantilizing by mother.

Patient is very obedient, does exactly as he is told, "too good," very considerate of mother's feelings and solicitous if she seems tired or worried. He enjoys any pleasure given him and very carefully thanks the giver. He is downcast if mother forgets to kiss him.

PERIOD OF ANTICIPATION

Child was wanted, although a female was preferred. Labor prolonged, low forceps, no asphyxia.

EXTRA HAZARD

Patient was placed in a day nursery at age 21 months, at the time of the birth of the second sibling. He was ill with some intestinal infection and swollen glands during and for six months following his stay at the nursery. During this illness, he did not recognize his parents. Mother neglected the second child to nurse him. Otherwise the medical history is negative. He was a quiet, healthy baby. There was no feeding difficulty.

MATERNAL FACTORS

Marital: Husband and wife rarely go out together. Mother explains this because of difficulty in getting someone to stay at home with the children. Husband goes out with friends from the office once a week. Besides, mother says, she does not want to neglect her housework. She is "completely absorbed in the children."

She is passive in sex relations, which she regards as always unpleasant. She never had an orgasm. There is no quarreling, but mother said she would leave the father, if it were not for the children, because of his gambling every Saturday night.

Social: Until recent years, mother never went out of the house at night. She now goes to a mothers' club at a neighboring settlement house once a week, where she is an active member and leads the discussions. She visits her mother daily. Previous to her marriage she was sociable but always preferred the company of women to men, and says she wondered why some girls always preferred boys.

Background: Her mother dominated, although neglecting her children, letting them eat and sleep when they wanted to. Her mother was an inadequate, poor, and very slovenly housekeeper. Patient's mother was neglected in childhood and very unhappy; she "never gave expression to any of her feelings." Her father was rather shiftless, a worker at odd jobs, and is now a janitor. Her mother always worked to supplement the income. Patient's mother is devoted to her mother and feels "protective" toward her.

Mother was the second and most responsible of the three children, all girls. She had complete charge of an epileptic sister from age 14 to 18 years, and the care of an older alcoholic sister. She managed and arranged the commitment of the younger sister to an institution.

At the age of 10, mother started working during summer vacations and after school hours, mainly office chores. She quit school in Grade VII to work in a factory and help support the family. She married at 18 to escape from her home environment.

She remains the responsible member of her family, to whom her mother also comes for aid. She is called over to manage the older sister when the latter is violently drunk, and has saved the younger sister from being run over when in an epileptic seizure.

PATERNAL FACTORS

Relation to patient: Father is interested in patient and siblings, plays with them and is very affectionate with the younger child. He distinctly prefers the younger boy, who is sturdy and independent. Father becomes irritated with patient's submissiveness and babyish behavior. Father leaves discipline entirely to his wife.

Background: Father is a steady, reliable worker and a good provider, except for occasional loss of money at Saturday night poker parties, which he started when his wife became "tied at home with the children." All family decisions are left to the wife.

Father's childhood was a happy one. His family was well-to-do. His mother was the dominating person in the household and was worshiped by her children. He saw very little of his father and was strongly attached to his next older sister. He is the eighth of nine siblings, all apparently successful. Father is described as a weak personality, domi nated by his efficient wife.

PATIENT

Behavior problems: Patient is generally submissive and obeys the orders of his two-year-old brother. Patient told the psychiatrist that he was two years old and the younger brother was four. Apparently he expects the younger brother to take the lead. He seldom opposes the younger brother's domination. "He takes the blame for brother's misdeeds rather than see him punished." At camp, when the patient was five years old, the complaint was that "he likes to be babied, whines, expects to be dressed, saying, 'I can't,' although able to dress himself."

He is too good, never destructive or quarrelsome. See also "Evidence of Overprotection" for obedience to parents and dependence on mother.

Patient has sucked his thumb since early infancy. This was encouraged by his grandmother on the basis that thumb-sucking babies are good babies. Thumb-sucking is now limited to the period before sleeping or when fatigued; he daydreams occasionally and then sucks his thumb. Efforts at cure—mittens, for example—were unsuccessful.

Patient has been afraid of dogs since infancy.

Delinquency: None.

Sex: Masturbation, that is, toying with penis observed at camp when patient was age five.

Friends: Besides brother and foster sister, with whom he plays nicely and never quarrels, he plays with a girl younger than himself. Otherwise, he refuses to play with other children, preferring always to be with mother.

Sibling relationship: See under "Behavior problems."

Developmental history: Breast fed for eight months; no weaning difficulty. Cut his first tooth at seven months; sat up at six months; never crept, but walked at 13 months; talked at one year.

Habit problems: Bowel and bladder control was established by 12 months, but there has been nocturnal enuresis since his stay in the nursery at age 21 months. No sleeping problems; sleeps alone. No eating problems except that he is a slow eater, in contrast with younger brother. He is very neat; puts all his toys back in their place.

INDEX

Norton Paperbacks on Psychiatry and Psychology

NORTON BOOKS
in Psychiatry and Psychology

GROTJAHN, MARTIN
Psychoanalysis and the Family Neurosis

HORNEY, KAREN
Feminine Psychology
Neurosis and Human Growth
The Neurotic Personality of our Time
New Ways in Psychoanalysis
Our Inner Conflicts
Self-Analysis

HORNEY, KAREN, ED.
Are You Considering Psychoanalysis?

KELLY, GEORGE A.
The Psychology of Personal Constructs, 2 Volumes

KELMAN, HAROLD, ED.
Advances in Psychoanalysis
New Perspectives in Psychoanalysis

LEWIN, BERTRAM D. and ROSS, HELEN
Psychoanalytic Education in the United States

LIFTON, ROBERT JAY
Thought Reform and the Psychology of Totalism

MAY, ROLLO
Man's Search for Himself

PEARSON, G. H. J.
Adolescence and the Conflict of Generations
Emotional Disorders of Children

ROSE, ARNOLD, ED.
Mental Health and Mental Disorder

RUESCH, JURGEN
Disturbed Communication
Therapeutic Communication

RUESCH, JURGEN and BATESON, GREGORY
Communication

SCHILDER, PAUL
Psychotherapy

SULLIVAN, HARRY STACK
Clinical Studies in Psychiatry
Conceptions of Modern Psychiatry
The Interpersonal Theory of Psychiatry
The Fusion of Psychiatry and Social Science
The Psychiatric Interview
Schizophrenia as a Human Process

VAN DEN BERG, J. H.
The Changing Nature of Man

WALTER, W. GREY
The Living Brain

WATZLAWICK, PAUL; BEAVIN, JANET; and
JACKSON, DON D.
Pragmatics of Human Communication

WHEELIS, ALLEN
The Quest for Identity

WYSS, DIETER
Depth Psychology

ZILBOORG, GREGORY and HENRY, GEORGE W.
History of Medical Psychology